THE
Chinese Kitchen

中式調煮我的歷史和記憶

中式調煮我的歷史和記憶

中國食譜

WILLIAM
MORROW
AND
COMPANY,
INC.
New York

THE
Chinese Kitchen

RECIPES, TECHNIQUES, INGREDIENTS,
HISTORY, AND MEMORIES FROM AMERICA'S
LEADING AUTHORITY ON CHINESE COOKING

Eileen Yin-Fei Lo

CALLIGRAPHY BY SAN YAN WONG
PHOTOGRAPHS BY ALEXANDRA GRABLEWSKI

It is the policy of William Morrow and Company, Inc., and its
imprints and affiliates, recognizing the importance
of preserving what has been written, to print the books we
publish on acid-free paper, and we exert
our best efforts to that end.

Library of Congress Cataloging-in-Publication Data

Lo, Eileen Yin-Fei.

The Chinese kitchen : recipes, techniques, ingredients,
history, and memories from America's leading authority on Chinese
cooking / Eileen Yin-Fei Lo; calligraphy by San Yan Wong.

p.   cm.

ISBN 0-688-15826-9

1. Cookery, Chinese.   I. Title.

TX724.5.C5L59442 1999

641.5951—dc21   99–30746

CIP

Printed in the United States of America

First Edition

1 2 3 4 5 6 7 8 9 10

BOOK DESIGN BY DEBORAH KERNER

www.williammorrow.com

This book is dedicated
to my family, tasters all,

to Fred,
tireless researcher
and holder of my hand,

and to my loving critics,
Christopher, Elena, and Stephen.

I thank my agent, Carla Glasser,
for pushing me and for her tenacity.

My editor, Justin Schwartz,
I thank for his faith in me,
his trust, and because he cares.

My deep appreciation to Stephen Wong, whom I call my "cookery
physician" in Hong Kong, for sharing the great depth of his knowledge of
foods and herbals.

Contents

THE
Chinese Kitchen

中式調煮我的歷史和記憶

The
Chinese Kitchen:
Memories *of* My Food

FOOD IN CHINA IS TRADITION, FOLK-LORE, MYTHOLOGY, RITUAL, AND RELIGIOUS OBSERVANCE AS WELL AS NUTRITION. NOWHERE ELSE IN THE WORLD IS THE DAILY TABLE SO ENTWINED WITH, SO MUCH A PART OF, A PEOPLE'S NATIONAL FABRIC. Food is what we Chinese eat. Food is what commonly binds our families together. Many of China's food preparations honor tales from both the imperial court and those everyday people called common. The gods eat with us at our table, and food is what we offer as gifts, as sacrifices to them. We hang their images in our kitchens and dining rooms to remind us of their continual presence. The altars of our ancestors are laden with food, which we symbolically send up to them. Whether we are Buddhists, Taoists, followers of the teachings of Confucius, Moslems, Christians, or Jews—and we are all of these—what we eat has enormous social, religious, and philosophical significance.

The importance of food in Chinese history cannot be overstated. Food customs, traditions, and practices, even the foods we Chinese eat and the way they are prepared, are rooted deeply in the country's culture, as far back as 5000 B.C., when the Chinese, in the northern regions of what we know today as China, were members of what is known as the Yangshao Culture. Through the millennia what China ate, what it cooked, and how have been well documented by archaeologists and anthropologists.

The cuisine that is distinctly Chinese evolved over many centuries from an initial collection of varied cooking experiences influenced by climate, land use, and native product into the codified traditions and styles espousing four distinct regions that comprise the great and vast Chinese table. The word *cuisine* is so overused, and misused, in these days of gastronomic hyperbole. Chinese cooking is a cuisine shaped by tradition and custom, by the foods that were available to it at different times, by climate. It is graced with a long literature, poets singing about it, philosophers theorizing. It is delicious history, created by the Chinese who cooked it, ate it, questioned it, and preserved it.

I am part of this history, an inheritor of its practices and its tastes. I was brought up to believe in the long, rolling swell of greater Chinese history, even though at times I, and my family, have been hurt by some of its excesses. I am devoted to China's foodways. I preach them and their purity, and I despair when this purity is compromised. Food in China is a living continuum, and I believe in, and partake of, the religion, folk tales, and mythology that we eat and in the long culinary tradition that is always with us.

What we Chinese eat to nourish ourselves we also eat to contribute to our interior balance and well-being. Food in China is to a great degree medicine. One food will bring us heat, necessary in the winter months or to balance what is cool within our bodies. Other foods will provide coolness, necessary in the summer, necessary for balance.

Our foods, we believe, are not eaten in a vacuum. One meat, one fish, one vegetable, even one herb is not advantageous in itself, despite the abundant newer interpretations that seek to confer health and healing properties on certain foods. In China a meat, a vegetable, a fish, a noodle, a bread, a spice, an herb or collection of herbs is health-giving, is advantageous, confers wellness only in the sense that it contributes to one's interior balance. Certain foods deemed to be inherently good, by their natures, in and of themselves, are not but must be considered and consumed in combination to establish or maintain desired balance.

Food is not only life-giving but also a source of familial or societal leanings. Our food is inextricably linked with manners, with form, with tradition, with history. I grew up with these beliefs. I remember my father, Lo Pak Wan, my first cooking teacher, telling me that we must eat our food first with our eyes, then with our minds, then with our noses, and finally with our mouths. He believed this. He taught this to my brother and me.

He would say, only partly joking, that fine vegetables should be chosen with as much care as one would a son-in-law. He would show me the correct way to prepare rice, telling me that if our rice was old then perhaps more water than customary might be needed to give our congee its fine and silky finish. "Keep an open mind," he would say. "Cook the way it has been written, but keep an open mind. If you keep walking only in a straight line, you will go into a wall. You must learn to make a turn if necessary. Do not be narrow." Or he would tell me, "*Yau mei haw yan tiu, mo mei haw yan tiu,*" an aphorism that translates as "If you don't have a tail, you cannot imitate the monkey; if you do have a tail, then do not imitate the monkey." By this he was telling me to follow the classical manner but not to be a simple, mindless imitator.

My mother, Lo Chan Miu Hau, encouraged me to cook as well. I recall her saying to me, "If you are wealthy and know how to cook, then servants cannot take advantage of you. If you are poor and know how to cook, you will be able to create wonderful meals with few resources." Cooking and its ramifications were that important to her, as well as to my father, when I was young and growing up in Sun Tak, a suburb of Canton, now Guangzhou. They and my grandmother, my Ah Paw, my mother's mother, insisted that I be involved in our family table. Ah Paw, despite her houseful of servants, despite the presence of a family cook, made certain whenever I visited her, which was every opportunity I had, every school holiday, that I was in her kitchen.

My Ah Paw knew instinctively, without ever having had to personally put a spatula into a wok, how things ought to be cooked, what foods wedded in combination, and what clashed. I am tempted to suggest that she was a brilliant, instinctive kitchen chemist. I will say it. Brilliant she was indeed, her knowledge of foods was encyclopedic, and she was never wrong about cooking, then or now, in my memory. I spent much of the Lunar New Year at her house. I liked her home, I liked her kitchen, and she spoiled me. Except when it came to imparting cookery lessons.

When we ate raw fish, *yue sahng,* she taught, one had to prepare the fish in the proper manner. You hit the fish at the front of its head to stun it, then, when it was still nominally alive, you scaled it, gutted and cleaned it, then sliced it for eating. This special dish, which we ate on important birthdays and on the eves of family weddings, had to be prepared this way, only this way, Ah Paw said.

When we steamed a fish, she taught me to softly lay the fish atop a bed of rice at the precise moment that the rice was in the final state of its absorption of water. It would then be perfectly prepared.

Once I steamed a fish, quite well, I thought, and proudly carried it to her at the family table. She sniffed. I had forgotten to pour boiled peanut oil over it just before serving. "Take it back to the kitchen and add the oil," she ordered. My grandmother's kitchen always had a crock of boiled peanut oil near the stove. To pour it over fish was to give the fish fragrance and to dispel any unpleasant odors. It does, even if the oil is not warm.

She would eat no vegetables that were older than two hours out of the ground, which necessitated repeated trips to the markets by her servants, a lesson of the importance of freshness that was not lost on me.

She cautioned me to eat every kernel of rice in my bowl, for if I did not, she warned, the man I married would have a pockmarked face, one mark for each uneaten rice kernel. I did as she cautioned, and I must have eaten well, for my husband's face is clear.

Do not shout in the kitchen, Ah Paw would insist. Do not use improper words in the kitchen. Do not show shortness of temper in the kitchen by, for example, banging chopsticks on a wok. All of these would reflect badly on us as a family, she would say, when done in front of Jo Kwan, the Kitchen God, whose image hung on the wall over the oven. For just before the Lunar New Year the image of Jo Kwan, his lips smeared with honey, was always burned so that he would go up to heaven and report only nice things about our family.

Ah Paw would consult her *Tung Sing,* an astrological book, for propitious days on which to begin preparing the special dumplings we made and ate during the New Year festival. She would specify to the second the time to make the dough, heat the oven, add the oil, in what we called "*hoi yau wok,*" or, literally translated, "begin the oil in the wok." So admired was she for her knowledge that young married couples, not even of our family, would consult with her. A memory I have is of pumping the pedal of the iron and stone grinding mill in our town square, at her orders, to get the flour that we would use for our dumplings.

She was an observant Buddhist who declined to eat either fish or meat on the first and the fifteenth of each month and for the first fifteen days of the New Year, and our family ate similarly out of deference to her. She was happy that my mother always encouraged me to cook, happy that my father brought kitchen discipline to me as well. She nodded with pleasure, in support of my father, I remember—not in sympathy with me—when I complained how boring it was when my father gave me the task of snapping off the ends of individual mung bean sprouts. "If you wish to learn how to make spring rolls well, learn the beginning of the spring roll. It must be done," Ah Paw said.

We had no grinders. We chopped meats and fish and other seafood with the cleaver on a chopping board. "Clean it," Ah Paw would say when I was finished. "If you do not, the food you chop next will not stick together. It will fall apart. There will be no texture. If it falls apart, I will know that you did not listen."

All of this she conferred on me without ever setting foot in the kitchen of her house. As a further example of her vision I should note in passing that my Ah Paw, a most independent woman, as is evident, refused to have bound the feet of my mother, her daughter, much the practice of high-born women. This despite the fact that her own feet had been bound since babyhood and were no more than four inches long. This extraordinary woman, never more than seventy-five pounds, who could not totter more than one hundred feet and was usually carried by servants, brought my mother and then me into modern times in her own way. I wanted nothing more than to be with her, and I would listen, wide-eyed and receptive, to her talk about food and its meanings.

Like many Chinese, our family, despite its religious beliefs, looked to Confucius and his teachings regarding manners, morality, behavior, and social order. Ah Paw would tell me stories of the time Confucius came from the North to our southern part of China. When he was young, she said, he would hold his writing brush at the top end, his forefinger hooked over the end, and he would write with precision and with grace. When he came south, he was aged, she said, and his hand would slide farther down the length of his brush until he wrote with the pad of his palm and his wrist resting on his writing desk. But his writing, Ah Paw, would tell us, remained beautiful. It is believed to this day by the Cantonese, in China's South, that the Cantonese hold their calligraphy brushes with their palms and wrists flat on their desks because that was the way they learned from the aging Confucius.

In her many and varied discourses on food, her advisories, Ah Paw would cite Confucius as she talked of techniques and the philosopher's opinions and dictates concerning food. He had been a simple man, she said of this most well known of Chinese philosophers, who lived and wrote in the fifth century B.C., who thought so much of food and its tastes and presentation that he would specify how foods ought to be cut up before cooking. Ah Paw told me that Confucius was a man satisfied to be paid for his teaching with a "small amount of dried meat" and that he was happy with "plain food to eat and pure water to drink."

It was as if she had learned by rote. Confucius, she said, desired rice to be at its whitest and meat to be finely chopped, but when food was overcooked he would not eat. When fish or meat had become tainted, or had lost its color, or had an odor he thought distasteful, he would not eat. He insisted that the food he ate be in season, not preserved, and sauce for it had to enhance it, and not change it. He drank wine, but not to excess. Nor did he overeat, she would say with a gesture of her finger, and "he would have no meal that did not have some ginger."

It was only later, as I grew up and studied, that I found that most of these dicta are included in Confucius's *Analects,* that collection of adages and dialogues Confucius wrote to, for, and with his followers. But for my Ah Paw they were valid and surely worth passing on to me, in particular her repetition of her favorite tale of Confucius, who, she told me, when asked for his opinions on war suggested that he knew more about meat preparation than about war. Good teaching. Though Ah Paw was an observant Buddhist, she did not reject some of the ways taught by Lao-Tzu, who wrote of the simple life, of direct, clean tastes, of foods prepared to reflect simplicity and honesty of flavor. In no other cuisine are the harmonies of color, appearance, tactile sensations, and textures so important.

There is much to be learned about the Chinese kitchen, perhaps the most widely known yet least understood of cuisines. Much, if not most of what has been written and continues to be written about Chinese foods is woefully inaccurate, filled with misinformation, replete with errors once made and repeated. Include in this most of the books reported to be concerned about the food of China. I exempt two exceptional, meticulously researched books concerned with the history and anthropology of food in China: *Food in Chinese Culture,* edited by K. C. Chang, and *The Food of China,* by E. N. Anderson, both published by Yale University Press. They are worth seeking out. Equally important, in my view, is a volume entitled simply *Gastronomy,* by Jay Jacobs (Newsweek

Books, 1975). He understands more about Chinese food than most.

The food of the vast country of my birth has a long, complex, exceedingly rich documented history, one that reaches further back than any other food tradition. Like other early people, the forerunners of the Chinese were hunters who gathered and cooked meats over fire, dried them, often preserved them. Even prior to them, as far back as 10,000 B.C., it has been written that rice as a basic life-giving food was cultivated in what is now southern China. The earliest Chinese, the people of the Yangshao Culture, flourished as farmers from 5,000 to 3,000 B.C. and knew about millet and wheat, rice and barley, and domesticated sheep and goats. They caught and cooked a wide variety of fish, most the same that are eaten in China to this day. Farms cultivated various melons and gourds, leeks, lettuces, cabbages and other greens, beans, and lotus roots. Domesticated pigs became a prime source of food, a custom that grew over the centuries to the point where "meat" in China meant pork primarily, occasionally solely.

Domestication spread in the Hsia and Shang dynasties, the first two in China's history, which spanned the years from 2200 to 1100 B.C. And the special nature of what would comprise the Chinese kitchen and its practices began to take form. In the Shang dynasty we know that chickens, geese, quail, and partridge were commonly eaten birds. We know that deer, rabbits, boars, bears, and foxes were hunted for food, that beef cattle began to be raised along with sheep and goats.

In the following dynasty, the Zhou, from 1122 to 770 B.C., we know that rice came gradually to be regarded as the country's major grain, one of status, even in the wheat-

and millet-dominated North, where it was relatively rare. Soybeans began to be cultivated widely, and there are even records containing instructions for food preparation, for cutting, for the proper amounts to prepare, for the length of time foods should be exposed to heat, for how to season. The Chinese began to smoke foods, sugar and salt them for preservation, pickle them, dry them either in the sun or in ovens for long keeping. In this dynasty food-related tasks were already designated by the imperial court. Manners at table and food rituals were evolving. So important was food, its preparation, and its presentation during this Zhou dynasty that nearly 3,000 of the 4,000 people who comprised the palace staff were responsible for its table.

A source for anthropologists studying food practices and rituals in this period is a book, or series of books, called *Chou Li*. Though this "Book of Rites and Ancient Ceremonies" was written 1,000 years later, it details the food history of that earlier period and includes recipes in the true sense for thousands of dishes. Yet another chronicler of Zhou gastronomic times was Cheng Hsuan, who in his *Li Chi*, written more than 1,200 years after the Zhou period, details prescribed methods for frying, baking, steaming, steeping, and preserving, the beginnings of characteristic Chinese methods of cooking, as well as how foods were to be cut into small pieces before cooking and eating and how the various foods were to be handled.

It was during the Zhou period that the concept of seasonal foods arose formally. It was specified that in spring lamb and suckling pig were to be eaten; in summer, chicken and dried fish; in fall, veal and venison, and in winter, fresh fish and game. We know that the Zhou people had pots and other food containers of bronze and pottery, ladles and other serving utensils, and chopsticks, all the better to serve meals that were the forerunners of the elaborate stratified, imperial feasts of later dynasties, and the meals of the less noble as well, both part of the fabric of Chinese food and preparation that has remained constant for thousands of years.

I place myself comfortably in this historical context when I consider the food of my ancestors, for I recognize my experience and the teachings of my grandmother and my parents as part of that fabric as well. Another patch in my personal quilt was another member of my family who helped mightily to make me a cook, my aunt, Pong Lo Siu Fong. That was her formal name, but we all called her Luk Gu Cheh, for "father's younger sister number six," which indeed she was. I often marketed with her, and she was known because she would have one of her servants follow her carrying an empty pail, the better to carry home a live fish. For her only that could be considered fresh.

She taught me how to kill and properly clean a fish. Another time I remember she asked, "Do you really want to cook?" and when I replied yes, I did, she took me to the market to buy a live chicken. We brought it home. As she watched and instructed, I spread its wings back, bent its neck, and made a cut in its neck, draining the blood into a bowl of salted water, where it congealed. I then steamed it into a blood pudding, which Luk Gu Cheh taught me to stir-fry with broccoli, a dish her husband favored. Her husband, my uncle, was a senator, and she supervised many grand political and social dinners at her home, even cooking with her servants. At one of these she created her version of lemon chicken, wherein chicken is steamed with fresh lemons instead of the customary concoction in which the fowl is fried, then doused with a lemon sauce thick with cornstarch. It has become my recipe. She taught me the discipline of carefully cutting meats and vegetables for *ding* dishes, which means "little squares."

Is not all of this in direct descent from those early Chinese days? Luk Gu Cheh had nothing to do with my killing and dressing my first snake, at the age of nine. That was a matter of pride, done on a dare. One of my playmates, a boy, had caught a snake, a nonpoisonous, edible water snake. He teased me, saying, "Sure, you know how to kill a fish. Sure, you know how to kill a chicken. But can you kill a snake?" I never had, but I had watched. So I cut the skin around the base of its head, with a broken shard of glass, as was the custom, then stripped the skin downward completely from its body. It became my snake, and I raced home with it, proudly, to tell my mother, who applauded me, for snakes, then as now, are expensive, luxurious foods, particularly during winter. Moreover, it was filled with eggs, which made it an even worthier prize. I confess I have never done it since, nor, I expect, could I do it again, nor could I similarly prepare a live eel or a turtle. I simply cannot. Yet what I had done that afternoon was, in a small though real way, a continuation of Chinese history.

I learned early, by doing and listening, the form and philosophy of the Chinese kitchen and its broad general categories of *fan* and *ts'ai. Fan* is grain, rice, wheat, millet, whole or milled into flour, and includes breads, noodles, and pancakes. *Ts'ai* includes basically everything else, vegetables and meats, which were to be cut into small, bite-sized pieces to be eaten with *fan.* Traditionally grains were, and are, the center of the Chinese meal, the basic, rice in particular; all else is complementary, secondary. They are not mixed but presented together, each retaining its essential character. What makes Chinese food unique in its preparation is the art of that mixture, which is why when I see, for example, foods tossed experimentally by chefs into a stir-fry mélange, just to see what taste might result, I become upset. What goes into a dish destined for the Chinese table should be prepared, and measured, with care and for the balance of tastes it should provide. All of my teachers, my family, taught me that the food at our table should be eagerly anticipated and talked about as it is prepared, it should be eaten with enjoyment and then discussed, with further enjoyment over tea.

It is usually believed that the Chinese preoccupation with food blossomed in the Han dynasty, which bridged the centuries from 206 B.C. to A.D. 220. To be sure the customs and practices of the Chinese kitchen were very much in place by that time, as we know from the *Chou Li*. Even in those fragmented times in Chinese history known as the Spring and Summer Annals, the Warring States, and the Chin, the years from 770 to 220 B.C., the literature about the practices of the Chinese kitchen flourished. It was, in fact, during these times that the five tastes of the Chinese kitchen—sweetness, sourness, saltiness, hotness, and bitterness—were enunciated and became common. Toward the end of the Warring States period, in 239 B.C., the *Lu Shih Chun Chiu,* or the "Spring and Fall Annals of Master Lu," was set down, a book of food flavors and flavorings. In the historic lore of Chinese cookery it is most important. It was the Han dynasty, however, that provided us with the most complete record of the development of the Chinese table. There is no doubt that the unearthing by archaeologists of Han tombs in the 1970s gives us the most minutely detailed picture of China's historic kitchen, its ingredients, its methods of preparation, its eating procedures, a picture that proved that Chinese food and its practices have been constants for many millennia.

The first archaeological site, in Hunan, yielded a vast treasure of gastronomic history. In the tomb was the preserved body of a woman, all around her kitchen artifacts: bamboo food storage cases, pottery, and perhaps most important, more than 300 bamboo slips carrying notations of cooking methods and ingredients. There are references to melons and melon seeds, which by the way were found in the digestive system of the woman in the tomb, bamboo shoots, taro, eggs, ginger, quails, ducks, salt, sugar, honey, soy sauce, with instructions for roasting, frying, steaming, salting, drying, and pickling, as well as details for stewing. And what was to be stewed? Sheep, deer, pigs, wild ducks, domesticated dogs, pheasants, chickens.

In this and other unearthed Han tombs there was information on butchering and cuts of meat not unfamiliar to us today: flank, chuck, shoulder, liver, stomach. In these tombs were wall murals and carved reliefs depicting cooking on stoves, serving, feasting, dough kneading, and firewood collecting, as well as overhead racks from which hung meats and fowl. An unimpeachable record. Evidence of rice and wheat cultivation were found, of soybeans, lentils, beans, garlic, scallions, leeks,

taro roots, and yams were found as well. The wok was in evidence, as was the *fu,* or cauldronlike stewing pot, and the *tseng,* the steamer, and the Hans are credited as well with formalizing three techniques for frying: slow-frying, deep-frying, and the ubiquitous stir-frying. This last, the most well-known technique of today's Chinese kitchen, was the brilliant answer to the need for cooking quickly, over the highest of heat provided by quick-burning, scarce fuel.

The Han also can be credited with creating that grand staple of the contemporary Chinese table, those darkened, salted, fermented beans, which they called *shih,* and which initially were a relish. Early mentions of soybean cakes and soybean curd occurred in this time as well, and the Hans also perfected the technique for extracting oil, for cooking, from seeds. Wines became important. All wines, liquors, fermented beverages in China are referred to as all-encompassing *shu,* and in the Han dynasty their manufacture became more intricate and refined. The simple, often rough, fermented alcohols of earlier times evolved into fine wines made from rice, usually glutinous rice; wines from millet, considered middle grade; and those from other grains, deemed to be inferior.

This dynasty was the time of Chang Chien, a far-ranging and inquisitive explorer, who is often credited with bringing back to China from his explorations grapes, pomegranates, walnuts, sesame and caraway seeds, onions, peas, cucumbers, and coriander. China's kitchen has always opened its arms to the foods of other lands, and this would continue during subsequent, often fragmented dynasties: the Three Kingdoms, the Tsin, the Southern and Northern, and the Sui, these from the end of the Han in 220 for 400 years to 618, and the beginning of the Tang dynasty. In terms of gastronomic literature the most important writing to come out of this period was the *Ch'i Min Yao Shu*, or "Important Skills for the Well-Being of the People," a collection of more than 300 actual recipes that the author, Jia Sixie, had gathered from previous food writings. This collection, first written in 535, toward the end of the Southern and Northern dynasty, became a reference in these early years, laboriously copied by hand, later printed more than 500 years later during the Sung dynasty. Its last edition, in 1875, is still a resource for researchers into the history and development of Chinese food.

Foods from other lands continued to come into China during this period, brought not only by Chang Chien but also by soldiers and other travelers on expeditions. Figs and pistachios came into China from the Middle East; spinach, kohlrabi, and sugar beets from the West. And in these times when even the Southern part of greater China was regarded as somewhat foreign and remote, the foods of the South, many of them exotic, became "imports" to the North. From below the Yangtze Basin came tangerines, from what is Canton, now Guangzhou, came litchis, longans, rambutans, bananas, coconuts, and dates from native palms, betel nuts. Nor was the culinary traffic one-way. The lovely, sweet oranges of Guangzhou, which I remember from my personal part of China, went west to become the Seville, the Valencia, and the navel orange.

Fruit, its preparation and consumption, has always been important to China's South. When I was growing up in Sun Tak, we were surrounded by fruits, which was so different from the North. We ate fresh melons and oranges, grapefruits and lemons, apples, peaches, and pears. We dried apricots and prunes and lightly salted them for snacks. Mangoes, bananas, and pineapples were staples. We preserved mangoes and tangerines as marmalades. Whole lemons were cooked, pressed flat, dried, then sugared and eaten as one would candy, but we also used these prepared lemons with steamed fish and steamed pork. We adored fresh papayas, which we also dried. I remember my Ah Paw telling me that papaya made into a soup with fresh fish was a necessity for a nursing mother. We candied citrus skins and dried grapes for raisins. As a child I adored fresh longans and litchis, and I recall my disappointment, when I first arrived in the United States, that no fresh litchis were to be had. This happily is no longer the case. We enjoyed those dates, peculiar to the South and known as jujubes, dried or steeped in honey or double-boiled with chicken. We even made a date tea from them. We pickled all manner of fruits, particularly pears and peaches, which we ate as snacks or sliced thinly and ate in stir-fried dishes, soups, or salads. It was this whole palette of fruit that went from the South north to the Hans, who appreciated it to such an extent that the imperial court designated couriers for the delivery of seasonal fruits.

Even if the Han had not contributed so much to the development, and later the understanding, of the complex and varied Chinese table, they would be remembered for perhaps their greatest contribution, noodles and all manner of "noodle foods"—cakes, breads, and buns, steamed, baked, or fried. A singular piece of Chinese gastronomic history. Say thank you, Marco Polo.

The food historians tell us that the Sui dynasty, which immediately preceded the Tang, saw the birth of two other familiar staples of the modern Chinese table, that Yangzhou fried rice of many ingredients, from the city of the same name, and those wonderful "dots on the heart," the little foods and dumplings of dim sum of the Chinese teahouse, the creations of the cooks in Guangzhou.

The Tang dynasty, so well known in its 618 to 907 period for the beauty and grace of its brilliantly glazed green and brown pottery and statuary, was no less prized for its preoccupation with food. Books about food and cookery, collections of recipes, and guides to diet multiplied. It was the time of Meng Shen, a seventh-century pharmacologist who codified food as medicine. The fruits of the South, as well as its chestnuts, pine nuts, and hazelnuts, were brought north to be grown in imperial orchards and hothouses, and there was even a palace retainer whose sole duty was to see to the health and plenitude of bamboo shoots. Elegance as well as variety increased, and spices poured into China in a flood: black pepper from South Asia, almonds from Turkestan, cardamom from Indonesia, saffron from Kashmir. Ice was gathered from the cold North in winter, then brought to the area that is now Beijing, there to be buried deep in hay-lined ground holes in preparation for the refrigeration of fresh fruits and vegetables. Vegetable carving became a court art. The importance of women in the kitchen was recognized to a limited extent.

In the food universe men were dominant in the imperial North. They were keepers of the food and its preparers, and women were expected to be properly concerned with sewing, embroidery, and music. In the South, however, I am happy to say, women were honored for their culinary skills, and because southern women were the cooks for those different and exotic foods so prized in the North, recognition was accorded them, grudgingly. Because the best, and freshest, food in China came from the South, and still does, it was natural that those who created wonders with this food should receive notice, if not honor. To cook expertly in southern China, where I was born and raised, brought respect and regard to women and made them desirable to marry.

The history of China has always been reflected in its table. By the Sung dynasty, which ran from 960 to 1280, with its population already at 100 million people China had turned to rice as its universal staple and was producing two crops each year. In the North there was still some obeisance to wheat, a condition that prevails even today, but rice by that time had become the country's *fan,* its main food. Cooking at the imperial court remained as rich and varied as it had been under the Tang, and among the people at large there was plenty. Philosophers and artists concerned themselves with food, declaring the "Seven Necessities" people could not do without: rice, tea, firewood, oil, salt, soy sauce, and vinegar. Only the fuel has changed in many parts of the country. Restaurants, which had sprung up initially as small travelers' inns, flourished, became elaborately decorated with extensive menus devoted to such specialties as noodles, fish, vegetables, pastries, and wines.

In this time food, its fineness on one hand, its broad appeal on the other, became identified with social, economic, religious, and intellectual status. There were spectacular palace feasts of countless courses and noble parties elsewhere, yet at the same time there was praise for simple food, as dictated in the writings of Confucius.

It was the Sung dynasty that gave us, as well, Meng Yuan-lao, probably the world's first restaurant critic. This peripatetic gastronome roamed the country, particularly Kaifeng, the capital under the Sung, looking in on the rising tide of restaurants. He wrote of these new public eating places, how sitting on the floor changed to chairs at table; about menus and markets and seasonal and prepared foods. A curious turn in the history of Chinese food came in the ensuing Yuan dynasty, in the 100 years from 1280 to 1368, when the Mongol invaders ruled the country. It was as if the traditions of China's food had been put on hold. The food of the Mongols, which they carried with them from the Far North, was coarse, bland, and simple. They drank mares' milk, by choice, and created great feasts around it. To be sure milk, from mares, sheep, cattle, and goats, had been tasted in China from time to time, but never to the extent as consumed by the Mongols. They boiled muttons whole. Intricate preparation was of little or no interest. All of this was abhorred by the Chinese people, who continued to eat the foods that had come to them, through the centuries, and they even managed to change some of those Mongol foods into cooking they considered edible. Huge cauldrons of boiled mutton became, later, the Mongolian hot pot. It is Mongol in name only, for the concept of grilling thin slices of lamb on a red-hot dome of iron is not Mongolian at all but the creation of twentieth-century Chinese Moslems.

Disorder was replaced with order under the Ming. Great reclamation projects were undertaken to make more land arable, and each Chinese ate well-balanced meals of 2,000 calories every day, according to anthropological studies. Rice was the standard staple, and sufficient amounts of it were produced to give every person 300 kilograms (660 pounds) each year. More open to the rest of the world, the Chinese saw corn, sweet potatoes, white potatoes, tomatoes, peanuts, and tobacco come into their country, additions that, along with bell peppers and chilies, brought even more variety and breadth to the national kitchen. We know that the Mings were preoccupied with food. In imperial Beijing, ceremony and ritual, discarded by the Mongols, were restored, and the vast array of palace retainers comprised thousands of people designated "people of skill" for the care and preparation of its foods. By the late sixteenth century, at the height of the Ming dynasty, about 8,000 people had duties that related to the purchase, acquisition, storage, cooking and otherwise preparing, and serving of food and drink.

There was even an official directorate of food stuffs, one of whose duties was to oversee fleets of barges designated to bring foods from all over China to the court. It has been written that fresh plums and strawberries, fresh bamboo shoots and fresh shad were sent, wrapped in layers of straw, more than 1,500 miles by barge to Beijing. Food in China was then, as it is today, pleasure. Writings about food, with males depicted as experts and professionals, females as talented amateurs, were numerous, with the latter being especially honored as supervisors of kitchens who saw to it that their daughters acquired cooking skills. It seems perfectly logical to me, though I do not know it to be fact, that my Ah Paw and my mother, as well as my aunt Luk Gu Cheh, would have read and been influenced by later editions of these writings.

Surely they would have known about the *Yin-Shih Hsu-Chih,* the "Essential Knowledge for Eating and Drinking," written by Chia Ming in 1368. This book of discourses on Chinese food is divided into eight sections of detailed food knowledge: 50 grains, beans, and seeds; 87 vegetables; 68 fish; 34 fowl; 42 meats; 63 fruits and nuts; 33 seasonings and condiments; and 43 kinds of water and fire methods of cooking. It details recipes and the inherent natures of all of these foods, a seminal writing on food as the source of health and as the provider of our necessary inner balance. It was the logical successor to earlier writings that simply regarded food as medicine, with little distinction, the most notable being the *Liang Fang,* "Good Descriptions," written two centuries before.

The last of the dynasties, the Ching, which bridged old and modern China, from 1644 to 1911, has become known for its excesses and extravagance not only in dress and ritual but also in food. In the imperial household there were officials whose services dealt individually, and only, with meats, tea, pastries, wines, pickles, and vinegars. During the reign of Ch'ien Lung a history of food in China was printed under court order, with entire chapters devoted to vinegars, wines, honey, sugar, oil, meats, and rice, augmented with writings on festival foods and poetry on the subject of the enjoyment of food. There were, in addition, two arbiters of food and cookery in the Ching dynasty who were highly regarded, Li Yu whose writings appeared in the seventeenth century, and

Yuan Mei, whose book of recipes, *Shih Tan,* was printed two centuries later.

Li Yu was much the esthete, suggesting that people who would eat meat were wastrels; that neither cattle nor dog ought to be eaten because these animals were friends of man, but that fish were permissible because they reproduced so plentifully. Scallions and garlic brought with them bad breath, he wrote, and should be avoided, and radishes caused hiccups. He would specify, for example, that roses, cassia, and citron ought to be added to the water in which rice was cooked to refine its taste. Li Yu was influential, but long after he was gone, Yuan Mei declared him an effete poseur, perhaps an instance of the pot calling the kettle black.

Yuan Mei, for example, wrote that pork before cooking should be inspected for the thickness of its skin, for only thin-skinned pigs should be eaten. Chickens were to be eaten only in their prime; no traces of feathers should be found in birds' nests before they were made into soup; mud should be cleansed from sea slugs and sand washed from sharks, and all meats should be free from gristle. Elementary precautions, I should think, but Yuan Mei also wrote extensively on balance in food, on the need for richness to be contrasted with blandness. He wrote on the correct amount of heat with which to cook particular foods and the need to have sauces that gave clarity to foods and did not change their nature.

These were writings of importance in a period when a Tao of food emerged, when excessive amounts of food were sacrificed to the gods, when there were countless numbers of banquets, each of different foods, each with differing numbers of courses, each connoting status and importance.

Among those less noble, corn, sweet potatoes, and peanuts, which had come from the West, became Chinese staples, and vast farmlands were devoted to them. In fact, writings of the Chings suggest that in many parts of China, particularly in the North and Northeast, sweet potatoes became the main staple of the peasant table. It was in this time that chefs came to be recognized. Cooks would apprentice in the court kitchens or fine restaurants and then depart to start their own establishments, and it was largely with these chefs, who came from various parts of the country, that the concepts of regional variations in China's cooking arose. The greatest chefs, those with the most skill, those who were most inventive, those most sought after, were customarily from the South, in Guangzhou, but those cooks from other regions gained fine reputations as well. Their work soon became formalized in cookbooks, often slight, yet nonetheless important, and many of them exist to this day.

Cooking came to be regarded as south-ern, from Guangdong, or Cantonese; north-ern, from Peking, now Beijing, and from the surrounding Shandong region; eastern, to include Shanghai and the cities and areas around Hangzhou and Suzhou; and western, with Sichuan the dominant style, but including Hunan and Yunnan. These distinctions exist today, yet as one delves deeply into the greater Chinese table there are carryovers, with spices and ingredients found in every region and with traditional dishes modified over time.

Yet they are all elements of the greater Chinese table, a cultural legacy that I regard as my palette. Whichever the section of China, good cooking respects the seasons as well as the food and honors its context. Good Chinese cooking, honest cooking, fine cooking, is precise. It is art. Its aim is to bring to the table foods that are balanced and healthful, to be sure, but Chinese cooking is foremost a cuisine of pleasure, given and taken. For my Ah Paw food was also a blessing, conferred and accepted.

The Chinese Larder

MOST OF THE FOODS OF THE CHINESE KITCHEN HAVE BECOME FAMILIAR. A FEW REMAIN FOREIGN. THERE WAS A TIME WHEN VIRTUALLY ALL OF THE FOODS OF CHINA WERE REGARDED CURIOUSLY, AS ARCANE, EVEN TOUCHED BY MYSTERY. *Exotic* was the overused word. No longer is this so. Though the variety of foods available to and cooked by the Chinese is wide, their tastes have become more known and accepted, and relished, by the Western palate, a happy state of affairs. With this familiarity and recognition has come more extensive use, and thus more and more people, including hordes of professional cooks, shop in Chinese and other Asian groceries with confidence.

Moreover, it appears that every market, no matter its size or orientation, has shelves stocked amply with Chinese ingredients. This too is a happy circumstance. Only a very few of the foods in this book, these quite specialized, are not available widely. Most are to be found in your local market or in Chinese and Asian shops. Most of the spices, oils, and condiments, as well as the canned, bottled, and jarred foods and the soy sauces, are of Chinese origin and are imported from the People's Republic of China, from Hong Kong, from Taiwan, and more recently from Southeast Asia, the Philippines, Indonesia, Malaysia, Korea, and Japan. A great many of these foods are available by mail order as well, particularly those dried, preserved, pickled, and otherwise prepared, and advertisements for them are to be found with increasing frequency in cookery magazines. Brands have also proliferated. In all of my writings I refrain from recommending brands except in those instances where I believe a particular one is far superior to others and thus, in my view, essential to the taste I wish to impart to a recipe. A note of caution: there is quite a bit of fanciful labeling of Chinese ingredients, with one food often being labeled several ways. I have given all of these variations. Read them with care. A suggestion I always make is to make photocopies of the ingredients needed, with their Chinese calligraphy, and present them to the shopkeeper. It helps.

ABALONE • A mollusk highly prized throughout Asia, particularly in China and Japan. Its meat, an oval-shaped disk, in a shell rough on the outside but with a lustrous mother-of-pearl interior, is usually tough and requires preparation before use in any recipe. The Chinese suggest that its name, *bau yue*, sounds like the words for "guaranteed wealth," and thus it is eaten symbolically at the Lunar New Year as well as at feasts.

The best abalone are those harvested in the waters off northern Japan, then dried. Rarely do the Chinese eat it fresh. Dried abalone, from those Japanese waters, can cost almost $1,000 a pound. It requires prolonged soaking, then is customarily simmered in a pot with a whole chicken and a piece of pork with bone. Once imbued with this rich stock, and tender, it is prepared further according to individual recipes.

In the United States, West Coast abalone is eaten fresh, generally pounded into paillard thinness, breaded and fried. Although quite tasty, in China it would never be cooked that way.

BAMBOO LEAVES • See *Lotus Leaves and Bamboo Leaves.*

BAMBOO SHOOTS • The pale yellow spear-shaped young beginnings of bamboo trees. At one time fresh bamboo shoots were unavailable outside of Asia, and the few that reached markets were often discolored or dried out. This is no longer the case. Fresh bamboo shoots are now available, usually in Chinese groceries. Quite often the shoots are tough and must be boiled for further use. Those imported cooked and canned are quite good. Winter bamboo shoots are considered more desirable because they are more tender and less fibrous. Cans will be labeled "winter bamboo shoots" or "bamboo shoots, tips." The latter are as good as those labeled "winter" and are less expensive. I prefer those that come in large chunks, so they can be cut as desired. Once a can is opened, the shoots must be removed to another container. Occasionally, shoots will be removed from cans and sold loose, by weight. They will keep for two to three weeks in water, in a closed container, if the water is changed daily.

To prepare fresh bamboo shoots, remove all outer husks down to the tender, cream-white core. Place the whole shoots in a pot with the water, cover, and bring to a boil over high heat. If very tender, simmer for 7 minutes; if a bit tough, simmer for 20 minutes. Turn off the heat, run cold water into the pot, and drain. Allow to cool, cut each shoot lengthwise into 4 pieces, and reserve overnight, refrigerated.

BEAN CURD, DRIED • When bean curd is being prepared, a film forms on top of the liquid, or milk. This is dried and cut into rectangular pieces about 1½ by 5 inches and about ⅛ inch thick. Ideally it is sun-dried, but more commonly the drying is done in factories under heat. It is then packaged in paper wrap and labeled "dried bean curd, slice type." It is brittle and should be handled carefully. Kept in a closed container in a cool, dry place, dried bean curd will keep for almost a year. Dried bean curd also comes in the form of large sheets that are packaged in plastic bags. These are even more brittle. Another form of dried bean curd is long, folded, hard strips that look like sticks. These "sticks," of a golden, sandy color, are often labeled, inexplicably and inaccurately, "bean thread," which they are not. This latter variety is tougher, requires more soaking time, and is usually reserved for long-cooked dishes such as stews.

BEAN CURD, FRESH • Called *daufu* by the Chinese, tofu by the Japanese, fresh bean curd comes in square cakes, 2½ to 3 inches on a side, that are sold loose (unpackaged) in water in some Asian markets. The custardlike cakes are made from soybean liquid called *milk*. Individual cakes are preferred rather than those that come several to a package or in large blocks. Bean curd has little taste of its own; its versatility lies in its ability to absorb the tastes of the foods with which it is combined. It may be kept refrigerated in a container of water, tightly closed, with the water changed daily. So treated, it will keep for two to three weeks. Japanese brands sold as "tofu" are packaged in larger sizes, 10 to 16 ounces. These brands are also sold in three distinct textures, soft or silken, firm or medium-firm, and extra-firm. For this cookbook, medium-firm

tofu is best in all recipes that call for fresh bean curd.

BEAN CURD, PRESERVED WITH WINE • Cubes of soybean curd in jars, preserved and fermented with salt, water, and wine, usually Shao-Hsing. These jars, which come from China, Hong Kong, and Taiwan, will be labeled either "preserved bean curd" or "bean sauce." The latter, incorrect, illustrates the mislabeling that sometimes occurs with prepared Chinese foods. I suggest that you photocopy the Chinese calligraphy and show it to the shopkeeper. Look for the cubes in the preserving liquid. After opening, preserved bean curd should be refrigerated. It will keep up to six months.

BEAN CURD, WET • Cubes of fermented bean curd, with salt, wine, and red rice. The labels on jars or crocks will read "wet bean curd," "red wet bean curd," or "fermented bean curd." This is very different from preserved bean curd. The only difference in packaging is the color—the flavor does not change. It is not spicy and is used for braising and barbecue recipes and always red in color. Note that these, like the preserved bean curd, are cubes but are larger and, as noted, always red. Opened, the bean curd must be refrigerated. It will keep in its container for at least six months. Japanese brands and markets sell wet bean curd as "soybean paste," which is fine to substitute in any of the recipes in this book.

BEAN CURD CAKES • These begin as fresh bean curd formed into smaller cakes. Pressed to remove almost all moisture, they are then cooked in water flavored with five-spice seasoning and soy sauce. They are dried and then packaged, six to an 8-ounce pack. They are brown in color and are usually labeled "soybean cake" as well as "spiced." They are even sold in an unflavored white variety. Bean curd cakes also come loosely bundled with smaller cakes, about two dozen to the pack, and in larger sizes in bags of 10 ounces to 1 pound. The larger cakes tend to be white inside and have a milder taste. The smaller ones are spicier, with an added taste of chili. I recommend those that come six to a package, with the faint taste of anise imparted by the five-spice seasoning.

BEAN CURD SKINS, FRESH • Like dried bean curd, this is a by-product of the cooking of soybean milk. Though it is made of the same film that forms in the cooking, it is thinner than dried bean curd, more flexible, and a bit moist. Usually it comes in round sheets, about 2 feet in diameter, folded in a plastic package and stored in the refrigerated cases of markets. These sheets usually come to the stores frozen, eight to a package; a retailer will separate them and create four packages of two skins each, which is often how they are sold. If you ask for them frozen, you may receive a package of eight.

BEAN SAUCE • This thick puree is made from those soybeans that remain after soy sauce is made and thus are fermented. They are mixed with wheat flour, to which sugar and salt have been added, and the result is this thick sauce which contains pieces of the soybeans. The jars are usually labeled "bean sauce." There is also a mixture labeled "ground bean sauce," which simply means the beans have been ground into a mash. These tend to be quite salty. Those labeled "bean sauce" containing bits of beans are my preference. You may also see jars labeled "yellow bean sauce" or "brown bean sauce." These are the same bean sauces, only the labels differ, and these latter two labels are rare these days.

BEAN SAUCE, SWEET • This sweet, pureed sauce of soybeans, often with sugar or maltose, garlic, and sesame oil, is quite like hoisin sauce, though a bit sweeter. In Chinese it is called *tim min jeung,* or "sweet noodle sauce," for it is often eaten with noodles. It comes in jars or cans, often labeled "sweet bean sauce" or simply "bean sauce," and is usually deep chocolate-brown in color.

BEAN SPROUTS • There are two varieties. The first, mung bean sprouts, are white and plump, with a decided crunch, and are grown from mung beans. They are sold by weight in Chinese markets and other markets as well. Stored in the refrigerator in plastic bags in which holes have been punched, they will keep for no more than four days, after which they soften and become colorless. The second, soybean sprouts, are also white but longer than mung bean sprouts, with yellow soybeans at the tips. They are also widely available, and storage is the same as for mung bean sprouts.

BEAN THREAD NOODLES • These are often called simply bean threads, vermicelli bean threads, or cellophane noodles. They are made when mung beans are moistened, mashed, strained, and formed into very thin, white noodles. They come dried in cellophane packs which contain eight small bundles or loose in ½-pound packages. Avoid other large packs of irregularly shaped sheets and long, thick rough sticks, both of which are labeled "dried bean thread" and are sandy brown in color. They are made with soybeans and should not be confused with bean thread noodles.

BIRD'S NESTS • These are truly nests, of the swallowlike swifts of Southeast Asia. They are actually the dried spittle of these birds, secreted for making nests. The nests are harvested, often under dangerous circumstances, from caves high up in cliffs in Indonesia, Malaysia, Thailand, and the Philippines or even in the eaves and under roof beams of houses in these countries. They command extraordinary prices, depending on their quality. The finest are those called *white nests,* almost completely of dried spittle and resembling small, white cups; or *blood nests,* because of the red color caused by the minerals in the diets of the birds. Some contain bits of twigs, grasses, leaves, and feathers and are referred to as "black" nests. A white or blood nest can cost as much as $200.

Bird's nests, the Chinese believe, will preserve the youthfulness of one's skin and are prized by young women, as well as by the aged of both sexes.

Like other dried and preserved traditional foods, bird's nests must be prepared for use. They are customarily soaked for several hours in cold water to soften them, then any impurities are picked out. Then they are steamed with a stock, usually chicken, if they are to be used in soup, or with rock sugar if they are to be a base for a sweet or dessert soup.

BLACK BEANS, FERMENTED • Fragrant black beans preserved in salt. They come either in plastic-wrapped packs or in cans. I prefer the packaged beans, which are lightly flavored with ginger and orange peel. Before the beans are used, the salt must be rinsed off. They will keep for as long as a year, without refrigeration, so long as they are kept in a tightly sealed container. I do not recommend jarred black beans, nor are they used in any of the recipes in this book.

白菜

BOK CHOY • This is surely China's most popular vegetable. Its name translates literally as "white vegetable" because of its lovely white bulbous stalk, which contrasts with its deep green leaves. Variations of it exist in China and other parts of Asia, though it is native to China. It is a most versatile vegetable because of its crispness and inherent sweetness. Though it is often referred to as *Chinese cabbage,* that is an error, for it bears no resemblance to cabbage. *Bok choy* will keep for about a week in the vegetable drawer of a refrigerator, but it tends to lose its sweetness quickly, so I recommend using it at its freshest.

上海白菜

BOK CHOY, SHANGHAI • Smaller than *bok choy*, with pronounced bulbous stalks, this is often called *ching bok choy,* which literally means "greenish white vegetable." It is an apt description, for its stalks are not as white as *bok choy,* its leaves less deep green. If you ask for Shanghai *bok choy,* you may be looked at strangely. If so, ask for *tong choy,* and there will be no problem. It also is quite sweet and crisp and should be stored as for *bok choy.* One caution: When cooked, Shanghai *bok choy* tends to become softer than *bok choy,* so care should be taken.

BOK CHOY, TIANJIN • See *Tianjin Bok Choy.*

枸杞子

BOXTHORN SEEDS • These are actually the tiny, red, raisinlike fruit of the boxthorn shrub. They have a faint, mild, sweet, licorice taste and are used generally in soups. They are considered to be helpful to eye health and are regarded as a restorative. Once they were available only in Chinese medicine or herbal shops, but now these dried red berrylike fruits can be found in packages in Chinese groceries. They are often called *wolfberries* but more familiarly labeled "boxthorn." The young leaves of the boxthorn shrub are often used in stir-fried preparations and in soups or tossed with scrambled eggs. Even the boxthorn twig is used to make soups, or infusions that are prized by the elderly for a perceived ability to cool one's inner heat and to help bone strength.

佛手

BUDDHA'S HAND • The gourd vegetable that is known familiarly in the West as chayote or christophine, or in the southern United States, particularly in Louisiana, as mirliton. It is pear-shaped and ranges in color from pale green, almost white, to darker green. In China it is called *fat su,* or "Buddha's hand," for it looks like Buddha's hands together, fingertips upward, in prayer. Related to the squash, it is eaten widely by Buddhist monks and nuns, perhaps more for its symbolism than for its taste, which is quite bland. Like some other vegetables, Buddha's hand's character is that it takes on the tastes of whatever it is cooked with. It is often cut up in stir-fries, used in soups, or braised.

CHILIES, THAI • Small thin chilies, colored deep red to deep green, about 1½ inches long. They are quite hot and impart a heat that tends to linger in the mouth, yet they are pleasant indeed. They are my chilies of choice. I also find them dependable in terms of the numbers used to obtain desired hotness. They will keep, refrigerated, for about four weeks in an open container, lightly covered with plastic wrap. Do not seal the container, or the chilies will deteriorate. They may be used dried as well, but their heat will be less intense.

CHILI PASTE • This jarred condiment of chilies, salt, soybean oil, and soybean paste is often labeled "chili paste with soybeans." It is used as a flavoring for stir-fried dishes and as a sauce ingredient.

CHILI SAUCE • This jarred sauce is a mixture of vinegar, chilies, salt, often with cornstarch and artificial coloring added. Better to make your own (see recipe, page 88).

CHINESE MUSHROOMS • See *Mushrooms, Chinese Black.*

CHINKIANG VINEGAR • See *Vinegar, Chinkiang.*

CHIVES, CHINESE • Also known as *garlic chives.* They are more pungent than the Western chive and are wider and flatter, though of the same deep green color. Yellow chives are the same vegetable, but as they grow they are deprived of sun and thus take on a lighter color. Their taste is more delicate than that of green chives, with more the taste of onion than of garlic. If you cannot find Chinese chives, you may use Western chives, but the taste of your recipe will be different.

CHOI SUM • A leafy vegetable with thin, tender stalks. It is all green, from its large outside leaves to the smaller inside leaves to the light green stalks, which are crisp and sweet. *Choi sum,* like other leafy vegetables, tends to lose its sweetness, so it should be eaten as quickly as possible. It is usually available in Chinese and Asian groceries.

CILANTRO • See *Coriander.*

CLOUD EARS • These are fungi that when dried look a bit like round chips, either brown or brown-black. When soaked in water, they soften and glisten and resemble flower petals. Dry, they may be kept indefinitely in a closed jar, in a cool, dry place. Once these cloud ears were interchangeable, at least in Chinese groceries, with tree ears, also known as *wood ears,* also a brownish fungus that grows on wood. However, cloud ears are smaller and more tender than the much larger, tougher, tree ears.

CONPOY • See *Scallops, Dry.*

CORIANDER • This aromatic leaf is also called *fresh coriander* (to distinguish it from the spice), *Chinese parsley,* and *cilantro.* It is similar only in appearance to parsley. It has an intense smell and imparts a distinctive taste when used as a flavoring agent or as a garnish. Often it is suggested that Italian parsley be used as a substitute. Do not follow such a suggestion. Their aromas are entirely different. There is no substitute for coriander. It should be used fresh so that its bouquet will be appreciated, but it may be refrigerated for a week.

CURRY POWDER • A blending of spices such as turmeric, cumin, fennel, and coriander seeds, plus others that might be used in an individual or personal mix. There are many brands of curry powder on the market, but I prefer the stronger, more pungent brands from India.

EGGPLANT, CHINESE • This bright lavender to purple eggplant, often white-tinged, is narrower than its Western counterpart, usually no more than 2 inches in diameter at its thickest. Its taste is like that of usual eggplant, but its skin is quite tender and need not be removed before cooking.

EGG ROLL SKINS • Food wrappers made from flour and water. Let me say that in China there is no such preparation as the egg roll. It is a Western hybrid of the spring roll. However, egg rolls are so pervasive that wrappers are made for them and so labeled. (For a fuller explanation, see *Spring Roll Skins* and *Wrappers.*)

EGGS, PRESERVED • The eggs preserved most often in China are duck eggs. The most common are those referred to as *thousand-year-old eggs.* Actually, they are considerably younger. Raw duck eggs are usually wrapped with a paste mix of salt, tea leaves, rice husks, and a preservative, sodium bicarbonate, and left to cure for 50 days. By that time the shell becomes a mottled gray, the inside of the egg like aspic, the yolk a deep, dull green, the white a deep brown. Once these eggs came shipped, loose, in huge brown earthenware crocks. Now they are packaged, usually six to a pack, and labeled "preserved duck egg." Though they are produced all over China, the thousand-year-old eggs from Fujian are generally considered the best and are often eaten as they are, sliced and accompanied by pieces of pickled ginger.

There is another treated duck egg in which the egg is covered with a mix of salt, water, and ashes from burned rice straw. After curing for about 20 days, the white of egg is still a viscous liquid, but the yolk becomes a hard orange-red ball. These are labeled "salted duck eggs." Both of these eggs are used in the Chinese kitchen. The Chinese also salt and preserve chicken eggs, but these are a home kitchen preparation and rarely available in the West.

EIGHT-STAR ANISE OR STAR ANISE • The tiny eight-pointed hard star fruit of the Chinese anise tree. This spice has a flavor more pronounced than that of anise seed. It should be kept in a tightly sealed jar in a cool, dry place. It will keep for a year, though it may gradually lose its intensity and flavor.

FISH SAUCE • A thin brownish liquid, made from fish essence or extract, with salt and water. In China it is called *yue lo,* or "fish mist." It is widely used by the Chiu Chow people of southern China and to some extent by the Cantonese. It is essentially the same as the *nam pla* of Thailand and the *nuoc mam* of Vietnam. It is made throughout Southeast Asia, China, and Taiwan and variously labeled as "fish sauce" or "fish gravy."

FIVE-SPICE SEASONING • The five spices can be of any combination from the following: star anise, fennel seeds, cinnamon, cloves, ginger, licorice, nutmeg, and Sichuan peppercorns. Different makes prefer different mixtures, though anise and cinnamon dominate. You may devise your own five-spice seasoning by asking for a ready-mixed packet at a Chinese herbal shop. The herbalist will be happy to oblige. Often the spices are ground into a powder that is quite pungent and used only sparingly in dishes that demand strong flavors. The mixture is also often used to flavor foods like soybean cakes and barbecued pork.

FLOURS • There are, of course, many brands of flour available, but I have chosen three, after much testing, as ideal for the doughs of the Chinese breads and dim sum:

*Pillsbury Best Bread Flour, enriched,
    bromide, naturally white, high protein,
    high gluten*
*Pillsbury Best All-Purpose Flour, enriched,
    bleached*
*Gold Medal All-Purpose Flour, enriched,
    bleached*

The properties of all flours and doughs are discussed at length in the chapter "Chinese Breads, Noodles, and Dim Sum."

GALANGAL • See *Sand Ginger.*

GARLIC CHIVES • See *Chives, Chinese.*

GINGER • Also referred to as *ginger root.* When selecting ginger roots, look for those with smooth outer skins, because ginger begins to wrinkle and roughen with age. It flavors extremely well. It serves as well to diffuse strong fish and shellfish odors. It should be used sparingly and should be sliced, and often peeled, before use. Its strength is often dictated by its preparation. I use ginger sliced, peeled and unpeeled, smashed lightly, julienned, minced, and shredded. When placed in a heavy brown paper bag and refrigerated, it will keep for four to five weeks.

I do not recommend trying to preserve it

in wine or freezing it, because it loses strength. Nor do I recommend ground ginger or bottled ginger juice as substitutes, because in the Chinese kitchen there is no substitute for fresh ginger. There is also young ginger, which is very smooth, slightly pink in color, and without the tough skin of older ginger. It is quite crisp. It is often called *spring ginger,* but that is a misnomer; it grows in China not in the spring but twice each year—late in the summer and in January and February. Occasionally there is even a third crop. I use this young ginger to make my own Ginger Pickle (see below).

GINGER JUICE • Although this is occasionally available in small bottles, you can make a better-quality juice yourself. Simply grate fresh ginger into a bowl, then press it through a garlic press. Make as needed; its shelf life, refrigerated, is only two to three days.

GINGER PICKLE • Slices of young ginger are pickled with salt, sugar, and white vinegar (see recipe, page 102). Pickled ginger is also available in jars and is an agreeable substitute.

GINKGO NUTS • These hard-shelled nuts shaped like tiny footballs are the seeds of the ginkgo tree, a common shade tree in China. The tree's fruit is not edible, but the nuts are, when cooked. Pale yellow when raw, they become translucent when cooked. They are available fresh or canned. When fresh they require cooking (see page 143). Those in cans are already cooked. Raw nuts will keep, refrigerated, in a plastic bag for four to six weeks. Cooked, they will keep for only four to five days. Canned nuts, when opened, should be used within a week. Both canned and raw ginkgos should be refrigerated.

GLUTEN • This is an elastic protein substance that is a component of wheat flour. It is called *mien gun* by the Chinese, a phrase that translates as "tendon flour," to illustrate its tensile nature. It is either doughlike or crisp after processing and is made in this manner: Wheat flour is made into a dough, with water, then kneaded. The dough is washed thoroughly to remove its starch, thus concentrating the gluten. The gluten dough is often simmered in a stock and not only acquires taste but becomes a spongelike mass. In China, where gluten is available fresh on a daily basis, it is eaten with frequency by monks and religious vegetarians as a meat substitute. It is sold both moist and doughy, and dried, often deep-fried to give it some body and texture. I am not as fond of this food as are some others. I prefer bean curd, in all of its forms, to gluten, as a basic food or as a protein substitute.

GLUTINOUS RICE • Often called *sweet rice,* this is shorter grained than other rices. When cooked, it becomes somewhat sticky. Its kernels stick together in a mass instead of separating the way extra-long-grain rice does. It is often referred to as *sticky rice.* Some packages of this rice are labeled "sweet rice." There are also black glutinous and long-grain glutinous rices, often used in Southeast Asia for sweets.

GLUTINOUS RICE POWDER • Often called *glutinous rice flour* as well, this is used as a base for dumplings and steamed rice cakes.

HAIR SEAWEED • Dried seaweed called *hair* because of its thin black strands. It comes in packages of various sizes. It will keep indefinitely, in a closed jar, in a cool, dark place. It must be soaked before use.

HAIRY MELON • This is a gourd-shaped green melon, generally larger than a cucumber, with a fine fuzz covering its exterior. It is a cousin to the winter melon, and like the winter melon it tends to take on the flavors of the foods with which it is cooked.

雲
腿

HAM, YUNNAN • A cured, salty ham from the western province of Yunnan, considered to be the best ham in China. It is unavailable in the United States, rare in the West in general. Jinhua ham, a similar cured ham, similarly unavailable, is from the Shanghai region. The use of Smithfield ham from Virginia is recommended as a substitute, the only substitute, for both. (See *Smithfield Ham*.)

海
鮮
醬

HOISIN SAUCE • A thick, chocolate-brown, sweetened sauce made from soybeans, garlic, sugar, and chilies. Some brands add a little vinegar to the mix; others thicken the sauce with flour. Often it is mistakenly called *plum sauce*, which it decidedly is not. Hoisin comes in jars and large cans. If purchased in a can, it should be transferred to a jar and refrigerated. It will keep for many months.

荳
瓣
醬

HORSE BEANS, PRESERVED WITH CHILI • The horse bean is the lima or fava bean. In Chinese it is called *dau ban jeung,* which translates as "bean mixed sauce." To make it, the beans are cooked, mashed, and mixed with ground chilies. It is a very spicy sauce and adds good heat to many dishes. It comes in jars that, once opened, must be refrigerated; or in cans, from which the sauce should be removed, then jarred, after opening. Refrigerated, it will keep for at least six months. This ingredient is a prime example of the confusion that can occur with labeling, because of the proliferation of brands. The one I prefer over all others is Lan Chi Preserved Horse Beans with Chili, jarred in Taiwan. However, on the shelves you will find the following: "hot bean sauce" or "hot bean paste" or "chili bean sauce" or "Sichuan hot bean sauce" or simply "bean sauce." All are essentially mixtures of beans and chili, but some add sugar, some flour, some sesame oil, some soybean oil, some garlic. One canned version labeled "bean sauce" even omits the chilies. Some substitute mashed soybeans for the horse beans and add chilies and oil. It can be confusing. As I have cautioned, look at labels with care. Hot pepper sauce could be used as a substitute, but the taste of the recipe will not be the same.

辣
椒
油

HOT PEPPER OIL • There are many brands of hot oil on market shelves. Often, however, they are based on inferior oils. It is preferable that you make your own with a peanut oil base. It is not difficult. Also, you will have as a by-product hot pepper flakes at the bottom of the oil, a bonus with many uses. (See recipe, page 87.)

JÍCAMA • See *Sah Gut.*

KETCHUP • Ketchup from China comes in bottles, like its Western counterparts. The best brand is Koon Yick Wan Kee, manufactured in Hong Kong, made from tomatoes, vinegar, and spices. The difference between it and Western ketchups with which we are familiar is its use. In China, ketchup is used more as a coloring agent than as a flavoring. The Chinese version is often difficult to find, however, so the use of Western ketchup will suffice. It is believed by some that ketchup originated in China. There is, in the South, on the island of Amoy, a concoction of fish essence and soy sauce called *keh chap* that could be, as has been suggested, a precursor.

LILY BULBS • These bulbs, from which lilies grow, look quite like garlic bulbs without skins. They are white, a bit glossy, and come fresh, wrapped in plastic, or dried. Fresh lily bulbs are crisp and sweet and peel off like petals from a flower. They are used in stir-fries, salads, sweet soups, and raw as snacks. Dried lily bulbs, packaged as loose individual petals, must be soaked to reconstitute them. The fresh variety, much preferred, are available whole, in refrigerated sections of markets, and usually are flown in from China. The best, traditionally, come from Lanzhou, near Xi'an, and were once regarded as one of those foods offered in tribute to the imperial court. Lily bulbs are often regarded as a relative to ginseng because it is said to reduce coughing and throat inflammation and to keep one's skin

clear. These fresh bulbs, refrigerated, will keep for up to two months.

LOTUS LEAVES AND BAMBOO LEAVES • These large dried leaves are used as wrappings for various steamed preparations. Lotus leaves impart a distinctive, somewhat sweet taste to the foods they are wrapped around, and they are preferable to bamboo leaves. Once lotus leaves were only sold commercially in 50-pound boxes to restaurants. Now they can be bought, by weight, in small quantities. Bamboo leaves can easily be bought in smaller quantities and make quite good substitutes, but their smell and taste are different. Kept in a plastic bag, in a dry place, the dried leaves will keep for six months to a year. If you are able to obtain fresh lotus leaves, then by all means use them fresh, or sun-dry them yourself for future use.

LOTUS ROOT • The gourd-shaped root of the lotus. These roots often grow four or five together, connected like a string of sausages, each about 3 inches in diameter and 4 to 5 inches long. When the root is cut across, there is a pattern of holes not unlike the holes found in Swiss cheese. The texture is light, a bit dry, and crisp. Lotus roots should be kept refrigerated in a brown paper bag and used within a few days of purchase, since they tend to lose both flavor and texture quickly.

LOTUS SEEDS • These are the olive-shaped seeds from the lotus pod. They are familiar to most as the cooked and mashed filling in some Chinese sweets. They are regarded as a delicacy and are sold by weight. They may be kept for as long as six months at room temperature in a tightly sealed jar. I do not recommend keeping them that long, however, for their flavor weakens and their texture toughens with time.

LOTUS SEED PASTE • A deep red-chocolate-colored paste made from lotus seeds cooked with sugar. It comes in cans, of many brands, generally all of which are of good quality. Once removed from the can, the paste will keep, refrigerated, in a closed container, for two to three months.

MALTOSE • A thick syrup made in China through malting from the starches of grains. It is pleasantly sweet, not as sweet as raw sugar, and is the ingredient of choice in the preparation of Peking Duck. When mixed with vinegar and boiling water, it is used to coat the duck skin before roasting. Once available in small ceramic pots, now it is sold in plastic containers.

MUSHROOMS, CHINESE BLACK • These dried mushrooms come in boxes or cellophane packs. They are black, dark gray, or speckled in color, and their caps range in size from about that of a nickel to 3 inches in diameter. Those in boxes are the choicest, in both size and color, and are priced accordingly. Chinese black mushrooms must always be soaked in hot water for at least a half hour before use, their stems removed and discarded, and they should be thoroughly cleaned on the underside of the cap and squeezed dry. In their dried form they will keep indefinitely at room temperature in a tightly closed container. If you live in an especially damp or humid climate, they should be stored in the freezer. These are the same mushrooms known as shiitake outside of China. I prefer the dried mushrooms to the fresh, because of the concentrated intensity of their flavor. I find fresh shiitakes lacking in flavor, perhaps a circumstance of overcultivation and quick harvesting.

MUSHROOMS, STRAW • Small mushrooms with elongated domelike caps. They are common in southern China and highly prized. It is a mark of respect to serve these mushrooms to a guest. Occasionally found fresh, more so lately, they are most often canned.

MUSTARD, HOT • This is made by mixing equal amounts of dry mustard powder and cold tap water. There are many hot mustards on the market, but I prefer the English-made Colman's Mustard, Double Superfine Compound. It must be the dried mustard powder, not the Colman's prepared mustard that comes in jars. For normal use, combine 2 to 3 teaspoons of mustard with a similar amount of water. For a quite pungent mix, using the same measurements, mix with Chinese white rice vinegar or distilled white vinegar.

MUSTARD, PRESERVED • See *Preserved Mustard*.

MUSTARD GREENS (SOUR MUSTARD PICKLE) • This leafy cabbagelike vegetable with large, round, green-tinged, bulbous stalks is called *kai choi*, or "leaf-mustard cabbage." Its taste is strong, and it is used fresh in soups or stir-fried with meats, but it is more commonly used in its preserved forms. Water-blanched and cured with salt, sugar, and vinegar, it is used in stir-fries and soups. Its heart is often used as a garnish. It can be bought, already cured in large crocks, loose, sold by weight, or in cans labeled "sour mustard pickle" or "sour mustard greens" or "mustard greens." If you buy

the cured greens loose, place them in a tightly closed plastic container and refrigerate them. They will keep for three months. Once cans are opened, greens should be stored in the same manner and will have the same storage life. There is also a smaller *kai choi*, called appropriately *kai choi jai*, or "baby *kai choi*." It differs in appearance. It is small, green, its stalks are straight instead of bulbous, and it is generally used in soups. It is too soft and tender to use in stir-fried dishes.

MUSTARD PICKLE • See *Sichuan Mustard Pickle*.

NOODLES • There are many variations on the noodle in China, all of them known collectively as *mien* or *min*. Because of their flour base, other foods made with doughs are often called "noodle fruit." There are wheat flour noodles, fresh and dried, of various widths, made from flour either mixed just with water or with eggs added. There are rice noodles, also fresh and dried, of various widths. Very fine rice noodles are often called *rice sticks*. (There is another food called *rice noodle* that is not a noodle. See *Rice Noodle*.) And there are mung bean noodles, in addition to the bean threads listed above. These are usually shaped like linguine and need only be soaked in hot water before use.

For most noodle dishes most types of noodle will be quite suitable. (Even fine vermicelli or capellini pasta, fresh or dried, will substitute quite well.) I have, however, given my preferences with individual recipes.

O ILS • Peanut oil is the preferred oil of the Chinese kitchen, not only for its healthful attributes but also for the fine nutty flavor it imparts. I have used peanut oil and sesame oil to create a series of flavored, spiced infused oils for use in specified recipes, to accompany different dishes, and to use as dips.

dried. The Chinese call this *mui choi*. Brown in color when dried and put into plastic bags, it is soft and pliable, with a texture quite like that of prunes. It is used in steaming as well as for stir-fried dishes, in braising, and in soups. The packages it comes in may also be labeled "salted mustard." Often you will see tiny salt crystals on it, but it does not affect the mustard. It should be stored in a sealed jar at room temperature and will keep for at least six months. The longer it is kept, the darker it becomes. Before use the leaves must be opened and the salt and sand thoroughly removed by washing.

O YSTER S AUCE • A rich sauce, the base of which is ground oysters that have been boiled and dried, then cooked into thickness. It is a highly prized seasoning in China, not only for its distinctive taste but also for the richness of its color. It is well regarded by Buddhists, because the oyster is a permitted food in their vegetarian diet, along with clams and mussels. Once opened, a bottle of oyster sauce should be refrigerated and will keep indefinitely. Unrefrigerated, it will also keep for a good period of time if used often and quickly, but I prefer to refrigerate it. I recommend Hop Sing Lung brand from Hong Kong, if available.

P RESERVED P LUMS • Small plums native to China. They look more like apricots. They come in jars, cured with salt and water. There is no sweetness at all to these plums; rather they are sour. In China it is believed that this sourness enhances the appetite.

R ED B EAN P ASTE • The most frequently used form of red beans. The beans are soaked and boiled, then mashed and cooked with sugar and traditionally with lard or with peanut oil into paste form. It comes in cans. Like lotus seed paste, most brands of red bean paste are of good quality. The paste is used for fillings in buns, pastries, and dumplings. Once a can is opened, the bean paste must be kept refrigerated in a closed container. It will keep for four to six weeks.

P RESERVED M USTARD • These are preserved mustard plants that have been cooked, then preserved in salt and sugar, then

RED BEANS • These small deep red beans are generally used in sweets, although occasionally they are combined with other foods in casseroles. The beans are sold in plastic sacks by weight and will keep indefinitely.

RED DATES • These dried fruit come in 1-pound plastic-wrapped packages, labeled either "red dates" or "dried dates." Once opened and removed from the package, the dates should be placed in a glass jar, covered, and stored in a cool place. They will keep for six months.

RED IN SNOW • A green, leafy vegetable, quite like collard greens, that is a Shanghai favorite. Its more mundane name is *snow cabbage,* but in China it is known as *hseut loi hung,* or "red in snow." It is rarely eaten fresh. More often it is water-blanched and preserved in salt. It is usually cut up for use in soups or with noodles, in stir-fries with meats, or in dumplings. It comes in small cans often labeled "snow cabbage" or "Shanghai cabbage" or "pickled cabbage," but it is the same vegetable, prepared identically. It also comes in plastic bags labeled with its correct name, "red in snow." It can also be bought fresh, and you may preserve it yourself, as the people of Shanghai prefer. Just ask for it by its Chinese name, take it home, water-blanch it,

drain, add salt, and allow to sit in a container for at least 48 hours at room temperature. Refrigerate after. The best time of the year to buy red in snow fresh, to preserve it yourself, is in September and October.

RICE • In its many forms rice, *fan,* is the universal staple of the Chinese kitchen. It exists in many varieties and can be prepared in many ways. For a discussion of rices and their preparations, including my recipe for cooking perfect, foolproof rice, see page 68.

RICE, RED • A very distinctive type of rice, deep red in color and short-grain. Rarely is it eaten by itself; rather it is used primarily as a coloring agent, most notably in a fermented preparation of the Southern Chinese of Fujian, Chiu Chow, and Hakka and in Southeast Asia that is simply called *red rice.* This rice comes in packages labeled "red yeast rice" or "yeast" or, inexplicably, "dried pearl barley." Ask for red rice.

RICE NOODLE • This is known as *sah hor fun* or "sand river noodle," though it is not strictly a noodle. It is made with rice flour and water. It does not come in strands and bunches but rather in sheets, occasionally round, usually square. It is snowy white with a glistening, shiny surface when fresh and is usually oiled and folded before packaging. This should be used only fresh. Rice noodle is sold in noodle factories in Chinese neighborhoods, and some markets will get it for you on request.

Before using it you must carefully unfold it and cut the pieces you need from it. It cannot be stored at room temperature but must be refrigerated. It will not last for more than three days. Or it can be frozen and will keep for one to two months. After refrigeration or freezing it must be returned to room temperature, then steamed to restore its pliability.

RICE POWDER • This is a coarse powder made from short-grain rice and Sichuan peppercorns that have been dry-roasted, then put through a blender so that the mixture has the consistency of bread crumbs. This is occasionally available in Chinese markets or Asian groceries, in boxes, lettered in Chinese except for the words *steam powder,* a reference to its use. It is far easier to make yourself than to search for it. I have different recipes for its use, depending on what will be steamed with it.

ROCK SUGAR (ROCK CANDY) • A compound of white sugar, raw brown sugar, and honey. It is used in sweet soups or in teas. It comes in 1-pound sacks and resembles a collection of small amber rocks.

SAH GUT • Commonly known in the West as jícama, this bulbous root is sweet and crisp, with a sand-colored exterior and white interior. It can be eaten raw or cooked. In Mexico and the Southwest its name, jícama, reflects its origin, but it has become widely cultivated in China and the rest of Asia. A fine use for it is, as noted, a substitute for water chestnuts. Stored in a brown paper bag and refrigerated, *sah gut* will keep its crispness for three to four days. Store on shelf, not in vegetable drawer.

SAND GINGER • A small, tender root, quite like ginger, also known throughout China and Southeast Asia as *galangal*. This root, quite like young ginger in appearance, is either yellow or sandy white in color; thus its name, *sah geun,* or "sand ginger." Its aroma, however, is unlike ginger; rather it has a fresh smell, reminiscent of fresh coriander. The white variety is preferred in China. It can be bought in its root form, but usually as a sand-colored powder, in packages labeled "sand ginger" or "dried ginger powder."

SAUSAGES, CHINESE • These *lop cheung* are traditionally made in China of coarsely diced pork, pork liver, and duck liver. Very little of the duck liver variety is made or is available in the United States. The most common is pork sausage, threaded through with pork fat, usually in pairs held together with string. Those of all liver are called *yun cheung* or "gold and silver" and are a favorite at the Lunar New Year. All of these sausages are cured, but not cooked, and thus must be cooked before eating. They can be kept refrigerated for about a month and frozen for two months. A somewhat leaner *lop cheung,* of ground pork, from Canadian processors is also available in some markets, but in my view it lacks the defined flavor of those made in the United States, which in my opinion are as good as those in China.

ing them for 1,000 years, and they are regarded as most warming and health-giving, often honored with the name "ginseng of the sea." The gray-black slugs, dried, command prices as high as $50 a pound, this for those about the size of a forefinger. They are allowed to dry to hardness, preferably in the sun, and are sold that way, loose, by weight. Again, as with most dried foods, the sea cucumber must be soaked until soft, then slit open and cleaned thoroughly. Often they are simmered in stock as a prepatory step, before being put into recipes. Sea cucumbers are often added to soups, cut up into stir-fries, or braised whole or in sections.

瑤
柱

SCALLOPS, DRY • These are sea scallops, known as *gawn bui,* anglicized as *conpoy,* that are dried at length to hardness, usually in the sun. They are a highly regarded delicacy in China and range in size from ½-inch disks to those as large as 2 inches in diameter. Prices can exceed $100 a pound for the largest. Usually they are sold loose, by weight, from large jars and are available in Chinese markets or herbal medicine shops. They are quite hard when dried and must be either soaked or steamed, after which they can be cooked further, either whole or separated into shreds, for other dishes.

蘇
油

SESAME OIL • This is a most aromatic oil made from pressed, often toasted, sesame seeds. It has a defined nutlike aroma. I prefer it as an additive to sauces or marinades or as a dressing. It tends to burn quickly when used to cook, and when this occurs there is no benefit of its fine aroma and little of its distinctive taste. Adding a bit of sesame oil as a finish to an already prepared dish imparts a fine flavor, in the case of some soups, or particularly to steamed fish. It is thick and brown in versions from China, thinner and lighter from the Middle East. I recommend the sesame oil from China. Stored in a tightly closed bottle at room temperature, it will keep for at least four months.

海
参

SEA CUCUMBER • This is a euphemism for sea slug, an oblong, occasionally large gelatinous creature that lives on the ocean floor. The Chinese have been harvest-

芝蔴醬

SESAME SEED PASTE • This is a paste made by mixing ground white sesame seeds with soybean oil. It is known in the Middle East as *tahini*. It comes in jars and is smooth, with the consistency of peanut butter. Its sesame taste is quite pronounced. After opening, the jar should be refrigerated. It will keep for six months.

芝蔴

SESAME SEEDS, BLACK AND WHITE • Black seeds, either roasted or not, are customarily used as a decoration or as an ingredient in the preparation of sweet pastry fillings. Roasted white seeds are generally used in dumpling fillings or as garnishes and occasionally in the making of sweets. Seeds should be stored in the freezer because they tend to become rancid quickly.

紹興酒

SHAO-HSING WINE • This is a sherrylike wine made and bottled in China and in Taiwan. There are several grades of differing degrees of alcohol. I use not only the basic wine but also the best refined grade of Shao-Hsing, which is labeled Hua Tiao Chiew. You may simply ask for *far jiu*, a generic term, like *burgundy*. Take care not to buy something called "Shao-Hsing Wine for Cooking," for it is inferior, with an inferior taste. I use Shao-Hsing widely, as you will see, in marinades, in sauces, or on its own, for it adds a great deal to individual dishes. A dry

sherry is an acceptable substitute, but again, do not use so-called cooking wine. Shao-Hsing wines are discussed at length in the chapter on the wines of China.

SHARK'S FINS • Usually refers to the top, dorsal fin of the shark, although five different shark fins are used in the Chinese kitchen, the two side fins, the bottom, and the tail as well. One of the most prestigious and traditional festive foods in China, shark's fins have been eaten by the Chinese for many hundreds of years, believed to be beneficial to heart, lungs, kidneys, and liver, as well as to the complexion.

The fins, cut from the shark, are dried, and when hard the black outer skin is scraped off with a curved knife and the fin split open to remove the structural cartilage. It is boiled, then soaked until all pieces of cartilage and skin are removed; then boiled again until it becomes yellow-white in color, clean, and odorless. It is dried for storage until use. As with other dried foods the fin must be prepared before cooking. To prepare it for consumption it is steamed until the strands of the fin separate; then steamed again, usually in a chicken broth with pork fat, ginger, and scallions, which imparts flavor to it. Not until this laborious process is complete is the fin used in recipes.

The whole fin can be braised or cooked in broth, so that it looks quite like a floating fan, the grandest of presentations. It can also be cooked, in sections, in broth, or its strands put into dim sum dumplings as a filling. There is much lore about fins, with special names bestowed on the choicest sharks with the choicest fins—Manila Yellow, Sea Tiger, Whole Skirt, Gold Mountain Hook, Tooth Root, Five Goats, and Sky Nine, to name a few. No banquet of any consequence is without some shark fin dish.

The finest of fins can be bought dried and cleaned for as much as $350 each. But packages of strands may be found in Chinese groceries and some herbal medicine shops, for use in soups. These require none of the time-consuming early preparation.

SHRIMP, DRIED • Precooked, shelled small shrimp, dried and salted for preservation. They come in packages. Before use they should be soaked in warm water for at least 30 minutes. They will keep for two to three months in a tightly closed container in a dry place. They can also be frozen for storage if they are not used often. They should be orange-pink in color, and a sure sign that they are aging and losing their strength is their change to a grayish color.

SHRIMP CHIPS • Small, hard, translucent, shrimp-flavored chips of various pastel colors, which when deep-fried puff up to three times their size. They are usually made from shrimp essence, potato flour, baking powder, and salt. They are eaten widely both in China and throughout Asia, quite extensively in Southeast Asia. They come in

boxes often labeled "shrimp chips," "shrimp-flavored chips," "imitation shrimp-flavored chips," or variations of these. Once fried, they are eaten as snacks or used as garnishes.

SHRIMP PASTE • A paste of tiny shrimp in jars with salt to prevent spoilage. The paste is made by mashing the shrimp, salting it, and allowing it to ferment, before putting the paste in jars. This extremely pungent paste is much favored by the Chiu Chow people in southern China, and is virtually identical to the *belachan* of Malaysia and the *kapee* of Thailand. In China it is used as a sauce additive and in steamed and stir-fried dishes. Occasionally it serves as a substitute for preserved bean curd.

SICHUAN MUSTARD PICKLE • This is also called *mustard pickle* and is made from Chinese radishes cooked with chili powder and salt. It can be added to soups and stir-fried with vegetables. It is never used fresh, only in its preserved form. It can be bought loose, by weight, but more often can be found in cans labeled "Sichuan preserved vegetable" or "Sichuan mustard pickle." As you can see, the labeling of some of the prepared foods of China is not always precise, so take care when you shop so that you obtain the correct vegetable. Sichuan mustard pickle should not, under any circumstances, be confused with sour mustard pickle.

SICHUAN PEPPERCORNS • Quite different from the usual peppercorns, these are reddish in color and not solid, but opened. They are often called *flower peppercorns* because of their appearance. They are neither hot nor peppery but rather mild. Store these peppercorns in a tightly closed jar as you would ordinary peppercorns. Several recipes call for ground Sichuan peppercorns. These cannot be bought; you must grind them yourself using a mortar and pestle or smash with the broad side of a cleaver blade, then strain through a sieve. Store the ground peppercorns in a tightly closed jar as well. Once ground, these can be used a base for an infused oil (page 86).

SILK SQUASH • An odd, thin, cucumber-shaped gourd, with pronounced ridges running along its length. It is deep green, but its flesh is white and faintly sweet with a soft texture. It is excellent in soups.

SMITHFIELD HAM • Cloth-wrapped hams, dry, salt-cured, aged, and smoked but uncooked, from Virginia. They replace, admirably, the traditional Yunnan and Jinhua hams of the Chinese kitchen. I use them often. It is not necessary to buy an entire ham; slices of up to 1 pound are available in butcher shops. To prepare for use, brush off the surface mold and wash well, then soak in

water for four hours to remove salt. Then place in a steamproof dish, add ⅓ cup of brown sugar, and steam for two hours. The ham is then ready for use. Once prepared, it may be kept, refrigerated, in a closed container for at least a month or frozen for six months.

SNOW PEA SHOOTS • These are the fine, tender tips of the vines on which snow peas grow. The leaves, called *dau miu*, are quite sweet when cooked and have been eaten happily by the Chinese for centuries. Recently they have been "discovered" and embraced by Western chefs for their freshness and delicate taste.

SOUR MUSTARD PICKLE • See *Mustard Greens.*

SOYBEAN • This bean is one of the richest sources of nourishment in the world and has been a Chinese food for thousands of years. A pound of soybeans contains twice the protein of the same weight of beef, more iron than a pound of beef liver, and is richer in digestible calcium than an equivalent amount of milk. In addition to being a source of many other vitamins, it is the most versatile of foodstuffs. It is the source of soy sauce, bean curd in all of its guises, soybean milk, and soybean sprouts. In China even the pods, with the beans inside, are eaten as a snack after being cooked in water, then baked over fire.

SOY SAUCE • This sauce, a staple of the Chinese kitchen for 3,000 years, since the Chou dynasty, is the product of the fermentation of soybeans, mixed with wheat flour, water, and salt. Evidence of its use has been found in the excavated Han tombs, and, a most democratic food, it was over the centuries enjoyed equally by the aristocracy and those people called common.

It comes in light and dark varieties. The light soys are usually taken from the tops of the batches being prepared, generally in earthenware crocks, the darker soys from the bottom. The best soy sauces are fermented in the sun, not in factories. Dark soys, which include such distinctions as dark, double dark, and a very thick and dark "pearl" sauce, are best for imparting a rich color to a dish. Some dark soys even have molasses added. I prefer dark soys with meats. Light soys are noted for their somewhat sweeter taste and marry well with fish and seafood. I prefer the soy sauces from Hong Kong and China to all others, including those produced in the United States and Japan, which I find a bit thin and too salty. The light and dark sauces I regard as superior are made in Hong Kong's New Territories by the Koon Chun Sauce Factory. Its light soy is labeled Koon Chun Thin Soy Sauce; its double-dark is labeled Koon Chun Double Black Soy Sauce. There is another dark soy I prefer, one to which mushrooms have been added, for a faint additional sweet-

ness. It comes from China and is labeled Pearl River Bridge Mushroom Soy.

The Chinese know that soys give body and richness to cooking. I often combine various soy sauces for different tastes and colorings. Most soys come in bottles, some in cans. If from a can, transfer to a bottle. Soy sauce can be kept six to nine months in a tightly capped bottle at room temperature. When not used as an additive to recipes, soy sauce can also be a dip. In general the Chinese use soy sauce more sparingly than do Westerners, many of whom I have observed pour it in large amounts over their food. Using it in that manner destroys its singular taste properties.

SPRING ROLL SKINS • These thin cooked skins are white in color and contain no eggs. (See *Wrappers.*)

SUGARCANE SUGAR • These are layered, caramel-colored blocks made from sugarcane. They come either plastic wrapped or loose, in crocks, and can be found in Chinese or Asian markets. The blocks are sold by weight.

TANGERINE PEEL, DRIED • This is the dried, wrinkled brown skin of the tangerine, used as a flavoring. The darker the dried skins, the older they are, and the older the better. The oldest dried tangerine skins are also the most expensive. The peel is sold in packages and can be stored indefinitely. Dry your own.

TAPIOCA FLOUR • Also called *tapioca starch*, this is made from the starch of the cassava root. Much of it comes packaged from Thailand. It is used as a basic ingredient in dumpling doughs. It is also used for dusting or coating in many preparations. It is also a thickener for sauces or a substitute for cornstarch. However, I cannot recommend that you substitute cornstarch for tapioca starch in these recipes. If you do substitute cornstarch, although it won't affect the taste, your recipes will not have the proper texture.

TARO ROOT • The starchy root of the taro plant, called *poi* in Hawaii. Taro is somewhat like a potato but is more fibrous and is tinged throughout its interior with fine purple threads. It must be eaten cooked, usually steamed or boiled. When the taro root steams, it emits a pleasant chestnutlike aroma. After cooking, it can be mashed. When stir-fried, it can be cooked in its raw state.

TIANJIN BOK CHOY • Often called *Tianjin cabbage* or *Tientsin bok choy*, the former spelling of its home city, *celery cabbage*, or *Napa cabbage*. It comes in two varieties, one a long-stalk type, the other rounder and leafier. It is the latter variety that is most often labeled with the city of its origin. It is also the sweeter of the two and my preference. It is at its best in spring. It may be kept refrigerated in a plastic bag for about a week, but like *bok choy* it tends to lose its sweetness, so I suggest eating it early, if not immediately.

TIANJIN PRESERVED VEGE-TABLE • This is a mixture of Tianjin *bok choy*, garlic, and salt. It comes either in crocks from China or in plastic bags from Hong Kong. The crocks are labeled either "Tientsin Preserved Vegetable" or "Tianjin Preserved Vegetable."

TIGER LILY BUDS • Elongated, reddish brown lily buds that have been dried, also known to the Chinese as *golden needles*. The best of these have a softness to them. When dry and brittle, they are usually old. Sold in packages, they will keep for at least six months in a tightly covered jar in a cool place.

TREE EARS • See *Cloud Ears*.

TURNIPS, CHINESE • These large white vegetables are about 8 inches long, occasionally longer, and 2 to 3 inches across at their thickest point. They have a fine crispness and can be as hot as radishes. They will keep for a week in a refrigerator vegetable drawer but are best if used promptly.

VINEGAR, CHINKIANG • This very strong, reddish black vinegar, made from glutinous rice, is widely used in China, particularly in the kitchens of the Chiu Chow and Hakka people of China's South. It has a distinct and direct taste and an aroma faintly reminiscent of balsamic vinegar. Throughout China there are various other red and white vinegars, the bases for which can be a mixture of glutinous rice and usual rice or each type of rice individually, depending on the distillation involved. I use one of two brands of white rice vinegar, Dragon Fountain Grain Vinegar and Swatow Rice Vinegar, both imported from the People's Republic of China, both widely available.

WATER CHESTNUT POWDER • Used to make cakes or to thicken sauces. Sauces containing this powder will give the foods over which they are poured a shiny, glazed appearance.

WATER CHESTNUTS • Not actually nuts. Rather they are bulbs, deep purplish brown in color, that grow in muddy water. To peel fresh water chestnuts is time consuming, but once done most rewarding. The meat of the water chestnut is white and sweet, juicy and crisp, and delicious even raw. Canned water chestnuts are a barely adequate, though serviceable, substitute. If you cannot find fresh water chestnuts, use *sah gut*, jícama, as a substitute instead. The water chestnut is quite versatile. It is used in stir-fries or in soups, even ground into a flour used to make pastries. It should be eaten fresh for greatest enjoyment. As water chestnuts age they become less firm, more starchy, less sweet. If you keep their skins on, with the mud remnants, and refrigerate them in a brown paper bag, they will keep for four to five weeks. Fresh water chestnuts, peeled, washed, dried, should be placed in a bowl covered with plastic wrap. They will keep four to five days. Canned water chestnuts should be placed in cold water in a container, and will keep four to five days, provided the water is changed daily.

WHEAT STARCH • The remains of wheat flour when the wheat's protein has been removed to make gluten. This starch is the basis for some dumpling wrappers and has other uses, as flour, as well. The starch will keep for at least a year if stored in a tightly sealed container and kept in a cool, dry place.

WHITE RICE WINE, CHINESE • I use Chinese white rice wine in many recipes. There are many types and brands, which I discuss in the chapter on Chinese wines. One brand that is usually available is Kiu Kiang, or "Nine Mountains." It is one of the kind that the Chinese refer to as Shuang Jim Chiew, and it combines quite well with foods.

WINE PILL • A yeast in the shape of a round, hard-crusted white ball about the size of a large marble. This yeast aids in the fermentation of the wine rice and red rice preparations. These balls come two to a plastic package and are not usually labeled in English. Ask for Shanghai Jao Bang Yeun, the translation of which is "Shanghai Wine Cake Pill."

WINE RICE • White glutinous rice that has been steamed, then fermented with a wine rice pill. A favorite of Shanghai, it can be eaten as it is or used in cooking other dishes. It comes in jars, often labeled "wine rice sweetened," but is best made yourself (see page 69).

WINTER MELON • A big melon that looks like a watermelon and grows to the same oblong-round shape. Its skin is dark green and occasionally mottled, while its interior is white with a very pale green tinge and white seeds. The winter melon has no taste of its own but has the characteristic of absorbing the flavors of whatever it is cooked with. When it is cooked, usually in soup, or steamed, the melon becomes translucent. Often the whole melon is used as a tureen, with other ingredients and stock steamed in it after it has been seeded and hollowed out. Winter melon should be used immediately, for it tends to dry quickly, particularly when pieces are cut from it. It is usually sold by weight, whole or by the piece. There is no reason to buy an entire melon unless you wish to try your hand at vegetable carving.

WON TON WRAPPERS • Also known as *won ton skins,* occasionally spelled *won tun,* these thin wrappers are made from wheat flour, eggs, water, and baking soda. They come in packages of 1 pound, about 75 to 100 wrappers to a package, and can be found in the refrigerated compartments of markets. They are also made without eggs if that is your preference.

WRAPPERS • Various other wrappers are used in the Chinese kitchen and are discussed in individual recipes. There are the won ton wrappers, above, spring roll skins, egg roll skins, Shanghai spring roll skins, water dumpling skins, and rice paper.

The Teas of China: Leaves and Legend

TEAS IN CHINA ARE OF LIMITLESS VARIETY. THEY ARE UNFERMENTED, PARTIALLY FERMENTED, FERMENTED, AND EVEN DOUBLE-FERMENTED TO INCREASE THEIR INTENSITY. THEY ARE MADE INTO PASTES, PRESSED INTO SMALL CAKES OR INTO BRICKS, OFTEN MIXED WITH FLOWERS, OCCASIONALLY FLAVORED WITH GINGER OR TANGERINE PEEL. Whatever the form, tea is regarded by the Chinese as one of life's necessities and, as with others of the foods of China, tea and its consumption are enriched with tradition and folklore.

There is little doubt that the tea tree is native to China and that tea as an herbal beverage has been known in China for thousands of years. It has been written that Shen Nung, an emperor of the third century B.C., in the time before the recognized dynasties began to be recorded, "discovered" tea. Shen Nung, a figure generally regarded as the father of Chinese herbal medicines, was sitting in the shade of a camellia tree, it is said, watching water boiling in a campfire cauldron, when a breeze rustling through the trees sent some leaves drifting into the water. The fragrance of the water tempted Shen Nung to sample it, and just like that, tea and tea drinking were born.

It is a gentler account than another bit of folklore that suggests tea was discovered accidentally by a Buddhist monk who, to prevent himself from sleeping and thus failing to fulfill his duty of keeping watch, cut off and discarded his eyelids. These eyelids fell to the ground and became the seeds for the first tea plants. A tale that suggests, in a rather direct and emphatic way, that tea is a stimulant.

Whichever one chooses to believe, lore or fancy, there is no doubt that the brewing of camellia leaves, later the leaves of its close cousin, the tea tree, in water to make tea, initially *t'u*, later *ch'a*, later *tei*, was written about as early as the twelfth century B.C. and widely practiced by the time of Confucius, 500 years before the birth of Christ. Tea emerged as a universal Chinese beverage in the Han dynasty. Under the Tang, tea was a valued court tribute, a tradition continued under later dynasties as well, and Taoists decreed that tea was so precious that to waste it constituted an offense against nature.

It was under the Tang, in the eighth century, that the greatest treatise on tea ever, *Ch'a Ching,* or "The Classic of Tea," was written by a philosopher and poet, Lu Yu. He imparted to the Chinese the necessity for ritual when one drank tea, not as rigid to be sure as that of the Chanoyu, the Japanese tea ceremony of a much later time, but rather a ritual of understanding that saw the need for tranquillity and serenity as one drank and the need for purity of water to honor the tea leaves, because the art of inhaling the fragrance of steeped tea and drinking it was an affirmation of self. The Tang dynasty was also the time of Lu T'ung, a poet who was granted the title of tea master, a tradition that continued into the ensuing Sung dynasty less than a century later under a sybaritic emperor, Hui Tsung. He became known as the tea emperor, who decreed for himself no fewer than forty-six personal imperial tea gardens.

Tea reached Japan in the ninth century when Japanese monks went home with seeds from China, and in the Ming dynasty tea went to Europe. It was under the Ching that tea made its way west and south to India and Ceylon, now Sri Lanka.

Tea was, and is, offered to the gods and at ancestral altars. It is the beverage that signifies a betrothal and that is served on a wedding day. Tea leaves grow on bushes that often are a century old and thus are regarded as symbols of longevity and fidelity. After a wedding in our family, the bride always presented cups of tea to our family's elders, and she would watch. For the moment that a recipient sipped from a cup it was a sign that the person accepted her into our family. In another of our customs, the bride would sit in a receiving room and present cups of tea as well as candied lotus seeds, lotus root, coconut, and winter melon rind to visitors.

Cups of tea were presented by all of us who were younger to our elders on the Lunar New Year, and a visitor to our house in Sun Tak or to the house of my grandmother, my Ah Paw, always received a cup of hot tea immediately as a welcome. My grandmother always drank tea with her meals and at the end of the meal insisted on a cup of Bo Lei tea, a double-fermented tea from Yunnan, which she insisted was the finest digestive.

Tea was, and is, a medium of business. Throughout Guangzhou and on up to Hangzhou and Shanghai, in later times, restaurants served dim sum and tea, and it was over these breakfasts in dim sum restaurants and in teahouses that business deals were consummated. To go to a dim sum teahouse was referred to as *yum cha,* which translates as "drink tea." So that business discussion would not be interrupted, when tea was poured, one tapped the fingers of one hand rapidly on the table top as conversation continued. This meant "thank you."

The hundreds, possibly thousands, of teas in China are classified as green, oolong, and black (also referred to as red). A few are white. Others are compressed into pastes or bricks. Green teas are unfermented; oolongs, semifermented; and blacks, fully fermented. In general the best teas grow at high elevations in soil that has good drainage for, as Lu Yu warned, too much water is not good for tea bushes. The smaller the tea leaf, the higher the quality; and if a leaf is whole and unbroken it is considered choice. Broken leaves are considered of lesser quality, and large leaves are held in still lesser regard. The leavings of the tea process, the small pieces called *fannings,* and tea dust, are of no interest to lovers of pure tea and are apt to find their way into tea bags. Powdered tea, though historically important, is rare these days in China. Although teas are grown all across China, in general it is thought that the best teas come from the Southern province of Fujian and its neighboring province to the north and west, Yunnan.

When we Chinese talk about our foodstuffs, we often invoke tradition, custom, and folktale, and tea is no exception. Many people will answer "Monkey Picked" when asked to name their favorite tea. And what is Monkey Picked? Tea picked by monkeys, of course, and here is the story they tell. Centuries ago a certain monastery in the Hangzhou hills, the land of green teas, was beset by hordes of wild monkeys, who hungrily would strip their vegetable, fruit, and tea plants of all buds. The monks decided not to get rid of the monkeys but to become their friends, so they took to leaving food for them, and one spring morning the monks came out of their monastery to find all of their tea leaves picked and packed in sacks, ready for them to make tea. Ever since then, the best teas, the smallest leaves, are said to be monkey picked and command enormous prices. Who could not believe such a lovely story?

Following are the various types of tea, some of their varieties, their methods of processing, and examples of some of the best and most familiar of China's teas.

GREEN TEAS

Picked leaves are usually spread in a thin layer on shallow bamboo trays, then dried in the sun briefly, after which they are heated to prevent any natural fermentation. They are further moved about to rid the leaves of moisture and then rolled into little balls. These are then heated again and left to dry. They become the dull emerald green that characterizes the best green teas. This is green tea, made with personal care, as I watched it made in the West Lake Peoples Commune near Hangzhou years ago. A shorter method is to steam the leaves to soften them, roll them, and heat them to dryness. The best known of the green teas are:

DRAGON WELL • Perhaps the choicest, surely the most famous of the green teas. In fact it is regarded as the crowning achievement of tea growing in China, and its cost reflects its regard. The best Dragon Well comes from Hangzhou. A tale in Chinese folklore suggests that the tea is named for a dragon that once lived in a Hangzhou Lake. It is known by a variety of spellings, Longjing or Lung Ching or Loong Tsing. Customarily this is the tea for state dinners. This tea, with its fine aroma and delicate, sweet taste, is usually drunk young, for it does not keep well. In China it is said Dragon Well stimulates the appetite and, as a medicine, is a remedy for cold and fever. It is my tea of choice for Tea-Smoked Duck.

SO MEI • Also known as *shao mei,* this strong green tea is hand-picked, massaged between the palms, and wind-dried, never in the sun. It has a pleasantly bitter taste, is quite cooling, and is thought to be beneficial to one's respiratory system.

PI LO CHUN • A delicate green tea whose poetic name translates as "green snail spring" for the tiny rolled shape of its cured leaves. It is said that as many as 80,000 tiny leaves are needed to create a pound of this tea, which was a favorite in the imperial court of the Ching dynasty. Its flavor is clean and faintly sweet.

GUNPOWDER • A grayish green tea rolled up into tiny balls that resemble gunpowder pellets. The Chinese also call this "pearl tea." Its taste is pungent, somewhat smoky.

OOLONG TEAS

Oolong teas are generally regarded as semifermented. These must be picked at precisely the right time, not too soon, and, it has been explained to me, processed immediately after picking. The leaves are wilted in sunlight, shaken, then spread loosely and the leaf fades slightly until the green becomes yellow-tinged and the edges almost reddish. At this point oxidation is halted by heating the leaves. Perhaps the best known of the many, many oolongs are:

IRON GODDESS • This very potent tea is called, in Chinese, *teh kuan yin* or *teet koon yum,* which translates as "Iron Goddess of Mercy." This dark, metallic coppery tea, with a strong, direct taste, is regarded both as a stimulant for one's appetite and by the Southern Chinese Chiu Chow

people as the ideal tea to drink, in very tiny cups, to help one's digestion immediately following a meal. This particular tea is often brewed by what the Chinese call a *gongfu* method, not to be confused with the similar-sounding form of martial arts. *Gongfu* means that there is a precise and disciplined way of doing something, in this instance the careful picking and precise preparation of the leaves. This particular oolong is usually steeped twice to make it exceptionally strong. The Chiu Chow people often say of themselves that they will become poor, "tea poor" they call it, because they use so many tea leaves to make their highly concentrated teas.

SHUI-HSIEN • Also called *soi sin,* this is one of the many oolongs favored by the Chinese. Its name translates as "water fairy" or "water sprite." This greenish brown tea comes from Fujian and has a slightly bitter taste that many people, including me, find enjoyable. For many Chinese it is the morning wake-up tea, as well as a fine tea to eat with morning dumplings.

POUCHONG • A lightly fermented oolong that is special because its leaves are wrapped in thin, porous paper during the limited fermentation process. This is also from Fujian and is so beloved by the Chinese that it is one of the teas taken to Taiwan and is now grown there as well. It is amber colored, sweet, and most refreshing, an afternoon tea.

RED (BLACK) TEAS

To process these teas (black in the West, red to the Chinese), the leaves are spread and allowed to wither, in the shade, not the sun, for the finer varieties. When they are limp they are rolled to break up their structure and then spread out to oxidize. They become a coppery red color. Finally the fermented leaf is heated, at which point it becomes black and acquires the aroma so familiar to black tea drinkers, which most of us are. Some well-known black teas are:

Bo Lei • This is the tea of my child-hood, a strong, direct, double-fermented tea from Yunnan. This is a robust tea that seems to get better as it ages. It is still possible to buy, in Hong Kong, hundred-year-old cakes of Bo Lei. This is another favored tea with dim sum and other dumplings because it is perfect, the Chinese believe, for digestion, a liquid that cuts through residual oils in one's system. It is also thought of as a cancer pre-ventative.

Luk On • A black tea that looks, even smells, as if it will be quite strong. Actually it is quite mild after it is brewed and illustrates its name, "Cloud Mist," quite well. It is a tea favored by the elderly for digestion. My aunt Luk Gu Cheh would not let a day pass without a few cups of Luk On, which for her was a tonic.

Ch'i-Men • A black tea named for the region in Anhui province where it originated. It is known around the world as Keemun, a Westernization of its Chinese name, and is perhaps the most famous of all black teas. This too is a *gongfu* tea in which the leaves are processed to be tiny strips. This is a deep brown tea in color with a pleasant aroma and a taste that is faintly sweet.

Lapsang Souchong • A special black tea of Fujian. After initial wither-ing and rolling, the leaves are pressed into bar-rels and covered with cloth to ferment fully. After fermentation they are again rolled, heated to halt the fermentation, and finally smoked over burning pine wood. This tea has a distinctive smoky aroma that carries over into its taste.

WHITE TEAS

These teas, allowed to ferment lightly and naturally, are exceedingly rare these days. Historically they were the most sought-after teas of the Sung dynasty. Today only a few exist, all from Fujian province. The buds of the bushes are picked before opening, then steamed and allowed to wither until all mois-ture has dried. These dried buds have a silvery color; thus their names such as Silver Needle, White Peony, and Noble Beauty. The tea made from them is pale yellow, and their tastes are equally faint.

PU-ERH TEAS

These are special teas from Yunnan, which throughout Chinese history have been held in special regard. Many of these teas are wild, and they include all of the usual varieties, but they are most notable because so many of these Yunnan teas are formed into pastes and bricks. In these forms they were offered as imperial tributes. The practice of making tea into solid blocks dates back a thousand years in China. Initially leaves were steamed, then compressed into molds, often molds that were intricately carved or embossed so that the resultant brick became sculptured plaques. Such bricks, currently made of tea that is not of the highest quality, are also fashioned into plaques, layered tiers, balls, and tiny bowllike shapes. Some people still swear by compressed teas, slicing off pieces to make teas they believe to be digestives or aids to control cholesterol.

FLAVORED AND SCENTED TEAS

All varieties of tea, after processing, are used to make flavored and scented teas. For example, black teas are mixed with litchis to make a favorite southern Chinese tea known as litchi black. Dried jasmine blossoms are mixed with green tea to make the highly regarded Jasmine Tea. Dried chrysanthemums are often mixed with fermented Bo Lei tea to create a scented tea the Chinese call Guk Bo, but chrysanthemum petals alone are often made into a tea. Teas in China are flavored with roses, orchids, cassia, gardenias, lotuses, and plums. A note here: Fruit bases, herbals, and flower infusions are not teas in the true sense unless they have some leaves from the tea bush in their mix. Which makes, I suppose, Chrysanthemum Tea not a true tea. It is, however, so regarded in Chinese tradition.

Whatever one's particular taste in tea, it is available in China and from China. If you are in China, you will have tea with your breakfast dumplings, surely your afternoon teahouse pastries, with your light meal in a noodle shop, or after your more substantial evening meal. Tins of tea abound on the shelves of Chinese markets in the West, and in many cities shops devoted to Chinese teas and to tea lore are increasing. Drop in—you will be taught the proper, Chinese way to drink tea, with a minimum of ceremony.

Tea drinking, the Chinese way, is simple, as Lu Yu suggested it should be. The water should be just at the point of boil, but not at a full, vigorous boil. First, you should boil water to pour into a clay or ceramic teapot to heat the pot, then that water should be discarded. Add your tea to the warmed pot and pour fresh, hot water—again, just at the point of boiling, but not actually boiling—over the tea. Tea should never be added to the water. How much tea? This truly depends on individual taste. The old English rule of thumb is one spoonful for each cup, plus one more for the pot. This may be too much. So you should experiment until you arrive at the threshold of taste, and aroma, you prefer. For particularly fine teas, such as a great Dragon Well, you may even pour off the first pot of tea brewed as a sort of first flush to be discarded, as some tea masters do, in the belief that the second pot will be the finest. In general tea should be steeped for three to five minutes before drinking. Care should be taken not to brew too long, for tea can become bitter.

A brief word about tea storage. Teas should always be kept in tightly closed containers. The tins that they come in are perfect. They should not be stored in transparent containers such as those of glass, for light over a prolonged period could lessen their potency. And these closed containers should be kept in a cool, dry place.

Cooking with tea is a Chinese custom. Smoking foods with fragrant woods and herbs was a culinary tradition in China for many centuries, a technique extended later to include teas. Smoking with dried, processed, and otherwise fermented teas imparts fine flavor to food, particularly fowl. Cooking with tea as an integral ingredient is another matter. Traditionally foods cooked with teas used freshly picked tea leaves; dried and processed leaves were never used. This was the case particularly in the region around Hangzhou, that home to Dragon Well tea. Access to fresh leaves these days is, however, limited, so this is what I do.

I brew the tea I am going to use, then pour off and reserve the liquid tea. I strain the leaves, and they are ready to cook with. In my recipes I will generally add a portion of the reserved brewed tea for additional flavor. This method successfully brings the full flavor of the tea to the food being cooked.

Over the years different Chinese teas have become associated with different foods, for their complementary characters. I have cooked fresh prawns with Dragon Well tea and scallops with that other lovely green tea, Pi Lo Chun. And I have cooked veal with Dragon Well too. All of these stir-fried dishes married the teas well with the food being cooked. I have tasted Sichuan foods with jasmine tea added to their benefit and enjoyed braised mushrooms with So Mei tea.

Younger Chinese chefs, particularly those in Hong Kong, have become adventuresome and adept at cooking various foods with specific teas and have set down some basic gastronomic marriages:

- *Green unfermented teas with seafood, because their taste can be so subtle*
- *Less strong black teas with more forthright foods such as preserved vegetables and spareribs*
- *Mild white teas with vegetarian dishes*
- *Strong oolongs with game*
- *Flower-scented teas with chicken*
- *Strong black teas with rich foods such as roasted pork*

These are, to be sure, but broad guidelines. One might have, as I did at one evening meal, a steamed fish finished with green tea juice. I have had scallops sautéed with rose-scented tea. In Myanmar I tasted, with a Chinese family, an unusual dish called *laphet,* of green tea leaves, dried, then salted in brine and combined with garlic, broad beans, roasted peanuts, and chilies, touched with lime juice. It was utterly wonderful.

A rule of thumb offered with foods being cooked with tea is that they should be eaten accompanied with cups of the same tea used in the recipe, for simple harmony. Lu Yu would like that.

The Wines of China: Grains, Flowers, and Grapes

中國酒，五穀香花葡萄

WINES IN CHINA ARE NOT ALWAYS WINES AS THEY ARE UNDERSTOOD TO BE IN THE WEST. ALL WINES, WHETHER FERMENTED FROM GRAPES OR GRAIN, ARE RE-FERRED TO AS *CHIEW* (LABEL VARIA-TIONS *CHIU* OR *JIEW*) IN MOST OF CHINA AND AS *JIU* OR *JAO* IN CANTON (GUANGZHOU) AND OTHER PARTS OF THE SOUTH. It is a generic word, one Chinese character, that describes not only wines but all alcoholic drinks, even distilled liqueurs flavored with flowers, herbs, or fruits and other distillations such as brandies and vodkas. I use both dialects because of the many labels on Chinese wines and spirits. Even beer is referred to as *beh chiew* or *beh jao*, which translates as "beer wine."

Thus there is a history of grape *chiews*, some produced in China for many centuries, others, the modern rieslings and muscats being made in China with input and techniques from French, Australian, and other Western oenologists. There are the traditional rice *chiew*, the most famous, and deservedly so, Shao-Hsing wine (also spelled Shaoxing) of fermented glutinous rice with the addition of wheat yeast. There are spirits of fermented grain alcohols scented with herbs or flowers, the most well-known Mei Kuei Lu Chiew, the base of which is rose petals. There are West-ern-styled brandies and bolder grain dis-tillations. All of these are *chiew*.

The processes of making *chiew* in China goes back as far as 2000 B.C. to the Hsia dynasty, when alcohols were fer-mented from grains, with millet the prime ingredient in any mash fermenta-tion. Drinking *chiew* was basic to the Chi-nese. *Chiew* were elements of feasts and special festive days, parts of rituals, tem-ple and ancestor offerings. As we have seen with other developments of the Chi-nese table, the making of *chiew* differed from North to South. In the north, gluti-nous millet and other cereal grains such as wheat and sorghum were used widely; in the South the base for *chiew* was cus-tomarily glutinous rice, as it is today. But also from the South came wines of fermented grapes, pears, and dates.

Those excavations of Han dynasty tombs, with their wall carvings and many examples of wine storage and serving pottery, tell us that *chiew*, made from all manner of grains, were common in China well before the birth of Christ. *Chiew*, designated either dark or white, were consumed widely, sufficiently so that we find writings cautioning against overindulgence on the one hand and on the other urging moderate drinking as a benefit for one's circulation and the health of the skin. It was the custom to serve wine warmed in the autumn and winter, cooled in the spring and summer.

It was in the Han dynasty that China imported from the Middle East and Persia grapes to eat and seeds to grow the vines that would yield wine grapes, this after many centuries of wine making with their own indigenous wild grapes. It was later, during the time of the Tangs, that *chiew* began to become alcoholic drinks of diverse flavors, made with chrysanthemums, pomegranate flowers, pepper, ginger, bamboo leaves, saffron, and honey. Centers for the production of *chiew*, fermented and distilled, arose in the provinces of Anhwei (now Anhui), Shandong, Kweichou (now Guizhou), Shansi (now Shanxi), Chekiang (now Zhejiang), and in Tianjin. Kweichou became famous, and remains so to this day, for its fiery drink, Mao Tai. These days Tianjing is perhaps China's most important grape-growing region and producer of what would be termed Western-styled wines, themselves, of course, *chiew*.

In our house in Sun Tak, when I was growing up, *chiew*, or *chiu*, or often in our case because we lived in the suburbs of Guangzhou, *jiu* or *jao*, was ever present. My father liked wines and was most fond of the white rice wines of Canton, now Guangdong Province. These wines, often labeled Kwangtung Mijiu, are still available occasionally. He would always ask what was being cooked for our main meal, or, when he cooked himself, which was often, he would specify particular varieties of these wines.

Our family favorites, actually his, were Sancheng Chiew, which translates as "triple-steamed," the most expensive of these white rice wines; Shuang Jin Chiew, or "double-steamed"; Mai Chiew, or ordinary white rice table wine; and Soi Chiew, or "water" wine, a very weak wine we used in ceremonies and ancestor offerings. If we had a special dish favored by my father, perhaps deep-fried oysters or a hot pot, he would specify Nor Mai Chiew, a special, strong glutinous white rice wine. I cannot recall a meal in our house that was without wine, nor can I ever remember cooking without wine.

My father used to say, "*Jao but sik yee yum, jao but sik yee tiu jeuh*," which translates literally from the Cantonese as "Wine not suitable to drink is not suitable for cooking" or, more familiarly, as I prefer, "If you cannot drink a wine, do not cook with it." It was his way of dismissing so-called cooking wines. He was correct, and I follow his advice to this day. I never use, nor do I recommend, Chinese "cooking wines," primarily because they are generally inferior and of lesser potency than wines destined for drinking. If you cannot drink it, do not cook with it.

My grandmother, my Ah Paw, never drank at all. She would pretend to sip for the sake of politeness at festivals or family occasions, at birthdays and weddings, but never would she drink. Yet she recommended, demanded, that wines be used in cooking, telling me that a good-quality wine dissipates strong, unpleasant meat or fish odors and adds fragrance to preparations. She insisted our family cook all meals with wine and with ginger, her other necessity.

And it was Ah Paw who supervised the arrangements of our rice wine ancestor offerings. She would see to it that three small wine cups were set before the portraits of our ancestors, along with three sets of chopsticks and a goodly number of foods. Then a small cup of Soi Chiew would be poured on the floor in front of the altar. This would eventually evaporate and thus rise to Heaven, our offering of *chiew*.

As a young girl I was never permitted to drink wine or any other *chiew*. Perhaps I might have a tiny sip, from a tiny cup, at a family feast, to join in a toast of *yamsing,* a wish for success, but nothing more, for it was impressed on me that properly brought-up young women never drank, and at least in our family that rule held until one married. It was a custom I followed, even though I cooked with wines and other *chiew* from an early age. My introduction to what is surely China's finest wine, Shao-Hsing, came as I entered my teen years and left Sun Tak for Hong Kong to live with an aunt. It became my favored cookery wine, which it remains, as well as a wine of many varieties that I enjoy often with food.

Shao-Hsing, like many of the wines of the world, is known for the place in which it is produced. This clear yellow wine, of varying degrees of age and intensity, reflects the mild region of the Southeastern coastal province of Zhejiang (formerly Chekiang), the abundance and quality of the native rice that is its base, and the mineral-rich water of Jiang Lake, with its peat-carpeted bottom, used to brew it. There are eighty wineries in and around Shao-Hsing, a city just to the south of Shanghai and to the east of Hangzhou. What more auspicious place of birth could there be for a drink that will eventually accompany food?

The history of rice wine in China extends back 4,000 years. In Shao-Hsing it began 2,400 years ago, and as with most other Chinese comestibles there is a historic tale that accounts for its origins. Shao-Hsing was, from 770 B.C. to 476 B.C., the capital of the Yue Kingdom during the Spring and Autumn Annals. It was a much fought-over city, and in 500 B.C. a warring house named Wu defeated the ruling house of Yue. As a consequence the Yues made great quantities of a superior rice wine to offer as tribute to the victorious Wu. Since that time the making of superior rice wine has been an unbroken tradition in Shao-Hsing. We know that the wine was so highly regarded in the North—where wines were usually made from sorghum, millet, and other cereal grains—that the imperial courts of many dynasties had great quantities of this yellow rice wine brought north to Beijing.

The wine begins with a cooked mash of fine glutinous rice, which produces the starches, which in turn yield the sugars, for fermentation. The mash is mixed with wheat yeasts and the particularly fine, clear water of Lake Jiang and allowed to ferment in huge pottery jars, sealed with lotus leaves, then with a fitted ceramic cover, and finally with mud. These covered jars rest in vast open fermentation houses through which breezes pass continuously. As the Shao-Hsing wines age, they darken from yellow to light amber, to dark, some as dark as a brandy. With some Shao-Hsing wines the older a wine becomes, the more aromatic it becomes, and the finer the wine. But not always. In general, Shao-Hsing wines of three, five, or eight years of age are more complex and better than those aged for a decade. But there are some that improve with age.

The wine-making cycle in Shao-Hsing begins normally on November 8, the first day of Chinese winter, when the cooked glutinous rice, the wheat yeast, and the lake water are mixed and poured into the crocks. By May 8 the liquid is separated from the solids and remains to be aged further, at least for three years. The solids, dried, are used for animal feed. After three years the wines are transferred to bottles or to ornamental ceramic jars or to carved pottery crocks. Some are aged further.

This aging can be for as long as twenty years. With such age the aroma of the Shao-Hsing becomes most pleasing, but its alcohol is reduced and the wine becomes less sweet. As a general rule, with most Shao-Hsing wines, the longer the aging, the better the smell but the weaker the taste. Experts say that it is best to drink before it reaches ten years of age.

The wines are categorized basically by their sugar content. Wines with below 1 percent sugar are referred to as *yuen hong;* those with 1 to 3 percent sugar are called *hua tiao;* those with 3 to 10 percent sugar are called *shan niang,* and those with more than 10 percent sugar are called *xiang xue.* The wines come in a variety of containers, in bottles to be sure, but also in jugs, in celadon-green ceramic bottles shaped like calabash gourds, others shaped like traditional Chinese ginger jars, others in earthenware urns of various shapes.

Following are some of the best-known Shao-Hsing wines and what makes them different, and special, within their family. I have listed them as they are usually labeled.

SUPREME *HUA TIAO CHIEW* • This is the wine exported most from Shao-Hsing. It is a fine and delicate yellow-to-amber wine in long-necked bottles with a blue label on which is a red seal with the wine's designation. I use it extensively for cooking and drinking. It is quite like a medium-dry sherry.

HUA TIAO, STATE BANQUET OR PEOPLE'S CONGRESS • This aged wine, usually eight to ten years, is mild and quite smooth, served at state banquets at the Diao Yu Tai Guest House in Beijing and at sessions of the People's Congress. It comes in a long-necked bottle similar to the first wine but with a large gold label, emblazoned with a red shield of identification.

HUA TIAO VINTAGE • This amber wine, very much like a traditional sherry, is usually aged for five to eight years. It is bottled in any of a variety of beautiful jars decorated with Chinese carvings, scenery, elaborately costumed women, or calligraphy. Some are boxed in brocaded cases, others in finely finished wood boxes, for presentation. They are meant usually to be gifts.

HUA TIAO CALABASH • A wine that is not dissimilar to the first of the Shao-Hsing wines listed. But for presentation purposes it is bottled in a gourd-shaped corked bottle. It has a concentrated sweet taste that is most pleasing, a lovely wine to sip, perhaps at meal's end.

ZHUANG YUAN HONG • It has been an old Shao-Hsing custom to select jars of special wine and commission artists to decorate their containers with drawings or incised carvings. These would then be sealed with mud and stored by a family in a cellar in anticipation of a male child. If the child was indeed a boy, the wine would be unearthed, called Zhuang Yuan Hong, or "Red of Number One Scholar," and the boy would be toasted with what was usually a well-aged, deep-brandy-colored wine.

NU ER HONG • A story is told of a tailor from Shao-Hsing who wished mightily to have a son and thus bought jugs of wine, had them decorated, buried them, and awaited his son. A daughter was born, however, and it is said the tailor was so upset he took his wine and reburied it, where it rested for 18 years. His daughter grew up, was beautiful and intelligent, and the tailor was so pleased he dug up the wine he had buried in anger to toast her betrothal. The wine turned out to be exquisite, soft, sweet, and mellow, and these days it comes in round, squat white ceramic containers labeled Nu Er Hong or "Scent of a Woman." It is usually aged eight years, not eighteen.

YUAN HONG • A dark-colored wine that is quite dry because it has less sugar content that the Hua Tiao wines, more like a drier sherry. I cook with this Shao-Hsing as well, and with as much success and gratification, though occasionally I find I must counter its dryness with a bit of sugar.

SHAN NIANG • This heavier Shao-Hsing comes in a deep brown bulbous earthenware container. It contains at least three times the sugar of Yuan Hong, and though that sounds like a good bit, it is not overly sweet at all and is often brown-orange in color.

CHIA FAN • A most fragrant Shao-Hsing, yellow-brown and rich, which also comes in a brown earthenware urnlike crock quite like the Shan Niang above. This is not only a fine cooking wine but also a favored wine for toasts at weddings and other banquets, where it is served warm. The wine also comes in bottles. There is as well a version of it from neighboring Anhui Province to the northwest, labeled either Te Jia Fan or simply Jia Fan, with the *Te* signifying "special."

All of these Shao-Hsing wines are excellent to cook with, and you should have no qualms about using, or drinking, any of them. The rule of thumb is, however, the older the more fragrant, but with a less defined taste. As time passes, more Shao-Hsing wines are making their way onto market shelves and into wine shops specializing in the wines and spirits of Asia.

Of the alcohols that are looked on as spirits rather than wines, the most famous *chiu* is Mei Kuei Lu Chiew, produced in Tianjin, in northern China, southeast of Beijing. Its name translates as "rose dew *chiu*," and it is a special spirit, based on sorghum, with the addition of liqueur made from soaked rose petals. Quite like an eau-de-vie, it is often drunk as an aperitif, yet it is an exceptionally fine *chiu* with which to cook.

Its manufacture is far from ordinary. Sorghum grains and yeasts are mashed and rest in distillery vats for fifteen days before being distilled into a crystal-clear liquid without sediment. To it rose liqueur is added. This *chiu* is made this way: Roses, preferably dew-laden buds, just about to bloom, are collected early in the mornings from gardens in the Miao Feng Mountains north of Beijing and brought to the distillery. There they are put into large crocks with their dew and with granulated sugar and left there for a year, with the sorghum spirit added bit by bit. At the end of this process Mei Kuei Lu Chiew results, a rose-scented alcohol with a long, lingering aftertaste, a *chiu* highly regarded throughout China. With this *chiu*, the longer the age the more intense it becomes.

It is marvelous to drink and a joy to cook with. When I make Beggar's Chicken, I rub Mei Kuei Lu Chiew well into the entire chicken. I marinate fish and shrimp in it and use it when roasting pork or goose or duck. It is a perfect ingredient in a braising mix. This rose-scented *chiu* is also the spirit of choice for Drunken Shrimp. I also recommend that it be drunk, as an accompaniment, to all of these preparations in which it is an ingredient.

Even as it ages, Mei Kuei Lu Chiew remains clear and colorless. I have had it aged for eight years and found it as fragrant and as potent as when it was young. I have even drunk a thirty-year-old vintage, and at that age it still filled the mouth, though its alcoholic strength had obviously waned.

Other spirit *chiu* from Tianjin include:

KAO LIANG CHIEW • A sorghum-based spirit, made with a yeast of barley and green peas. *Kao Liang* translates as "sorghum." It comes in glass bottles and is clear white and most fragrant. It is used in cooking, and the Chinese also drink it because they believe it to be a powerful restorative.

WU CHIA PI CHIEW • This reddish amber spirit is made by mixing Kao Liang Chiew with a mixture of Chinese herbs. It is slightly sweet and is drunk widely in China as a tonic to help blood circulation and to relieve the pains of rheumatism. This comes in glass bottles, in squat brown earthenware crocks, and in artfully decorated white ceramic presentation jugs.

NG GA PEI • In Tianjin this is another name for Wu Chia Pi Chiew. It is also made in other parts of China, in Hong Kong and Taiwan, and often labeled Nga Pei or Ng Ka Pay. Usually this deep-amber spirit is based on sorghum and occasionally is referred to by the Chinese as simply "whiskey." In Taiwan it is labeled similarly as Ng Ka Pay but is made from maltose, cane sugar, and various plant extracts and herbs.

FEN CHIEW • This is a clear, exceptionally strong, sorghum-based spirit that is quite like gin. It is a fine, occasional ingredient in a seafood stock and with fish and other seafood.

Tianjin also produces a range of grape-based brandies patterned after French production techniques and methods, as well as a wide selection of white wines in the Western manner, all from grapes. In Shansi Province, west of Tianjin, a version of Fen Chiew is produced, as is a version of Chia Fan, that special festive rice wine that originated in Shao-Hsing. But Shansi is most famous for its *Chu Yeh China Chiew,* or "Bamboo Leaf Clear

Chiu," a clear, greenish sorghum spirit, Kao Liang, to which has been added the essence of bamboo leaves and sugar. Often peas, green leaves, dried orange peel, and herbs are added to its mix. Though it is quite strong, its green mintlike taste is not unpleasant.

Anhui Province, in southeastern China, west of Nanjing and Shanghai, is home to a historic *chiu* that had its origins in the Ming dynasty. It is called *Gu Jing,* which translates as "Ancient Well," and was first made as a tribute wine to present to the imperial Ming court, a practice continued through the Ching dynasty. The spirit is produced in the town of Jian Dian in Anhui from sorghum, barley, wheat, peas, sugar, and the water from the town's old well, covered by a lovely pagoda roof supported by bright red columns, the same well that supplied the water more than 500 years ago. It is crystal clear, smells somewhat like orchids, and is pleasantly sweet.

Less sweet and quite strong is another Anhui *chiew* with imperial roots, Long Xing Yu Ye—he translation of which is "Rising Dragon Liquid." This too can be traced to the Ming dynasty court, which, it is said, drank this *chiew* on visits to the Ming dynasty tombs outside of Beijing and to ensure its continued quality supervised its production. Like other such spirits, it is a Kao Liang, based on a distillation of a sorghum, wheat, and peas mash, heated and steamed over very low fires, a particular method, to arrive at a clear state. It is notable for its container, a lovely white and blue porcelain vase decorated with the traditional symbol of the imperial court, the five-taloned dragon.

In southwestern China, sandwiched between the provinces of Hunan and Sichuan, lies Guizhou, where Moutai, perhaps the best known strong spirit of China, is made. Until the brewing of that special banquet Shao-Hsing, Moutai was the drink of state visits, the drink that was offered to all visiting foreign dignitaries. Moutai can be traced as another of those *chiu* offered as tributes to the emperor, in its case, to the Tang dynasty 1,400 years ago and the subsequent Sung dynasty. Another sorghum-based spirit, it is clear with an assertive, pungent aroma and a strong taste. It has often been called "Chinese grappa," and its alcoholic strength is equal to, or stronger than, vodka's. Another notable Guizhou *chiew,* Guiyang Da Qu, is also a Kao Liang, a sorghum spirit, the name of which translates as the "Great Wine of Guiyang." This is an unusual, particularly rich *chiew* because wheat is added to the base. Like Moutai, it is a strong spirit to drink, virtually without fragrance. Some Chinese suggest that it is a restorative that gets one's blood flowing, and I would not argue with that.

Throughout China there are various of these spirits based on sorghum, wheat, barley, rice, and other grains, and each province, each region, has its own. For example, there are any number of ginseng *chiew,* usually made from ginseng root, sugar, glutinous rice, and sorghum spirits. In China's South, among the Hakka nomads, there are Tung Kiang wines based upon glutinous rice, and in Fujian there is a wine called Chengang, which translates as "sunken urn," named because it is aged by burying a sealed jar of wine in the earth.

It is said that more than 700 of these *chiew* exist in China. I have given a sampling, just to indicate the scope and types of *chiew,* wines and spirits, in the Chinese larder.

In the
Chinese Kitchen
with Wok *and* Cleaver

To the Chinese, preparing and cooking a meal that will eventually please and satisfy others is an art or an honor. From a personal perspective there is no more satisfying way of preparing foods than in the Chinese manner. It is cooking that requires rudimentary skills, to be sure, skills such as learning to manipulate the wok and becoming familiar with it; the proper positioning of the hands and fingers when cutting with the cleaver; the use of spatula and strainer. But as you will discover, these are skills learned easily and quickly, and once you have learned them the Chinese kitchen will become accessible and certainly without mystery.

The classic techniques of the Chinese kitchen, its implements, its basics, differ from those in the West. There is no collection of knives; instead there is the cleaver. There is no array of pots; instead there is the wok, perhaps the world's finest all-purpose cookpot. The wok is used to fry, steam, blanch, bake, and boil. Can these processes in this single pot be daunting? Initially, many people believe so, but with familiarity comes content. And confidence. Dismiss the words *difficult* and *cannot* from your thoughts and your vocabulary.

I have taught many, many people, professionals and amateurs, to cook everything from perfectly boiled rice to vegetable, meat, and fish preparations of many steps and many ingredients. While it is true that representations of the foods from all regions of China can be eaten in restaurants these days, that should not be an excuse for not learning how to prepare what I deem the most creative, innovative, and varied cuisine in the world. Not to learn it is to cheat yourself out of the satisfaction and well-being that comes with accomplishment.

Chinese cooking, true Chinese cooking, perhaps more than any other, is an art that changes constantly. It is added to, altered by the talents of its practitioners. It is a living cuisine. But it is not unsolvable. Really. It has only to be learned, and learning the techniques of the Chinese kitchen is anything but tedious. Rather it is a delight, a discovery. Nor should you be awed by the idea of preparing a meal of several courses. Many dishes can be prepared ahead, or those that require less preparation can be paired with those needing more. The fun is in the challenge. The reward is in the eating. It seems to me that a few hours spent to prepare something that will be both beautiful to contemplate and delicious to taste is time well spent. I remember my grandmother, my Ah Paw, telling me when I was a little girl and she and my father were teaching me how to cook that the most important asset you could bring to learning to cook was patience. With that and with practice you could then create something that would bring happiness and smiles of satisfaction to the faces of those who were enjoying your efforts. Is that not a fine reward? To me it is.

I had to learn *chui fong, ngai seut,* or "kitchen techniques," my grandmother would preach to me, impressing on me that in these lay the steps to excellence. And my father would repeat, *chui ngai,* a shortened, conversational way of saying, and conveying, the same thing. Along that path I would find both satisfaction and enjoyment, he said. My grandmother and my father were correct. This is the sort of thinking I have tried to transmit to my students through the years: that the process itself is delicious.

The key to this enjoyment is to do things correctly and with economy. Ingredients and utensils must be at the ready. Any cookery can be overpowering and frustrating if you are ill prepared, and Chinese cuisine, with its disciplines, is no different. Yet it can be relatively free of most concerns if you attend to basics. *Basics* means not only coming to know your

cooking equipment and familiarizing yourself with the different vegetables, meats, fish, and fowl, with the sauces, spices, and oils of the Chinese kitchen, but also learning their properties and the techniques that will enhance them. It also means learning the capacities of the tools necessary to working with these foods.

Welcome to the Chinese kitchen. Here are its tools and the ways to use them.

THE WOK

There is nothing more traditional in Chinese cookery than that creation of thousands of years, the wok. Historically, first made of iron, later of carbon steel, still later of stainless steel and aluminum, it was, and is, shaped like an oversized soup plate. Its concave shape places its belly right into the flame or heat source of a stove and makes it the ideal cooker. In carbon steel it is as perfect a cooking utensil as can be. It conducts heat almost instantaneously. Though it is not a pot or a pan, it functions as both. Its shape permits food to be stir-fried, tossed quickly through small amounts of oil so that food cooks yet does not retain oil. The shape of the wok permits one to make it a steamer simply by placing bamboo steamers in its well. Wok cooking, more than any other sort, is natural cooking.

The most useful carbon-steel wok is one with a diameter of about 14 inches. It is all purpose, used for stir-frying, deep-frying, dry-roasting, and sauce making. With the addition of bamboo steamers it is also perfect for all manner of steaming foods. A carbon-steel wok, as described, available in Chinese or

Asian markets, will cost only about $6 and will be perfect when properly seasoned. Many other kinds of woks are available, made of stainless steel, aluminum, and various thicknesses of iron. I do not recommend any of these for general use, particularly stir-frying, although a stainless-steel wok is fine for steaming. In most cases these woks are more expensive than the best carbon-steel ones. Nor do I favor any of those nonstick-coated woks. Chinese stir-frying requires intense, direct heat, and such heat can damage or loosen this coating. Avoid plug-in electric woks because you cannot properly control their heat as you must in wok cooking. Nothing is as versatile or as desirable as the carbon-steel wok.

I should mention flat-bottomed woks. They come in carbon and stainless steel. I prefer the round-bottomed woks because of the ease with which stir-frying can be accomplished, the spatula whooshing through the foods with no change of plane to hinder it. But I recognize that the flat-bottomed woks are well suited to electric ranges. There are also one-handle woks, both round bottomed and flat. These are perfect in a traditional Chinese kitchen with a special wok stove. I do not recommend them for general use.

A carbon-steel wok is not pretty when it is new, because of a coating of sticky oil used as a preservative. Once cleansed and seasoned, however, it is ideal and will last for many years. A new wok should be immersed in extremely hot water with a little liquid detergent. The interior should be cleaned with a sponge, the outside with steel wool and cleanser; then the wok should be rinsed and, while wet, placed over a flame and dried with a paper towel to prevent instant rust. Discard the paper towel

and, with the wok still over a burner, tip 1 teaspoon of oil into its bowl and rub it around with another paper towel. Repeat this oiling process until the paper towel is free of any traces of black residue. The wok is then ready for use.

A new wok "drinks" oil until it is properly seasoned. Once seasoned, very little oil is necessary to cook in it. What I usually do with a new wok is make a batch of French fried potatoes in it. That is the perfect way to season it initially. I pour in 4 cups of peanut oil, heat the wok until I see wisps of white smoke rising, then put in the potatoes.

After the first washing, detergents should never be used in the bowl of the wok. It should be scrubbed with extremely hot water with a stiff-bristled wok brush. After rinsing, it should be dried quickly with a paper towel, then placed over a flame for a thorough drying. If you have finished cooking in it for the day, reseason it with a bit of peanut oil rubbed around inside the bowl with a paper towel. Do this for the first fifteen or twenty uses, until it becomes shiny and dark colored, which indicates it is completely seasoned. If the wok is to be used several times in the course of one day's cooking, then wipe it with a paper towel, over heat, before each use. The wok is best used with a wok ring that steadies it over the flame.

WOK COVER
Usually of aluminum, this cover, about 12 to 13 inches in diameter with a top handle, sits firmly in the wok. It enables the wok to be

used for stews, for steaming, and for boiling. Years ago in China, the covers were of wood. Today there are covers of stainless steel as well. Either the aluminum or the steel cover is adequate.

WOK BRUSH

This is a slightly oversized, oar-shaped wooden brush with long, very stiff bristles. It is used, with exceedingly hot water, to clean all cooking residues from the wok without any detergent.

WOK RING

This is a hollow steel base that nestles over a single stove burner. The round base of the wok settles into it firmly, thus ensuring that the wok is steady on the stove and that flames from the burner will surround it.

CHINESE SPATULA

This is a shovel-shaped utensil available in either carbon steel or stainless steel and in different sizes. The carbon-steel spatula has become somewhat rare in recent years, and either carbon or stainless steel is fine. If a carbon-steel one is to be used several times in the course of one cooking session, wash and wipe it with a paper towel, over heat, before each use.

CHINESE LADLE

Usually of stainless steel, it is bowl-shaped, with the bowl and the long handle of a single piece of steel. At the end of the handle is a wood inset. These ladles come in various sizes, but one with a 4½-inch-diameter bowl is perfect for all uses. The ladle occasionally can be found in carbon steel with a larger bowl, but I do not recommend these because they rust quite easily.

CHINESE STRAINERS

One is a circular steel-mesh strainer attached to a long split-bamboo handle. This type comes in many sizes, from as small as a person's palm to as large as 14 inches in diameter. For all-purpose use I prefer one 10 inches in diameter. As an option there are other, rather large stainless-steel strainers made by piercing holes in a bowl-shaped circle of steel. These may either have wood handles or be of one piece of steel, their handles hollow steel tubes. Both of these come in a 10-inch-diameter size.

BAMBOO STEAMERS

Bamboo steamers consist of circular frames of bamboo with woven bamboo-mesh bases and covers. They come in various sizes, but those 12 to 13 inches in diameter are preferred because they sit quite nicely in the wok. Foods rest on the woven bamboo, and steam passes up through the spaces and to the food. The steamers can be stacked two or three high so that different foods may be steamed simultaneously. Steamers are also made of aluminum and of wood with bamboo-mesh bases. There are also small steamers, usually of bamboo or stainless steel, that are often used for individual servings or for individual dim sum presentations.

Also to be found, usually in Chinese or Asian food supply markets, are steaming sets of stainless steel. These consist of a base pot, into which are set two steamers. Usually one of them has a base of crosshatched steel strips, the other of bamboo strips, this latter removable. And there is a pot cover. This set is valuable for those with limited storage space because the set's base is an 8-quart pot, which is useful. The same kind of unit comes in aluminum as well, the pot and steamers larger. I prefer the steel.

Also useful for steaming are the steel insets that fit into pots usually used for such foods as asparagus, corn, and pasta. Finally, for steaming large items, such as whole fish, or a whole winter melon, a clam steamer will serve nicely.

CHINESE CLEAVER

This is the other all-purpose tool of the Chinese kitchen. It cuts and dices, slices and minces. Its flat blade and its handle can mash. Usually of carbon steel with a wood handle, it is also available in stainless steel, either with a wood handle or with blade and handle of one continuous piece of steel. The blades of cleavers are gently rounded at their ends. There are different sizes and weights of cleavers, from 12 ounces to 2 pounds. I prefer a 12-ounce stainless-steel cleaver with a wood handle, the blade about 8 inches long and 3½ inches wide. It is a professional cleaver made by Dexter in the United States. I regard it as superior for slicing, cutting, dicing, or mincing vegetables, meats, and seafoods, and it should be used only for those purposes.

A heavier cleaver, of carbon steel, with a wood handle, weighing 1 pound, its blade measuring 8¼ by 4 inches, is ideal for cutting up a whole fowl and chopping its meat and bones.

There is another cleaver of stainless steel, its blade and handle of one piece. It weighs 18 ounces, its blade measures 8½ by 4 inches, and it is a good all-purpose cleaver, for cutting, mincing, and slicing as well as for chopping chickens and other fowl. It is, I feel, too heavy for continued use. I prefer the Dexter.

A still heavier cleaver, of carbon steel, with a wood handle, weighs 26 ounces. Its blade measures about 8 by 5 inches and is the knife of choice for cutting and chopping large bones, such as spareribs.

Finally, there is a smaller, narrower cleaver that is usually used to carve a Peking Duck. It is not for everyday use because it is too light. Its blade is 8½ by 2 inches. I mention it only because of its prominence on market shelves. It is a handsome all-steel knife.

Most cleavers are rather formidable looking and occasionally cause trepidation. Some people think that the first time they use a cleaver they will slice off one or more of their fingers. Nonsense. The cleaver, when held correctly so that its weight and balance are used properly, can do virtually anything a handful of lesser knives can. It slices, shreds, dices, and hacks, all with great ease. It scoops and can also function as a dough scraper.

There are correct ways to hold the cleaver. It should be held comfortably and in such a way as to make the weight of the cleaver do the work, firmly and efficiently. Two grips will be helpful:

First, for chopping and mincing, grip the handle in a fistlike grasp and swing it straight down. The strokes are long and forceful if cutting something quite thick. If mincing, the strokes are short, rapid, and controlled. The wrist dictates the force.

Second, for slicing, dicing, and shredding, grip the handle as for chopping, but permit the index finger to stretch out alongside the side of the flat blade to give it guidance. The wrist, which barely moves with this grip, is virtually rigid and becomes almost an extension of the cleaver as the blade is drawn across whatever food is being cut. When this grip is used, your other hand becomes a guide. Your fingertips should anchor the food to be cut, and your knuckles should guide the cleaver blade, which will brush them ever so slightly as it moves over the food.

To use the blade to mash, hold the handle tightly in the same grip you would for chopping. With the flat of the blade, come down hard on the food to be flattened, such as garlic, ginger, scallions, and leeks. The handle of the cleaver is perfect for mashing as well. Hold the handle firmly with the index finger and thumb at the base of the blade where it meets the handle. The other fingers are clenched. The blade faces upward and outward. The handle thus becomes a hammer that can be used to make a paste, such as that of fermented black beans and garlic.

Most kitchens these days are equipped with electric food processors and mixers. Slicing and chopping can be done in a food processor if you wish, but I prefer the control I can exert with my hand on the cleaver and the uniformity of size I can maintain. It is the traditional way, the way of the finest Chinese chefs, and I recommend it. Once you have become adept with the cleaver, I think you will prefer it as well.

CUTTING BOARDS

Many cutting boards are available. I recommend those of wood or of a rubberized composition sold in Chinese cooking supply stores. These beige-to-yellow boards are square, rectangular, or circular, of various sizes, and are quite heavy. They will never warp and are used in all professional Chinese kitchens because they are dense and their surface is both easy to scour clean and easy on cleaver blades. I do not recommend those boards of opaque white plastic since they tend to dull knife blades easily. Whichever chopping board you use, clean it thoroughly after use with hot water and detergent.

SAND CLAY POT

This is a pot of baked clay, its almond-beige exterior with a rough sandlike texture, its interior a brown glaze. It comes with a fitted glazed lid and with either two handles or one. Its bowl is banded with steel wire crosshatching. This is a historic, traditional Chinese cookpot that, despite its appearance, is used atop the stove directly over heat. This goes back to the time when Chinese kitchens had no ovens, only fire. It is used for stews and for braising, for congees and soups, and to cook rice. The Chinese believe that foods cooked in these sand pots retain more flavor and fragrance than those cooked in metal pots.

The sand pots come in many sizes and shapes. For most uses one 10 inches in diameter, with a single handle, is recommended. There are larger ones that might be considered after becoming familiar with the smaller one. Before use, submerge a sand pot totally in cold water for 24 hours. Remove it, allow it to dry, then fill with cold water to the brim and bring to a boil over medium-low heat. Boil for 30 minutes. Turn off the heat and allow the water to come to room temperature. The sand pot is now "cured," ready for use. This procedure prevents cracking and need be done only once. A caution: Never put a sand pot on a flame without liquid inside.

CHOPSTICKS

Bamboo chopsticks, in addition to being what the Chinese eat with, are marvelous cooking tools. They make fine stirrers, mixers, and servers and are usually available in packages of ten. Avoid plastic chopsticks, which should never be used for cooking and are more difficult to manipulate than bamboo when eating. Use longer chopsticks with rounded tips rather than those short versions with pointed ends. Chopsticks, because they are so important to the Chinese, come in a variety of materials. They can be ivory; jade; teak, ebony, and palisander woods; and silver. The emperors of China often used chopsticks of gold. In the imperial court, a bit of folklore has it, ivory chopsticks were used to test foods for poison. If the ivory blackened after touching food, the food had been poisoned.

The following implements will complete your Chinese kitchen:

Frying pan, cast iron, 10 inches in diameter
Round cake pan, 9 inches in diameter
Selection of steamproof dishes
Strainer, fine, all-purpose
Small hand grater, single panel
Garlic press
Kitchen shears
Cooking thermometer, for deep-frying

COOKING TECHNIQUES

The techniques of the Chinese kitchen are as important as its foods. There are specific ways to do things—to cut, to stir, to put foods together in proper, precise order. I urge you to read this section of my book before even planning a meal.

STIR-FRYING

Surely the most dramatic of all Chinese cooking techniques. It is fascinating to watch finely sliced and chopped foods being whisked through a bit of oil and tossed with a spatula. The hands and arms move as the wok is often tipped and rocked back and forth. Stir-frying is all movement and rhythm. The Chinese call this *wok hei,* or "wok air," and it indicates that the proper amount of fire is made to curl up around the bowl of the wok to cook foods precisely to that point of optimum flavor. What leads to it is careful preparation.

The object of stir-frying is to cook foods to the point at which they retain their flavors, colors, textures, and nutritive values. All foods to be stir-fried should be cut to indicated size and placed next to the wok, ready to be tipped into the oil. Sauces should be mixed and ready as well. This is simply organization, so that as you cook everything will be within reach and the rhythm of stir-frying will not be interrupted. The best stir-fried foods are those that retain their natures while at the same time absorbing and retaining the heat of the wok.

When I am ready to stir-fry, I heat the wok for a specific time, usually from 30 seconds to a minute. I pour oil into the wok and coat the sides by spreading it with the spatula. I drop a slice of ginger into the oil; when it turns light brown, the oil is ready.

When cooking vegetables, I usually add a bit of salt to the oil, to bring out the flavors of the foods. Place what is to be cooked in the wok and begin tossing it through the oil with the spatula, 1 to 2 minutes for such soft vegetables as bok choy and scallions, perhaps a minute longer for firmer vegetables such as cabbage, carrots, and broccoli. Scoop out the vegetables with the spatula, and they are ready to be served.

If vegetables are too wet, they will not stir-fry well, so they should be patted dry with paper towels (a bit of moisture will remain). If they are too dry, however, you may have to sprinkle a few drops of water into the wok while cooking to create steam, which aids the cooking process.

Meats are usually cut into uniform bite-sized pieces. They should always be placed in the oiled wok in a thin single layer, cooked to a specified time, then turned over and mixed briefly. At this point the meat will be cooked to about 70 percent of doneness. When it is stir-fried with other ingredients, it cooks through.

Seafood stir-frying varies. Shrimp should be cooked in a single layer, exactly like a meat. With crabs and lobsters it is occasionally necessary to cover the wok for a time to allow them to cook through their shells. Individual recipes specify. Clams, mussels, and oysters are usually blanched to make them open before stir-frying.

A gas range is best for cooking Chinese food because of its greater heat and the height of its flame, particularly for those stir-fries that require such direct, high heat. There is a technique, however, for obtaining high heat as well as necessary variance on an electric range. It is a method I have devised and taught with success.

I use two electric burners, side by side. Turn one burner to the highest setting and allow it to heat for 10 minutes. After 5 minutes, turn on the other burner to medium. Place a flat-bottomed wok on the highest heat and allow it to heat for 1 to 1½ minutes, until the wok is very hot. Begin the cooking process. Place the food in the wok. If it begins to cook too quickly or looks as if it is about to burn, switch the wok to the burner with medium heat. Go back and forth between the burners as necessary. Once you have become accustomed to this method, you will cook Chinese perfectly, without a gas range and with ease.

As a general rule, never just double a recipe for stir-frying unless you have a restaurant range. Otherwise, cook in two batches, or the heat will not really be adequate.

DEEP-FRYING

The object of deep-frying foods is to cook them thoroughly inside while outside they are golden, tender, and lightly crusted. Most foods that are to be deep-fried are first seasoned, marinated, and dipped into a batter. Ideally the oil combines with these other tastes to create fresh, new flavors. The taste of oil should never be dominant.

When I wish to make my wok into a deep-fryer, I heat it briefly, then pour in 4 to 6 cups of peanut oil and heat the oil to 325° to

375°F, depending on what is being cooked. The oil should be heated to a temperature a bit higher than that required for frying the food, because when the food is placed into it, the oil temperature will drop. Then it will begin to rise again, so I use a frying thermometer, which I leave in the oil, to help regulate the temperature. When the oil reaches the proper temperature, slide the food into it from the outer edges of the wok. Remember to keep the temperature of the oil steady by turning the heat up or down as required.

The utensil to use for moving ingredients in deep-frying is the Chinese mesh strainer. Its large surface and stout bamboo handle are ideal for removing foods from oil and straining them as well. In my view the strainer is far more useful than a slotted spoon.

OIL-BLANCHING

This relatively simple cooking technique is basically a sealing process. Its aim is to seal in flavor and juices, in the case of meats, and to help them retain their color, in the case of vegetables. Heat the wok, pour 3 cups of peanut oil into it, then heat to about 300°F (this temperature will vary slightly; see individual recipes). Vegetables should be added to the oil for no longer than 30 to 45 seconds, then removed with a Chinese strainer. Meats will be blanched for 1 to 2 minutes, depending on the individual recipe. When foods are removed from the oil, all excess oil should be drained off and the oil-blanched foods set aside to be cooked further as required.

WATER-BLANCHING

Water blanching removes water from vegetables. Pour 3 to 4 cups of water into a wok, add ¼ teaspoon of baking soda, and bring to a boil. The baking soda is optional; it ensures a bright green color for vegetables. I like to say that the intense green of green vegetables blanched this way is imperial jade green. Place the vegetables in the water and immerse them. When their color becomes bright, remove them. This process usually takes no more than 30 seconds. Immediately drain them through a strainer, place them in a bowl, and run cold water over them to halt the cooking process. Alternatively, the blanched food may be placed in a bowl of cold water with ice cubes, which also will stop the cooking process. The use of bowls of ice water is best for large amounts of food. See individual recipes. Drain the blanched foods and set aside.

STOCK-BLANCHING

This is a method designed to impart taste and lessen the amount of oil used in preparation. Heat stock in a wok, the amount determined by the amount of food to be blanched, from 1 to 2 cups. Heat to boiling. Place the food to be blanched in the stock for 10 to 30 seconds, 10 seconds for thinly sliced fowl or meats, 30 seconds for hard vegetables such as asparagus, broccoli, and cauliflower. Remove and drain. The foods are then ready to use further. Stocks can be reserved for another use, such as in soups.

DRY-ROASTING

The advantage of dry-roasting is that there is no need for oil, salt, or anything else in the wok except the food to be roasted. To dry-roast nuts, heat the wok over high heat for 30 to 45 seconds. Add the nuts and lower the heat to very low. Spread the nuts in a single layer and use a spatula to move them about and turn them over to prevent burning. This process takes about 12 to 15 minutes, or until the nuts turn brown. Turn off the heat, remove the nuts from the wok, and allow them to cool. Nuts can be dry-roasted two to three days in advance of their use. After they cool, place them in a sealed jar.

Use the same process to dry-roast sesame seeds, except that the roasting time should be 2 minutes.

TEMPERING DISHES FOR STEAMING

Porcelain or Pyrex dishes may be used inside steamers but first should be seasoned and tempered. Fill a wok with 5 to 6 cups of cold water. Place a cake rack in the wok and stack the dishes to be tempered on the rack, making certain they are completely covered by the cold water. Cover with a wok cover and bring the water to a boil. Let the water boil for 10 minutes, turn off the heat, and allow the wok to cool to room temperature. The dishes are then seasoned and can be placed in steamers without fear that they will crack. They may also be used in place of steamers on occasion.

Foods are placed in the seasoned, tempered, steamproof dishes, which are in turn placed on cake racks within the wok. Once tempered, the dishes will remain so for their lifetime. They need not be tempered again.

It has been suggested that it is unnecessary to temper Pyrex because it is already tempered glass. However, this applies only if Pyrex is to be used in the oven. It has been my experience, and that of my students, that Pyrex may indeed crack during steaming. So it is best to temper Pyrex along with porcelain. The process is simple and quick and provides a good measure of safety.

STEAMING

Steaming in the Chinese manner is a life-giving process. Natural tastes are preserved well when food is steamed. Dry food becomes moist when subjected to steam's wet, penetrating heat. Breads become softened. That which has shrunk expands. Steaming bestows a glistening coating of moisture to foods. It is artful as well, because foods can be arranged in attractive ways within bamboo steamers, and once steamed they can be served in their container. Steaming requires no oil at all, except that which is used to brush the woven bamboo at the bottom of the steamers to prevent sticking.

To steam, pour 2 quarts of water into a wok and bring it to a boil. Place the steamers in the wok so that they sit evenly above, but not touching, the water. You will be able to stack two steamers or more, should you wish.

Cover the top one and the contents of all will cook perfectly. Boiling water should be on hand at all times during the steaming process to replenish any water that evaporates from the wok. Steaming times vary with the foods being prepared. See individual recipes.

You may also steam in a wok without bamboo steamers. Use a large cake rack. Place it in the wok over boiling water. Place the food to be steamed in a steamproof tempered and seasoned porcelain or glass dish. Cover the wok and steam. You may also steam in a metal dish, cake pan, or pie plate. If steaming in a metal dish the steaming time, in general, will be half that of porcelain or glass.

You may also use steamers of stainless steel or aluminum. There are Chinese steamers, self-contained, of holed insets that nestle into pots. These are available in stainless steel, occasionally in aluminum (see page 58). Using these, the process is again the same, with times indicated in the recipes. With these, most foods must be in steamproof dishes. Some vegetables, however, may be steamed directly in the insets. You may also use asparagus, pasta, and clam steamers to steam foods if you wish; with these, foods must go into steamproof dishes, as before. When steaming with metal, there will always be more residual moisture, either in the food, in the steamer, or both. So I recommend the traditional bamboo steamers for the best results.

It should be noted that metal is easier to clean and maintain than bamboo. Bamboo steamers must be washed and brushed, then allowed to dry thoroughly before storage. Allowing for this, I still prefer the results obtained with the bamboo steamer.

Basics,
Traditions,
and Innovations

基本傳統現代

BASIC TO COOKING IN THE CHINESE MANNER, IN ADDITION TO THOSE FOODS I HAVE ALREADY LISTED, ARE PREPARATIONS THAT BECOME BUILDING BLOCKS ON WHICH OTHER DISHES RELY. MANY PROCEED FROM CHINA'S LONG CULINARY TRADITION; OTHERS REFLECT SOME NEW THINKING, NEW INPUT INTO THE CHINESE KITCHEN, MUCH OF IT MY OWN. Virtually all of the essential prepared foods that appear in my Chinese larder can be bought in markets these days, Chinese, Asian, and, more and more, in neighborhood markets. As far as bottled, canned, jarred, and dried ingredients are concerned, I find many of them very good indeed. I choose, however, to make as many of these as I can fresh in my own kitchen, and invariably they are better.

Some are traditional tastes of China that are best made rather than bought, simply because their flavors will be more pronounced. I would put condiments, pickles, and snacks in that category, foods the Chinese love to nibble on as they await service of a meal or in the teahouse. Others are variations on Chinese themes—sauces, seasoning mixes, flavored infused oils that enhance foods. Others are the stocks on which rest the best of the Chinese kitchen, as well as prepared, cooked rices, *fan,* that are central to virtually every Chinese meal.

SPECIAL RICES

Surely nothing is more basic to the Chinese kitchen than rice. Cooked rices are always at the center of every dining table, with the accompaniments, the *t'sai,* arrayed around the rice. An entire collection of recipes later in this book, devoted to rice in its Chinese context as a universal staple and to its types and variations as well. What follow here are basic rice recipes, one for a perfect cooked rice to accompany other dishes, others that are used either as ingredients in or as bases for other dishes.

BASIC COOKED RICE

Fan

*I*t has been said often, too often, that making properly cooked rice is virtually impossible. This is of course not so. Rather than being difficult, it is easy, in fact simple. Here is a virtually foolproof recipe for cooking perfect rice, fluffy, separated grains, the rice I recommend be eaten with most of the cooked recipes in this book.

Use extra long-grain rice, preferably Texas-grown.

Place it in a pot with cold water. Wash the rice 3 times in the cold water in the pot by rubbing it between the hands. Drain well after washing. Then add water to the rice and allow it to rest for 1 hour before cooking. A good ratio is 2 cups of rice to 1⅞ cups (15 ounces) of water, sufficient for 2 people. (The common 2 cups water–to–2 cups rice ratio will not yield satisfactory results. The rice will be too soft for Chinese tastes.) So-called old rice, that which has been lying about in sacks for extended periods, is the rice I prefer, for it will absorb more water and will be easier to cook.

Begin cooking the rice, uncovered, over high heat, by bringing the water to a boil. Stir the rice with chopsticks or with a wooden spoon and cook for about 4 minutes or until the water is absorbed or evaporates. Even after the water is gone, the rice will continue to be quite hard. Cover the pot and cook over low heat for about 8 minutes more, stirring the rice from time to time.

After turning off the heat, loosen the rice with the chopsticks or wooden spoon. This will help it retain its fluffiness. Cover tightly until ready to serve. Just before serving, stir and loosen the rice once again. Well-cooked rice will have absorbed the water but will not be lumpy, nor will the kernels stick together. They will be firm and separate. The rice may be kept hot in a warm oven for an hour without drying it out.

MAKES 4½ TO 5 CUPS,

THE OLDER THE RICE THE LARGER THE YIELD

SWEET WINE RICE

Jau Long

*T*his is a well-known preparation in Shanghai, where it is eaten as a snack or used to prepare Shanghai's famous Wine Rice Soup. The sweetness of the rice is due to its fermentation. Only when a soup is made is more sweetness added, in the form of sugar.

2 cups glutinous rice
2 cups cold water
2 quarts boiling water
3 wine pills, crushed
1 teaspoon flour

1. Wash the rice 3 times; drain off excess water thoroughly. Place the rice in a round cake pan, add the 2 cups of cold water, and place the cake pan in a steamer. Add the boiling water to a wok, bring to a boil, and steam the rice for 30 to 40 minutes (see steaming, page 64).

2. Place the cooked rice in a large bowl and allow to cool for 20 minutes. Run cold water into the bowl and loosen the rice with your fingers. Drain off the water. Place the crushed wine pills in the rice and mix it well into the mixture with your hands. When mixed, use your fingers to punch 8 to 10 holes into the rice to aid fermentation.

3. Sprinkle the flour on top of the rice, cover the bowl with a damp cloth, and set in an unheated gas oven or in a warm place. The rice will ferment in 24 to 48 hours. You know fermentation has occurred when you see bubbles and liquid in the holes made in the rice. The smell of wine should be strong.

N O T E : *Sweet Wine Rice may be stored in a tightly closed jar in the refrigerator for up to 6 months.*

MAKES 3 ½ TO 4 CUPS

RED WINE RICE

Hong Jau

This is a very popular dish in Fujian. It is never eaten as it is cooked but as the basis for, or as an ingredient in, other dishes. The color of this dish comes from the red rice used.

2 cups glutinous rice
4½ cups cold water
2 quarts boiling water
¾ cup red rice
2 wine pills, crushed
2 teaspoons flour

1. Wash the rice 3 times in a bowl and drain off the excess water thoroughly. Place the rice in a round cake pan and add the cold water. Place the cake pan in a steamer and cover. Add the boiling water to the wok and bring back to a boil over high heat. Steam the rice (see page 64) for 50 to 60 minutes or until the rice is cooked. It will be quite soft.

2. Place the cooked rice in a large bowl. Loosen with chopsticks and allow to come to room temperature. Meanwhile, pulverize the red rice into a powder in a blender.

3. Add the red rice powder and crushed wine pills to the room-temperature rice and mix in thoroughly. Place the mixture in a glass jar. Sprinkle with flour. Cover with 2 paper towels, and tie tightly with a string around the neck of the jar. Allow to stand at a temperature of about 55°F for 48 hours to ferment. (If it's too warm, mold may form. Do not cover the opening with paper towels. Place a dish towel loosely over the top and store for 48 hours.) There will be a strong wine smell. Remove the paper towels, cover the jar, and place in the refrigerator to ferment further for 1 month.

4. After 1 month, drain off the red liquid. In China this is used to color foods. You may wish to experiment. (Store the liquid for use in other recipes in a closed jar, refrigerated, for up to 6 months.) The red wine rice may be used at this point. Stored in the refrigerator, it will keep for up to 6 months.

MAKES 7 TO 7½ CUPS

SICHUAN ROASTED RICE

Sichuan Jing Mai Fun

*T*his is a classic preparation from Sichuan. It is used to coat meats before steaming them, thus its name, jing mai fun, which translates as "steamed rice powder." Traditionally this was a dish for the common folk, not recognized as fine, but it is said that those of higher social orders liked it so much that they would patronize smaller restaurants where foods were cooked with it. These days it is loved by rich and poor alike.

1 cup short-grain rice
1 tablespoon Sichuan peppercorns

1. Place the rice in a large bowl and fill to the top with cold water. Wash the rice 3 times by rubbing it together between your hands. Drain the rice, cover with cold water, and allow to soak for 2 hours. Drain off the water and allow the rice to dry thoroughly. (It is best to do this the night before.) This may seem to be a good deal of effort for a mixture that is going to be dry-roasted, then ground up, but it is necessary. The rice must be washed to rid it of starch and must be soaked—unsoaked raw rice in a powder will dry out the meat it coats.

2. Heat a wok over high heat for 30 seconds. Add the rice and Sichuan peppercorns and stir to mix well. If the rice browns too quickly or you smell burning, lower the heat to medium. Stir-fry for about 7 minutes, controlling the heat so the rice does not burn, until the rice turns a sandy color and the peppercorns release their fragrance. Turn off the heat. Transfer to a bowl and allow to cool to room temperature.

3. Place the rice-peppercorn mixture in a blender and blend coarsely to the consistency of bread crumbs. Place in a glass jar immediately, so no fragrance is lost. It will keep for 2 months.

MAKES 1 CUP

CINNAMON ROASTED RICE POWDER

Guai Jee Chau Mai Fun

*T*his preparation is not eaten by itself as prepared but used as a coating for steamed meats and poultry. This version from Beijing differs from the preceding Sichuan recipe in that cinnamon and eight-star anise are added to the ground mix. The flavor imparted is different indeed.

1 cup short-grain rice
One 3-inch cinnamon stick, crushed
   into small pieces
1 whole eight-star anise, crushed
¼ teaspoon Sichuan peppercorns

1. Wash, soak, and dry the rice precisely as in the previous recipe.

2. Heat a wok over high heat for 30 seconds. Add the crushed cinnamon and anise and the peppercorns. Stir together for 1 minute, then lower the heat to medium. Add the rice and cook, stirring, for 7 minutes, controlling the heat carefully so the rice does not burn, until the rice is a sandy color. Turn off the heat, transfer to a bowl, and allow to cool to room temperature. Place the rice-peppercorn mixture in a blender and blend coarsely to a consistency like bread crumbs. Place in a glass jar immediately, so no fragrance is lost. It will keep for 2 months.

MAKES 1 CUP

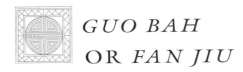

GUO BAH
OR *FAN JIU*

This basic rice preparation, for those soups usually called guo bah *(which evolved into the* wor bar *seen on menus), probably had its genesis in Shanghai, though it is known and used throughout China, Hong Kong, and Taiwan. Traditionally, in China, a hardened rice layer is left at the bottom of a pot, particularly if the heat has been high, after the cooked rice has been removed. This layer, if left in the pot and subjected to low heat, will eventually harden, brown slightly, and come away from the pot surface in a crisp layer. The Chinese call this* fan jiu, *which translates as "rice left at the bottom of a pot."*

If this rice is not too burned, it can become the basis for a guo bah *dish, that is, deep-fried, placed in a tureen, and soup poured over it in a sizzle. To the Chinese the* fan jiu, *or rice layer, becomes* guo bah, *or the bastardized* wor bah, *when used with soup. For those who do not wish to cook a pot of rice to get a crisp layer, what follows is a way to make a foolproof* fan jiu.

½ cup extra-long-grain rice
½ cup cold water

1. Place the rice in a bowl, cover with cold water, and wash 3 times by rubbing between your hands. Drain the rice, place in a 10-inch nonstick skillet, and add ½ cup cold water. Spread the rice in a thin, even layer. Allow to sit for 1½ hours. Most of the water will be absorbed.

2. Place the skillet over medium heat, cover, and cook for 5 minutes. Reduce the heat to low and cook for 2 minutes more. The rice should be white and translucent. Remove the cover and cook for 2 to 3 minutes more. Move the pan from side to side to loosen the rice. If it is loose and moves, it is done. Turn off the heat and allow to cool in the pan.

3. Place a large platter over the skillet and invert so the rice round falls out. It should be cooked, dry, and hardened, with no moisture. It is now considered to be a *fan jiu* and ready to be used in *wor bah* soups. Allow to cool to room temperature and to dry completely, then store in a closed container in a cool, dry place for as long as 6 months.

    To use for a sizzling *wor bah* soup, deep-fry the rice cake in 3 cups peanut oil heated to 375°F for 2 minutes or until it expands to about double its size. Drain. This is now, the Chinese say, a *wor bah,* to be used to sizzle soup.

MAKES 4 TO 6 SERVINGS

S tocks are more than basic to the Chinese kitchen; they are a necessity. One stock or another is a component of any well-prepared dish, whether it be a soup, a sauce, or a marinade. Stocks impart flavor, to be sure, but more important they provide the bedrock intensity essential to the best of Chinese food and obviate the need for flavor-enhancing substances of any kind.

I believe it essential to use specific stocks for specific dishes, simply because of their different flavor bases. However, you may choose to limit your supply to chicken or vegetable stocks, and they will be sufficient for most dishes in this book. I do urge, though, that you have all of the following stocks at hand. As you will see, they can be frozen for storage. ◆

SUPERIOR STOCK

Chiu Kop Seung Tong

T his rich mixture is the stock of choice throughout China. The words "superior stock" on restaurant menus are familiar to most of us. To the Chinese the words indicate that great care has been taken to raise the level of taste in a dish with the use of such a stock. And it is indeed rich in China, where Yunnan and Jinhua hams are available. The better chefs use this stock in virtually everything they cook. Because it is generally made in huge amounts, it is not unusual for a stockpot to contain whole chickens, pounds of pork, and whole ham shank bones. It is such a special stock that it is often called *seung tong*, or "best soup," from which all other soups proceed. For the

ham, Smithfield ham from Virginia is an admirable substitute.

1 gallon water
4 pounds pork neck bones
3 pounds lean pork butt, cut in half
5 pounds chicken, cut into 8 pieces
2½ pounds shank bone of Smithfield ham or ham bones
½ pound fresh ginger, lightly smashed
1 bunch fresh scallions, trimmed and cut in half
¼ cup fried shallots (page 84)
½ cup fried scallions (page 82)
2 gallons cold water
Salt

1. In a large stockpot, bring 1 gallon water to a boil. Add the pork neck bones, pork butt, and chicken and bring to a boil. Allow to boil for 1 minute to bring the blood to the top of the water. Turn off the heat. Pour off the water and run cold water into the pot to rinse the meats. Drain.

2. Place all the pork bones and meat, chicken parts, ham, ginger, fresh scallions, and fried shallots and scallions in the pot. Add 2 gallons cold water, cover, and bring to a boil over high heat. Add salt to taste, lower the heat, and simmer, leaving the lid slightly cracked, for 5 hours. Skim off the residue from the surface during the simmering.

3. Turn off the heat, allow to cool, and strain the stock. Pour the stock into containers to store for further use. Cover and refrigerate for 3 to 4 days or freeze for up to 3 months.

MAKES 1 GALLON

CHICKEN STOCK

Gai Seung Tong

3 quarts water
2 whole chickens (8 pounds total), including giblets, fat removed and each chicken cut into 4 pieces
2 pounds chicken wings
7½ quarts cold water
½ pound fresh ginger, cut into 3 pieces, lightly smashed
6 garlic cloves, peeled
1 bunch scallions, trimmed and cut into thirds

4 medium onions, peeled and quartered
¼ pound fresh coriander (cilantro), cut into thirds (1 cup)
¼ cup fried onions (page 83)
½ teaspoon white peppercorns
¼ pound boxthorn seeds, soaked for 10 minutes
Salt

1. In a large stockpot, bring 3 quarts water to a boil. Add the chicken, chicken wings, and giblets, bring back to a boil, and boil for 1 minute. This will bring the blood and juices to the top of the liquid. Turn off the heat. Pour off the water and run cold water into the pot to rinse the chicken. Drain.

2. Place the chicken and giblets back into the pot. Add 7½ quarts cold water and all the remaining ingredients except salt. Cover the pot and bring to a boil over high heat. Add salt to taste and lower the heat to simmer. Leaving the lid slightly cracked, simmer for 4½ hours. Skim off residue from the surface during simmering.

3. Turn off the heat. Allow to cool for 10 to 15 minutes. Strain and pour into containers to store for later use. Cover and refrigerate for 4 to 5 days or freeze for up to 3 months.

MAKES 5 QUARTS

SEAFOOD STOCK

Hoi Sin Tong

12 pounds fish heads and bones, well
    washed in cold running water
5 quarts cold water
2 pounds onions, peeled and quartered
6 scallions, trimmed and cut into
    ½-inch pieces

½ pound fresh ginger, lightly smashed
6 garlic cloves, peeled
¼ pound fresh coriander (cilantro)
¾ cup fried scallions (page 82)
¼ cup fried garlic (page 84)
2 teaspoons fried Sichuan peppercorns

1. Place all ingredients in a large stockpot. Bring to a boil over high heat. Lower the heat
   and partially cover the pot, but keep at a boil at all times. Cook for 3 hours.

2. Turn off the heat. Strain the stock and pour it into containers to store for later use.
   Cover and refrigerate for up to 2 to 3 days or freeze for about 3 months.

MAKES 3 QUARTS

VEGETABLE STOCK

Jai Seung Tong

7 quarts cold water
1½ pounds carrots, cut into thirds
3½ pounds onions, peeled and cut into
    quarters
1½ pounds scallions, trimmed and cut
    into thirds
1 pound fresh mushrooms, cut into
    thirds
12 celery stalks, cut into thirds
½ pound fresh coriander (cilantro),
    cut into 3-inch pieces

½ cup red dates, soaked in hot water
    for 30 minutes
⅓ cup boxthorn seeds, soaked in hot
    water for 30 minutes
1 teaspoon white peppercorns
½ pound fresh ginger, lightly smashed
3 tablespoons Scallion Oil (page 82) or
    peanut oil
1 cup fried scallions (page 82)
¼ cup fried garlic (page 84)
Salt

1. In a large pot, bring the water to a boil over high heat. Add all the ingredients, including salt to taste, to the boiling water, reduce the heat, and cook at a slow boil in a partially covered pot for 5 hours.

2. Remove the pot from the heat and strain the liquid into containers, discarding the solids. Cover and refrigerate for up to 4 to 5 days or freeze for up to 3 months.

MAKES 4 TO 4½ QUARTS

VEGETABLE STOCK II

Jai Seung Tong

*T*his second vegetable stock is almost identical to the first, except that it is made without red dates or boxthorn seeds. The familiar pitted sweet dates and preserved figs are widely available.

7 quarts cold water
1½ pounds carrots, cut into thirds
3½ pounds onions, peeled and cut into quarters
1 pound fresh mushrooms, cut into halves
1 pound leeks, trimmed, well washed, and cut into 4 pieces
12 celery stalks, cut into thirds
½ pound fresh coriander (cilantro), cut into 3-inch pieces
3 tablespoons Scallion Oil (page 82) or peanut oil
¾ cup fried scallions (page 82)
¼ cup fried shallots (page 84)
½ pound fresh ginger, lightly smashed
6 preserved figs
7 pitted sweet dates
2 teaspoons white peppercorns
Salt

1. In a large pot, bring the water to a boil over high heat. Add all the ingredients, including salt to taste, to the water. Reduce the heat and cook at a slow boil in a partially covered pot for 5 hours.

2. Remove the pot from the heat and strain the liquid into containers to store for later use. Discard the solids. Cover and refrigerate for up to 4 to 5 days or freeze for up to 3 months.

MAKES 4 TO 4½ QUARTS

MILK STOCK
Nai Tong

Although this is a popular stock in Shanghai, it is widely used throughout China. Its name translates as "milk soup" or "milk stock," but its color is not like that of white milk. When it is made it is milky, opaque, almost an almond-white color. It is an extraordinarily rich stock that is ideal for soups and sauces. You may wish to interchange it with other stocks for different tastes in recipes, particularly soups.

4½ pounds pork feet, cut in half lengthwise by the butcher
2 pounds lean fresh ham with skin
20 garlic cloves, peeled
½ pound white parts of scallions (16 scallions)
7½ quarts cold water
½ teaspoon white peppercorns
1 large onion, quartered
2 tablespoons salt
6 tablespoons Mei Kuei Lu Chiew or gin

Use a paring knife to scrape impurities from the skin of the pork feet until the roughness is gone and the feet become almost white. Place all the ingredients in a large stockpot except 1 tablespoon salt and the Mei Kuei Lu Chiew. Cover the pot and bring to a boil over high heat. Uncover the pot, lower the heat to simmer, and stir to make certain that the food does not stick to the bottom of the pot. Cook for 4½ hours or until the skin falls off the bones of the pork feet. Add the remaining tablespoon of salt or to taste. Add the Mei Kuei Lu Chiew, stir, and cook for 10 minutes more. Turn off the heat and strain the liquid into containers to store for later use. Cover and refrigerate for up to 4 days or freeze for up to 3 months.

N O T E : *The pork meat may be eaten if desired.*

M A K E S   5   Q U A R T S

SMITHFIELD HAM

For Tui

*T*he name for ham in China, for tui, translates as "fire leg" to illustrate that it is a pork leg that has been treated and cured. In China there are many regional hams, but the finest are Yunnan, from that province, and Jinhua, from the Shanghai region. Smithfield ham from Virginia closely resembles these hams. Like them, it is cured but not cooked. Once prepared, as here, it fills in for them quite nicely.

One 2½-pound slab Smithfield ham, cross-cut to include skin and center bone, about 2 inches thick
9 quarts cold water
5 ounces sugarcane sugar or dark brown sugar

1. Under warm running water, with a stiff brush, remove the black pepper coating of the Smithfield ham. Soak in 5 quarts cold water overnight.

2. In a large pot, place 4 quarts cold water and the ham and bring to a boil over high heat. Lower the heat and simmer for 1 hour. Turn off the heat, drain the water from the pot, then refill the pot with ice water to cover the ham. Allow to cool for 30 minutes.

3. Remove the ham from the water, dry with paper towels, and place in a round cake pan. Break up the sugarcane sugar and place it under, atop, and around the ham. Place the cake pan in a steamer and steam for 1 hour, turning the ham over after 30 minutes. Baste the ham with liquid 4 to 5 times during steaming.

4. Turn off the heat. Remove the ham from the steamer and allow to cool. The ham is now ready for use. It can be eaten as it is. For recipes that call for Yunnan or Jinhua ham, this is perfect. Once cooked, the ham will keep, in a closed container and refrigerated, for up to 10 days.

N O T E : *If the piece of ham you buy is smaller than that specified, or has been boned and trimmed, you need boil it for only 20 minutes to remove the salt. Continue the process from the point of placing it in ice water and steam with 1 tablespoon brown sugar for 15 to 20 minutes.*

STEAMED DRY SCALLOPS

*T*hese are expensive delicacies, used sparingly, to enhance other preparations.
Occasionally these flavorful dry scallops,
gawn bui, *anglicized and known widely as
"dried scallops," are added to rich seafood
stocks. I use them, steamed, as here, in many
recipes, for their different, pungent taste.*

*8 Chinese dry scallops, the diameter of
a quarter*
2 teaspoons Mei Kuei Lu Chiew or gin
2 tablespoons Chicken Stock (page 75)

Place the scallops in a steamproof dish; add the Mei Kuei Lu Chiew or gin and the stock.
Place 2 quarts boiling water in a wok, place the dish in a steamer and the steamer in the
wok, cover, and steam for 35 to 30 minutes. The scallops are done when they fall apart
into strands when prodded with chopsticks. They can be used immediately after steaming or refrigerated in a closed container for 7 to 10 days. Do not freeze them.

MAKES ABOUT 1 CUP

STEAMED BLACK MUSHROOMS

Gai Yau Dong Gu

*T*his basic preparation is a widespread tradition eaten throughout China. The mushrooms, once steamed, can be served as a small appetizer, a full course, or an accompaniment. I go several steps further and use them in many dishes, in a variety of ways, which is why I regard these mushrooms as a basic necessity.

30 dried Chinese black mushrooms, caps about 1½ inches in diameter
½ teaspoon salt
1½ teaspoons sugar

1 tablespoon dark soy sauce
3 scallions, trimmed and cut into 2-inch pieces
2 ounces raw chicken fat, cut into 4 pieces, or 2 tablespoons Scallion Oil (page 82)
One ½-inch slice fresh ginger, lightly smashed
1 tablespoon Mei Kuei Lu Chiew or gin
¾ cup Chicken Stock (page 75) or Vegetable Stock (page 76)

1. Soak the mushrooms in hot water for 30 minutes. Wash thoroughly and squeeze out excess water. Remove the stems and place the mushroom caps in a steamproof dish. Mix all the other ingredients and toss well with the mushrooms. Place 2 quarts boiling water in a wok, place the dish and the steamer in the wok, cover, and steam for 30 minutes.

2. Remove the dish from the steamer. Discard the scallions, ginger, and chicken fat and gently toss the mushrooms in the remaining liquid. Allow to cool to room temperature, cover with plastic wrap, and refrigerate for up to 4 to 5 days. Serve at slightly cooler than room temperature.

MAKES 10 SERVINGS AS A FIRST COURSE

*T*here has been a tendency to regard infused and flavored oils as newcomers over the culinary horizon. This is not the case at all. Flavored oils have existed in many countries, certainly in China, for centuries. Oils pressed from sesame seeds, turnips, and rapeseed have been used in China for more than 2,000 years, long before the peanut made its way there and became the prime source of cooking oil. Peanut oil, I have found in developing these infused oils, is most receptive and welcoming to other flavors, absorbing the scent and taste of whichever spice or vegetable it is wedded to by heat. Such oils, when used sparingly, judiciously, imbue dishes with a subtlety of taste that is most desirable. This is particularly so in Chinese cooking, where the emphasis is always on inherent flavor, not on massive alteration.

I suggest that a wok be used to make these oils, because the simple process of heating oil in the wok serves to season it. All of the oils that follow can be stored for significant lengths of time, which are specified, and an added, recurring, bonus are the cooked spices and vegetables that remain after the oils have been blended with them. These tasty residuals are used repeatedly, particularly in stocks and soups, but in stir-fried dishes as well, as are the sauces and flavorings that follow.

As with my stocks, I recommend various infused oils because of their different tastes. However, simple peanut oil may be used in their stead. ◆

SCALLION OIL

Chung Yau

*S*callion oil is a favorite, often used ingredient that finds its way into many soups, sauces, and marinades.

1½ cups peanut oil
3 to 4 bunches scallions (1 pound),
    trimmed, white parts lightly
    smashed, each scallion cut into
    2-inch pieces

1. Heat a wok over medium heat. Add the peanut oil, then the scallions. Bring to a boil, and lower the heat to simmer for 20 to 30 minutes, stirring occasionally. When the oil turns golden brown, it is done.

2. Turn off the heat. Strain through a fine strainer into a bowl and cool to room temperature. Pour the scallion oil into a glass jar and refrigerate until needed. The oil will keep at room temperature for 1 week or refrigerated for up to 6 months.

N O T E : *Do not discard the scallions. Place in a plastic container and refrigerate. They will keep indefinitely and are a fine addition to stocks and soups.*

M A K E S 1¼ C U P S

ONION OIL

Yung Chung Yau

1½ cups peanut oil
1 pound yellow onions, very thinly
sliced (4 cups)

1. Heat a wok over high heat for 30 seconds. Add the peanut oil and onions. Stir, making certain the onions are coated. Cook for 7 minutes, stirring and turning often to prevent burning and to ensure even browning. Lower the heat to medium and cook for 15 minutes more or until the onions turn light brown.

2. Strain the oil into a bowl, using a ladle or large spoon to press the onions as they drain. Allow to cool. Place in a glass jar and close tightly. The oil will keep at room temperature for 1 week or refrigerated for up to 6 months.

N O T E : *The browned onions remaining are used in many recipes. Place in a plastic container and refrigerate. They will keep indefinitely.*

M A K E S 1¼ C U P S

GARLIC OIL

Seun Yau

*T*his oil imparts a fine aroma to cooked foods and to salads. As a finishing oil, it is often stirred into soups just before serving.

2 cups peanut oil
3 cups thinly sliced garlic (4 heads)

1. Heat a wok over high heat for 30 seconds. Add the peanut oil and garlic and stir. Lower the heat to medium and bring to a boil. Reduce the heat to low and cook for 10 minutes or until the garlic turns light brown.

2. Strain the oil into a bowl and allow to cool. The oil will keep at room temperature for 1 week or refrigerated for up to 6 months.

N O T E : *The fried garlic that remains should be drained on paper towels and refrigerated in a closed container for use in other recipes for up to 2 months.*

M A K E S   1½   C U P S

SHALLOT OIL

Chung Tau Yau

1½ cups peanut oil
1 pound shallots, thinly sliced (2 cups)

1. Heat a wok over high heat for 40 seconds. Add the peanut oil and shallots. Stir and cook for 5 minutes. Lower the heat to medium, and cook for 10 more minutes or until the shallots turn golden brown, stirring frequently to ensure even cooking.

2. Strain the oil and allow to cool. Pour into a glass jar. The oil will keep at room temperature for 1 week or refrigerated for up to 6 months.

NOTE: *The crisp shallots that remain should be drained on paper towels and kept in a closed container for use in other recipes. They will keep for 1 month at room temperature or refrigerated for 2 months.*

MAKES 1 CUP

WHITE PEPPERCORN OIL

Bok Chiu Yau

白椒油

White pepper is a spice used throughout China and is much preferred to black pepper. I use white pepper by choice in most of my recipes for its fragrance and flavor. This infused oil has that subtle white pepper aroma.

1 cup peanut oil
½ cup white peppercorns

1. Place the oil and peppercorns in a wok over medium heat and bring to a boil. Reduce the heat to low and cook for 2 minutes.

2. Turn off the heat and allow to cool in the wok. Do not strain this oil. Place the oil and peppercorns in a glass jar and close tightly. Because it is so delicate, this oil will not keep long, so I only make a small amount at a time. It will keep, refrigerated, for no longer than 2 months.

MAKES 1 SCANT CUP

SICHUAN PEPPERCORN OIL

Chun Jiu Yau

¼ cup Sichuan peppercorns
1 cup peanut oil

1. Heat a wok over high heat for 30 seconds. Add the Sichuan peppercorns to the dry wok and stir. Reduce the heat to low and stir for 1½ minutes or until the peppercorns release their fragrance. Add the peanut oil, raise the heat to medium, and bring the oil to a boil. Lower the heat to a simmer and cook for 4 to 5 minutes, stirring, or until the peppercorns turn black and release their fragrance.

2. Strain the oil, allow it to cool, and pour into a glass jar. The oil will keep at room temperature for 1 week or refrigerated for up to 6 months.

N O T E : *The peppercorns will keep indefinitely, refrigerated, in a closed container.*

M A K E S   1   S C A N T   C U P

CORIANDER OIL

Yeun Sai Yau

This oil resembles the first-press green of an extra-virgin olive oil, but there the resemblance ends. The green is from the fresh coriander leaves and stems, which may be added later to vegetable stocks.

1 cup tightly packed fresh coriander (cilantro) leaves and stems (1 large bunch), stems cut into 2-inch pieces
1¼ cups peanut oil

1. Make sure the coriander is completely dry. Heat a wok over high heat for 40 seconds. Add the peanut oil, stir briefly, and add the coriander stems. Stir and bring to a boil. Boil for about 4 minutes. Add the coriander leaves and stir, making certain they are coated. Cook until the coriander becomes dull in color, then brown, about 15 minutes.

2. Strain the oil and allow it to cool. Pour into a jar and close tightly. The oil will keep at room temperature for 1 week or refrigerated for up to 6 months.

M A K E S   A B O U T   1   C U P

HOT PEPPER OIL

Lot Jiu Yau

The hot pepper flakes that remain after this infusion should be kept in the oil. They will rest at the bottom of the oil and are used in various recipes.

½ cup hot red pepper flakes
⅓ cup sesame oil
½ cup peanut oil

Place all the ingredients in a large jar and mix well. Close tightly and place in a cool, dry place for 2 weeks. The oil will then be ready for use. The longer it is stored, the more potent it becomes. Because the heat of hot pepper flakes varies, the oil may be ready for use in 1 week instead of 2. Taste it. The oil will keep at room temperature for 1 week or refrigerated for up to 6 months.

VARIATION: *Place the hot pepper flakes in a bowl. Bring the peanut and sesame oils to a boil and pour over the flakes. (I caution you not to have your face over the bowl, because the fumes may cause throat discomfort or coughing.) After the oil cools, it is ready for use. Store as directed.*

MAKES 1⅓ CUPS

RED OIL

Hung Yau

*T*his is an oil favored by the chefs of Sichuan. Make certain you buy cayenne that is bright orange-red in color, which is an indication of freshness. Old cayenne is dull in color.

¾ *cup peanut oil*
3 tablespoons cayenne pepper

Heat a wok over high heat for 30 seconds. Add the peanut oil and reduce the heat to low. Add the cayenne and stir well to mix. Cook until wisps of smoke can be seen rising from the wok, stirring occasionally so that the cayenne will not stick to the wok bottom, clot, and burn. Bring to a boil and immediately turn off the heat and cool the mixture in the wok. Place the oil and cayenne in a jar. Close the jar. It will keep at room temperature for 4 weeks or refrigerated up to 6 months.

MAKES ½ CUP

CHILI SAUCE

Lot Chiu Jeung

*T*here are more brands of chili and pepper sauces on the market than one can possibly count. Many of these contain preservatives or added oil. I suggest you make your own, one that is pure and intense. You may use any of the hot red chilies available; my only caution is that you judge the degree of hotness you prefer. Depending on your taste, you may alter the amounts of salt, sugar, and vinegar. I like the amounts set down, and I prefer mature jalapeños, for the more mature, the more intense the heat.

2 pounds mature red jalapeños, stems removed
3½ teaspoons salt
3 tablespoons sugar
7 tablespoons Chinese white rice vinegar or distilled vinegar

1. Place the jalapeños and salt in a pot. Add ¼ cup cold water, cover the pot, and bring to a boil over high heat. Reduce the heat to medium-low and stir the peppers. Cook for 20 minutes, removing the cover to stir frequently, until the peppers are completely softened. (Do not add more liquid, for the mixture will then become watery.)

2. Place the peppers and remaining liquid in a blender, add the sugar and vinegar, and blend into a puree. The sauce can be used immediately. Place some in a container and refrigerate for up to 4 weeks. Freeze the rest for up to 6 months.

MAKES ABOUT 1 QUART

SICHUAN PEPPERCORN SALT

Jiu Yim

This is a marvelous use of the Sichuan peppercorn for a flavored seasoning of many uses. It complements poultry, meat, and seafood. It is widely used throughout China.

4 teaspoons iodized or kosher salt
1 teaspoon five-spice powder
½ teaspoon Sichuan peppercorns

1. Heat a wok over medium heat for 45 seconds. Lower the heat to low and add all the ingredients. Dry-roast until the peppercorns turn black, stirring constantly, until the fragrance is released, 3 to 4 minutes.

2. Strain out and discard the peppercorns. The salt should be a pleasant tan color. It is ready for use and is best served in small individual dipping dishes. Place whatever is not used in a tightly closed jar and store at room temperature for at least a month.

SICHUAN PEPPERCORN PASTE

Far Jiu Fun

*T*his is what is often referred to in the kitchens of Sichuan as a "secret ingredient." Chefs there will never reveal to you this fragrant paste, which adds so much to the tastes of the Sichuan kitchen. It took quite a lot of detective work to find it.

1½ teaspoons Sichuan peppercorns
1 tablespoon minced fresh ginger
⅓ cup trimmed and finely sliced scallions

Place all the ingredients in a small stainless-steel bowl and crush into a coarse paste with the handle of a cleaver. Or use a mortar and pestle. Store in the refrigerator for 2 to 3 days.

MAKES ¼ CUP

CONDIMENTS, PICKLES, AND LITTLE DISHES ◆

*W*e Chinese love to nibble before a meal, with wines or tea, particularly just after we have settled at the table and are preparing for a banquet. Arrayed in front of us as we sit might be as many as eight different small dishes of pickles and condiments, tart and sweet, spiced and not, that we will pick at with our chopsticks. As a matter of fact there is a type of dinner banquet that is called bot dai, bot siu, which translates as "eight big, eight small" to denote the number of dishes that will be served.

However, one need not be at a banquet to enjoy some of these small dishes. A few at any meal will satisfy, either as appetizers, even as small first courses, or as snacks. Such dishes are a long tradition in China, and there are literally hundreds of them throughout the country. Some are pickles, which the Chinese enjoy hugely. Some are sweet and soft. Others are crisp. Some are sour, a taste that we believe stimulates the appetite. And they are most versatile. Most can be eaten as prepared. Others can be ingredients as well. A pickle, to be sure, is a pickle, but it may become a component in a larger dish; and the same can be said of many condiments, which of course might be eaten as accompaniments. You will note that most of these pickles and condiments appear in other recipes. ◆

LOTUS ROOT CHIPS

Lin Ngau Pin

*T*his is a gift from Hong Kong. I ate these chips recently before a dinner and found them not only tasty but also texturally satisfying. A simple and wonderful use of a traditional vegetable.

1½ pounds lotus root, washed, peeled, and dried
5 cups peanut oil

1. Slice the lotus root paper-thin, and spread the slices on a cookie sheet lined with wax paper to dry for about 1 to 1½ hours.

2. Heat a wok over high heat for 40 seconds. Add the peanut oil. When a wisp of white smoke appears, place half the lotus root slices in the wok, loosening them with chopsticks or a wooden spoon so they fry evenly. If the slices burn or make too much smoke, lower it to medium. Fry for 4 to 5 minutes or until the lotus slices are golden. Remove with a Chinese strainer and place on paper towels to drain. Repeat with the remaining slices.

3. Serve them either warm or at room temperature. Or you may pack them in a plastic container and freeze for up to 4 to 6 weeks. Serve directly from the freezer to the table. They will be cold but taste great.

FRIED PEANUTS AND SEAWEED

Ji Choi Far Sung

This is most popular before meals, a favorite with either tea or strong beverages. It involves tossing together fried peanuts and fried laver, a kind of seaweed. I suggest strongly that you use the very deep purple sheets of laver, available in Chinese and Asian groceries, rather than nori, *because* nori *does not fry as crisply as laver and tends to remain soggy.*

5 cups peanut oil
One 14-ounce package raw peanuts
    with skins on (2½ cups), not roasted
1 sheet laver
½ teaspoon salt

1. Heat a wok over high heat for 40 seconds. Add the peanut oil. When a wisp of white smoke appears, place half the peanuts in the oil. Stir and cook for 2 minutes. (If smoke appears, lower the heat to medium.) Remove the nuts with a strainer and place on paper towels to drain. Repeat with the remaining nuts. Allow the nuts to cool.

2. Lower the heat to medium. Place the sheet of laver into the oil and press down with the strainer, making certain it is completely immersed. Fry for 1 minute. Remove and drain on paper towels. Allow to cool.

3. Place the peanuts in a bowl, sprinkle with salt, and mix well. Crumble the laver in your hands and mix the small pieces thoroughly with the nuts until well coated. Serve or transfer to a container. They will keep at room temperature for a week or frozen up to 2 months. Serve directly from the freezer. They will be cold but taste great.

FIVE-SPICE BOILED PEANUTS

Ng Hung Far Sung

五香花生

*T*his is a traditional condiment that I first enjoyed as a child at the Lunar New Year. Far sung, or "flower alive," are also eaten widely before other meals and banquets. The Chinese also call peanuts dei dau, or "nuts from the ground," which of course they are. There is also another kind of peanut loved in China, very small and round, that is roasted and served in its shell. We call these jiu dau, or "pearls."

One 14-ounce package raw peanuts with skins on (2½ cups), **not** roasted

One 1- or 2-inch square piece dried tangerine peel

3 cups cold water

Two 5-inch cinnamon sticks, broken into halves

4 whole pieces eight-star anise

10 cloves

1 whole nutmeg

1 teaspoon salt

1. Place all the ingredients in a pot and bring to a boil over high heat. Stir, reduce the heat to low, and simmer with the pot lid open a crack for 1½ hours. Stir often to prevent the peanuts from sticking to the bottom of the pot.

2. Turn off the heat, cover the pot, and allow to come to room temperature. Drain the peanuts and allow to dry on a cookie sheet lined with wax paper. They should not be totally dry, just free of liquid but a bit moist. Discard all the spices. Serve immediately or refrigerate in a closed container for up to 1 week—any longer and their fragrance vanishes.

SHANGHAI LIMA BEANS

Seut Loi Hung Boon Chan Dau

A tradition beloved in Shanghai, where limas, broad beans, or favas are cooked with that wonderful preserved green known as red in snow. This can be eaten as a premeal appetizer with tea or wine, as a first course, or as an accompanying side dish. I have served it as part of a buffet of many dishes.

½ pound fresh or frozen baby lima beans

2½ cups cold water
2½ teaspoons Garlic Oil (page 84) or peanut oil
1 garlic clove, peeled and lightly smashed
One ½-inch-thick slice fresh ginger, lightly smashed
⅔ cup red in snow, cut into ½-inch sections
⅛ teaspoon salt

1. Place the fresh lima beans and water in a large pot and bring to a boil over high heat. Lower the heat to medium and cook for 10 to 12 minutes or until the lima beans are tender. Turn off the heat. Run cold water into the pot and drain. (For frozen lima beans, defrost to room temperature, then place directly into boiling water for 20 to 30 seconds. Run cold water into the pot and drain.)

2. Heat a wok over high heat for 30 seconds, add the garlic oil, and coat the wok with the oil using a spatula. Add the garlic and ginger. When the garlic turns light brown, add the lima beans, stir, and mix for 1 minute. Add the red in snow and mix well, then add all the salt. Lower the heat to medium and stir again. Cook for 3 more minutes. Turn off the heat and transfer to a serving dish or 4 small dishes. Serve.

CAULIFLOWER PICKLES

War Mei Yeh Choi Far

These are good anytime. My husband eats them, at will, directly from their refrigerated storage jar. They are best as a premeal appetite enhancer.

3 quarts cold water
5 garlic cloves, peeled
One 1-inch-thick slice fresh ginger

3½ pounds fresh cauliflower, cut into
   1½-inch florets
1¾ cups sugar
1¾ cups Chinese white rice vinegar or
   distilled vinegar
5½ cups cold water
4 teaspoons salt

1. In a large pot, bring the 3 quarts of water to a boil with the garlic and ginger. Add the cauliflower and blanch for 30 to 45 seconds. Do not overcook. Remove from the heat and run cold water into the pot. Drain. Fill the pot with cold water and let the cauliflower rest in cold water for 15 minutes, then drain.

2. In an oversized glass jar, place the sugar, vinegar, 5½ cups water, and salt. Stir with a wooden spoon to ensure that the sugar and salt are completely dissolved. Add the cauliflower, garlic, and ginger. Cover the jar. (A jar with a plastic screw top is preferred; if unavailable, place a piece of plastic wrap over the top before closing.) Refrigerate for at least 24 hours before serving. Serve cold. The cauliflower pickles will keep, covered and refrigerated, for up to 6 months.

PICKLED JÍCAMA

Wor Mei Sah Gut

*T*his crisp tuber is known as sah gut *in China and is as popular there as it is, under its Spanish name, in the American Southwest. In China it is eaten in many ways, in soups, in stir-fried dishes, in salads, and as a pickle. Its texture makes it a perfect pickled vegetable.*

1 whole jícama, 1½ pounds
1½ teaspoons salt
5 tablespoons Chinese white rice vinegar or distilled vinegar
5 tablespoons sugar

Peel, wash, and dry the jícama. Cut into ½-inch dice. Place in a bowl with all the other ingredients and mix well. Place the bowl in the refrigerator, covered with plastic wrap, and allow to rest for 3 days. It will keep, refrigerated, for 2 to 3 weeks. Serve as a condiment or a snack.

CUCUMBER PICKLE

Wor Mei Ching Gua

*A*s early as the fifth century the Chinese *were growing the cucumber, which is deemed to be simply another squash. In China there are two kinds of cucumber, yellow and green. Unfortunately the word for yellow is* wong, *and for yellow squash* wong gua, *and people named Wong object to being referred to as yellow squashes, thus the green cucumber,* ching gua, *is used, because* ching *is no one's last name. This quite versatile cucumber pickle is eaten simply as a pickle or a condiment or in salads. It is quite a favorite in Sichuan.*

2 pounds small cucumbers (Kirbys, usually used for pickles)
1½ teaspoons salt
4½ tablespoons Chinese white rice vinegar or distilled vinegar
4½ tablespoons sugar
1 teaspoon Red Oil (page 88)
1 red jalapeño, minced, with seeds

Wash the cucumbers, cut off both ends, and cut in half lengthwise. Scoop out the seeds. Cut into ½-inch strips, then into ½-inch dice. Place the cubes in a bowl. Add all the other ingredients and toss together thoroughly. Place in a closed container and refrigerate for at least 3 days before use. The pickles will keep, refrigerated, for up to 3 weeks.

Following are two recipes for sweetened nuts. The Chinese have a long tradition of snacking on sweet or salted nuts of various kinds, often with teas or with wines. These are my variations, new versions of nut presentations that I sampled years ago in Hong Kong. They are tasty indeed as snacks, and I always serve one or both of them to guests at holiday gatherings. ◆

SESAME WALNUTS

Ji Mah Mot Hop Toh

¼ cup white sesame seeds
12¼ cups water
1 pound freshly shelled walnuts

⅓ cup sugar
5 cups peanut oil

1. Roast the sesame seeds. Heat the wok over high heat for 30 seconds. Lower the heat to medium. Add the sesame seeds. Stir and mix, roast for 1½ to 2 minutes, until the fragrance is released. Turn off the heat, remove, and reserve.

2. In a wok, bring 6 cups of the water to a boil over high heat. Place the walnuts in the water for 5 minutes. This will remove their bitter taste. Remove from the water and strain, then run cold water over the walnuts and strain again. Then place the walnuts back in the wok with 6 cups more water and bring to a boil over high heat. Cook for another 5 minutes. Repeat the straining process. Set the walnuts aside and allow to drain thoroughly.

3. Wash and dry the wok. Add the remaining ¼ cup water and bring to a boil. Add the sugar, stirring constantly. Allow to boil for 1 minute. Add the walnuts and stir until well coated with a glaze and the remaining liquid in the wok has evaporated. Transfer the walnuts to a Chinese strainer and set aside.

continued

4. Wash the wok and spatula with extremely hot water to remove the sugar. Dry. Heat the wok over high heat for 30 seconds. Place the peanut oil in the wok and bring to a boil over high heat. When you see a wisp of white smoke, lower the strainer of walnuts into the oil, fry for 1½ minutes, then remove the strainer, allowing the nuts to remain in the oil and fry for another 3 minutes. The walnuts should be brown. Remove with the strainer and drain over a bowl.

5. Remove the nuts to another bowl and sprinkle with the roasted sesame seeds, mixing with a wooden spoon as you sprinkle. Make certain the walnuts are coated well and separate. When they come to room temperature, remove to a container, discarding any loose sesame seeds. These may be kept for 1 week at room temperature, or for at least 3 months frozen.

HONEY PECANS

Mot Wu Toh

12¼ cups water
1 pound freshly shelled pecans

⅓ cup sugar
5 cups peanut oil

1. In a wok, bring 6 cups of the water to a boil over high heat. Place the pecans in the boiling water for 5 minutes. Remove from the water and drain, then run cold water over them. Drain again, then place back in the wok with 6 more cups water. Bring to a boil and cook for another 5 minutes. Turn off the heat. Repeat the draining process. Set aside and allow to drain in a strainer.

2. Wash the wok. Add the remaining ¼ cup water and bring to a boil over high heat. Add the sugar, stirring constantly. Boil for 1 minute. Add the pecans. Stir until coated with a sugar glaze and the remaining liquid in the wok has evaporated. Remove the pecans and set aside. Wash the wok and spatula with extremely hot water to remove the sugar. Dry.

3. Heat the wok over high heat for 40 seconds. Add the peanut oil and bring to a boil. When a wisp of white smoke appears, add the pecans. Fry for 4 to 5 minutes, until they turn golden brown. Remove and allow to cool, loosening the nuts to prevent clumping. Serve or place in a closed container. The pecans will keep at room temperature for 1 week. Frozen, they will keep for at least 3 months.

SICHUAN PEPPER PICKLE

Bau Lot Chiu

*A*nother of the traditional condiments from Sichuan, that home to fine chili peppers. These pickles are used in many dishes in Sichuan and have been adopted joyously in Shanghai. Red jalapeños are hotter, I find, than green. They are more colorful as well.

1 pound red or green jalapeños
  (about 18)

4½ cups cold water
1 piece fresh ginger, 1 by 1½ inches,
  lightly smashed
½ teaspoon Sichuan peppercorns
1½ tablespoons salt
3 tablespoons sugar
½ cup Chinese white rice vinegar or
  distilled vinegar
2 tablespoons Chinese white rice wine
  or gin

1. Wash and dry the peppers. Use a large needle or skewer to pierce 6 holes in the base of each, around the stem.

2. In a large pot, place the cold water, ginger, Sichuan peppercorns, salt, sugar, and vinegar and bring to a boil over high heat. Lower the heat, cover the pot, and simmer for 5 minutes. Turn the heat back to high, add the wine, and stir. Turn off the heat and allow the liquid to come to room temperature. Place the peppers in a large jar and pour the liquid over them to cover. Close tightly and refrigerate. Allow to rest for 48 hours before use; they become better pickles, however, if left for a week. Refrigerated, the peppers will keep for at least 3 months, though they tend to soften with age.

HOT TIANJIN *BOK CHOY*
Lot Bok Choy

Here is a Shanghai classic "little dish" using those pickled peppers from Sichuan in combination with that snowy white bok choy from Tianjin. Its Chinese name translates as "hot white vegetable," which it is. It is a perfect appetizer, often served in a "big 8, small 8" banquet. It is also perfect as a salad, a small course, by itself, or as an accompaniment. Its intense heat is the result of those fine Sichuan Pepper Pickles.

2¾ pounds Tianjin bok choy, outer leaves removed (2½ pounds)
2½ teaspoons salt
1½ tablespoons Sichuan Pepper Pickle (preceding recipe), julienned
1½ tablespoons sesame oil
6 small dried Thai chilies
⅛ teaspoon Sichuan peppercorns
½ tablespoon shredded fresh ginger
3 tablespoons Chinese white rice vinegar or distilled vinegar
2 tablespoons sugar
1 teaspoon light soy sauce

1. Separate the individual stalks of Tianjin *bok choy,* wash, and drain well. Cut the *bok choy* crosswise into ⅓-inch pieces. Place in a large bowl, pour in the salt, mix, and let stand for 2 hours. Drain well and squeeze off all liquid. Place back in the bowl and add the Sichuan pepper pickles.

2. Heat a wok over medium-low heat for 10 seconds. Add the sesame oil. When a wisp of white smoke appears, add the dried chilies, stir, and cook for 20 seconds. Add the Sichuan peppercorns and ginger, stir, and cook for 10 seconds. Turn off the heat, pour the sesame oil, dried chilies, and peppercorns over the *bok choy.* Add the vinegar, sugar, and soy sauce and mix thoroughly. Allow to stand for at least 4 hours or preferably overnight to allow the flavors to mix and the pepper pickles to take hold. Serve cold. Kept in a closed container, refrigerated, this *bok choy* will keep for a week.

PICKLED PEARS

Wor Mei Lei

When making these pickles I use the Bosc pear, for it is quite close to the hard, crisp pear of China referred to as sah leh, or "sand pear," which is almost round and quite hard. To use these as an appetizer, they are best julienned.

2 pounds pears (5 or 6 pears), very hard, barely ripe
1⅓ cups Chinese white rice vinegar or distilled vinegar
1⅓ cups cold water
½ cup sugar
2 teaspoons salt

Peel, wash, and dry the pears. In an oversized glass jar, place the vinegar, water, sugar, and salt. Mix well with a wooden spoon to dissolve the sugar and salt. Add the pears to the jar, mix well, and cover the jar tightly. Allow to rest, refrigerated, for 3 days before use. These pears will keep, refrigerated, for at least 6 months.

PICKLED PEACHES

Wor Mei Toh

A most versatile preparation is this pickle. I use it in salads, in stir-fries, and in steaming, because of its pleasing sweet and sour taste. As an appetizer the peaches should be julienned for serving. If you prefer them sweeter, add more sugar, but only as you prepare them. Adding sugar later on will not penetrate the fruit.

2 pounds fresh peaches (about 8), very hard but with rosy color, indicating they are about to ripen
2 cups Chinese white rice vinegar or distilled vinegar
3¾ cups cold water
⅔ cup sugar
2¼ teaspoons salt

Wash the peaches well and dry thoroughly. Do not slice or peel them. In an oversized glass jar, place the vinegar, water, sugar, and salt. Mix well with a wooden spoon until the sugar and salt are dissolved. Add the peaches and stir well. Cover the jar tightly. Refrigerate for 3 days before use. These will keep, refrigerated, for at least 6 months.

SHALLOT PICKLES

Seun Kiu Jau

*T*he Chinese name for this preparation translates as "sour shallots." Traditionally in China, shallots are picked white, with their stalks, before they ripen and then pickled. I use mature, purple-streaked shallots, and they are as satisfying as those I remember, if not more so.

5 cups cold water

4 teaspoons salt

1 pound shallots, peeled

⅔ cup sugar

⅔ cup Chinese white rice vinegar or distilled vinegar

1. In a large pot, place the cold water and 2 teaspoons of the salt. Cover and bring to a boil over high heat. Add the shallots, stir, and cook for 1½ minutes. Turn off the heat, run cold water into the pot, and drain. Transfer the shallots to a bowl of ice water and allow to rest for 10 minutes. Drain off the water and reserve the shallots.

2. Place the remaining 2 teaspoons salt, the sugar, and the vinegar in a jar and mix well to dissolve the salt and sugar. Add the shallots and mix well. Cover the jar. Refrigerate for 24 hours before use. They are better pickles if permitted to cure longer. Store for 2 to 3 months in the refrigerator.

PICKLED GINGER

Wor Mei Gee Geung

*L*ike other pickles, this is a preparation of many uses. It is an appetizer, an ingredient, and a garnish. Only fresh, young ginger should be used for this pickle. Once difficult to find, young ginger is widely available today. It is recognized by its thin skin, creamy-white interior with a pinkish cast, and the green shoots that protrude from the root. Pickled ginger is also available in jars, and it is adequate, but not at all as pleasing as freshly made pickle, with sweetness contrasting with its faint hotness.

2 quarts water

1 teaspoon baking soda

1½ pounds fresh young ginger, washed thoroughly to remove thin outer bark but thin skin left on, cut into ⅛-inch slices with shoots

For the marinade

1¼ teaspoons salt

½ cup plus 2 tablespoons Chinese white rice vinegar or distilled vinegar

1 cup sugar

1. In a large pot, bring the water and baking soda to a boil over high heat. Add the ginger and boil for 30 seconds. Remove from the heat. Add cold water to the pot to reduce the temperature. Drain. Add water again, drain, then repeat a third time. Place the ginger in cold water and rest it for 10 minutes. Drain and place in a bowl.

2. In a small bowl, combine the marinade ingredients. Add the marinade to the ginger and mix well. Cover and refrigerate for at least 24 hours before use. Serve cold. This pickled ginger will keep in a tightly closed jar in the refrigerator for at least 3 months.

 # PICKLED MUSTARD GREENS

Ham Seun Choi

This method of pickling is popular in my region of China, in Sun Tak, near Canton. This particular pickle was a favorite of my family at the New Year when, after it had cured 4 hours, we ate it as a snack, not diced, but a whole length, spread with mustard.

1 gallon cold water
3½ tablespoons salt

3½ pounds mustard greens (2 bunches), washed well to remove sand, drained, each bunch cut in half lengthwise

For pickling
½ cup sugar
4 teaspoons salt
3½ cups cold water
1½ cups Chinese white rice vinegar or distilled vinegar

1. Place 1 gallon cold water and 3½ tablespoons salt in a large pot and bring to a boil over high heat. Add the mustard greens, using a pair of chopsticks or tongs to immerse completely. Cook for 2 minutes or until the mustard greens turn bright green. Turn off the heat, run cold water into the pot, and drain. Repeat twice more and drain.

2. In a large bowl, dissolve the sugar and 4 teaspoons salt in the 3½ cups cold water. Add the vinegar and mix well.

3. Squeeze all residual liquid from the mustard greens and place the greens in the pickling mixture. Mix well and make certain the greens are totally covered by the liquid. Allow to rest at room temperature for 4 hours.

4. To serve as a condiment, cut the stems into ½-inch dice. Reserve the leaves for another use. To use as a pickle in other recipes, allow the mustard greens, leaves and stems, to remain in the pickling mixture overnight. The pickled greens will keep, refrigerated, in a glass jar or plastic container, in their pickling liquid, for at least 3 months.

Classics
from China's Regions

中國各地正宗名菜

THE VAST CHINESE MENU HAS MANY COURSES, ALL OF THEM INFLUENCED BY HISTORY AND TRADITION, SOCIAL PHILOSOPHY AND INHERITED CUSTOM, FOLKTALE AND LEGEND, BY THE NEEDS AND WANTS OF PARTICULAR ERAS, BY TOPOGRAPHY AND CLIMATE, AND, OF COURSE, BY HEALTH AND SENSORY ENJOYMENT. It is a legacy of taste that encompasses the meat and wheat culture of China's North, the diverse and changeable finesse of the vegetable-rich South, the intensity of the spices and peppers of the West, and the sweetness and oil surrounding the East's culture of sea and lake. Though it is true that the great Chinese table divides generally into these loosely recognized regions, there is, particularly these days, a great deal of cross-pollination. No city in China is without the elegant, subtle foods of Canton, a tacit acknowledgment that this elegant southern kitchen is regarded as the country's best, its most inventive. Dim sum has migrated north to Shanghai and to Beijing, and the fire, salt, and devotion to spices of Sichuan and Hunan are everywhere. The distinctive cooking of Shanghai and its nearby regions of Hangzhou and Suzhou has traveled to all parts of China, altering its sweetness and oiliness as it has moved. The Hunan and Yunnan kitchens are now recognized as distinctive pockets of China's western cooking. The old gastronomic divisions, which in centuries past were so defined because of insulation and isolation, exist, to be sure, but the lines blur.

It is a saying throughout China: *Jui lei seung dik sung wood hai, sahng joi Suzhou, jiuk joi Hangzhou, see joi Luzhou, sik joi Guangzhou.* "A perfect life is possible if one is born in Suzhou, dressed in Hangzhou, dies in Luzhou, but eats in Guangzhou." This pays homage to the women of Suzhou, of surpassing beauty, with soft skin, the color of glowing marble; to the finest silks of China in Hangzhou; to the best willow wood for coffins in Luzhou; and to the Southern Chinese table centered in Guangzhou, Canton and its food. I offer the adage in Cantonese, the language of Guangdong, where I am from, and because I am proud of the traditional cooking of my region. There has been no doubt in China, through the centuries, that the food of the South has always been regarded as China's finest, sought by the northern emperors for shipment by barge and caravan for their pleasure, eaten with enjoyment by everyone else.

To a large extent, Cantonese is what people think of when they think of Chinese food. It is the cooking, albeit altered by circumstance, of those men from southern China who migrated to the West to search for gold and to build the transcontinental railroad. But pure Cantonese cooking is grand indeed, with its belief in the sanctity of freshness and that the essential nature and taste of a food ought not to be changed. Overcooking is a sin in the Cantonese kitchen, which relies heavily on stir-frying and steaming, though it roasts and stews as well. This kitchen is ingenious, innovative, inventive, and most welcoming. Over the centuries it has accepted foods and spices from other parts of China and from foreign countries, and made them part of its repertoire. The culinary tradition of the South goes back 2,000 years, along with its vaunted adaptability. The Cantonese say, and mean, *Saw yau dong mut, soi mut, lan gah com, fei com, du hor lung sik tak.* This nineteenth-century saying translates as "Anything that walks, swims, crawls, or flies with its back to Heaven is edible." And so it is, in this kitchen that historically has creatively incorporated into its menu frogs, bears, dogs, snakes, civets, and turtles.

The cooking of the South has come to include the cookery of the Hakka and Chiu Chow people and those creators of Chinese sweets, the people of Fujian. Though many of their dishes differ, happily, their bases are identical: Use the many vegetables and fruits that are products of this subtropical part of China. Spare not ginger, sugar, salt, vinegar,

and wines. Live off lake and sea. Rice is the core of the table; where China talks of *fan* and *ts'ai*, its accompaniments, the Cantonese say *sung fan*, or "eat with the rice." It was the Cantonese whose inventiveness made pork the meat of choice throughout China. Canton has enriched the greater Chinese table with melons, squashes, and gourds; with taro, water chestnuts, and lotus root; with oranges, persimmons, peaches, and tangerines; litchis, kumquats, and longans, apricots, coconuts, and mangoes; and joyfully taught the rest of China to eat those foods it adopted and grew—eggplant from India; okra from Africa; corn, tomatoes, potatoes, and peanuts from the West. It was Canton that recognized the versatility of the soybean and how its curd could become "meats" and "seafood" when artfully cooked. The historical, traditional cooking of the North, of Beijing, Tianjin, and the Shandong region, is a wondrous mixture of the elegant and the rough. Except for brief periods in China's history, its capital has always been Beijing, once Peking. Thus there has always been an imperial kitchen tradition, of elaborate preparations, often of meals of hundreds of courses, of exotic foods demanded, brought to the imperial kitchens at great cost of riches and labor, and cooked in excessively ornate ways. But from Beijing have also come written recipes, cooking precepts, food philosophies, all the blossoms of a court life that dwelt on art, music, the musings of scholars, and consideration of moral precepts.

Historically the North was a food culture based on millets, wheat, barley, and other grains. Only later did rice come into its existence, and this because the imperial court deemed rice to be a *fan* of great luxury. A good deal of mutton and goat was eaten in the

North, and there still is. Where the South was surrounded by freshness and green, the harsh northern winters forced the drying and preservation of foods and great use of hardier vegetables such as cabbage, ubiquitous in the North, and all manner of roots. The North cooked with pork fat and favored the direct tastes of garlic, scallions, onions, and leeks, of pickled cabbages and pickled greens.

Yet there was that imperial tradition. Ice was cut into huge blocks in the far North and brought south to be placed in vast holes in the earth, these to be the "refrigerators" of foods brought from the South. Every court had hundreds of retainers, whose duties were devoted only to aspects of food. Those great banquets dictated by court rank, social and professional caste reached their zenith in the Ming and Ching dynasties, where eating utensils of silver, jade, ivory, and gold were dictated. Many dishes we regard today as typical of grand Beijing cookery include such marvelous presentations as Peking Duck and Beggar's Chicken. These rich and varied dishes gave rise to that overused misnomer "Mandarin cooking." There is no such school, despite what has been written; the words suggest rather a style in which dishes presented at court should have the appearance that great effort had been expended in cooking and arranging them.

The North is justly famous for its grain-based foods, its breads and buns, both steamed and fried, its dumplings and pancakes, often decorated with sesame seeds or stuffed with onions, and its noodles. Ordinary citizens not invited to court banquets, or to state banquets in modern times, ate, and eat, a good deal of millet and sorghum gruel, food

that protects them in the cold. Most of the fish they ate was salted.

The cooking of the East is particularly rich because of the access to fish in the seas of Shanghai and the coast and in the thousands of lakes and river tributaries that course through this region. Crustaceans such as the hairy crab abound, as do those tiny, succulent clams, *hoi dai gua jee,* or "watermelon seeds from the sea bottom," their shells often no bigger than the nail on one's smallest finger. And fish, particularly the prized yellow fish, tender freshwater eels, and the carp, are loved so much in Shanghai and its environs that the people there have farmed them for many centuries.

The people in Suzhou and Hangzhou are renowned for their artistic vegetarian cooking, their vegetables and fruit carving, but the core of eastern cooking is in Shanghai. By the circumstance of geography, Shanghai sits as a great deepwater international shipping and receiving port, once home to scores of foreign concessions. It is also at land's end and on the eastern shore of the great Yangtze River. Shanghai received and kept cookery traditions from all parts of China and from foreign countries as well. Its pastries, some traditional fried red bean and turnip concoctions, are well known throughout China, as are its soup buns and soup dumplings, dough mounds that contain hot soup and pork, occasionally crab as well; scallion pancakes; and those pan-fried dumplings we know as potstickers.

The people of this eastern region eat very little lamb or beef; they prefer chicken and duck and pork and prefer to cook with pork fat rather than oil. They love sweetness, and a dish of tradition in Shanghai will be sweet and oily. It is cooking I love because of its liberal use of wines, soys, and vinegars. From the time when China's capital was in Nanjing, nearby to the west, the cooks of this region have doted on presentation dishes, quite like those cooks in Beijing, and will spend hours flavoring chicken with fermented wines or cooking a tea-smoked duck.

In many ways the cooking of China's West is perhaps most interesting. The region itself, encompassing Sichuan, Hunan, and Yunnan, is bordered by Pakistan and India, by Nepal, Myanmar, Laos, and Vietnam, and spice influences abound. Its geography is a curious mix of fertile plain along the Yangtze and barren mountains. Buddhism spread into China through this western region, which also was crisscrossed by trade routes. Rice is plentiful in its plains, though not to the extent of the South, where two crops a year are commonplace. It is generally believed that the cooking of China's West is always searingly hot. It is not. To be sure, there are hot dishes and a liberal use of chilies, but there are just as many preparations cooked without heat. The West is the home of tea-smoked and camphorsmoked ducks, of garlic, salt, and those peculiar, aromatic Sichuan peppercorns, otherwise known as *fagara*.

Pungent flavors all, and the cooks of the West blend them expertly. The heat of their food, provided by chilies, is not by whim but because they stimulate the palate and prepare it for the more subtly spiced dishes. People in this region love their poultry and eat more beef and lamb than do other sections of China, beef because of the traditionally wide use of cattle as beasts of burden in the region's salt mines. Meats in the West are simmered, roasted, oil-blanched. Dishes such as *wui wor yuk*, which translates as "return to the pot pork," and which most of us would recognize as twice-cooked pork, illustrate a classic technique of China's West. The meat is cooked first in water, then stir-fried. This region pickles and salts, and there is sufficient carp from its many lakes. Both Sichuan and Hunan dishes tend generally to be heavier than those of China's East. Yunnan cooking is spice-laden as well, but the meat of choice is pork, and Yunnan's hams constitute its major claim to culinary fame.

From these diverse regions come the classic preparations of the Chinese kitchen. They are dishes of history, plates of tradition, that have been made in essentially the same manner for many centuries. Many dishes can be made in a prescribed way. Others may be adapted, modernized, often shortened, but only if their essential nature is left untouched and they remain true to their roots. A classic is, after all, a classic.

Duck is a basis for many classics of the Chinese kitchen. Wild and domesticated, it has been eaten in China for 2,000 years, and in the Tang dynasty domesticated duck was a prize to be enjoyed at the imperial court. Later, in the Ching dynasty, a recorded banquet included pot-boiled duck, smoked duck, and salted duck. Surely the best known of China's duck preparations is Peking Duck.

PEKING DUCK
Beijing Op

This duck from China's imperial city is as universal as any dish can be. In Beijing there are restaurants that serve only duck, in fact whole banquets in which some part of the duck is each course. Peking Duck, served in the traditional manner, is regarded as elegant and special, a dish for a feast. Rarely is the preparation served as it should be. What follows is Peking Duck in the traditional manner. The size of the duck is important when it is to be served in the classic manner, as 3 separate courses. The larger the duck, the more skin, the more meat.

The way to prepare Peking Duck in the classic manner, without being overtaken by details, is to simply prepare ahead. Make your pancakes ahead, as the duck dries; they will keep well for steaming. Prepare your vegetables for stir-frying in advance. Prepare your soup ingredients ahead. Thus, when your duck roasts, your pancakes can steam. As your guests eat the duck skin folded into the pancakes, you can cut up the duck meat and stir-fry it with the vegetables as, simultaneously, the duck bones are boiling into soup. In this way you will be able to serve seamlessly from course to course.

Peking Duck, served in this manner, as 3 courses, can be a complete meal served for 6 people.

One 7-pound duck, freshly killed preferred, including head, wings, and feet
¼ cup salt
1 quart boiling water, to scald duck

For the coating
3 cups boiling water
3 tablespoons Chinese white rice vinegar or distilled vinegar
3 tablespoons maltose or honey

12 Peking Duck Pancakes (page 113)

For the sauce
⅓ cup hoisin sauce
1 teaspoon sugar
1 teaspoon sesame oil
1 teaspoon Shao-Hsing wine or sherry
6 scallions, white parts only, cut into 2-inch pieces, edges cut to make fringes

Special equipment
1 air pump
1 chopstick, cut to 7-inch length

1. Prepare the duck. Clean, remove all membranes and fat, and rinse inside and outside with cold running water. Sprinkle the outside of the duck with salt and rub in well. Rinse all salt off. Allow the water to drain. Tie off the neck of the duck with string and insert the nozzle of the air pump into the neck opening. Inflate with the pump until the skin separates from the flesh.

continued

2.   Remove the pump nozzle. With a cleaver, remove the first 2 joints of each of the duck's wings and feet. Insert the 7-inch chopstick under the wings through the back to lift them away from the body.

3.   To scald the duck, holding the duck with one hand, use the other hand to ladle 4 cups boiling water onto the skin. The entire outside must be scalded. It is advisable to hang the duck on a hook over a sink to ease this step. The skin will darken and tighten when scalded. Allow 30 minutes for the skin to dry. (On humid days this may take longer.)

4.   To coat the duck, in a wok mix together 3 cups boiling water, the vinegar, and the maltose, and bring to a boil. Ladle the coating mixture over the hanging duck, making certain the skin is coated completely and thoroughly. Allow 10 to 12 hours of drying time. (You may use a fan blowing air onto the duck to reduce the drying time by half.)

5.   As the duck dries, make the pancakes.

6.   To roast the duck, heat the oven to 450°F for 30 minutes. Place a large roasting pan containing at least 1½ inches of water on the bottom shelf of the oven. Place the duck directly on the oven rack over the roasting pan, not in the roasting pan. The pan serves only to catch the fat drippings as the duck roasts. Roast the duck, breast side down, for 10 minutes, then reduce the temperature to 425°F. Turn the duck over and allow the other side to roast 10 minutes. If the duck begins to burn, reduce the temperature to 400°F. Allow the duck to roast evenly for another 35 to 45 minutes, turning frequently to ensure the head and tail do not burn. The duck is ready when the skin is a deep brown color and crisp. Remove from the oven and allow to cool for 7 minutes.

7.   Combine the sauce ingredients, except for the scallions, in a small bowl and set aside.

8.   To serve, make certain the pancakes are hot and ready for serving. Slice the duck skin carefully away from the meat in irregular scallops about 2½ inches long. Serve the duck skin slices in pancakes: Brush each pancake with 1½ teaspoons of the sauce mixture with a fringed scallion brush. Then lay the brush down, cover with 2 slices of skin, and wrap by overlapping the pancakes over the skin, then folding up one end. Serve.

MAKES 6 SERVINGS OF
2 WRAPPED PANCAKES EACH

STIR-FRIED PEKING DUCK MEAT

1¼ to 1½ cups duck meat, depending
  on size of duck
¾ cup julienned carrot
¾ cup julienned celery
1 cup green parts of scallions, cut into
  2-inch pieces
1 cup bean sprouts

For the sauce
¼ cup Chicken Stock (page 75)
1 tablespoon oyster sauce
2 teaspoons soy sauce
1 teaspoon sesame oil

2 teaspoons Shao-Hsing wine or dry
  sherry
1 teaspoon sugar
1 teaspoon Chinese white rice vinegar
  or distilled vinegar
2 teaspoons cornstarch
Pinch freshly ground white pepper

3 tablespoons peanut oil
1½ teaspoons minced fresh ginger
½ teaspoon salt
1½ teaspoons minced garlic

1. Julienne the duck meat and reserve. Prepare all vegetables and reserve. In a small bowl, combine the sauce ingredients and reserve.

2. Heat a wok over high heat for 30 seconds. Add 1½ tablespoons of the peanut oil and coat the wok with the oil using a spatula. When a wisp of white smoke appears, add the ginger and salt and stir. Add the carrots and celery and cook, stirring, for 10 seconds. Add the scallions and cook, stirring, for 10 seconds. Add the bean sprouts and stir all together for 20 seconds more. Turn off the heat, remove to a bowl, and reserve.

3. Wipe off the wok and spatula with paper towels. Heat the wok over high heat for 20 seconds. Add the remaining peanut oil and coat the wok with it using a spatula. When a wisp of white smoke appears, add the garlic and stir briefly. Add the duck meat and cook, stirring, for 1½ minutes, until very hot. Add the vegetables and cook, stirring everything together thoroughly, for 1 minute. Make a well in the center of the mixture, stir the sauce ingredients, pour in, and stir until the sauce thickens and turns light brown. Turn off the heat, transfer to a heated serving dish, and serve.

MAKES 6 SERVINGS

PEKING DUCK SOUP

1 quart Chicken Stock (page 75)
3 cups cold water
Duck bones and giblets
One 1-inch-thick slice fresh ginger,
    lightly smashed

1 pound Tianjin bok choy, stalks and
    leaves separated and sliced into
    ½-inch diagonal pieces
Salt

1. Place the stock and water in a large pot. Add the duck giblets and ginger, cover the pot, and bring to a boil over high heat. Lower the heat to a low boil and cook for 15 minutes. Turn the heat back to high, add the duck bones, and return to a boil. Lower the heat to medium and simmer for 45 minutes with the lid cracked.

2. Turn off the heat. Strain through a strainer. Discard the bones and giblets. Place the soup back into the pot and return to a boil. Add the *bok choy* stalks, stir, and allow to return to a boil. Lower the heat to medium and cook for 5 minutes. Return the heat to high, add the *bok choy* leaves, stir, and cook for 3 minutes, until tender. Add salt to taste. Turn off the heat, transfer to a heated tureen, and serve.

MAKES 6 SERVINGS

PEKING DUCK PANCAKES

Bok Bang

These are the classic pancakes used in Peking Duck service. It has been suggested that tortillas be used in their place. Do not use them. Their taste is different and inadequate; they tend to be thick and chewy, and they subvert the elegance of the duck. There are ready-made pancakes as well, imported frozen from Taiwan.

I do not recommend them either. They lack elasticity and tend to crumble and fall apart when heated.

1¾ cups high-gluten flour
¾ cup boiling water
½ cup flour, for dusting
1½ teaspoons sesame oil

1. Place the flour in a bowl. Slowly add the boiling water and mix with a wooden spoon or 4 chopsticks in one direction. When the flour absorbs the water and cools, knead the dough into a ball, then place on a work surface dusted with flour. Knead for about 2 minutes, until the dough is thoroughly mixed. Place in a bowl, cover with plastic wrap, and allow to rest for 30 minutes.

2. On a work surface dusted with flour, roll the dough into a 12-inch sausage shape, then divide it into 12 equal pieces. Flatten each piece with your palm, dusting if the dough sticks. As you work, cover unused dough with plastic wrap.

3. Working with 2 pieces at a time, wipe the top of one gently with sesame oil and place the other flattened piece on top. Dust with flour, if necessary, and roll them into a double-layer round pancake, 7 inches in diameter.

4. Heat a wok over medium-low heat for 1 minute. Put the double pancake in the hot, dry wok and cook for 1 minute, until the pancake begins to bubble up. The heat in a dry wok must be controlled carefully. If too high, the pancakes will burn. Turn the pancake over and cook until a few brown spots are visible. Remove from the wok and separate the layers. You will have 2 pancakes, each browned lightly on one side, white on the other. Repeat until all the dough is used.

5. To steam the pancakes for Peking Duck service, invert a steamproof dish in a steamer and lay the pancakes, stacked on top of one another, over it. Steam for 5 to 7 minutes, until hot and pliable. Serve as directed for Peking Duck. The pancakes may be frozen for up to 3 months.

MAKES 12 PANCAKES

CANTON ROAST DUCK

Siu Op Guangzhou

*L*ike Beijing, Canton has its own classic duck preparation, a roast duck of many uses, many ways of serving. Roasted, it is often the centerpiece of a banquet. It can be eaten cold, as a first course, and its meat is often cut to create edible art on a plate. This roasted, glazed duck is what one sees hanging, often in lines, from racks in the windows of restaurants.

One 6-pound duck, freshly killed
  preferred, head on, feet removed,
  wing tips removed
Salt
3 tablespoons Chinese white rice wine
  or gin

For the marinade
2 tablespoons bean sauce
2 tablespoons soy sauce
3 tablespoons light or dark brown
  sugar
¼ teaspoon freshly ground white pepper
2 tablespoons minced fresh coriander
  (cilantro)

One 1-inch-thick slice fresh ginger,
  lightly smashed
2 scallions, trimmed and cut in half
3 pieces eight-star anise
One 3-inch cinnamon stick

1. Heat the oven to 400°F for 20 minutes.

2. Wash the duck inside and out under running cold water. Remove all membranes and fat. Sprinkle ¼ cup salt on the outside of the duck, rub well, rinse, and allow to drain. Rub the body and cavity of duck with the wine. Sprinkle salt on the body and rub in well.

3. In a small bowl, stir together the marinade ingredients. Place the marinade in the body cavity and rub well. Place the ginger, scallions, anise, and cinnamon in the cavity. Close the body cavity with a poultry skewer.

4. Line a shallow baking pan with heavy-duty foil. Place the duck on a roasting rack in the pan, breast side up. Roast for 15 minutes, turn over, and roast for 15 minutes more. Turn back over. Pierce the skin with a fork repeatedly over the body to allow the fat to run out. Roast for 20 minutes more, until well cooked and glazed.

5. Remove from the oven and allow to cool for 10 minutes. Remove the skewer. Transfer the juices from the duck cavity to a sauceboat.

6. Traditionally this duck is cut up into bite-sized pieces and served. It may also be carved and sliced and served with the reserved juices.

MAKES 6 TO 8 SERVINGS

STEAMED DUCK WITH PRESERVED PLUMS

Seun Moi Op

*T*his Cantonese classic is very much a wedding of opposite tastes, the sweetness of sugar, the sourness of preserved plums. This sourness, accented by the sugar of the rock candy, is what gives this duck its particular quality. A very special preparation, it is, like those roasted ducks, most often a component of banquets. This steamed duck is seen less and less these days, a circumstance I should like to change.

One 4½-pound duck, freshly killed preferred, head on, wings intact, feet removed
Salt

For the stuffing
7 to 9 preserved plums, pitted (2½ tablespoons)
5 large garlic cloves, mashed and minced
2 tablespoons bean sauce
1 teaspoon salt
⅓ cup rock sugar (rock candy), finely mashed with a mallet
⅓ cup light or dark brown sugar

1½ tablespoons double dark soy sauce, regular dark soy sauce, or mushroom soy sauce, to coat duck
1½ tablespoons peanut oil

1. Clean the duck thoroughly, removing all membranes and fat, and wash under cold running water. Sprinkle ¼ cup salt on the outside of the duck and rub in well. Rinse off and drain. Allow the duck to drain over a bowl so all the water drips out. Dry thoroughly with paper towels.

2. Combine the stuffing ingredients in a bowl. Place in the duck cavity. Secure the opening with a poultry skewer. Coat the duck well with the soy sauce.

3. Heat a wok over high heat for 40 seconds, add the peanut oil, and coat the wok with it using a spatula. When a wisp of white smoke appears, sear the duck in the wok, breast side down, for 1 minute. Turn over and continue to sear, turning frequently until the whole duck is browned.

4. Remove the duck to a steamproof dish, place on a rack in a wok over 2 quarts boiling water, cover the wok, and steam for 1¾ to 2 hours. Keep boiling water on hand to replenish any that evaporates; check every 20 minutes. The duck should be very tender, its skin only slightly brown, and the duck will have shrunk a bit. Most of the fat between the skin and meat will have run off during the steaming, but some will be left. This is the way the dish is enjoyed in Canton.

5. Allow the duck to rest for 15 minutes. As it rests, remove the skewer and pour off the stuffing and its liquid from the cavity into a saucepan. Add the ½ cup liquid (not the fat) from the dish in which the duck steamed. Mix and bring to a boil. Turn off the heat. Cut the duck into bite-sized pieces and serve, with the sauce poured over it.

MAKES 6 SERVINGS

TEA SMOKED DUCK

Long Jing Op

The most important ingredient in this classic duck preparation from Shanghai is Dragon Well Tea, long jing, an unfermented green tea from the high hills near Shanghai, a tea that many consider China's finest. The taste of this green tea, imparted to the duck during its smoking process, is as distinctive as its aroma during smoking. A most desirable festive dish, all the more so because it is prepared with 4 distinct cooking techniques.

One 5-pound duck, freshly killed preferred, head on, wings intact, feet removed
¼ cup salt to rub duck
Three 2-inch-long cinnamon sticks
3 pieces eight-star anise
Three ¼-inch-thick slices fresh ginger
2 teaspoons sugar
2 teaspoons salt
⅓ cup Shao-Hsing wine or dry sherry
⅔ cup long jing green tea leaves
6 cups peanut oil
24 fried shrimp chips (see Note)

1. Clean the duck thoroughly, remove the fat and membranes, and wash under cold running water. Sprinkle ¼ cup salt on the outside of the duck and rub thoroughly. Rinse and dry well with paper towels.

2. Place the duck in a steamproof dish with the cinnamon sticks, anise, and ginger and sprinkle the duck inside and out with sugar and 2 teaspoons salt. Pour the wine over the duck. Place the dish on a rack over 2 quarts boiling water in a wok, cover, and steam for 1¼ to 1½ hours. Have boiling water on hand to replenish any water that evaporates. Check the water every 20 minutes. Remove the duck from the wok and allow to cool.

3. Heat the oven to 350°F. As the oven heats, smoke the duck. Place the tea leaves in a dry wok over high heat until the leaves smoke. Reduce the heat to medium-high and place the duck on a rack over the leaves. Cover the wok, and where the cover meets the wok place a wet cloth around the seam to seal it. Smoke the duck for 7 to 10 minutes.

4. Remove the duck from the wok and transfer to a rack in a roasting pan. Roast for 1 hour, until the duck has rendered its fat. If very crisp skin is desired, turn the duck over halfway through roasting. Remove the duck from the oven and allow to cool.

5. Wash and dry the wok and heat it over high heat for 1 minute. Add the peanut oil and heat to 400°F. Carefully lower the duck into the oil with a large Chinese strainer. Fry on one side for 5 minutes, carefully ladling hot oil over the duck. Turn over and repeat the process, cooking for 5 minutes more, until the duck is deep golden brown. Remove the duck from the oil with a strainer and allow to drain for 10 minutes. To serve, cut into bite-sized pieces and serve with Sichuan Peppercorn Salt (page 89) and fried shrimp chips as a garnish.

NOTE: *The shrimp chips may be fried ahead. Heat 1 quart of peanut oil in a wok to 350°F. Place the chips in the oil. They will puff up within seconds. Remove and drain on paper towels. If fried ahead, place the chips in a closed container at room temperature until needed. They should be eaten within 2 days.*

MAKES 6 SERVINGS

Poultry in China dates back to the beginning of its recorded history. Chickens have been domesticated there for at least 3,000 years. So it is not surprising that chicken, which in China is steamed, braised, smoked, fried, roasted, boiled, and stir-fried, and minced and sliced for soups, dumplings, congees, noodles, and stuffings, should be regarded as symbol as well as food. In Chinese folklore, the chicken symbolizes the phoenix, the bird of rebirth that rises from ashes; and it is the symbol of the empress as well. Chicken is offered in temples and at ancestor altars, and it is a food that must be eaten on the second day of the Lunar New Year, for its symbolism of rebirth. Small wonder that festive classic chicken dishes abound. ◆

BEGGAR'S CHICKEN

Hot Yee Gai

*T*his famous and most elaborate dish from Beijing derives its name from a folktale: A beggar, without a home or food, stole a chicken from a farm. To cook it, he covered it with mud, made a fire in a hole in the ground, and baked the chicken, peeling the feathers off as he ate. It is said that despite this tale, the people in Beijing think their special chicken is too rich a preparation to carry the name beggar, *and prefer to call it Fu Guai Gai, or "Rich and Noble Chicken." I think I prefer that too, though here it is given its classic name.*

One 3- to 3¼-pound chicken
¼ cup salt

For the marinade
3 tablespoons Mei Kuei Lu Chiew
    or gin
One 3-inch cinnamon stick, broken
    into 4 pieces
2 pieces eight-star anise

1 tablespoon sugar
1½ teaspoons salt
Pinch freshly ground white pepper

For the stuffing
1½ tablespoons peanut oil
1½ cups diced onion
½ cup pork fat, cut into ⅛-inch dice
6 dried black mushrooms, washed,
    soaked to softness, stems discarded,
    and caps diced into ½-inch pieces
¾ cup preserved mustard greens,
    washed 5 times to cleanse of sand
    and salt, leaves opened and rinsed,
    squeezed dry, and finely sliced
1 tablespoon Shao-Hsing wine or dry
    sherry
1½ teaspoons sesame oil
1 teaspoon five-spice powder
¾ teaspoon salt
1 tablespoon sugar
Pinch freshly ground white pepper

For the dough
5 cups high-gluten flour
2 cups hot water
2½ teaspoons peanut oil

Special equipment
1 yard cheesecloth or 2 large lotus
*   leaves, soaked in water for*
*   20 minutes until soft, washed, and*
*   dried*
2 feet heavy-duty foil

1. Clean the chicken thoroughly, remove fat and membranes, and wash under cold running water. Sprinkle ¼ cup salt on the outside of the chicken, rub well, rinse, and dry. In a small bowl, stir together the marinade ingredients and rub the inside and outside with it. Set the chicken aside.

2. To prepare the stuffing, heat a wok over high heat for 30 seconds, add the peanut oil, and coat the wok with it using a spatula. When a wisp of white smoke appears, add the onion and cook until light brown, about 5 minutes. Lower the heat to medium, add the pork fat, and cook, stirring, until translucent. Add the mushrooms and mustard greens and mix well. Turn the heat back to high, add the wine, and mix all the ingredients together. Add the sesame oil, five-spice powder, salt, sugar, and pepper and mix. Remove from the heat, place in a bowl, and reserve.

3. To prepare the dough, place the flour in the center of the work surface and make a well in the center. Add the hot water slowly with one hand as you mix with the other. When the water is absorbed, knead for about 2 minutes to make a dough. Coat your hands with peanut oil and rub the dough with some pressure to coat it. Rub your hands on the work surface as well. Flatten the dough until it is large enough to wrap the chicken completely.

4. Stuff the chicken by loosely putting the stuffing into the body cavity. Close the neck and tail openings with skewers.

5. Wrap the chicken completely in the cheesecloth or in overlapping lotus leaves. Place the wrapped chicken in the center of the flattened dough and wrap the chicken, sealing the edges by pressing closed with your fingers. Spread out the foil and place the chicken, breast side up, on it. Enfold the chicken, closing the foil.

6. Heat the oven to 350°F for 15 minutes. Place the wrapped chicken in a roasting pan and bake for 1 hour. Lower the heat to 325°F and bake for 3 hours more. Turn off the heat, remove the chicken from the oven, and remove the foil. Cut through the dough with kitchen shears and make a large opening. Scoop out pieces of chicken and stuffing with a serving spoon and serve together.

NOTE: *The covering insulates the chicken. It will remain hot enough to serve if removed from the oven 1 to 2 hours before serving.*

MAKES 6 SERVINGS

PERFUMED CHICKEN

Heung So Gai

*T*he perfume of this classic chicken preparation from Sichuan comes from the cinnamon, anise, and rose-based spirit that flavor it and illustrates a significant and often overlooked aspect of the Sichuan kitchen. The cooking of this region is not always heat and pungent spices, as is widely believed. It can be most delicate, as with this aromatic chicken.

One 3½-pound chicken
¼ cup plus 1 tablespoon salt
4½ cups cold water
⅓ cup Mei Kuei Lu Chiew or gin
One 1-inch-thick slice fresh ginger, lightly smashed

3 pieces eight-star anise
¼ teaspoon Sichuan peppercorns
Three 2-inch cinnamon sticks
One 1- by 2-inch piece dried tangerine peel
2 scallions, trimmed and cut in half
3 teaspoons sugar
1½ tablespoons dark soy sauce
1 egg, beaten
½ cup tapioca flour, or enough to coat chicken

5 cups peanut oil
Sichuan Peppercorn Salt (page 89) for serving

1. Clean the chicken and remove the fat and membranes. Wash under cold running water, rinse, and drain. Sprinkle ¼ cup salt on the outside, rub in well, rinse off, and drain. Place the chicken in a large oval Dutch oven. Add the next 9 ingredients, from cold water to sugar, and the remaining tablespoon salt, cover, and bring to a boil over high heat. Add the soy sauce, then cover the pot and simmer for 20 minutes.

2. Turn the chicken over and simmer for another 20 minutes. Remove the chicken from the pot and allow to cool and dry for 4 to 5 hours or refrigerate overnight.

3. Place the chicken in a large dish and coat with the beaten egg. Place the tapioca flour on a sheet of wax paper and coat the chicken thoroughly by rolling it in the flour. Set aside.

4. Heat a wok. Add the peanut oil and heat to 350°F to 375°F. Place the chicken in a large Chinese strainer and lower into the oil. Fry for 5 to 7 minutes, until golden brown, ladling hot oil over it to ensure even frying.

5. Turn the heat off. Remove the chicken from the oil with a strainer and allow to drain in the strainer for 10 minutes. Cut into bite-sized pieces and serve with Sichuan peppercorn salt.

MAKES 6 TO 8 SERVINGS

DRUNKEN CHICKEN

Joi Gai

This traditional dish from Shanghai is often referred to as "wine chicken," but not in Shanghai, where those who cook it and those who eat it with pleasure call it joi gai, or "drunken chicken." The classic way of cooking this chicken is to steam it whole. I have done a version of it in which I boil it, and it is a fine dish, but what follows is "drunken chicken" as it is supposed to be cooked, accompanied by its "drunken" sauce.

One 3½-pound chicken
¼ cup plus 2 teaspoons salt
1 tablespoon sugar
3 scallions, trimmed and cut in half
Three ¼-inch-thick slices fresh ginger

For the wine sauce
3 tablespoons Shao-Hsing wine or dry sherry
3 tablespoons steamed chicken liquid
¾ teaspoon salt
1 teaspoon sugar
Pinch freshly ground white pepper

1. Clean the chicken and remove the fat and membranes. Wash under cold running water, rinse, and drain. Sprinkle with the ¼ cup salt, rub the outside well, rinse, drain, and dry well with paper towels.

2. Place the chicken in a steamproof dish, and sprinkle with the remaining 2 teaspoons salt and the sugar inside the cavity and out. Place 1 scallion and 1 slice of ginger in the cavity, the others along its sides. Bring 2 quarts water to a boil in a wok. Place the dish containing the chicken on a rack over the boiling water, cover, and steam for 45 minutes to 1 hour. Have boiling water at hand to replenish any water that evaporates.

3. Turn off the heat, remove the chicken from the steamer, and reserve. In a small bowl, combine the sauce ingredients.

4. When the chicken is cool to the touch, cut into bite-sized pieces and place in a deep serving dish. Pour the sauce over the chicken, place in the refrigerator, and marinate for at least 4 hours, to become "drunk." Serve as either a small dish appetizer or a first course.

MAKES 6 TO 8 SERVINGS

CRISP CHICKEN

Jah Ji Gai

*T*his twice-cooked chicken is a classic of Canton and southern China, often served at banquets and family feasts. The words ji gai *mean a chicken that has never laid an egg, which is young and tender, usually small. Elders like to pretend that this is so tender that when cooked its bones may be eaten. This is of course not true, but it is a lovely story. In the West this preparation is often misnamed "Peking Chicken" and served with pancakes or steamed breads. Do not be deceived; there is nothing at all "Peking" about this chicken, although it can indeed be served with pancakes or steamed breads. Dried tangerine skin is best in this recipe. If you substitute fresh, the flavor and aroma will not be as intense.*

One 3- to 3¼-pound chicken
¼ cup plus 2 tablespoons salt
3 pieces eight-star anise

One 1- by 2-inch piece dried tangerine
    peel
Three 2-inch cinnamon sticks
One ½-inch-thick slice fresh ginger,
    lightly smashed
8½ cups cold water
½ cup Chinese white rice wine or gin
1 whole nutmeg

For the coating
1 teaspoon maltose or honey, melted
    with 2 tablespoons boiling water
1 teaspoon Shao-Hsing wine or dry
    sherry
1 teaspoon Chinese white rice vinegar
    or distilled vinegar
½ teaspoon cornstarch

6 cups peanut oil
Sichuan Peppercorn Salt (page 89) for
    serving

1. Clean the chicken inside and out and remove the fat and membranes. Wash under cold running water and drain. Sprinkle ¼ cup of the salt on the outside of the chicken, rub well, rinse, and drain well. Place the chicken in a strainer and let drain for 1 hour.

2. Combine all the other ingredients, including the remaining 2 tablespoons salt, except coating ingredients, in a large oval Dutch oven, and bring to a boil over high heat. Cover, lower the heat, and simmer for 30 minutes. Turn the heat back to high and return to a boil. Place the chicken in the pot, breast side up. Cover. When the liquid begins to boil, lower the heat immediately and simmer for 10 to 12 minutes. Turn the chicken over and repeat, cooking for 10 to 12 minutes more.

3. Turn off the heat and allow the chicken to rest in the liquid for 10 minutes. Remove and discard all the other ingredients in the pot. Allow the chicken to drain and pierce it with a cooking fork to help the draining process.

4. In a small bowl, combine the coating ingredients. With a pastry brush, coat the chicken thoroughly with the coating mixture. Allow the chicken to dry thoroughly, about 6 hours. (The use of an electric fan can reduce this by half.)

5. Heat a wok over high heat for 1 minute. Add the peanut oil and heat to 350°F to 375°F. Place the chicken, breast side up, in a large Chinese strainer, lower into the oil, and fry for 4 minutes, ladling hot oil over it as it fries. The chicken should be golden brown.

6. Turn off the heat. Remove the chicken with a strainer and drain well over a bowl. Allow to rest for 7 minutes. To serve, chop into bite-sized pieces and serve with Sichuan peppercorn salt.

MAKES 6 SERVINGS

In most of China meat is pork. Early in its agricultural history China domesticated the pig, and over the centuries pork has become dominant. To this day the Chinese raise a third of all the domesticated pigs in the world, more than Europe, the United States, and Canada combined.

Historically, no part of the pig is wasted. The Chinese eat virtually all of the pig—its skin, its meats, its innards. So enamored are the Chinese of pork that in parts of the country suckling pigs are bred so that they and their tender skin may be roasted for special banquets. No region of China is without pork, as a meat for the everyday table or as festive dishes. ◆

BARBECUED PORK

Char Siu

The Chinese in Canton, where roasting pork is an art form, call this char siu, which translates as "held by fork over fire." It harks back to the times when there were few ovens in China, and all meats, marinated or not, were roasted over an open fire. This pork, with its glossy glaze, is what you see hanging in the windows of restaurants. Commercially this pork is colored with red vegetable dye. I do not dye my pork.

Char Siu *is surely one of the most versatile preparations in China. It can be eaten hot or cold. It can be used in a stir-fry with other ingredients or as a filling for dumplings, put into soups, and it is often used as one of those small dishes in a* bot dai, bot siu, *"8 large, 8 small" banquet.*

4½ pounds lean boneless pork loin
3 tablespoons dark soy sauce
3 tablespoons soy sauce
½ cup honey
½ teaspoon salt
3 tablespoons oyster sauce
2 tablespoons Mei Kuei Lu Chiew or gin
3 tablespoons hoisin sauce
⅛ teaspoon freshly ground white pepper
1½ cakes (1½ ounces) wet (or red) preserved bean curd
1 teaspoon five-spice powder

1. Cut the pork into lengthwise strips 2 inches wide and 1 inch thick. Using a small knife, pierce the meat repeatedly at ½-inch intervals to help tenderize it.

2. Line a roasting pan with foil. Place the pork strips in a single layer at the bottom of the pan. In a small bowl, combine all the other ingredients and pour over the strips. Coat well and marinate for 4 hours or overnight in the refrigerator.

3. Heat the oven to broil. Place the roasting pan in the broiler about 4 inches from the heat and roast for 30 to 50 minutes. To test for doneness, remove one strip of pork after 30 minutes and slice it to see if it is cooked through. During the cooking period, the pork should be basted 5 or 6 times and turned over 4 times. If the sauce dries out, add some boiling water to the pan. When the meat is cooked, remove from the pan, allow to cool, and refrigerate until ready to use.

N O T E : Char Siu *may be made ahead. It can be refrigerated for 4 to 5 days and frozen for a month. Allow to defrost before use.*

RED COOKED PORK SHOULDER

Jau Yau Tai Pong

*S*urely one of the foremost classics of Shanghai. It is said that the dish is at least 300 years old, a dish for weddings and special birthdays, for the celebration of a son's first month of life, even for a funeral banquet. The people of Shanghai love this dish. The pork is braised, the process the Chinese call "long cooking," after the meat has been seared. It is also perhaps the best example of "red cooking," for in most instances it is colored with dye. I prefer to color it with red rice, a food. Like many others of these classics, this preparation requires time, but the result is exceptional. Although the recipe will taste the same if you omit the powdered red rice, the color of the dish will not be authentic.

One 5½- to 6-pound pork shoulder

1 cup plus 2 tablespoons double dark soy sauce, regular dark soy sauce, or mushroom soy sauce

4½ cups peanut oil for blanching

¾ cup sugar

3 pieces eight-star anise

Two 3-inch-long cinnamon sticks

4 scallions, trimmed and cut into thirds

Two 1-inch-thick slices ginger, peeled

10 cups cold water

⅓ cup Shao-Hsing wine or dry sherry

1½ teaspoons red rice, pulverized into a powder (optional)

continued

1. Wash the pork shoulder and with a small knife scrape the skin clean. Run cold water over it, rinse, and dry with paper towels.

2. Rub the shoulder with 2 tablespoons of the soy sauce, covering it thoroughly. Allow to rest for 15 minutes. Heat a wok over high heat for 1 minute. Add the peanut oil and heat to 375°F. Place the shoulder in a Chinese strainer and lower into the oil for 45 seconds to 1 minute to seal it, ladling oil over it until the skin turns a deep, rich brown and small white bubbles appear on it. Turn the shoulder over and blanch for another 45 seconds to 1 minute, repeating the ladling process. Turn off the heat, remove the shoulder in a strainer, and drain over a bowl. Remove the oil from the wok.

3. Place a shallow rack at the bottom of a large pot and place the pork shoulder on it. Add the sugar, anise, cinnamon, scallions, ginger, and water. The liquid should cover the pork. Cover the pot and bring to a boil over medium heat. Raise the heat to high, add the remaining 1 cup soy sauce, and bring back to a boil. Add the wine and powdered red rice, if using, and bring back to a boil. Lower the heat and allow the shoulder to simmer, leaving the lid cracked.

4. After 1 hour, turn the pork over and cook for another 1½ hours. Turn over again and cook for 1 more hour. Turn over again and cook for 1 to 1½ hours more. At this point the pork should appear about to fall from the bone. Taste the liquid—it should be sweet, with a faint touch of saltiness. You may have to adjust it a bit.

5. Turn off the heat. Allow the pork to rest in the pot until it cools to room temperature. Transfer the pork and liquid to a large bowl and allow to rest in the refrigerator overnight. It may, of course, be eaten warm, out of the pot, but it is far better eaten a day later, which allows its tastes to blend. (I suggest a test: Cut and taste a slice right after cooking. Then reserve for a day, reheat the pork as I suggest, and taste.) To serve, heat the shoulder and liquid until hot. Transfer the pork and some liquid, now a sauce, to a deep serving dish. Serve with fork and spoon, for the meat will fall from its bone.

MAKES 10 SERVINGS

LION'S HEAD

See Ji Tau

*T*his is a traditional dish from Shanghai, oversized pork and pork fat meatballs cooked in a clay pot with bok choy, *the
size of the meatballs responsible for their
grand name. Generally the meat mixture is
half pork, half pork fat, but it is not
unusual to find the ratio to be two-thirds
fat to one-third meat. For my rendition, I
use lean pork, which yields a firmer ball
and better taste.* Bok choy *is always served
with Lion's Head. I have used Shanghai*
bok choy, *smaller and paler than regular*
bok choy, *which has distinctive white stems
and deep green leaves. Either* bok choy *is
suitable. This dish is best cooked the way it is
done in Shanghai, in a "sand clay" pot (see
page 59). Any other casserole may be used,
clay or with a nonstick interior.*

For the meatballs
1 pound coarsely ground lean pork
6 scallions, white and pale green parts
    only, trimmed and sliced thinly
3 tablespoons flour
2½ tablespoons egg white, lightly
    beaten
1 tablespoon Shao-Hsing wine or dry
    sherry
1 teaspoon minced fresh ginger
2 teaspoons soy sauce
2 teaspoons sugar
1 teaspoon sesame oil
¾ teaspoon salt
Pinch freshly ground white pepper

2 tablespoons peanut oil
8 heads Shanghai bok choy (about
    2½ pounds), washed thoroughly
    and halved lengthwise
3 cups Chicken Stock (page 75)

1. Place all the meatball ingredients in a bowl and stir together with your hands, in one
    direction, until well blended. Form into 4 large meatballs and flatten slightly.

2. Place the peanut oil in a skillet and heat the oil over moderate heat until it is hot but
    not smoking. Cook the meatballs for 5 minutes on each side or until golden brown.

3. As the meatballs cook, arrange the *bok choy* halves at the bottom of a sand clay pot or
    other casserole and add the stock. Place the meatballs on top of the *bok choy*. Bring the
    stock to a boil, lower the heat to medium, and cook the mixture at a slow boil, with the
    pot lid cracked, for 25 minutes. Turn the meatballs over and cook the mixture 20 min-
    utes more or until the *bok choy* is tender.

4. To serve, present the clay pot at table, then serve the lion's head and *bok choy* in indi-
    vidual bowls.

MAKES 4 SERVINGS

MAH PAW DAU FU

This wonderful Sichuan classic defies adequate translation. It is bean curd in a hot, chili-flavored sauce, but that seems flat. Best to ask for it, phonetically, by its traditional name; better yet, make it. This is one of those dishes of folklore. It is said that an old woman, with a pockmarked face, opened a restaurant in Sichuan and created this dish. It and she became so famous that people would journey great distances just to eat it. But it had no name. So the dish was named for the old woman, mah paw dau fu, or "the pockmarked grandmother's bean curd," and so it is known today.

For the sauce
1 tablespoon Shao-Hsing wine or dry sherry
2½ teaspoons Chinese rice wine vinegar or distilled vinegar
1 tablespoon sugar
¼ teaspoon salt

2 teaspoons soy sauce
2½ teaspoons dark soy sauce
¼ cup ketchup
2½ tablespoons cornstarch
1 tablespoon sesame oil
Pinch ground Sichuan peppercorns
1⅓ cups Chicken Stock (page 75)

¼ cup peanut oil
2 teaspoons minced fresh ginger
5 small fresh red Thai chilies, minced
3 tablespoons minced mustard pickle
1½ teaspoons minced garlic
½ pound lean ground pork
1½ tablespoons Chili Sauce (page 88)
6 cakes fresh bean curd (medium-firm tofu), cut into ¼-inch dice
⅓ cup trimmed and thinly sliced scallion
1 pound fresh Chinese egg noodles or capellini
1 tablespoon sesame oil

1. In a bowl, mix together the sauce ingredients and reserve. Bring a pot of water to a boil to cook the noodles.

2. Heat a wok over high heat for 30 seconds, add the peanut oil, and coat the wok with it using a spatula. When a wisp of white smoke appears, add the ginger, chilies, and mustard pickle and cook, stirring, for 1 minute. Add the garlic and cook, stirring, for 30 seconds. Add the pork and cook, stirring, breaking the pork up with a spatula, for 1 minute or until the pork is no longer pink. Stir in the chili sauce until well combined,

then add the bean curd and cook, stirring together, for 3 minutes or until it begins to boil. Make a well in the center of the mixture, stir the sauce, pour in, and stir well for 1 minute or until it begins to bubble and thicken. Turn off the heat, stir in the scallion until well combined, and transfer to a heated serving bowl.

3. Cook the noodles in the boiling water, stirring, until the water returns to a boil. Remove the pot from the heat, add the cold water to the pot, and drain well. Return the noodles to the pot and toss with the sesame oil. Add the noodles to the bean curd and pork mixture and toss gently to mix. Serve. If you prefer, you may eliminate the noodles and serve the Mah Paw Dau Fu over cooked rice. Either choice is fine.

MAKES 6 TO 8 SERVINGS

RETURN TO THE POT PORK

Wui Wor Yuk

*T*his is a most loved, and famous, masterpiece of Sichuan cookery. Often on menus it is referred to as "twice-cooked pork," which is accurate to a point, but "pork returned to the pot" precisely describes the dish as it is known in Sichuan. It is notable as well for its lack of chilies, conferring just a hint of heat from its horse beans cooked and preserved with chili.

¾ pound fresh pork belly or bacon (see Note)
3 cups cold water

For the sauce
2 teaspoons sweet bean sauce
1 tablespoon horse beans preserved with chili or Chili Sauce (page 88)

1½ tablespoons ketchup
½ teaspoon soy sauce
2 teaspoons sugar
1½ teaspoons Chinese white rice vinegar or distilled vinegar
6 Sichuan peppercorns, crushed

⅓ cup sliced leeks in ¼-inch diagonal pieces
1 teaspoon minced fresh ginger
2 scallions, trimmed and cut into ½-inch diagonal pieces
1 tablespoon Shao-Hsing wine or dry sherry
1 cup chopped green bell pepper in 1- by ½-inch pieces

1. Place the pork and cold water in a pot, cover, and bring to a boil over high heat. Lower the heat and simmer, leaving the lid cracked. Simmer for 30 minutes. Turn off the heat and allow the pork to cool in the pot. Remove from the pot, cut off the skin, slice thinly, and reserve.

2. As the pork cooks, mix the sauce ingredients together in a bowl and reserve.

3. Heat a wok over high heat for 40 seconds. Add the sliced pork and cook, stirring constantly, for 2 minutes. Add the leeks and ginger and cook, stirring, for 30 seconds. Add the scallions and cook, stirring, for 30 seconds. Add the wine and mix well. Add the bell pepper and cook, stirring, for 45 seconds. Add the sauce and stir well to mix, making certain the pork and vegetables are well coated, about 1½ minutes. Turn off the heat, transfer to a heated dish, and serve.

N O T E : *Fresh pork belly or bacon often comes with bone and skin. If so, 1 pound is needed to arrive at the ¾ pound required for this recipe.*

MAKES 4 TO 6 SERVINGS

MU SHU PORK

Muk See Yuk

*W*ho has not heard of mu shu pork, that tradition from Beijing? How, you might ask, does mu shu pork become muk see yuk? Well, muk see yuk is a dialect translation for "shaved wood pork" to indicate that the pork in this recipe is shredded, as a carpenter's plane might shave wood. This fine preparation of many ingredients is a perfect example of elaborate imperial court cooking.

12 Peking Duck Pancakes (page 113)

For the sauce
3½ teaspoons sugar
¾ teaspoon salt
1½ teaspoons Shao-Hsing wine or dry sherry
2 tablespoons dark soy sauce
1 tablespoon cornstarch
2 tablespoons Chicken Stock (page 75)
2 tablespoons hoisin sauce

3 cups peanut oil
1 cup julienned boneless lean pork
1 teaspoon minced fresh ginger
1 teaspoon minced garlic
4 cups finely shredded cabbage
3 scallions, trimmed and cut into 1½-inch pieces, white parts quartered lengthwise
½ cup julienned bamboo shoots
2 tablespoons cloud ears, soaked in hot water for 30 minutes
40 tiger lily buds, soaked in hot water for 30 minutes, hard ends removed, and cut crosswise into halves
5 Steamed Black Mushrooms (page 81), julienned
Pinch freshly ground white pepper
4 large eggs, lightly scrambled
1 tablespoon sesame oil

1. Make the pancakes and reserve. In a bowl, combine the sauce ingredients and set aside.

2. Heat a wok over high heat. Add the peanut oil and heat to 350°F. Add the pork and oil-blanch for 1½ minutes, until the pork loses its pinkness. Remove the pork from the oil with a strainer and allow to drain over a bowl.

3. Empty all but 2 tablespoons of the oil from the wok. Heat the wok over high heat for 20 seconds. Add the ginger and garlic and stir briefly. Add the cabbage, stir, and cook for 3 minutes. Add the scallions, bamboo shoots, cloud ears, tiger lily buds, mushrooms, and white pepper and cook, stirring, for another 3 minutes. Return the pork to the mixture and cook, stirring, for 2 minutes. Make a well in the center of the mixture, stir the reserved sauce, pour in, and mix thoroughly. Add the scrambled eggs and mix well. Turn off the heat, add the sesame oil, toss, and serve folded in the pancakes, to make 12 equal portions.

MAKES 6 SERVINGS

ANTS CLIMB A TREE

Mah Ngai Seung Seuh

This Sichuan classic has a most fanciful name. It is supposed that the "ants" are the ground-up morsels of pork, the "tree" the noodles they eventually rest upon. Suffice it to say that throughout Sichuan it is cooked and enjoyed, and elsewhere it is envied. This dish can be made with soft cooked noodles as well, but I prefer mine because of its textures.

6 ounces rice noodle
6 cups peanut oil
6 ounces lean ground pork
2 teaspoons Sichuan Pepper Pickle
   (page 99) or jarred pickled hot
   peppers

2 tablespoons preserved horse beans
   with chili or Chili Sauce (page 88)
1 tablespoon double dark soy sauce,
   regular dark soy sauce, or mushroom
   soy sauce
2 teaspoons Chinese white rice vinegar
   or distilled vinegar
1½ teaspoons minced ginger
1 tablespoon Shao-Hsing wine or dry
   sherry
2½ teaspoons sugar
⅛ teaspoon salt
¼ cup Sweet Wine Rice (page 69)
⅓ cup plus ¼ cup Chicken Stock
   (page 75)
1 scallion, trimmed and finely sliced

1. Separate the rice noodle into 3 equal portions. Heat a wok over high heat for 40 seconds, add the peanut oil, and heat to 350°F. Place 1 portion of rice noodle in the wok for only seconds. When it fluffs up and becomes snow white, it is done. Remove from the oil and drain on paper towels. Repeat with the 2 other portions.

2. Empty the oil into a large bowl. Heat the wok over high heat, add the ground pork, loosen with a spatula, and cook until the pork loses its pinkness and all liquid from it is absorbed. Add the pepper pickle and horse beans and stir well. Add the soy sauce and mix well. Add the vinegar and mix well. Add the ginger and mix well. Add the wine and mix well. Add the sugar and salt, stir, and cook for 2 minutes. Add the wine rice, stir, and cook for 3 minutes.

3. Place 1 portion of fried rice noodle on a heated serving dish. Add the other 2 portions to the wok mixture and stir briefly. Add the ⅓ cup stock, stir, and cook for 2 minutes. Add 2 tablespoons more stock and mix well. The noodles should blend with the pork mixture into a deep brown color. Add the remaining 2 tablespoons stock and mix well. When all the stock is absorbed, turn off the heat. Transfer to a serving dish lined with rice noodle, sprinkle with the scallion, and serve.

MAKES 8 SERVINGS

ORANGE BEEF

Chun Pei Ngau Yuk

*B*eef is not now, nor was it before, consumed as widely as pork in China.
*Traditionally beef was not eaten because
cattle were deemed too important, vital as
draft and farm animals. Better to eat the
easily domesticated and plentiful pigs. Beef
is nonetheless an important food in the western parts of the country. And as with most
foods in China, great and special preparations arose in the cooking of beef. One such is
this classic from Hunan. Its name,* chun pei
ngau yuk, *translates as "old beef," very old,
or as we say in China, so old it gathers dust.
The main reason for this is that this dish is
most often cooked with old, dried, hard
orange peel, and it is fine that way. I prefer
fresh orange peel. As the beef cooks, it emits a
pleasing aroma, and as it is eaten the bits of
orange are refreshing. Different chefs have
different renditions of orange beef. This is
mine.*

*½ pound thick flank steak, weighed
    after trimming, cut into strips
    2½ inches by ¼ inch
½ teaspoon baking soda
1 tablespoon egg white, lightly beaten*

*½ teaspoon Shao-Hsing wine or
    dry sherry
Pinch freshly ground white pepper
1 tablespoon peanut oil
2 tablespoons cornstarch*

*For the sauce
2 teaspoons dark soy sauce
1 tablespoon sugar
1 teaspoon sesame oil
1 teaspoon Chinese white rice vinegar
    or distilled vinegar
2 tablespoons Chicken Stock (page 75)
Pinch freshly ground white pepper*

*3½ cups peanut oil, to deep-fry the beef
5 small dried chilies
2 teaspoons minced fresh ginger
1 teaspoon minced garlic
1 fresh Thai chili, minced
1½ tablespoons ½- by ⅛-inch pieces
    fresh orange peel, most of pith
    removed
2 scallions, trimmed and cut into
    2-inch sections
6 slices fresh orange*

1. Marinate the beef with baking soda in the refrigerator for 8 hours or, preferably, overnight. After marinating, wash thoroughly, twice, with cold water. Drain and dry with paper towels. Place the beef in a bowl, add the egg white, and mix well until the beef is coated. Add the wine, white pepper, 1 tablespoon peanut oil, and cornstarch, mixing with your hand each time an ingredient is added. Allow to rest for 1 hour, refrigerated. There should be no residue. *continued*

2. In a bowl, combine the sauce ingredients and set aside.

3. Heat a wok over high heat for 1 minute. Add the 3½ cups peanut oil and heat to 400°F. Place the beef strips, one at a time, in the oil and cook for 1½ minutes, loosening the beef with a spatula. Remove with a strainer and drain. Heat the oil again to 425°F. Place the beef strips again in the oil and cook for 2 minutes, until the beef becomes crisp. Remove and allow to drain.

4. Drain off all but 1 tablespoon oil from the wok and heat over high heat for 20 seconds. Add the dried chilies, stir, and cook until darkened. Add the ginger and garlic and stir briefly. Add the fresh chili and orange peel and stir briefly. Add the scallions, and mix well. Add the beef and cook, stirring, for 45 seconds. Make a well in the center of the mixture, stir the sauce mixture, and pour in. Mix well until the sauce is absorbed and the beef acquires a shiny coating. Remove to a serving dish and serve, garnished with the orange slices.

MAKES 4 SERVINGS

SICHUAN BEEF

Sichuan Chau Ngau Yuk

If this is not the most well known of China's classics, it surely ranks close to it. It is familiar throughout China, where it is known, more properly, as gawn chau, *or "dry fried," beef of Sichuan, which means that no liquid is used in its cooking, no sauces, except for the peanut oil necessary to brown it. Sichuan beef is familiar in the West as well, though interpretations of it differ widely, by chef and by menu. What follows is the traditional way of cooking this great dish from Sichuan.*

For the sweet bean sauce
1½ tablespoons sweet bean sauce
1 tablespoon preserved horse beans with chili or Chili Sauce (page 88)
1 tablespoon sugar

⅛ teaspoon cayenne pepper
¼ teaspoon Hot Pepper Oil (page 87)
¼ teaspoon salt

2 tablespoons peanut oil
¾ pound London broil, cut across the grain into 2½-inch julienne
1¼ teaspoons minced fresh ginger
1¼ teaspoons minced garlic
2 teaspoons Shao-Hsing wine or dry sherry
1 tablespoon Sichuan Peppercorn Paste (page 90)
3 large celery stalks, cut into 2½-inch fine julienne
3 tablespoons julienned white parts of scallions

1. In a bowl, combine the sweet bean mixture ingredients and reserve.

2. Heat a wok over high heat for 40 seconds, add 1 tablespoon of the peanut oil, and coat the wok with it using a spatula. When a wisp of white smoke appears, add the beef and spread in a thin layer. Cook for 30 seconds, turn over, stir, and cook until the beef loses its redness. At this point the beef has released some liquid, about ¼ cup. Turn off the heat, remove the beef to a strainer, drain, and reserve.

3. Wash and dry the wok and spatula. Heat the wok over high heat for 40 seconds, add the remaining tablespoon of peanut oil, and coat the wok. When a wisp of white smoke appears, add the ginger and garlic and stir. When the garlic turns light brown, add the beef and cook, stirring, for 2 minutes or until very dry. Add the wine and cook, stirring, until the wine is absorbed, about 40 seconds. Add the sweet bean sauce mixture and stir well, making certain the beef is coated a deep brown. Add the Sichuan peppercorn paste and stir well until blended. Add the celery and cook, stirring, for 2½ minutes or until the celery wilts. Add the scallions and stir to mix well. Turn off the heat, transfer to a heated platter, and serve.

MAKES 8 SERVINGS

*A*ny discussion of fish consumption in China must begin in Canton, to a lesser but significant extent in Shanghai. The Cantonese catch, raise, and eat an extraordinary variety of fish and shellfish, and for them the premium is freshness, not cost. To this day I strive to buy only fish that are alive. When I was growing up in China, our markets had bewildering arrays of fish, shellfish, and crustaceans, all freshly caught, all live, every day, and our family delighted in them. My grandmother's servants would go twice to market each day, before the afternoon and evening meals, and most often would return with a fat fish, or live shrimp and prawns, flipping and bouncing about in a pail of water, ready to be prepared for our table, usually by steaming. Fish are quite important in Shanghai as well, but in this eastern region of China fish and shellfish are cooked more with oil and spices. Farther north, and in the West, fish are not as significant as in the South. Yet throughout China the fish, a symbol of plenty, has been honored by masterful cooking that has produced traditional classics as well as everyday wonders. ◆

STEAMED SEA BASS

Ching Jing Seh Bon

*T*his epitomizes the essence of Cantonese cooking, simplicity, freshness, and honesty of flavor. Steaming a fish, any fish, whether it be a bass, garoupa, wrasse, or snapper, is the favored method of preparation in Canton. A steamed fish is a particularly important component in a family dinner or an elaborate banquet, where usually it is the final course that graces the meal. And precision is demanded in steaming. I can recall an evening in a restaurant when my cousin sent a fish back to the kitchen, refusing it because he simply knew that it had been steamed 30 seconds too long.

For the marinade
2 teaspoons Chinese white rice vinegar
   or distilled vinegar
1 teaspoon salt
1½ teaspoons sesame oil
2 tablespoons soy sauce
2 tablespoons Chinese white rice wine
   or 1½ tablespoons gin
2 tablespoons julienned fresh ginger

One 2½-pound sea bass, striped bass,
   flounder, or red snapper, cleaned
   thoroughly, intestines and extra fat
   removed, washed inside and out, and
   dried well

2 quarts boiling water
2 tablespoons White Peppercorn Oil
(page 85) or peanut oil

3 scallions, trimmed and finely sliced
1½ tablespoons fresh coriander
(cilantro), finely sliced

1. In a bowl, combine all the marinade ingredients. Coat the fish inside and out with the marinade. Place in a steamproof dish and marinate, refrigerated, for 15 minutes.

2. Place the boiling water in a wok and place a rack over but not touching the water. Place the fish in the dish on the rack, cover the wok, and steam for 25 to 30 minutes (see steaming, page 64) or until a chopstick can be inserted easily into the flesh. (If flounder is used, the steaming time will be about 15 minutes.) If the fish is too large, it may be cut in half, though it is preferable aesthetically to keep it whole.

3. Turn off the heat, remove the fish in the dish from the wok, pour white peppercorn oil over it, sprinkle scallions and coriander on it, and serve.

MAKES 8 SERVINGS

CRISP SWIMMING FISH

Soh Jah Seh Bon

A classic Hunan banquet preparation. It is important that this festive fish, once cooked, look as if it is swimming, even though it has been soh jah, *fried crisp. So it is carefully arranged upright, as if about to dart away. This is meant to impress, and does. Presenting any fish, in any context, is good luck to the Chinese. If it is swimming, it is considered good fortune of high order.*

1 whole sea bass or red snapper, 1½ to 1¾ pounds, cleaned thoroughly, intestines and extra fat removed, washed inside and out, dried well
1½ teaspoons Chinese white rice vinegar or distilled vinegar
2 tablespoons Shao-Hsing wine or dry sherry
1 teaspoon salt
¼ teaspoon freshly ground white pepper
½ cup cornstarch
5½ cups peanut oil

For the sauce
2 tablespoons Chinese white rice vinegar or distilled vinegar
2 tablespoons sugar
½ teaspoon salt
2 tablespoons Shao-Hsing wine or dry sherry
1 tablespoon double dark soy sauce, regular dark soy sauce, or mushroom soy sauce
1½ teaspoons cornstarch
¼ cup Chicken Stock (page 75)
2 tablespoons Sweet Wine Rice (page 69)
Pinch freshly ground white pepper

½ cup diced onion
1 tablespoon minced fresh ginger
2 small fresh Thai chilies, minced
2 tablespoons diced carrot
2 tablespoons diced bamboo shoot
2 tablespoons chopped scallion
10 sprigs fresh coriander (cilantro), for garnish

1. Place the fish on a chopping board. Cut 5 slits diagonally into each side of the fish, but do not cut to the bone. Sprinkle vinegar all over, inside and out. Repeat with the wine, salt, and white pepper. Place the cornstarch on a sheet of wax paper and coat the fish thoroughly on both sides, including the cleaning opening.

2. Heat a wok over high heat for 40 seconds. Pour the oil into the wok and heat to 375°F to 400°F. Place the fish in a Chinese strainer and lower into the oil. (If it cannot be lowered completely, ladle oil over it and tip the strainer so the fish is completely cooked, brown and crisp, including the head.) Fry for 10 to 12 minutes, until cooked.

3. Remove to a heated serving dish. Use a cloth to protect your hands and place the fish upright, stomach and cleaning opening down. Press it down gently so that it is firmly set. Reserve. Empty all but 1½ tablespoons of the oil from the wok.

4. In a bowl, combine the sauce ingredients and set aside. Heat the wok for 20 seconds. Add the onion, stir, and cook for 5 minutes. Add the ginger and stir briefly. Add the chilies, carrot, and bamboo shoot. Stir the sauce, add to the wok and cook, stirring, until the sauce thickens. Pour it over the fish, sprinkle with the scallion, garnish with the coriander, and serve.

MAKES 6 SERVINGS

EMPEROR'S FISH

Keh Lun Yue

*T*his artistic fish preparation was, it is said, a favorite in the imperial dining rooms of the Ching dynasty. It name, keh lun, *represents a mythological animal with the body of a horse and the head of a dragon, a symbol of surpassing good fortune. The dragon, itself, customarily represents the emperor. In the kitchens of Beijing, Yunnan ham would be used in this dish; Smithfield ham serves equally well.*

1 whole striped bass, 1¾ to 2 pounds,
   cleaned thoroughly, intestines and
   extra fat removed, washed inside
   and out, and dried well

For the marinade
1 teaspoon Chinese white rice vinegar
   or distilled vinegar

1½ tablespoons Chinese white rice wine
   or gin
1½ tablespoons soy sauce
2 tablespoons peanut oil
1 tablespoon julienned fresh ginger
1 teaspoon salt
Pinch freshly ground white pepper

6 slices prepared Smithfield Ham
   (page 79)
3 large Steamed Black Mushrooms
   (page 81), caps halved
2 tablespoons Scallion Oil (page 82) or
   peanut oil
4 scallions, white parts only, julienned
20 thin strips red bell pepper
10 sprigs fresh coriander (cilantro)

1. Place the fish on a chopping board. Score the fish by making 6 slices approximately the width of the fish in its sides, about 1 inch apart. The cuts should be made up to, but not into, the bone and with the blade held at an angle, these on both sides of the fish. Place the fish in a steamproof dish. Combine the marinade ingredients, add to the steamproof dish with the fish, and set aside.

2. Slice the ham into 6 rectangular pieces, 3 inches by ½ inch and about ⅛ inch thick. Slip a ham slice and a half mushroom cap into each of the scores on the side of the fish facing up. The cuts in the down side will absorb the marinade.

3. Place the fish in a steamproof dish in a wok, cover, and steam for 10 to 12 minutes (see steaming, page 64). (If steamed in a metal dish instead of porcelain, steaming time will be 6 to 8 minutes.) Remove the wok cover and pour the scallion oil on the fish. Add the scallions, pepper strips, and coriander atop the fish and around its sides. Serve with cooked rice.

MAKES 6 SERVINGS

ABALONE

Bau Yue

This exotic mollusk is prized, even revered, by Chinese gastronomes to such an extent that they demand abalone by specific type, from specific breeding grounds. That the Chinese words for abalone, bau yue, sound almost identical to the words for "guaranteed wealth" does not diminish the desire for them, nor lessen their mystique. In fact abalone shells are often ground into a fine powdered medicine believed by the Chinese to improve eyesight, and to relieve high blood pressure.

The finest abalone come from Japan, a small area at the northern tip of Honshu, Japan's largest island, where the waters separate it from the northernmost island of Hokkaido. Abalone are also found off Mexico, the Pacific coast of the United States, Australia, and the Persian Gulf, but those from Japan are the finest and most expensive. Most abalone are harvested, eaten fresh, or canned. The best Japanese abalone are harvested, removed with precision from their shells, bathed in salt water, boiled, air and heat dried, finally dried in the sun, and then stored in tightly closed jars until used. Three abalone are considered the world's best: Oma, small and scarce, from the straits between Honshu and Hokkaida, dried to an oval beige disk, and hoarded by collectors; Yoshihama, from the northeastern

tip of Honshu, are larger, meaty, and dry to a redness; and Amidori, the largest of the three, though still small, aromatic, and, when dried, golden in cast. These finest of all abalone are never eaten fresh. Traditionally, dried abalone in China must be prepared to be eaten, and there is one classic way to do this.

Select good abalone at a reasonable price. Chinese groceries have a full range. If you buy too cheaply, you will get abalone usually cut up for use in other recipes.

One more note: The classic recipe here uses a small bit of lard. If you do not wish to use it, eliminate it; but do not substitute for it. It is there for the taste and texture it provides.

8 dried abalone
1 quart water
1½ pounds fresh pork spareribs
1 pound chicken wings
1 pound chicken legs
2 tablespoons lard
3 tablespoons Shao-Hsing wine or dry sherry
3 tablespoons oyster sauce
1½ cups Superior Stock (page 74) or Chicken Stock (page 75), to cover
2½ tablespoons tapioca flour mixed with 2½ tablespoons cold water

1. Place the abalone and water in a sand clay pot (page 59) or any large nonstick pot, cover, and bring to a boil. Lower the heat and simmer for 30 minutes. Turn off the heat. Allow the abalone to rest in the water and soak overnight. *continued*

2. Rinse the abalone under running water. Place the spareribs in the bottom of the sand pot, place the abalone in a layer atop them, then place the chicken, wings first, atop the abalone. Add enough water to cover and bring to a boil over low heat. Simmer for 4½ hours. Turn off the heat. Remove the abalone from the pot and reserve. Only a very small amount of liquid should remain, about 1 cup. (At this point the abalone may be reserved for use as long as 2 to 3 days before final preparation. The spareribs and chicken parts may be eaten as they are or saved for future use.)

3. Wash and dry the sand pot. Heat over low heat for 20 seconds. Add the lard, wine, oyster sauce, and abalone to the pot, and cover with the stock. Cover the pot, raise the heat to medium, and bring to a boil. Lower the heat and simmer for 20 minutes. Raise the heat back to medium. Stir the tapioca flour mixture and pour into the pot. Stir continuously until the liquid thickens.

4. Turn off the heat. Transfer the abalone to 8 individual heated dishes, divide the sauce among the dishes, and serve. Eat the abalone as the Chinese do, by tradition, with knife and fork. Cut tiny slices around the edges of the abalone, saving the center, the *tung sum*, or "sugar heart," for last.

MAKES 8 SERVINGS

BUDDHA'S DELIGHT

Lor Horn Jai

*T*his classic vegetarian preparation is known all across China. Its ingredients will vary slightly from region to region, but essentially it is a soft mixture of many vegetables, usually 10, occasionally more. In my version I use 11. Buddha's Delight is a Lunar New Year tradition but served at other festive times as well. I remember my grandmother always having it served on my birthday and those of other family members. Even though it is a vegetarian dish, honoring Buddha, and bearing what is said to be the name of one of his famous monasteries, it is a dish that vegetarian Taoists enjoy as well. I should note that though this preparation demonstrates well the art of the stir-fry, it does not result in a crisp mix. It is intended to be quite soft and thus suitable for all ages, the youngest to the elderly.

½ cup fresh or canned ginkgo nuts
2 cups water

For the sauce
¼ cup Vegetable Stock (page 76)
1 teaspoon sesame oil
1¼ teaspoons sugar
2 teaspoons dark soy sauce
1 tablespoon cornstarch
Pinch freshly ground white pepper

3 tablespoons peanut oil
1 tablespoon minced fresh ginger
½ teaspoon salt
*½ cup julienned lotus root in
    2- by ½-inch pieces*
*½ cup julienned carrot in
    2- by ½-inch pieces*
*¼ cup julienned bamboo shoot in
    2- by ½-inch pieces*
2 water chestnuts, julienned (¼ cup)
*½ cup Chinese celery cut in 2-inch
    pieces*
*⅓ cup snow peas cut in ½-inch pieces,
    strings removed*
*5 Chinese black mushrooms (⅓ cup),
    soaked in hot water for 45 minutes,
    squeezed dry, stems removed, and
    julienned*
*30 dried tiger lily buds, soaked in hot
    water for 30 minutes, squeezed dry,
    hard ends removed, and cut in half*
*4 slices dried bean curd, soaked in hot
    water for 30 minutes and julienned*
*Very light 1-inch hair seaweed, torn
    from a bundle, soaked in hot water
    for 20 minutes, washed, and drained*
*3 tablespoons Vegetable Stock
    (page 76)*

1. To prepare fresh ginkgo nuts, crack the shells, remove the nuts, and boil in the water for 20 minutes. Remove from the pot and allow to cool. Remove the skins and interior shoot and reserve. Or use canned nuts.

continued

2. Combine the sauce ingredients in a bowl and reserve.

3. Heat a wok over high heat for 45 seconds. Add the peanut oil and coat the wok with it using a spatula. When a wisp of white smoke appears, add the ginger and salt and stir briefly. Add the lotus root and stir for 30 seconds. Add the carrot and stir briefly. Add the bamboo shoot and stir briefly. Add the water chestnuts and stir briefly. Add the celery and stir briefly. Add the snow peas and stir briefly. Add the mushrooms and stir briefly. Add the tiger lily buds and stir briefly. Add the bean curd and stir briefly. Add the hair seaweed and stir to mix well. Add the 2 tablespoons of the stock and stir well. Add the reserved ginkgo nuts and stir well.

4. Let all the vegetables cook together for 5 minutes, stirring. It may be necessary to add the remaining tablespoon of stock during this period if the mixture dries. Make a well in the center of the mixture, stir the sauce, pour in, and mix well. When the sauce bubbles and darkens, the dish is done. Turn off the heat, transfer the mixture to a heated platter, and serve.

MAKES 6 SERVINGS

STEAMED WHOLE WINTER MELON SOUP

Dun Dong Gua Jung

*T*his is another of those special preparations known throughout China, from Hangzhou where traditionally China's great food carvers have practiced their art, north to the imperial court and south to where the great melons grow. What makes this classic feast dish so unusual is that the melon itself becomes a cookpot for a variety of ingredients, then the tureen in which they are served. The winter melon resembles a watermelon in size and shape, but its interior is translucent white and it absorbs the tastes of what it is cooked with. Which makes it ideal, in all ways, for this presentation.

1 winter melon (8 to 10 pounds)
⅓ cup Canton Roast Duck meat (page 114), cut into ⅓-inch dice
⅓ cup Barbecued Pork (page 124), cut into ⅓-inch dice
⅓ cup prepared Smithfield Ham (page 79), cut into ⅓-inch dice
2 Steamed Dry Scallops (page 80), julienned by hand
6 Chinese black mushrooms, soaked for 30 minutes in hot water, washed, stems discarded, and cut into ¼-inch dice

3 fresh water chestnuts, peeled and cut
    into ¼-inch dice
1½ teaspoons minced fresh ginger
1½ teaspoons minced garlic
2 tablespoons White Peppercorn Oil
    (page 85) or peanut oil
5½ cups Superior Stock (page 74) or
    Chicken Stock (page 75)
1½ cups silk squash, ridges peeled,
    leaving most of green skin, cut into
    ½-inch pieces

For blanching
¼ teaspoon baking soda
1 teaspoon salt

2 ounces crabmeat

1. Use a large clam steamer with a rack for this preparation. Place the winter melon in a steamproof bowl in the steamer pot initially for measurement purposes only. Put the rack in the pot and place the melon on it. With a pencil, mark the melon around where it is even with the top of the steamer. Remove from the steamer. Cut the melon straight across at the drawn line. Discard the top.

2. With a serrated knife, remove the seeds and soft center pulp of the melon. With the same knife, create a serrated edge around the edge of the melon. Place all the ingredients, except the silk squash, blanching ingredients, and crabmeat in the melon.

3. Tie 6 lengths of string to the rack. Place the melon in the bowl on the rack. Tie the string ends together over the open top of the melon. Place 2 to 3 inches of water in the steamer and bring to a boil. Lower the melon on the rack into the steamer. Cover and steam for at least 1 hour.

4. While the melon steams, to blanch the silk squash, put 2 cups water in a pot with the baking soda and salt. Bring to a boil, add the silk squash, and blanch for 8 to 10 seconds, until the squash turns bright green. Run cold water into the pot, drain, and repeat. Remove and reserve.

5. After 1 hour, check the melon sides inside to see if they are tender and softened. If they are, immediately add the silk squash and crabmeat and cook for another 10 minutes over reduced heat. The melon is done when its insides are tender and can be scooped with a spoon.

6. When done, lift the melon and rack from the steamer and place on a serving plate. Cut the strings and remove them. Stir the soup and ladle it into individual bowls, then carefully shave pieces of melon insides and place 1 or 2 in each bowl. Serve.

MAKES 10 SERVINGS

HOT AND SOUR SOUP

Seun Lot Tong

*T*his is surely one of the most recogniz-able dishes in China, known virtually everywhere in the West. There is no Chinese restaurant, it seems, where it does not appear on the menu. This classic most prob-ably had its roots in Beijing, though it is claimed, as a tradition, with equal fervor by both Sichuan and Hunan. Suffice it to say that it could be the pride of any region that cares to claim it.

5 cups Chicken Stock (page 75)
1 garlic clove, peeled
One ½-inch-thick slice ginger, lightly
    smashed
2 tablespoons cloud ears, soaked in hot
    water for 3 minutes until soft, washed,
    hard ends broken off, and broken into
    pieces by hand

30 dried tiger lily buds, soaked in hot
    water for 30 minutes until soft,
    hard ends discarded, and halved
3 tablespoons julienned Sichuan
    mustard pickle
1½ teaspoons hot pepper flakes
    (page 87)
6 slices dried bean curd, soaked in hot
    water until soft and julienned
¼ pound lean boneless pork, julienned
¼ cup Chinese red wine vinegar
¼ cup cornstarch mixed with ¼ cup
    cold water
3 large eggs, beaten
½ pound fresh bean curd (medium-
    firm tofu), sliced into ¼-inch strips
1 tablespoon double dark soy sauce,
    regular dark soy sauce, or mushroom
    soy sauce
2 teaspoons sesame oil
1 scallion, trimmed and finely sliced

1. Place the stock, garlic, and ginger in a pot, cover, and bring to a boil over high heat. Add the cloud ears, tiger lily buds, mustard pickle, and hot pepper flakes and return to a boil. Add the dried bean curd, stir to mix, cover the pot, lower the heat, and simmer for 15 minutes.

2. Raise the heat to high, add the pork, and stir. Add the vinegar, mix well, and return to a boil. Slowly add the cornstarch mixture, stirring constantly with your other hand until the soup thickens. Add the eggs in the same manner. Add the fresh bean curd, stir to mix well, and return to a boil. Turn off the heat, add the soy sauce, and stir in. Add the sesame oil and stir in. Taste the soup. If necessary, adjust for hotness and sourness to taste. Transfer the soup to a heated tureen, sprinkle with the scallion, and serve.

MAKES 6 TO 8 SERVINGS

SHARK'S FIN SOUP

Yue Chi Tong

*N*o banquet, no feast, of any consequence is considered complete in
China unless it includes Shark's Fin Soup.
This is a grand classic, known in many
variations from northern China to the
South, where it is especially loved. Chefs in
Canton and Shanghai are particularly
adept at creating dishes with shark's fins,
braising and stewing them, fitting them
into dumplings, and making soups of them.
I have already spoken about the processes of
cleaning and readying shark's fins for cooking (page 33). But these fins, already
reduced to strands, may be bought dried or
frozen. I caution you to select a reputable
merchant, for occasionally it has been found
that strands of processed, dried fish have
been mingled with them. Once you have
your strands of fins, however, you are ready
to make shark's fin soup in the traditional
manner.

3 ounces dried shark's fin
2 cups cold water
1 tablespoon Chinese white rice
 vinegar or distilled vinegar
1 tablespoon Chinese white rice wine
 or gin
2 scallions, trimmed and halved
One 1-inch-thick slice fresh ginger,
 lightly smashed
2 ounces pork fat, cut into 6 to 8 cubes
6 cups Superior Stock (page 74) or
 Chicken Stock (page 75)
¾ cup julienned prepared Smithfield
 Ham (page 79)
3 tablespoons cornstarch mixed with
 3 tablespoons cold water
1 teaspoon sesame oil
1 cup mung bean sprouts, washed and
 both ends removed
3 tablespoons Chinese red vinegar

1. Soak the shark's fin in warm water to cover until soft, at least 2 hours. Wash and rinse through a fine strainer. Soak overnight in a bowl with the cold water and white rice vinegar. Drain, then place in a steamproof dish with the wine, scallions, ginger, pork fat, and 1 cup of the stock. Place the dish in a steamer, cover, and steam for 30 minutes. (See steaming, page 64.) Turn off the heat, remove the dish, and discard all ingredients except the shark's fin. There should be about ¾ cup of fins. Reserve.

2. Pour the remaining 5 cups stock into a pot, add the shark's fin, and bring to a boil over high heat. Lower the heat and simmer for 20 minutes, leaving the lid cracked. Add the Smithfield ham and continue to simmer for 5 minutes more. Raise the heat to medium and slowly add the cornstarch mixture, stirring constantly with your other hand until the soup thickens. Turn off the heat, add the sesame oil, and serve the shark's fin in individual heated bowls.

continued

To serve in the Chinese manner, into each bowl, after the soup has been ladled, sprinkle some bean sprouts, what the Chinese call *ngon jum,* or "silver needles." Then add the red vinegar, usually 1 to 2 teaspoons per serving, depending on individual tastes.

CROSSING THE BRIDGE NOODLE SOUP

Guor Kiu Mai Fun Tong

A traditional soup from Hangzhou, with a tale. It is said that long ago in Hangzhou, a scholar studying for examinations that would advance him in the imperial court moved away from his home, wife, and family so he would have no distractions. To be away was to be "across a bridge." His wife would make this soup with noodles and carry it to him; thus its name.

6 ounces lean boneless pork loin, placed in the freezer until half frozen and sliced paper-thin
6 ounces large shrimp, shelled, deveined, each shrimp halved lengthwise, then sliced lengthwise into 4 thin slices each
1 quart Superior Stock (page 74)
1 quart water
½ pound dry rice noodles, soaked in hot water for 20 minutes and drained

1. Arrange the pork and shrimp slices at the bottoms of 4 individual large soup bowls.

2. Place the stock in a pot, cover, and bring to a rolling boil over high heat for 1 minute. At the same time, in another pot, bring the water to a boil over high heat. Add the noodles to the boiling water, immediately turn off the heat, and drain.

3. Pour the boiling stock into the bowls over the pork and shrimp. Divide the noodles equally among the 4 bowls. Serve with the following soy chili sauce to taste.

Soy Chili Sauce
2 fresh Thai chilies, minced
2 tablespoons soy sauce

1 tablespoon Sichuan Peppercorn Oil (page 86) or peanut oil

Combine the ingredients in a bowl and serve with the soup above.

SHREDDING

Thinly slice.

Cut the slices into a fine julienne
or "threads as fine as silk."

KNIFE-HOLDING TECHNIQUE

Grip the handle with a fistlike grip with the index finger
stretched out alongside the side of the flat blade to give it
guidance. With the other hand, anchor the food with
your fingers curled under and use your knuckles as a
guide for the thickness of the slice.

DICING

To cut into $1/4$-inch dice, first slice into $1/4$-inch slices. Cut the slices into $1/4$-inch matchsticks.

Cut the matchsticks into $1/4$-inch dice.

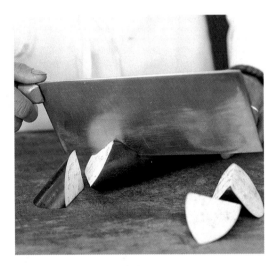

ROLL-CUT TECHNIQUE

Beginning at one end, cut the eggplant diagonally into approximately $3/4$-inch slices. Turn the eggplant one-quarter turn between each cut. The shape will be a kind of rounded, edged triangle the Chinese call fu tau, or the "axe."

BEEF WITH EGGPLANT

BEGGAR'S CHICKEN

*Use lotus leaves to wrap
the stuffed chicken.*

*Use the dough to wrap the lotus
wrapped chicken. Wrap the whole
thing in heavy-duty aluminum foil.*

*To serve, unwrap the foil and, using
kitchen shears, cut a hole in the top
through the dough and the lotus leaves.*

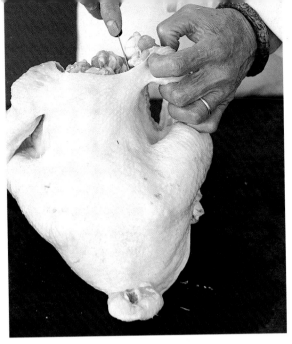

BONELESS STUFFED CHICKEN

To debone the chicken without breaking the skin: Set the chicken vertically on its tail and, using a sharp, pointed peeling knife, start loosening the skin around the neck cavity. Use the knife to cut the wing joint.

Detach both wings, but do not remove, and keep loosening the skin down the body of the bird.

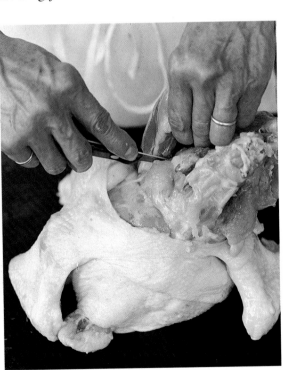

When the skin is halfway down the body of the bird, cut along the backbone but do not remove yet. Cut both breastbone joints and remove the entire breastbone with the meat on it.

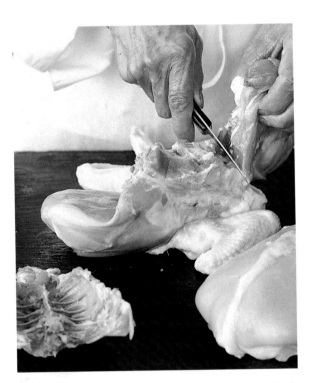

Cut out the backbone and remove. Cut both thigh joints and remove the thighs with the meat on them.

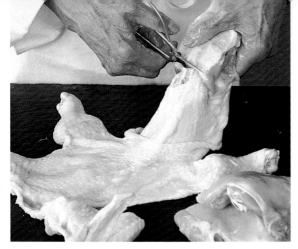

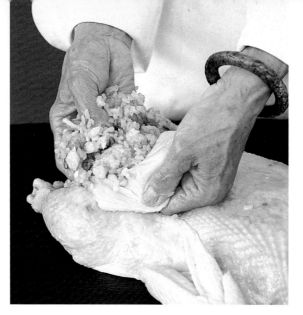

Use the kitchen shears to cut the last piece of back-bone off, making sure you leave the tailbone intact. Cut the drumsticks in half crosswise and remove the larger end. Sew up the neck with a needle and thick nylon thread. Now the chicken is ready to stuff. The meat from the thighs, drumsticks, and breastbone should be removed from the bone, cut into 1/4-inch dice, prepared and added to the stuffing mixture.

Use a Chinese strainer to carefully lower the stuffed chicken into the hot oil.

Using your hands, insert handfuls of stuffing into the body cavity. When stuffed, use a needle and thick nylon thread to sew up the tail opening. Use your hands to plump it so that it looks like the chicken before it was boned.

BONELESS STUFFED CHICKEN

SALT-BAKED CHICKEN

Heat the salt in the oven for about 1/2 hour before using. Spread a layer of hot salt in the bottom of the Dutch oven, form a shallow well, and nestle the chicken into it. Cover the chicken with the remaining salt.

Wearing oven mitts, push off the hot salt and lift out the cooked chicken. Unwrap the lotus leaves and discard.

SALT-BAKED CHICKEN

EMPEROR'S FISH

To score, hold the cleaver at an angle and cut slits into the flesh to the bone but not through the bone.

Insert the mushrooms and slices of ham into the slits.

Place the fish into a steamproof dish, pour over the marinade to cover, and steam.

RED COOKED
PORK SHOULDER

*Using a Chinese strainer, carefully lower
the marinated pork shoulder into the hot oil.*

*Use a ladle to carefully spoon the hot oil
over the pork shoulder.*

RED COOKED PORK SHOULDER

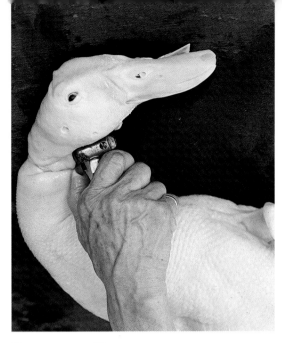

PEKING DUCK

Place the air pump nozzle into the neck opening under the tie. Start pumping to separate the skin from the meat.

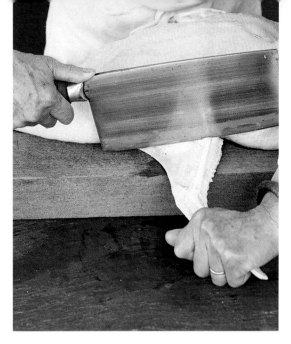

Cut the first two wing joints off with a cleaver.

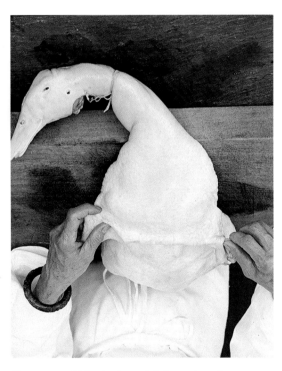

Insert one 7-inch chopstick into the wing opening, pushing it through the back of the bird between the meat and the skin and out through the other wing hole. Now the duck is ready for scalding.

Holding the duck over a large pot or wok of boiling water, ladle the hot liquid over the duck to scald. Let hang to dry for 1/2 hour. Repeat the scalding process with the coating liquid. Hang the duck over a pan to catch the drippings. Air-dry for 6 hours with an electric fan blowing.

FOR THE PANCAKES: *Flatten the balls of dough with the palm of your hand and use your fingers to brush sesame oil on one side of one round of dough. Place another round of dough on top and using your hands, press the 2 rounds together. Roll out to a 7-inch pancake.*

Heat a dry wok over medium heat until very hot. Place the pancake in the wok and cook on one side for 45 seconds. Turn it over using your fingers or a spatula. After 45 seconds to 1 minute it should begin to puff up. When it is all puffed up, remove to a plate.

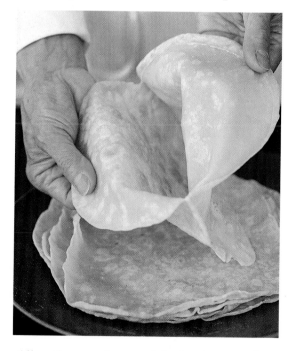

Allow the pancake to cool for 1 minute and then peel apart to make 2 pancakes.

TO SERVE PEKING DUCK: *Place a pancake in a dish and using a scallion brush, brush on hoisin sauce. Place 2 to 3 pieces of duck skin and the scallion brush on the pancake and fold.*

SALT-BAKED SHRIMP

*Lightly coat the shrimp in cornstarch
and place in a Chinese strainer before
stir frying.*

SALT-BAKED SHRIMP

BAKED PORK BUNS

*Hold a round of dough in one hand. Press
with fingers to create a well. Scoop a portion of filling into the round. Wrap the
dough up around the filling, turning the
bun and using your thumb to keep the
filling inside. Press with your hand to
continue closing until you have a knob of
dough at the top. Twist it off and place
the bun upside down on wax paper.*

BAKED PORK BUNS

SPRING ROLLS

Place the spring roll skin in a diamond shape with the point facing you. On the corner closest to you, place 2 tablespoons of filling in a 3-inch line. Lift the corner closest to you and start rolling very tightly.

Before you roll it up halfway, dip your fingers in beaten egg, wet the edges of the wrapper, and fold up the left and right sides to the center.

Brush the exposed area with egg again and continue to roll up to finish.

DEEP-FRIED SPRING ROLLS

STEAMED PORK BUNS

Flatten a round of dough. Holding it in one hand, scoop the filling onto the round.

Wrap the dough up around the filling. Use your fingers to pleat and close the bun.

Twist and pinch off the last bit of dough and place the bun, pinch side up, on a piece of wax paper.

The top of the bun will open while steaming.

WON TON

Holding the won ton skin in one hand, spoon on some of the filling and pat it down to flatten. Brush the edges with water to moisten.

Using two hands, fold the dough in half over the filling.

Use your fingers to seal the edges closed.

Wet two corners to bring them together. Overlap the corners and pinch them so they adhere.

WON TON SOUP

SHRIMP DUMPLINGS

Use the wheat starch tapioca dough for this recipe. Press the ball of dough down with your hand to flatten. Oil the blade of the cleaver so it won't stick to the dough. Using the flat side of the blade, press the dough down in a half circle, turning to flatten thin. Repeat in the opposite direction, forming a 3-inch round. If necessary, repeat the flattening motion.

Holding the skin in one hand, place some filling in the center and press it down to flatten. Fold the dumpling into a half-moon shape but do not close. Use your fingers to pleat only one side, sealing it closed.

STEAMED SHRIMP DUMPLINGS

CHIVE DUMPLINGS

Using the same dough and technique as for shrimp dumplings, flatten the dough into a 4-inch round. The rounds should be a little bit thicker than the shrimp dumpling rounds. Holding the skin in one hand, place some filling in the center and pat it down to flatten. Gather up the sides of the dough around the filling.

Press to close flat between thumb and forefinger. Turn the dumpling and pinch between the thumb and forefinger again. Pinch off the extra knob of dough. Place upside down on an oiled steamer.

Siu Mai

Holding a round dumpling skin in one hand, place some filling in the center and pat it down to flatten.

Use your fingers to fold u the sides while turning and flattening the filling on the top. Continue turning and flattening until the basket shape is formed. The diameter should be about $1/4$ inch across. Tap the bottom to flatten and place in an oiled steamer.

STEAMED SIU MAI

FISH CONGEE

ROLLED FISH
WITH OYSTERS

Following page:
CRABS WITH STEAMED
GLUTINOUS RICE

Previous page:
DOUBLE-BOILED CHICKEN WITH HONEY DATES

SNOW PEA SOUP WITH TWO EGGS

FISH WRAPPED IN BEAN CURD SHEETS

POACHED PEARS WITH HONEY,
LEMON BALM, AND RAISINS

STEAMED PEACHES
WITH HONEY DATES

HAINANESE CHICKEN RICE

From the top:
UNCOOKED GLUTINOUS RICE, RED WINE RICE, WINE PILLS, WINE RICE, UNCOOKED RED RICE

Opposite page:
CHINESE COOKING UTENSILS

a. stainless-steel strainer
b. Chinese strainer
c. Chinese ladle
d. clay pot for stock or congee
e. stainless-steel steamer
f. bamboo steamers
g. earthenware crock
h. sand clay pots
i. wok with cover and wok ring
j. Chinese spatula
k. Chinese kitchen shears
l. small grater
m. wok brush
n. bamboo steamer for dim sum

a

b

c

d

e

f

g

h

i

j

k

l

m

n

CHINESE WINES AND SPIRITS

TAINAN NOODLE SOUP

Tainan Tan Tsu Mien

A traditional soup from the town of Tainan, in southern Taiwan, where it was created in a small noodle shop called Du Shao Yueh. This soup became so famous, it is said, that people would journey, many days, from all over Taiwan simply to enjoy a bowl of it. The words tan tsu *indicate the old way of carrying things in China, at both ends of a bamboo pole balanced on the shoulders, in this case the wok and stove at one end, the food on the other. As with most of these dishes of tradition, special work is involved. But as with others, the result is surely worth the effort.*

6 ounces lean ground pork for garnish
¼ teaspoon baking soda
½ teaspoon salt
½ teaspoon sugar
1 teaspoon Shao-Hsing wine or dry
   sherry
2 teaspoons beaten egg white
1 teaspoon sesame oil
2 teaspoons cornstarch
Pinch freshly ground white pepper
1½ cups peanut oil

For the meatballs
½ pound lean ground pork
½ teaspoon grated fresh ginger
1 teaspoon Shao-Hsing wine or dry
   sherry
1 teaspoon sesame oil
1 tablespoon beaten egg white
½ teaspoon salt
1 teaspoon sugar
½ teaspoon soy sauce
1½ tablespoons cornstarch
Pinch freshly ground white pepper

1 quart Chicken Stock (page 75)
2 quarts cold water
½ pound egg noodles (vermicelli #11)
½ pound medium shrimp (about 24),
   shelled and deveined
¼ pound chive flowers (2-inch pieces
   with flowers)
1 teaspoon minced garlic
1 tablespoon preserved horse beans with
   chili or Chili Sauce (page 88)
2 tablespoons finely sliced green parts
   of scallion
1 tablespoon sesame oil

1. To make the pork garnish, toss the pork with the baking soda and allow to sit for 30 minutes. Add the salt, sugar, wine, egg white, sesame oil, cornstarch, and white pepper and mix together well to blend. Heat the peanut oil to 350°F in a wok. Stir in the pork mixture, loosen with a spatula, and fry until golden brown and crisp. Remove the mixture from the oil, drain, and reserve.

2. To make the meatballs, place the pork and all other meatball ingredients in a bowl. Mix well, stirring in one direction, until blended. Pick up the mass and throw back into the

bowl. Repeat 10 to 12 times. This strengthens the consistency. Form the mixture into 24 small meatballs.

3. Place the stock in a large pot, cover, and bring to a boil over high heat. Add the meatballs, cover, and bring back to a boil. Boil for 2 minutes. When the meatballs float to the top, they are done.

4. As the meatballs are cooking, prepare the noodles. Bring the cold water to a boil. Add the noodles and stir, loosening them. Cook for 30 seconds, until al dente. Turn off the heat, run cold water into the pot, and drain. Repeat. Remove the noodles with a strainer and drain over a bowl. Divide the noodles among 6 large soup bowls.

5. Add the shrimp, chive flowers, garlic, preserved horse beans, scallion, and sesame oil to the meatball soup and bring to a boil for 20 seconds. Turn off the heat. Ladle the soup and meatballs into the bowls over the noodles. Garnish each bowl with the reserved fried pork and serve.

MAKES 6 SERVINGS

SINGAPORE NOODLES

Sing Jau Chau Mai Fan

*T*his dish is an example of the openness of the greater Chinese table. Its curried antecedents are rooted in India, the Malay Peninsula and Indonesia, and earlier India. The Cantonese welcomed all of these influences, adapted them to the Chinese way of cooking, and have made this preparation a classic of their kitchen. Many versions of this exist, some with greater or lesser concentrations of curry, some with egg, some with chicken, but this is the classic way to make Singapore noodles.

2 quarts hot water
6 ounces very fine dry rice noodles

For the curry mixture
1 tablespoon peanut oil
1 garlic clove, minced

1½ tablespoons curry powder mixed
   with 1½ tablespoons cold water
2½ tablespoons cold water
2 beef bouillon cubes

¼ cup peanut oil
One ¼-inch-thick slice fresh ginger
½ cup julienned celery
⅓ cup julienned carrot
2 fresh water chestnuts, peeled and
   julienned
½ cup julienned green bell pepper
½ cup mung bean sprouts
3 scallions, trimmed and cut into
   1½-inch pieces
1 garlic clove, minced
6 large shrimp, shelled, deveined, and
   quartered
¾ cup julienned Barbecued Pork
   (page 124)
1 tablespoon oyster sauce

1. Prepare the noodles at least 2½ hours before assembling this preparation. Place 2 quarts hot water in a bowl. Place the rice noodles in water and allow to soak for 20 minutes. Drain off the water. Loosen the noodles and drain to dry.

2. To make the curry mixture, heat the peanut oil in a saucepan over high heat. Add the garlic and stir. When the garlic browns, add the curry mixed with water. Stir and cook for 1 minute. Add the cold water and mix. Add the bouillon cubes. Cover and cook for 10 to 15 minutes, stirring 3 to 4 times, until smoothly blended. Set aside.

3. Heat a wok over high heat for 30 seconds, add 1 tablespoon of the peanut oil, and coat the wok with a spatula. When a wisp of white smoke appears, add the ginger and stir for 30 seconds. Add all the vegetables and cook, stirring, for 2 to 3 minutes, until their colors brighten. Remove from the wok and reserve.

4. Wipe the wok and spatula clean. Heat the wok over high heat for 20 seconds, add another tablespoon of the peanut oil, and coat the wok with it using a spatula. When a wisp of white smoke appears, add the garlic. When the garlic turns light brown, add the shrimp and cook, stirring, for 20 seconds, until the shrimp turn pink. Add the pork and cook, stirring, for 30 seconds. Add the oyster sauce, mix well, then add the reserved curry mixture and stir together well. Turn off the heat, remove the contents of the wok, and reserve.

5. Wipe the wok and spatula clean. Heat the wok over high heat for 45 seconds, add the remaining 2 tablespoons peanut oil, and coat the wok with it using the spatula. When a wisp of white smoke appears, slide the noodles into the wok and loosen with chop-sticks. If they start to burn, lower the heat. Cook for 5 minutes, until very hot, then add the shrimp-pork-curry mixture and combine well with the noodles. Add the reserved vegetables and stir to mix thoroughly. When combined, turn off the heat, transfer to a heated platter, and serve.

MAKES 4 TO 6 SERVINGS

*A*mong China's regional cuisines, those covering broad areas of the country and those nestled into small niches, none are of more historical interest or more enticing than two from southern China. One, the Chiu Chow cooking of a small region around Swatow, now Shantou; the second, the cooking of the Hakka, which evolved from the experiences of these Chinese nomads.

The Chiu Chow, centered in the coastal city of Shantou, were seafarers, and they are to be found in Taiwan and elsewhere along China's coast, as well in cities in Southeast Asia. Though they are referred to as Chiu Chau, Ch'ao Chou, Chaozhou, Teochiu, or Teochew, depending on where they are, they refer to themselves as Chiu Chow, at home and in Hong Kong, where they live by the millions. I shall therefore defer to them and call them Chiu Chow.

The cooking of the Chiu Chow, long overlooked, has become more familiar in recent years. Once thought to be simply another facet of Cantonese cooking, which it is by geography, it truly is unique, what I have called in other of my writings a defined gastronomic subculture. This is cooking that is pungent and direct. The Chiu Chow relish those delicacies of China, shark fin's and sweet bird's nest soups. Their soups, largely of seafood, are flavored with their fish sauce, strong and salty, virtually identical to the nam pla of Thailand, the nuoc mam of Vietnam, to which they have historically migrated, and with whose people they have intermarried. The Chiu Chow love sweet marmalades and preserves. They preserve cabbages and mustard pickles in salt; they pickle shallots and ginger and pack mustard greens and garlic in earthenware pots. They flavor with ginger and with what they call lam geung, or "southern ginger," about the size and shape of common ginger, but with an aroma like galangal, that "sand ginger." They bottle their own white rice vinegar, tangerine oil, and a "sweet soy" made by cooking soy sauce with sugar. They drink tiny cups of bitter "iron goddess" teas to heighten their appetites and after meals to digest them.

Perhaps what the Chiu Chow are best known for in terms of food is a particular preparation that is both stock and sauce, lo soi, which translates as "old water." This is a mother sauce that is used over and over, through the years, replenished by the poultry and seasonings that are cooked in it. There are chefs I know who have had lo soi for nearly fifty years, who carry it with them from restaurant to restaurant. All one need do is start one. ◆

LO SOI
Old Water

Once made, this stock-sauce may be kept and used indefinitely, its flavor continually enhanced by the geese, ducks, and chickens cooked in it. This recipe is the legacy of Chef Lui Sum Hon of Hong Kong, who has lived for more than 75 years and cooked for most of them. His lo soi *is half a century old.*

Three 3-inch cinnamon sticks
5 pieces eight-star anise
¾ teaspoon Sichuan peppercorns
¾ teaspoon whole cloves
2 teaspoons fennel seeds
1 whole nutmeg

8 pieces licorice root
One 3-inch-long piece fresh ginger, lightly smashed
4 pieces sand ginger (galangal)
4 pounds fresh boneless pork butt or shoulder in one piece
14 cups cold water
2½ cups double dark soy sauce, regular dark soy sauce, or mushroom soy sauce
1½ cups soy sauce
¼ cup Mei Kuei Lu Chiew or gin
1 pound rock sugar or light or dark brown sugar

1. Wrap all the spices, from cinnamon to sand ginger, in cheesecloth and sew closed.

2. Wrap the pork in cheesecloth and sew closed.

3. In a large, covered stockpot, bring the water, spice package, and wrapped pork to a boil over high heat. Reduce the heat, leave the lid cracked, and simmer for 3 hours. Turn off the heat, remove the pork, and save for another use. (It will be an enjoyable meal.)

4. Add the soy sauces, Mei Kuei Lu Chiew, and sugar to the pot. Raise the heat back to high and bring to a boil. Stir to make certain all ingredients are blended and the sugar is dissolved. The *lo soi* is ready for use.

LO SOI
MY ALTERNATIVE

All ingredients remain the same, including the spice package, but replace the pork and the 3½ quarts cold water with 1½ quarts of my Chicken Stock (page 75) and 1½ quarts cold water. Boil for 30 minutes, add the soy sauces, Mei Kuei Lu Chiew, and sugar, and return to a boil. Stir to make certain the sugar is dissolved. My version of *lo soi* is ready.

BOTH RECIPES MAKE ABOUT 3 QUARTS

NOTE: *Chiu Chow chefs never store* lo soi, *never remove it from the pot, for it is always in use. For the rest of us, it should be stored, refrigerated, in a closed container. Each month it should be removed, placed in a pot, and boiled for 5 minutes, then allowed to return to room temperature before being returned to the refrigerator. So treated, it will last for at least a year. Until it is used the first time, the spice package should remain in the* lo soi. *Also, each time it is used, taste it. You may wish to replenish spices, soy sauce, rose spirits, or sugar.*

LO SOI DUCK

Lo Soi Op

A simple preparation, transformed into a classic treasure by the lo soi, a dish with a deep, intense flavor that transcends its name, which translates as "old water duck." A goose or chicken may be cooked in this as well, with no alteration of the recipe.

One 5-pound duck, feet removed, head on, or a freshly killed, beheaded duck
3 quarts Lo Soi (preceding recipe), spice package retained

1. Place a rack at the bottom of a large pot. Place the duck on the rack. Pour in the *lo soi.* The duck should be completely immersed. Cover the pot, raise the heat to high, and bring to a boil. Reduce the heat, leave the lid cracked, and simmer for 1¾ to 2 hours, turning the duck 2 or 3 times.

2. Turn off the heat and cover the pot. Allow the duck to rest in the liquid for 30 minutes. Remove the duck, cut into bite-sized pieces, and serve with vinegar ginger dip.

Vinegar Ginger Dip
2 teaspoons Chinese white rice vinegar or distilled vinegar
2 teaspoons grated fresh ginger
½ teaspoon sugar
4 teaspoons water
Pinch salt

Mix together all of the ingredients in a bowl.

MAKES 10 SERVINGS

CHINJIEW CHICKEN
Chinjiew Gai

This traditional Chiu Chow dish uses 2 ingredients that these southern people dote on: chinjiew, *their term for Sichuan peppercorns, and green leaves, shaped quite like small maple leaves, which the Chiu Chow call* jun jiu choi, *or "pearl vegetable." These grow wild and are fried, as garnishes, with many of their dishes. These are simply unavailable outside of their region, so large leafed basil is usually used in their stead.*

For the marinade
1 teaspoon double dark soy sauce, regular dark soy sauce, or mushroom soy sauce
1 teaspoon Thai fish sauce
1 teaspoon sugar
1 large egg white, beaten
1½ teaspoons sesame oil
1 tablespoon oyster sauce
½ teaspoon ginger juice

1 teaspoon Shao-Hsing wine or dry sherry
3 tablespoons cornstarch

1 pound boneless, skinless chicken breasts, cut into 1-inch cubes

For the sauce
1 teaspoon oyster sauce
½ teaspoon sugar
1¼ teaspoons cornstarch
3 tablespoons Superior Stock (page 74) or Chicken Stock (page 75)

1 teaspoon Sichuan peppercorns
3 cups peanut oil
1 cup basil leaves, washed and well dried
3 scallions, trimmed and finely sliced
1 tablespoon Shao-Hsing wine or dry sherry

1. In a large bowl, combine the marinade ingredients. Place the chicken in the marinade and allow to rest 30 minutes. In another bowl, combine the sauce ingredients and reserve.

2. Dry-roast the peppercorns in a skillet over high heat for 30 seconds, reduce the heat, and toss for 2 minutes, until they become dark. Transfer to a bowl to cool. Crush or grind coarsely, then reserve.

3. Place the oil in a wok and heat to 300°F. Quickly deep-fry half of the basil leaves for 45 seconds, until crisp and bright green, turning once. Drain on paper towels. Repeat with the remaining leaves. Reserve.

4. Raise the heat under the wok and bring the oil to 350°F. Add the chicken and marinade, spreading to prevent it from sticking together, and turn repeatedly until golden brown, about 3 minutes. Drain and reserve, keeping warm.

5. Drain all but 2 tablespoons of the peanut oil from the wok and heat for 20 seconds over high heat. When a wisp of white smoke appears, add two-thirds of the scallions and all the peppercorns and cook, stirring, for 45 seconds. Add the chicken and cook, stirring, for 1 minute. Add the wine and stir, turning the chicken to coat it. Make a well in the center of the mixture, stir the sauce, and pour in. Stir until the sauce is absorbed and the chicken well coated. Remove to a heated serving dish, arrange the fried basil leaves around the chicken, sprinkle with the remaining scallions, and serve.

MAKES 6 SERVINGS

SUPERIOR SOY NOODLES
See Yau Wong Chau Mien

*T*his traditional preparation is in every Chiu Chow kitchen and illustrates essentials of that cuisine. The combination of sugar and very dark soy sauce and the use of that exceedingly rich Superior Stock are distinctive among the Chiu Chow, so much so that they call attention to the dish with the words *superior soy.*

6 cups cold water
1 teaspoon salt
9 ounces fresh egg noodles, such as
    fettuccine

For the sauce
1½ teaspoons double dark soy sauce,
    regular dark soy sauce, or mushroom
    soy sauce

2½ teaspoons sugar
1½ teaspoons Thai fish sauce
1 tablespoon Shao-Hsing wine or dry
    sherry
2 teaspoons sesame oil
1 tablespoon oyster sauce
¼ cup Superior Stock (page 74) or
    Chicken Stock (page 75)

½ tablespoon black sesame seeds
3 tablespoons peanut oil
⅓ cup plus 2 tablespoons trimmed and
    finely sliced scallion
2 teaspoons minced garlic
2 teaspoons Tianjin preserved
    vegetable

1. Place the water and salt in a pot and bring to a boil over medium heat. Add the noodles and cook for 2 minutes or until al dente, stirring to separate them. Turn off the heat, run cold water into the pot, and drain. Run cold water again into the pot and drain in a strainer for 30 minutes, stirring occasionally to prevent sticking.

2. In a bowl, combine the sauce ingredients and reserve. Dry-roast the sesame seeds (see dry-roasting, page 63) and reserve.

3. Heat a wok over high heat for 30 seconds, add the peanut oil, and coat the wok with it using a spatula. When a wisp of white smoke appears, add ⅓ cup of the scallion, the garlic, and the preserved vegetable and stir together for 1 minute. Add the sauce to the wok and stir well. When the sauce bubbles, add the noodles, stir well, and simmer until all the sauce is absorbed. Turn off the heat and sprinkle the noodles with the roasted sesame seeds. Transfer to a heated serving dish, garnish with the remaining 2 tablespoons of scallion, and serve.

MAKES 4 TO 6 SERVINGS

THE HAKKA

The Hakka are China's historic wanderers. Originally from the North, they were persecuted initially by the Mongols and driven from their homes. Over the centuries they became China's "guest people," often not welcomed into other cities and regions, often victims of prejudice. Eventually they settled in the Southern area of China, below Guangzhou, Canton, and elsewhere in the province of Guangdong, and in the New Territories area adjacent to Hong Kong. Their circumstances dictated that they would be insular, wary of outsiders, and dedicated to succeeding economically, for this became the path to acceptance. They have succeeded. They are recognized as shrewd and tenacious businesspeople, and to this day many Hakka still live in small walled communities by themselves.

Their distinctive cooking is a culinary evolution, formed by their nomadic history. They had no permanent homes, no permanent stoves. But they had the land and the water, even though often only temporarily, and this was reflected in their food. They ate what they caught from the sea, what they raised in herds, what they grew, and they absorbed cooking methods, as well as prepared foods, from those with whom they came in contact. Because they found their most permanent welcome in the South, around Canton, their food, like that of their fairly close neighbors, the Chiu Chow, has similarities to the Cantonese kitchen. But there are important differences. They preserved vegetables so they could be portable. They boiled vegetables and ate them with cold sauces so that they would not have to be heated. They boiled soybeans, drank their exuded milk, ate their curd.

The Hakka are willing to eat virtually anything and prefer strong flavors, fried foods, and saltiness. They boast few banquet and festive dishes, but there are a few, one that is a glorious, elaborate treasure known as Eight-Jewel Duck.

EIGHT-JEWEL STUFFED DUCK

Bot Boh Cheun Op

For the Hakka this is important and symbolic. It must have 8 ingredients stuffed into it, these to represent the 8 auspicious signs of Buddha, the 8 organs of his body, the 8 immortals of Taoism, the 8 famous horses of Mu Wang of the Chou dynasty, the 8 paths to everlasting happiness. A most noble, meaningful presentation, yet favorable and beautiful as well.

One 5- to 5½-pound duck, freshly killed, head and neck cut off where they meet the body
¼ cup salt for rubbing into duck
2 cups glutinous rice
2 cups Chicken Stock (page 75)
¾ cup lotus seeds
1 quart cold water
1½ tablespoons peanut oil
1 teaspoon minced fresh ginger
¼ teaspoon salt
½ pound shrimp, shelled, deveined, and cut into ¼-inch dice

2 teaspoons Chinese white rice vinegar or distilled vinegar
3 teaspoons Shao-Hsing wine or dry sherry
½ cup peeled and diced fresh water chestnuts
½ cup dried Chinese black mushrooms (6 to 8), soaked in hot water for 30 minutes, washed, stems discarded, and cut into ¼-inch dice
4 scallions, trimmed and finely sliced
¼ cup diced bamboo shoot
3 tablespoons oyster sauce
1½ tablespoons sesame oil
2½ teaspoons soy sauce
2 teaspoons dark soy sauce
1½ tablespoons sugar
2 teaspoons minced garlic
⅛ teaspoon freshly ground white pepper
2 tablespoons dark soy sauce, to coat duck for roasting

1. Clean the duck thoroughly and remove any fat and membranes. Wash under cold running water and drain. Sprinkle the outside with the ¼ cup salt, rub in, rinse, and drain.

2. Wash and drain the glutinous rice 4 times. After washing the last time, drain thoroughly through a strainer. Place the rice in a cake pan with the stock, place in a steamer, cover, and steam for 30 to 45 minutes (see steaming, page 64). When cooked, remove and transfer the rice to a large bowl.

3. Place the lotus seeds and cold water in a pot and bring to a boil over high heat. Lower the heat, partially cover the pot, and simmer for 1½ hours, until tender. Drain and reserve. (Alternately, use 1 cup canned cooked lotus seeds. Though fresh are preferred, canned are adequate.)

4. To prepare the shrimp, heat the wok over high heat for 45 seconds, add the peanut oil, and coat the wok with it using a spatula. When a wisp of white smoke appears, add the ginger and salt. Stir for 30 seconds and add the shrimp. Spread in a thin layer. When they begin to turn pink, turn over and cook, stirring, until they completely change color, about 1½ minutes. Turn off the heat, remove from the wok, and reserve.

5. Bone the duck. This is a bit difficult. The object is to remove its bones but keep the meat and skin intact. Set the duck upright, as if in a sitting position. The head and neck have been removed. With a sharp paring knife, loosen and remove the fat and gristle around the neck area. Keep the meat and skin intact. Cut into the wing joint to loosen, and detach the wishbone and breastbone. Work the wishbone out of the bird with care. Work to remove the shoulder blade and small backbones from the spinal column. Detach the rib cage joint from the breast plate. Once the plate is removed, the rest of the boning will be easier. You must gently tease and work the meat from the breast plate. Slowly detach the skin from the back, working downward to the legs. Detach the thighs from the backbone by cutting through the joint. Work, carefully cutting both sides, continuing to pull the skin back over the hip bone. Pull the skin over the legs. It should begin to come off easily of its own accord. Keep working the skin carefully so it does not tear.

   Using kitchen shears, cut through the tailbone and pull the skin completely off from the backbone. To remove the thighbone, slowly cut the meat from the thighbone. Cut through the joint and remove. Leave the drumstick in place. Pull off all excess fat from the skin. Cut off the wing tips. (Do not become frustrated if in the course of your work you make slight tears in the skin. It happens to everybody. Simply sew the holes with needle and thread.)

6. At this point, coat the duck, inside and out, with a mixture of white vinegar and wine. Sew the neck opening closed. To the bowl of cooked glutinous rice, add the shrimp, lotus seeds, water chestnuts, mushrooms, scallions, bamboo shoot, oyster sauce, sesame oil, soy sauces, sugar, garlic, and white pepper. Mix together by hand until well blended. Stuff the mixture into the duck cavity. Sew the duck closed. Pat the duck into its former shape. Coat thoroughly with dark soy sauce.

7. Heat the oven to 400°F for 20 minutes. Place the duck on a rack in a foil-lined roasting pan, place in the oven, and roast for 40 minutes. Turn the duck over and roast for 20 minutes. Lower the heat to 350°F and roast for another 20 minutes, until the duck is a deep brown color. Remove from the oven to a large serving platter. Slice across the duck as you would a terrine and serve.

MAKES 10 SERVINGS

NOTE: *Both boning and lotus seed preparations may be done a day ahead. If so, they must be covered and refrigerated.*

SALT-BAKED CHICKEN

Tum Guk Gai

This is the most famous dish of the Hakka people, a true classic. Traditionally the Hakka would dig a shallow hole in the earth, place the stones in it, heat them, and add the sea salt before placing the chicken in the hole, covering it, and baking it. There is less romance these days, to be sure, because a Dutch oven is perfect for cooking this preparation. It is often believed that this is a most salty dish; this is not so. The salt acts as the chicken's "oven" and imparts only a faint touch of salt to it. Unfortunately, this lovely dish is feigned these days; often a chicken is placed in a boiling water and salt solution and presented as salt-baked. Best to make it yourself, for it is not difficult.

One 3- to 3¼-pound chicken

¼ cup salt, for rubbing chicken

¾ teaspoon powdered sand ginger mixed with 2 tablespoons Shao-Hsing wine or dry sherry

2 scallions, trimmed, flattened with the flat of a cleaver blade, then each cut into 4 equal pieces

One ¼-inch-thick slice fresh ginger

One 1- by 2-inch piece dried tangerine peel, soaked in hot water for 30 minutes until soft

2 lotus leaves, soaked in hot water for 20 minutes until soft, washed, drained, and reserved

6 pounds kosher salt

1. Clean the chicken and remove any fat and membranes. Wash under cold running water and drain. Sprinkle the outside with the ¼ cup salt, rub in, rinse, drain, and pat dry with paper towels.

2. Rub the sand ginger–wine mixture inside the chicken cavity and out. Place the scallions, ginger, and tangerine peel inside the cavity. Wrap the chicken with overlapping lotus leaves to cover completely.

3. Heat the oven to 450°F. Place half of the kosher salt in a Dutch oven, the other half in a roasting pan. Place both the Dutch oven and the roasting pan in the oven. Allow the salt to become hot, about 30 minutes. Remove both from the oven. Make a shallow well in the salt in the Dutch oven and nestle the chicken into it. Pour the salt from the roasting pan over the chicken to cover.

4. Place the Dutch oven, uncovered, in the oven and roast the chicken for 1 hour and 10 minutes. Turn off the heat, remove from the oven, and allow the chicken to rest for 15

minutes. Remove the chicken from the salt to a large platter. Unwrap it and discard the lotus leaves. Chop the chicken into bite-sized pieces and serve with the following sauce.

Salt-Baked Chicken Sauce
3 tablespoons soy sauce
2 tablespoons peanut oil
1 teaspoon sesame oil
1 teaspoon Chinese red vinegar

1½ tablespoons finely julienned fresh
  ginger
1½ tablespoons finely julienned white
  part of scallion

Mix all the ingredients together and serve in small individual condiment dishes.

MAKES 6 TO 8 SERVINGS

PRESERVED VEGETABLE WITH FRESH BACON

Mui Choi Kau Yuk

This is truly a local classic. It is a preparation unique to the Hakka and is to be found nowhere else in China. For a Westerner the prospects of eating a fatty piece of pork can be less than appetizing, but some astonishing cooking chemistry occurs as this is cooked. Fat vanishes, and flavors are enhanced. In making this dish, I boil the fresh bacon rather than fry it as most Hakka would.

¼ pound preserved mustard greens
2½ pounds fresh, uncured bacon in
  1 piece
2 quarts cold water
5 ounces sugarcane sugar or brown
  sugar
3 tablespoons Shao-Hsing wine or dry
  sherry
1 cup mushroom soy sauce

1. Wash the preserved vegetable carefully and thoroughly to remove sand and salt. Remove each stalk, open the leaves, and wash 4 times.

continued

2. In a large oval Dutch oven, place all the ingredients except the mushroom soy sauce. Bring to a boil over high heat. Add the mushroom soy sauce and return to a boil. Cover the pot, reduce the heat, leave the lid cracked, and simmer for 3 hours. Test the bacon with a chopstick: If it goes easily into the bacon, it is done. If not, cook for another 30 minutes to an hour. When the meat is done, allow the pot to cool.

3. Remove the meat and vegetable to a large plate, allow to cool to room temperature, cover, and refrigerate for 8 hours or overnight. Reserve 1 cup of cooking liquid.

4. Remove the vegetable from the plate, cut into ⅛-inch slices, and make a bed of these in a steamproof dish. Slice the bacon across into ⅓-inch slices. Reassemble the slices atop the vegetable. Coat the bacon with the reserved cooking liquid to give it a dark coating. Place the dish in a steamer, cover, and steam for 30 minutes (see steaming, page 64). Turn off the heat, remove from the steamer, and serve with cooked rice.

MAKES 10 SERVINGS

HAKKA STUFFED BEAN CURD

Hakka Yeung Dau Fu

This is another Hakka staple, a tradi-tional food that is made in the several Hakka restaurants that exist in Hong Kong exactly the way it has been for hun-dreds of years. It is taken for granted that when you go for a meal in a Hakka restau-rant, this stuffed bean curd will be included.

6 ounces shrimp, shelled and deveined

For the shrimp filling
1 tablespoon dried shrimp, soaked in hot water for 20 minutes to soften, drained, dried, and minced
½ teaspoon ginger juice mixed with 1½ teaspoons Chinese white rice wine or gin
½ teaspoon soy sauce

1 teaspoon sesame oil
2 teaspoons oyster sauce
¼ teaspoon salt
¾ teaspoon sugar
½ large egg, beaten
Pinch freshly ground white pepper
1½ tablespoons cornstarch
3 scallions, trimmed and finely chopped

24 ounces (6 cakes) fresh bean curd (medium-firm tofu), drained well and thoroughly dried with paper towels
1 tablespoon tapioca flour
3 tablespoons peanut oil
2 tablespoons trimmed and sliced scallion

For the sauce
1½ tablespoons oyster sauce
2 teaspoons double dark soy sauce,
   regular dark soy sauce, or mushroom
   soy sauce

1 teaspoon sugar
Pinch freshly ground white pepper
1½ tablespoons cornstarch
1 cup Seafood Stock (page 76)

1. Chop the shrimp into a paste, place in a bowl, and add all the filling ingredients fromdried shrimp to finely chopped scallions. Mix thoroughly to blend well and refrigerate for 2 hours.

2. Cut each cake of bean curd diagonally and, with a pointed knife, cut out a pocket in the inside of the diagonal cross-cut section. Dust each pocket with tapioca flour, then fill with a tablespoon of the shrimp mixture. Pack smoothly with a knife or with your fingers.

3. Pour the peanut oil into a cast-iron skillet. Heat over high heat until a wisp of white smoke appears. With the diagonal stuffed side of the bean curd down, pan-fry the cakes over medium heat for 6 minutes. Turn the bean curd cakes and fry each side for 2 minutes. Turn the heat off, remove to a plate, and place in a warm oven.

4. To make the sauce, mix the sauce ingredients in a pot over medium heat, stirring continuously until the sauce thickens and bubbles. Turn off the heat, remove the stuffed bean curd from the oven, pour the sauce over them, sprinkle with sliced scallions, and serve.

MAKES 6 SERVINGS

Buddha
Jumps *over the* Wall:
A Singular Feast

佛跳牆宴慶

THIS IS PERHAPS THE ULTIMATE FEAST IN A LAND OF FEASTS, AMONG A PEOPLE WHO DEARLY LOVE FESTIVE FOODS AND THE TRADITIONS THAT OCCASION THEM. THIS GREAT DISH HAILS FROM FUZHOU, IN FUJIAN PROVINCE. IT REQUIRES AN ENORMOUS AMOUNT OF EFFORT, IS BEST MADE OVER A PERIOD OF TWO DAYS, AND CAN CONTAIN AS MANY AS THIRTY DIFFERENT MAIN INGREDIENTS. It is a perfect family endeavor, with many hands involved in its preparation and cooking. It can be described perhaps, though the description begs the dish, as a giant pot-au-feu, though it is infinitely more complex. Because of this complexity, because of the effort needed to make it, I have given it its own chapter, deservedly, because to eat it in the traditional way it must be part of a feast, with five accompanying side dishes, all from Fujian, which I have included.

As with many of China's culinary traditions, stories surround Buddha Jumps Over the Wall and its origins. In the last century of the Ching dynasty, it is said, a Fuzhou merchant, wishing to impress a high official whom he had invited to his home, asked his cook, together with the merchant's wife, a woman of Shanghai and knowledgeable in the ways of food, to create a special dish for the dinner. They hit on the idea of immersing chicken, duck, and pork in an earthenware crock with Shao-Hsing wine to cook it. A fine fragrance arose, the taste was equally fine, and the official was so taken with the dish that he is said to have raced home and ordered his cook to make the dish, an unsuccessful effort. So the official took his cook to confer with the merchant's cook. They spoke, and the official's cook, Jang Chun Fat, made the dish, adding many more ingredients, including shark's fin, sea cucumber, abalone, and dried scallops to it. This made him so famous that he left the official's employ and in 1877 opened his own restaurant, Joy Chun Yeun, in Fuzhou.

One day a scholar chanced to come to the restaurant, attracted, he said, by the fragrance of the cooking that went out of the restaurant and into the street. He tasted many dishes through the evening and then asked Chef Jang to create a special dish just for him.

Out came this dish of many ingredients, many layers, of rich aroma. What was it called, the scholar asked?

Chef Jang said it had no name. The scholar, it is said, thought, with eyes closed, then wrote his thoughts out and announced that it would henceforth be called Buddha Jumps over the Wall. Why? Because, even though Buddha is a vegetarian, the smells of this dish would be so overpowering that Buddha would forget his beliefs, would race to Fuzhou, even jump a wall, just to taste it. Is that not a fine story?

Traditionally, Buddha Jumps over the Wall can have as many as thirty main ingredients, as I have said. My version has more than twenty. I have omitted fish lips, sea cucumber, fish stomach, pork tendon, pork stomach, and duck gizzards, some of which were probably in Chef Jang's Fuzhou dish. Different versions exist, however. I have divided the preparation and cooking into two days, and I believe that if you approach this dish in a spirit of adventure, even as a group cooking party, you will enjoy yourself immensely.

BUDDHA JUMPS OVER THE WALL
Fat Tiu Cheung

Day 1

¼ pound shark's fin

2 tablespoons white vinegar

1 cup Superior Stock (page 74)

¼ cup Shao-Hsing wine or dry sherry

2 ounces lard or peanut oil

One ½-inch-thick slice fresh ginger, lightly smashed

3 scallions, white parts only

4 whole abalone

1 cup Superior Stock (page 74)

2 tablespoons Shao-Hsing wine or dry sherry

4 dry scallops, each 1 inch in diameter

2 tablespoons Shao-Hsing wine or dry sherry, for scallops

12 quail eggs

3 small fresh bamboo shoots (1½ pounds)

1 quart cold water, for bamboo shoots

One 4-pound chicken

¼ cup salt

One 4-pound duck

¼ cup salt

1½ pounds pork feet (3 halves), each half cut into 4 pieces by butcher

2 pounds lamb filet

2½ pounds pork (fresh ham)

1 pound Smithfield ham

2 quarts cold water, for Smithfield ham

12 Chinese black mushrooms

Day 2

3½ cups peanut oil

2½ pounds Chinese turnips, peeled, both ends discarded, cut into 4 pieces lengthwise, then into 1-inch pieces

1 pound carrots (3 large), peeled, cut into 1-inch sections

Four 3-inch-long cinnamon sticks

4 pieces eight-star anise

6 scallions, trimmed and cut into thirds

5 cups Shao-Hsing wine or dry sherry

7 cups Chicken Stock (page 75)

6 ounces rock sugar (rock candy)

½ cup plus 3 tablespoons double dark soy sauce, regular dark soy sauce, or mushroom soy sauce

1 cup Superior Stock (page 74) or Chicken Stock (page 75)

4 bamboo leaves, soaked in hot water for 20 minutes, until softened, and washed

1 large lotus leaf, soaked in hot water for 20 minutes until softened, washed, and dried

continued

DAY 1

1. To prepare the shark's fin, the night before, soak the fins in a bowl of water with the white vinegar for at least 4 to 6 hours, rinse, and drain. Place the soaked shark's fins in a steamproof dish with the stock, wine, lard, ginger, and scallions and steam for 30 minutes (see steaming, page 64). Turn off the heat, discard the ginger and scallions, strain off and discard the liquid, and reserve overnight, refrigerated.

2. To prepare the abalone, the night before (at the same time you soak the shark's fins), wash the abalone, place in a pot with 3 quarts water, bring to a boil over medium heat, lower the heat, and simmer for 10 minutes. Turn off the heat and allow to rest in the liquid in the pot overnight. Place the abalone in a steamproof dish with the stock and wine and steam for 1½ to 2 hours, until softened. Discard the liquid and reserve the abalone overnight, refrigerated.

3. To prepare the scallops, place the scallops and wine in a steamproof dish and steam for 20 minutes, until softened. Turn off the heat, discard the liquid, and reserve the scallops overnight, refrigerated.

4. To prepare the quail eggs, cook them in boiling water for about 7 minutes, until hard-boiled. Remove from the pot and cool. Shell and reserve overnight, refrigerated. Remove from the refrigerator and allow to come to room temperature on Day 2.

5. To prepare the bamboo shoots, remove all outer husks down to the tender, cream-white core. Place the whole shoots in a pot with the water, cover, and bring to a boil over high heat. If very tender, simmer for 7 minutes; if a bit tough, simmer for 20 minutes. Turn off the heat, run cold water into the pot, and drain. Allow to cool, cut each shoot lengthwise into 4 pieces, and reserve overnight, refrigerated.

6. To prepare the chicken, wash and remove the fat and membranes. Rinse under cold running water and drain. Sprinkle the outside with the salt and rub in well. Rinse, drain, and dry. Cut the chicken into 12 pieces and reserve overnight, refrigerated.

7. To prepare the duck, prepare precisely as the chicken in the preceding step.

8. To prepare the pork feet, cut up the pork feet, if necessary, and reserve overnight, refrigerated.

9. To prepare the lamb and pork, cut the lamb into 12 equal pieces and reserve refrigerated, overnight. Cut the pork into 12 equal pieces and reserve refrigerated, overnight.

10. To prepare the Smithfield ham, place the ham and the water in a pot, cover, and bring to a boil over medium heat. Lower the heat to medium and simmer for 30 minutes. Turn off the heat, allow to rest in the liquid, and return to room temperature. Remove, discard the liquid, cut into 12 equal pieces, and reserve, refrigerated, overnight.

11. To prepare the mushrooms, soak the mushrooms in hot water for 30 minutes, until softened. Wash, drain, remove the stems, and reserve overnight, refrigerated.

DAY 2

1. Heat a wok over high heat for 1 minute. Add the peanut oil and heat to 350°F. Place the turnips in a Chinese strainer and lower into the oil. Blanch for 2 minutes, remove, drain over a bowl, and reserve. Bring the oil back to 350°F, blanch the carrots and bamboo shoots similarly for 3 minutes, remove and drain, and reserve. Bring the oil again to 350°F, add the quail eggs to the wok, and deep-fry for 2 minutes or until the eggs brown lightly. Remove, strain, and reserve.

2. Remove all but 2 tablespoons of the oil from the wok and set aside. Heat the wok over high heat for 20 seconds. When a wisp of white smoke appears, add 2 cinnamon sticks, 2 pieces of star anise, and half the scallions. Stir-fry until the fragrance is released, about 1 minute. Add the reserved chicken and duck, stir, and cook for 5 minutes. Turn off the heat, remove the entire contents of the wok to a bowl, and reserve.

3. Wash the wok and spatula. Heat the wok over high heat for 1 minute. Add the 3 tablespoons of the reserved peanut oil and coat the wok with it using a spatula. When a wisp of white smoke appears, add the remaining cinnamon, anise, and scallions and stir for 1 minute. Add the pork feet, lamb, and pork and cook, stirring, for 5 minutes. Turn off the heat.

4. Place the contents of the wok into a large pot. Add the wine, chicken stock, and rock sugar and stir. Cover and bring to a boil over medium heat. Add ½ cup of the soy sauce and stir well. Lower the heat and simmer for 30 minutes. Raise the heat to high, add the reserved chicken and duck and the contents of the bowl, and simmer for 15 minutes. Turn off the heat. Allow all the contents of the pot to rest in the liquid for 10 minutes. Empty the contents into a bowl, including the cooking liquid, discard the scallions, and allow to cool sufficiently to handle.

5. While all the meats are cooking, place the reserved blanched turnips, carrots, and bamboo shoots in a wok. Add the superior stock. Raise the heat to high, mix well, stirring, and bring to a boil. Add the remaining 3 tablespoons soy sauce and stir. Lower the heat and simmer for 5 minutes. Turn off the heat, strain, and reserve. Reserve the liquid for another use.

6. Wrap the reserved shark's fin, abalone, scallops, and Smithfield ham in cheesecloth. Sew or tie to close.

continued

7. For this final step, a large pot, about 3-gallon capacity, should be used. Pour 2 cups of reserved cooking liquid from the bowl into the pot. Place a rack on the bottom and cover with bamboo leaves trimmed to fit the shape of the rack. Begin layering the ingredients.

   Place the pork feet in a single layer on the bamboo leaf–lined rack. Place a single layer of lamb atop the pork feet. Place a single layer of chicken atop the lamb. Place a single layer of duck atop the chicken. Place a single layer of pork atop the duck. Place the cheesecloth bundle atop the pork. Ladle 1 quart of cooking liquid over the layers. Place the mushrooms over the bundle. Layer the turnips, carrots, and bamboo shoots over the mushrooms. Pour the remaining liquid, including the spices, over the top. Lay the lotus leaf over the top of the pot. Place the pot cover on the leaf to seal the pot.

8. Over low heat, allow the contents of the pot to simmer for 1¼ to 1½ hours. Turn off the heat and allow the pot to rest for 10 minutes. Remove all the foods from the pot to a large heated serving platter. Garnish the platter with the quail eggs. Place the liquid, now a rich broth, in a heated tureen. Remove the cheesecloth bundle to another heated plate, discard the cheesecloth, remove the contents, slice the abalone thinly, and arrange it with the other ingredients as an accompaniment.

9. Serve in the Chinese manner: the meats and vegetables together, with some of the broth poured over them, the rest of the broth divided into bowls to drink.

MAKES 12 SERVINGS

*T*raditionally, Buddha Jumps over the Wall is served with a selection of five special accompaniments, these to complete the feast and to offer tastes that complement the central dish of the feast. Following are those traditional dishes, as prepared and eaten in Fuzhou. Each of the dishes yields six servings, but since they are meant to accompany Buddha Jumps over the Wall, they will be eaten casually and thus are adequate for twelve. It has been suggested that even these dishes would be enough to have Buddha jump a wall. They might. ◆

SNOW PEA SHOOTS WITH STEAMED MUSHROOMS

Dau Miu Dong Gu

2 quarts cold water
One ½-inch-thick slice fresh ginger, lightly smashed
2 teaspoons salt
¾ teaspoon baking soda
1 pound snow pea shoots, hard stems removed, broken into small, irregular pieces, washed, and drained

12 Steamed Black Mushrooms (page 81)
2 teaspoons Garlic Oil (page 84) or peanut oil

1. To blanch the snow pea shoots, place the cold water, ginger, salt, and baking soda in a pot, cover, and bring to a boil over high heat. Add the snow pea shoots, making certain they are completely immersed. Cook for 10 seconds. Turn off the heat, run cold water into the pot, and drain thoroughly.

2. Place the steamed mushrooms around the edge of a heated serving platter.

3. Heat a wok over high heat for 30 seconds, add the garlic oil, and coat the wok with a spatula. When a wisp of white smoke appears, add the pea shoots and cook, stirring, for 3 minutes. Turn off the heat, transfer to the heated platter, and serve with the mushrooms.

CHOI SUM WITH YUNNAN HAM

Choi Sum Boon For Tui

2 quarts cold water
One ½-inch-thick slice fresh ginger,
  lightly smashed
1 tablespoon salt
1½ pounds choi sum, hard ends and
  old leaves removed, washed and
  drained thoroughly

2 teaspoons Onion Oil (page 83) or
  peanut oil
½ cup prepared Smithfield Ham
  (page 79), cut into pieces 2 inches
  long, ½ inch wide, and ¼ inch thick

1. To blanch the *choi sum*, place the water, ginger, and salt in a pot, cover, and bring to a boil over high heat. Add the *choi sum* and stir, making certain the *choi sum* is completely immersed. Allow the water to return to a boil. Turn off the heat, run cold water into the pot, and drain thoroughly.

2. Place the *choi sum* in a heated serving dish. Pour the onion oil over it and toss well. Garnish with Smithfield ham around the edge of the platter and serve.

MUSTARD GREEN STEMS
IN SWEET MUSTARD SAUCE

Lot Gai Choi Sum

This is a very distinctive dish, using only the stems of the mustard green. Usually these stems are sold alone, with only small remnants of leaves attached. If not available, use mustard greens, remove all leaves, and use only the stalks.

For the sweet mustard sauce
2½ teaspoons Colman's mustard
  powder

2½ teaspoons cold water
½ teaspoon salt
2½ teaspoons sugar
2 teaspoons sesame oil

2 teaspoons Coriander Oil (page 86) or
  peanut oil
1¼ pounds mustard green stems, sliced
  into ¼-inch-thick rounds

1. Combine the sweet mustard sauce ingredients in a bowl and reserve.

2. Heat a wok over high heat for 30 seconds, add the coriander oil, and coat the wok with it using a spatula. When a wisp of white smoke appears, add the mustard green stems and cook, stirring, for 2 minutes. Turn off the heat and transfer to a heated serving bowl. Stir the sweet mustard sauce, pour over the stems, and mix well. Serve.

N O T E : *This dish is quite pungent. You may wish to add the sweet mustard sauce gradually, to taste.*

LOTUS ROOT
WITH PICKLED PEACH SAUCE

Seun Toh Ngau

Traditionally the sauce for this condiment is made with jarred sour plums. On occasion I have found these not to be sufficiently tart or balanced, often too salty. So, I have adapted the recipe for my own pickled peaches.

1¼ pounds lotus root
½ Pickled Peach (page 107), cut into 1-inch pieces (½ cup)
¾ cup Pickled Peach liquid

1. To prepare the lotus root, wash, peel, cut in half lengthwise, then cut into ¼-inch-thick half moons. Place in a bowl and cover with ice water.

2. Place the pickled peaches and liquid in a blender and blend for about 1 minute into a coarse puree.

3. Drain the lotus root. Divide the pieces equally into 2 dishes, one for each end of the table. Divide the sauce equally into 2 bowls, one for each end of the table.

To eat this condiment, dip the lotus root into the sauce.

This completes the feast, except for hot steamed breads, one small loaf per person (see page 364), to be used to sop up the exquisite broth of Buddha Jumps over the Wall. These steamed breads can be made well in advance and simply resteamed on the final day of preparation. *Ho ho sik,* or "Eat well," as my father would say.

The
Rice Bowl

RICE IN CHINA IS UNIVERSAL. IN EARLY CHINA, WHEN ITS RECORDED LIFE WAS CENTERED IN THE NORTH, RICE WAS CONSIDERED AN EXOTIC GRAIN FROM THE SOUTH TO BE BROUGHT NORTH FOR IMPERIAL PLEASURE. GRADUALLY, HOWEVER, EVEN IN THE NORTH, WHERE WHEAT, MILLET, SORGHUM, AND OTHER GRAINS WERE ITS HERITAGE, RICE EVOLVED INTO CHINA'S GRAIN OF CHOICE. Today China grows one third of the world's rice, most of that still in the South, where, particularly in the area of Guangdong, two rice crops a year is commonplace.

Rice is the core of virtually every Chinese meal, and to be invited to dine one is asked to *sik fan,* or "eat rice." If a family is provided for, it is said to have a full rice bowl; if impoverished, its rice bowl is considered empty, or broken. It is a tacit acknowledgment of a family's status to have a container always filled with rice in its larder. In our house in Sun Tak this was a large crock with a small piece of red paper pasted to its side, on which were the characters *seung moon,* or "always full." This demonstrates for us, as well as to others who might see it, that our family was solvent and provided for. Among the Chiu Chow people, cooked rice is always included among offerings at ancestral altars.

The history of rice in China goes back 5,000 years. Evidence of rice grains and straw have been found in archaeological sites in southeast and central China and carbon dated, particularly in Yaurhermuduh in Chekiang province, where proof of rice grown in paddies has been uncovered. In other sites, impressions of rice have been found in clay. The origins of rice are probably as a wild grass growing on the fringes of lakes, but we Chinese like legends and folklore, and we tell the story of a hunter, Houh Jir, who, as people multiplied and game became scarce, prayed to heaven for another source of food. The god of heaven and earth gave Houh Jir five sacks, one for each of his sons, and told him to send them out in search of grain foods. They collected wheat, millet, beans, hemp, and rice, and because the son who found rice was named Pahdi, rice became known as the paddy crop. To this day rice is grown in paddies, a tribute to that son of Houh Jir.

Rice in China is short, medium, and long grain, with extra-long-grain rice considered the choicest. It is this extra-long-grain rice that is used most often, cooked, as the center of any meal. In China there is a distinction between long grain and extra long grain that is often not made in the West. The basic long-grain rice is about four times as long as it is wide; extra long grain is longer and thinner. This is the rice I favor, for when properly cooked its grains are separate, fluffy, and have a pleasing bite. China also grows a red long-grain rice that is cooked mainly for decorative dishes.

Short-grain rice tends to soften when it cooks and tends to become clumps of grains. This rice is favored in Japan and to a large degree in Taiwan. I use it, together with gluti-nous rice, in congees. Glutinous rice, often called *sweet rice,* or *sticky rice,* tends to stick together after cooking as well. Because it can be molded, it is used often in stuffings or in cakes. A long-grain black glutinous rice, often labeled "black sweet rice," is grown in South-east Asia and generally used in sweet pastries. Brown rice is rice that has been partially milled to remove only its outer husk. Brown chaff is left on. The Chinese prefer their rice to be white, the whiter the better, for white-ness is prized. I recall eating brown rice only

in one period, near the end of World War II, when our family was forced to eat it. We did not like it. There are even red rices, grown near the Chinese border with Thailand and in Thailand. This country is also the source for an utterly delicious jasmine-scented extra-long-grain rice. The Chinese eat rice in a vast number of ways: cooked in water, steamed, boiled, fried, in porridgelike congees, as dim sum, in pastries, as fresh rice noodle, in sweet or savory steamed cakes, wrapped as bundles and steamed in lotus or bamboo leaves, as stuffings. White rice powder, cooked with sugar water, is often used as a substitute for mothers' milk.

The Chinese distinguish between rice as a crop and rice as food. Uncooked, rice is called *mai;* cooked, it is *fan.* Once cooked, rice was traditionally taken as food at least three times each day, first for *jo chan,* or early meal, break-fast, either as congee or, if the weather was cool, cooked and served with a spoonful of liquid lard, soy sauce, and an egg. To eat rice is to *sik fan,* and there is, in addition to those morning preparations, *n'fan,* or "afternoon rice," and *mon fan,* or "evening rice." There is even a custom called *siu yeh,* which translates literally as "cooked midnight" and means rice eaten as a late evening snack. No time of any day in China is without its rice.

YANGZHOU FRIED RICE

Yangzhou Chau Fan

F*ried rice of any sort is highly regarded. Fried rice from Yangzhou is a prize. This dish of many centuries was first concocted, it is said, in the city of Yangzhou, in Jiangsu province, just north of Nanjing. This rice appears on virtually every Chinese restaurant menu, but in name only. Often, carelessly, different ingredients are tossed into this classic dish—sliced lettuce, green peas, chunks of Western ham, chunks of chicken. None of these should be in the classic fried rice from Yangzhou, presented here. My only break with tradition is to replace the lard with which the rice is traditionally cooked with peanut oil.*

3 cups Basic Cooked Rice (page 68), cooled to room temperature
1 cup peanut oil

¼ pound shrimp, shelled, deveined, and cut into ¼-inch pieces
3 eggs, beaten with a pinch freshly ground white pepper and ¼ teaspoon salt

For the sauce
1 tablespoon soy sauce
1 tablespoon Chinese white rice wine
½ teaspoon salt
1 teaspoon sugar
½ tablespoon oyster sauce
1 teaspoon sesame oil
Pinch freshly ground white pepper

2 teaspoons minced fresh ginger
2 teaspoons minced garlic
1 cup Barbecued Pork (page 124), cut into ⅓-inch dice
3 scallions, trimmed and finely sliced

1. Prepare the cooked rice. Reserve.

2. Heat a wok over high heat for 45 seconds. Add the peanut oil and heat to 325°F. Add the shrimp and oil-blanch them for 30 seconds (see oil-blanching, page 62). Turn off the heat, remove the shrimp, drain, and reserve. Transfer the oil from the wok to a bowl and reserve.

3. Heat the wok over high heat for 10 seconds. Add the beaten eggs and scramble until medium soft. Turn off the heat and, with a spatula, cut the egg into small pieces. The egg will harden slightly as you do this. Remove and reserve.

4. In a bowl, combine the sauce ingredients and reserve.

5. Wipe off the wok and spatula with paper towels. Heat the wok over high heat for 20 seconds, return 2 tablespoons of the reserved peanut oil to the wok, and coat the wok

with the oil using the spatula. When a wisp of white smoke appears, add the ginger and stir briefly. Add the garlic. When it turns light brown, add the pork. Cook, stirring, for 1 minute. Add the cooked rice. Cook, stirring well, for 2 minutes. Add the reserved shrimp and stir well. Stir the sauce, drizzle into the rice, and stir well.

6. Reduce the heat to low and stir, making certain the rice is completely coated and mixed. Add the scrambled egg and mix well. Add the scallions and mix well. Turn off the heat, transfer the rice to a heated bowl, and serve.

MAKES 4 TO 6 SERVINGS

STIR-FRIED GLUTINOUS RICE

Nor Mai Fan

*T*his is a traditional dish of the cooler winter months in parts of Canton and Shanghai. Glutinous rice is considered a "hot" food, one that brings heat to the body, as do bacon and sausages, so when I was young this rice was served only in winter. And all summer I thought about it longingly.

2 cups glutinous rice
2 cups water
½ cup chopped Chinese bacon in ¼-inch dice

½ cup chopped Chinese sausage in ¼-inch dice
2 tablespoons dried shrimp, soaked in warm water for 20 minutes and cut into ½-inch dice
¾ teaspoon salt
1 teaspoon soy sauce
1 teaspoon dark soy sauce
2 tablespoons oyster sauce
3 scallions, trimmed and finely sliced
1 tablespoon sesame oil

1. Place the rice in a bowl, cover with water, and wash 4 times, rubbing between your palms. Drain well. Place the rice and the 2 cups water in a cake pan in a steamer. Cover and steam for 35 minutes (see steaming, page 64). Turn off the heat, remove the pan, and reserve.

2. Wash and dry the wok. Heat over high heat for 30 seconds. Add the bacon and cook, stirring, for 30 seconds. Push to one side and add the sausage. Cook, stirring, for 1 minute, and combine with the bacon. Add the shrimp and stir for 15 seconds. Add the salt and stir for another 15 seconds. Add the reserved rice, reduce the heat to medium, and continually turn the rice, mixing well, for 1½ minutes. Add the 2 soy sauces and mix thoroughly. Add the oyster sauce and stir until the rice acquires an even pale brown color and is well mixed. Add the scallions and mix well. Turn off the heat, add the sesame oil, and mix well.

3. Serve in individual bowls. Another way of serving this rice is to pack it well into individual bowls, then upend them on plates to create smooth mounds.

MAKES 4 TO 6 SERVINGS

GREEN RICE

Luk Fan

The origin of this very different, distinctive fried rice preparation is Taiwan. Its name translates simply as "green rice," which is what it becomes when rice is blended with spinach. I have modified this basic recipe by adding tartness with pickled ginger and peaches and with capers, to make the rice as refreshing as it looks.

4 cups Basic Cooked Rice (page 68)
3 extra-large eggs, beaten with ¾ teaspoon salt and 1½ teaspoons sugar

3½ tablespoons Shallot Oil (page 84) or peanut oil
⅛ teaspoon salt
½ teaspoon sugar
1 pound fresh spinach, washed well and dried, stems removed, and leaves shredded (4 cups tightly packed)
3 tablespoons drained capers
2½ tablespoons minced Pickled Peach (page 101)
2 tablespoons minced Pickled Ginger (page 102)

1. Place the cooked rice in a bowl, add the beaten eggs, and mix thoroughly, making certain the rice is completely coated with egg.

2. Heat a wok over high heat for 20 seconds, add 1 tablespoon of the shallot oil, the salt, and the sugar, and coat the wok with it using a spatula. Add the spinach, stir well,

reduce the heat to medium, and cook for 1½ minutes or until the spinach turns bright green. Turn off the heat, remove the spinach, and reserve.

3. Wash and dry the wok and spatula. Heat the wok over high heat for 30 seconds. Add the remaining shallot oil and coat the wok with it using the spatula. When a wisp of white smoke appears, add the rice-egg mixture and stir well. Reduce the heat to medium, cook, stirring for 2 minutes, add the capers, and stir. Add the spinach and stir, separating the spinach leaves, until the rice is hot. Add the pickled peaches and pickled ginger, stir together, and cook for 7 minutes or until the rice becomes green and is blended well with the spinach. Turn off the heat, transfer to a heated dish, and serve.

MAKES 6 SERVINGS

JASMINE RICE

Moot Lei Fan

*T*his extra-long-grain rice of Thailand has a natural jasmine scent. It is lovely to smell and delicious to taste. I use it constantly. Its name helps to explain how the Chinese describe rice. Moot lei mai trans-lates as "jasmine rice uncooked"; moot lei fan is "jasmine rice cooked." The Chinese also call it heung mai, or "uncooked fra-grant rice," and heung fan, or "cooked fragrant rice." Whichever you call it, this fried rice from Thailand is special.

1 recipe Basic Cooked Rice (page 68), using jasmine rice

½ *pound thick-sliced bacon, fat separated from meat, fat cut into ¼-inch dice, meat into ½-inch dice*

2½ *tablespoons peanut oil*

5 *eggs, beaten with a pinch freshly ground white pepper*

3 *medium shallots, minced*

4 *large broccoli stalks, peeled and cut into ¼-inch dice (about 1¼ cups)*

2 *tablespoons oyster sauce*

1 *teaspoon sugar*

6 *scallions, trimmed and finely sliced*

½ *teaspoon salt*

1. Heat a wok over high heat for 40 seconds. Add the diced bacon fat and cook, stirring, until golden brown and crisp, about 2 minutes. Remove from the heat, drain on paper

towels, and reserve. Pour off the fat from the wok and discard. Rinse and dry the wok and spatula.

2. Heat the wok over high heat for 40 seconds, add 1½ tablespoons of the peanut oil, and coat the wok with it using the spatula. When a wisp of white smoke appears, add the beaten eggs and scramble until firm, about 2 minutes. Turn off the heat, remove the wok from the burner, and with the spatula, cut the eggs into ½-inch pieces. Remove to a plate and reserve. Rinse and dry the wok and spatula again.

3. Heat the wok over high heat for 40 seconds, add the remaining peanut oil, and coat the wok with it using the spatula. When a wisp of white smoke appears, add the bacon meat and spread in a single layer. Cook for 1 minute. Turn over and cook until well browned, about 1 minute longer. Stir in the shallots and cook until softened, about 2 minutes. Add the broccoli stalks, stir, and cook for 2 minutes. Add the cooked rice, stir well, and cook until the rice is hot, about 2 minutes. Stir the oyster sauce and sugar together, pour in, and mix well. Add the reserved eggs and stir well. Add the scallions and stir well. Add the salt and mix thoroughly. Turn off the heat, transfer the rice to a heated platter, sprinkle with the reserved crisp cracklings, and serve.

MAKES 6 SERVINGS

HAINANESE CHICKEN RICE

Hoi Lam Gai Fan

This is an immigrant Chinese dish. The people from Hainan, an island off southernmost China, were historically among the most daring of China's voyagers, sailing to, trading with, and settling into various parts of Southeast Asia. This preparation, thoroughly Chinese, has become a tradition in Singapore. The separate elements of it—rice, chicken, and soup—are served together as a single course and eaten any way one wishes.

One 4- to 4½-pound chicken
Chicken giblets and neck bones
¼ cup plus 2 teaspoons salt

3 tablespoons Chinese white rice wine
 or gin
5 onions (1¼ pounds), quartered
One 1½-inch-thick slice fresh ginger,
 peeled and coarsely chopped
2 garlic cloves
18 sprigs fresh coriander (cilantro)
10 cups cold water
2 tablespoons peanut oil
6 medium shallots, finely diced
2 small fresh Thai chilies, minced
1 large ripe tomato, cut into ½-inch
 dice
1 medium cucumber, peeled, halved,
 seeded, and cut into ¼-inch dice
2 cups extra-long-grain rice

1. Wash the chicken and remove the fat and membranes. Wash, dry, and reserve the giblets and neck bones. Rinse the chicken under cold running water, sprinkle ¼ cup of the salt over the outside, rinse thoroughly inside and out, drain, and pat dry with paper towels. Rub the chicken with the rice wine and sprinkle the remaining 2 teaspoons salt on the skin and inside the cavity.

2. In a casserole or Dutch oven, combine the onions, ginger, and garlic, 12 coriander sprigs, the chicken giblets and neck bones, and the cold water. Cover and bring to a boil over high heat. Reduce the heat to low and simmer for 45 minutes, leaving the lid cracked.

3. Add the chicken to the pot, breast side up, increase the heat to medium, and bring the pot back to a boil. Cover, reduce the heat to low, and simmer for 30 minutes, leaving the lid cracked. Turn the chicken over and simmer for 15 minutes longer. Turn the chicken breast side up again and simmer for another 15 minutes. Remove the pot from the heat and allow the chicken to rest in the liquid, covered, for another 15 minutes. Remove the neck bones and giblets. Transfer the chicken to a platter and allow to cool sufficiently to handle. Strain the cooking liquid, now a stock, and skim off the fat, to have 2 quarts. Reserve.

4. Cut the chicken meat into bite-sized pieces, transfer to a platter, and garnish with the remaining coriander sprigs.

5. To prepare the soup, in a large pot, heat the peanut oil over high heat until very hot, about 1 minute. Add the shallots and cook, stirring, until they begin to brown, about 3 minutes. Stir in the chilies and tomato. Add the all but 2 cups of the stock, stir well, and bring to a boil over high heat. Reduce the heat to low, cover, leaving the lid cracked, and simmer for 20 minutes. Add the cucumber, return to a boil, and remove from the heat. Keep the soup tightly covered.

6. To prepare the rice, as the soup cooks, place the rice in a medium pot and add water to cover. Wash the rice by rubbing it between your palms. Drain. Repeat twice more. Return the rice to the pot, add the remaining 2 cups stock, and bring to a boil over high heat. Stir and cook until bubbles begin to appear on the surface of the rice, about 3 minutes. Reduce the heat to low, cover, and cook for 6 minutes. Stir, cover again, and cook until tender, 3 to 5 minutes. Turn off the heat and transfer to a heated bowl. Serve in the traditional way. Pour the soup into individual bowls and serve with the chicken and rice and with small individual dishes of these 2 dipping sauces, one of ginger and garlic, which is traditional, the other one of my own design.

Ginger Garlic Sauce
3 tablespoons peanut oil
4 teaspoons grated fresh ginger
2 garlic cloves, minced

In a small bowl, combine all of the ingredients.

Chili Soy Sauce
¼ cup soy sauce
4 teaspoons Coriander Oil
   (page 86)
3 fresh Thai chilies, minced

In a small bowl, combine all of the ingredients.

MAKES 6 SERVINGS

CRABS WITH STEAMED GLUTINOUS RICE

Hoi Bah Wong Hai Fan

This special rice dish from Taiwan has a wonderful name, which translates as "sea pirate crab rice." Whether that refers to its origins I do not know, but that is what it is called in Taiwan, where, you will be told, this dish is best in the autumn, when the native crabs, called chrysanthemum yellow *because of the color of their roe, are at their biggest and best. These Taiwan crabs are as highly regarded as the so-called hairy crabs of Shanghai, also at their best in autumn.*

1½ cups glutinous rice
1½ cups cold water
4 live blue crabs or 2 larger crabs
  (1½ pounds)
2 tablespoons peanut oil
⅓ cup minced shallot

2½ tablespoons dried shrimp, soaked in
  warm water for 20 minutes until
  softened
4 medium Chinese black mushrooms,
  soaked in hot water for 30 minutes,
  washed, stems discarded, and cut
  into ¼-inch pieces (⅓ cup)
¼ pound lean boneless pork loin, cut
  into ¼-inch dice
1 tablespoon soy sauce
1 tablespoon oyster sauce
1 teaspoon sesame oil
1½ teaspoons sugar
1 tablespoon Shao-Hsing wine or dry
  sherry
¾ teaspoon salt
Pinch freshly ground white pepper

1. Place the rice in a bowl, add water to cover, and wash the rice 3 times by rubbing between your palms. Drain well. No water should remain. Place the rice in a cake pan, add the 1½ cups cold water, place in a steamer, cover, and steam (see steaming, page 64) for 25 to 30 minutes, until done.

2. As the rice steams, prepare the crabs. Clean them, remove the claws, and wash the claws and crabs under cold running water. Remove the flap, open the shell, and remove the gills. If 2 larger crabs are used, clean in the same manner, but leave the claws on and cut each crab into quarters. Reserve.

3. Heat a wok over high heat for 30 seconds, add the peanut oil, and coat the wok with it using a spatula. When a wisp of white smoke appears, add the shallot and cook, stir-

ring, until their fragrance is released, about 1 minute. Add the shrimp and mushrooms and stir together for 1 minute. Add the pork and cook, stirring, until the pork turns white, about 2 minutes. Add the cooked rice and mix thoroughly. Add all the other ingredients except the crabs, reduce the heat to low, and mix to combine thoroughly. The rice mixture should turn light brown.

4. Transfer the cooked rice mixture to a larger cake pan and spread evenly. Lay the crabs and claws atop the rice and steam, as above, for 12 to 15 minutes, or until the crabs turn pink, the roe hardens, and the meat turns white. Turn off the heat, transfer the rice and crabs to a heated platter, and serve.

MAKES 4 SERVINGS

CONGEE

Jook

These days congee is understood to be a rice gruel, or porridge, eaten most often at breakfast, generally with other ingredients added to it for taste and texture, a dish eaten and enjoyed in every corner of China. Historically, however, congee was made with many bases—wheat, barley, sorghum, millet, tapioca, even corn—sometimes in mixture with rice, sometimes not. The use of other grains was, in general, a circumstance of the North. The South, from Shanghai to Canton, most often used rice, 2 rices, in combination for congees.

As near as can be determined, congees date from the Zhou dynasty, a thousand years B.C., and were thick gruels of grain flavored with foods such as pears, lily buds, chrysanthemums, ginger, ginseng, lotus and bamboo leaves, sugarcane, and mint leaves. During the Ming dynasty congees were regarded, in addition, as vehicles for medicinal herbs.

Its name, jook, means in today's context "soft rice," and it is considered a most nourishing food by young and old. Babies are raised on it, and the elderly like it for the ease with which it can be digested. It can be eaten sweetened with rock sugar, one way it is eaten in Canton, or savory with cabbage, as the people in Shanghai like it occasionally, There is, as with so many of China's foods, a bit of folklore surrounding congee.

It is told that once a miserly man, faced with a need to produce rice for 10 guests, told his cook to stretch his rice, as needed, by ladling water into the cooking rice. He would do this, he said, by calling the cook's name, Ah Fook, which would be a code signal. The name spoken aloud meant another ladle of water. But confusion reigned. Even before the guests arrived, the miser, forgetful, would call to the chef on a different matter. But every time Ah Fook heard his name, he would pour another ladle of water into the cooking rice. What resulted, it is said, was a frustrated cook with a rice porridge, rather than rice, and a rhyme—Ah Fook, Ah Fook, Ah Fook, Ah Fook. Fook Mut Yeh. Bin Jor Wok Jook—which translates as the miserly man calling the cook repeatedly and the cook angrily telling him to stop calling because his rice had already become a thin congee. Ah Fook rhymes with jook. When I was a child, we used to chant this rhyme and laugh.

Congee, or jook, is considered a rice dish these days, and not only for breakfast. In Hong Kong, for example, it can be lunch as well as dinner. And it seems there is no limit to what may be added to a congee: fish, meats,

vegetables, herbs, other grains, condiments, spices, different broths and
stocks. Congee is most accommodating. I have set down a basic congee; one
with preserved eggs that is a tradition of centuries in Canton; another,
made only with glutinous rice, from Fujian, with a history as long; and
finally a thoroughly modern congee, a lobster, or "dragon shrimp jook"
from Hong Kong. I urge you to experiment.

BASIC CONGEE

½ cup short-grain rice
¼ cup glutinous rice

4½ cups water
1 quart Chicken Stock (page 75)

1. Place both rices in a large pot, with water to cover. Wash the rice by rubbing between your palms. Drain. Repeat twice more.

2. Return the washed rice to the pot, add the 4½ cups of water and the stock, and bring to a boil over high heat. Reduce the heat to medium-low, cover the pot, leaving the lid cracked, and cook for 1 hour, stirring occasionally to prevent the rice from sticking to the pot bottom. A nonstick pot is preferred. Cook until the rice thickens almost to a porridge consistency.

3. Heat a tureen by pouring boiling water into it. When the congee is done, turn off the heat, pour the congee into the heated tureen, and serve. For a vegetarian congee, substitute Vegetable Stock (page 76) for the chicken stock.

MAKES 6 TO 8 SERVINGS

PRESERVED EGG CONGEE

Pei Dan Sau Yuk Jook

1 recipe Basic Congee (preceding
   recipe)

For the sauce
1½ tablespoons Coriander Oil
   (page 86) or peanut oil
1 tablespoon soy sauce

2 tablespoons Chicken Stock (page 75)
1 tablespoon sugar
⅛ teaspoon freshly ground white pepper

2 preserved eggs
2 cups salted pork, cut into thin slices,
   1½ inches by ½ inch

1. As you prepare the congee, in a bowl, combine the sauce ingredients and reserve. To prepare the eggs, remove the shells, wash and dry, cut into ⅓-inch dice, and reserve.

2. After the rice has cooked for 40 minutes, or two thirds of its cooking time, add the preserved eggs. Cook for 10 minutes more and add the pork. Stir and cook for the remaining 10 minutes. Turn off the heat, ladle the congee into individual bowls, and pour in the sauce to taste.

MAKES 6 TO 8 SERVINGS

FUJIAN PORK CONGEE

Fujian Yuk Jook

¾ *cup glutinous rice*
¾ *pound fresh pork butt in 1 piece*
1 *quart cold water*
1 *medium onion, peeled and quartered*
One ½-*inch-thick slice fresh ginger,*
  lightly smashed
4 *scallions, trimmed and cut into*
  thirds

2 *teaspoons salt*
3 *cups Chicken Stock (page 75)*
⅔ *cup raw peanuts, skins removed*
3 *tablespoons finely sliced green parts*
  of scallion, for garnish
2 *tablespoons finely sliced fresh*
  coriander (cilantro)

1. To prepare the rice, place it in a bowl with water to cover and wash 3 times, rubbing between your palms. Drain. Place back in the bowl with water to cover, and soak for 2 hours.

2. In a large pot, place the pork butt, cold water, onion, ginger, scallions, and salt. Cover and bring to a boil over high heat. Reduce the heat to low, leave the lid cracked, and simmer for 45 minutes. There should be 3 cups of liquid. Turn off the heat and strain the cooking liquid into a bowl. Remove the pork and allow it to cool until it can be handled. Discard all other ingredients.

3. Place the stock, pork cooking liquid, and peanuts in a pot and bring to a boil over high heat. Reduce the heat to low, leave the lid cracked, and cook for 30 minutes. Raise the heat to high and return to a boil. Strain the rice, add to the pot, stir well, and return to a boil. Reduce the heat to low, leave the lid cracked, and simmer for 45 minutes, stirring every 10 minutes. As the congee is cooking, cut the pork into ½-inch cubes. Five minutes before the end of the cooking time, add the pork and stir well into the congee. Turn off the heat, transfer to a heated tureen, and serve, garnished with scallions and coriander.

MAKES 4 TO 6 SERVINGS

LOBSTER CONGEE

Lung Har Jook

1 recipe Basic Congee (page 189)
1 scallion, trimmed and finely sliced
3 tablespoons finely sliced fresh
   coriander (cilantro)
3 tablespoons finely julienned fresh
   ginger
¼ pound won ton wrappers
3½ cups peanut oil
Three ½-pound lobster tails

For the marinade
1 teaspoon ginger juice mixed with
   1½ tablespoons Mei Kuei Lu Chiew
   or gin
2 teaspoons soy sauce
1½ teaspoons sugar
½ teaspoon salt
1½ teaspoons Chinese white rice
   vinegar or distilled vinegar
Pinch freshly ground white pepper

1 egg, beaten

1. While the congee is cooking, prepare the accompaniments. Place the sliced scallion, coriander, and julienned ginger in 3 small bowls and reserve. Scrape the cornstarch coating from the won ton wrappers and slice into ¼-inch strips. Heat a wok over high heat, add the oil, and bring to 350°F. Place the won ton strips in the oil and deep-fry, separating the strips with a spatula, for 30 to 45 seconds, until brown. Turn off the heat, remove the strips with a Chinese strainer, drain over paper towels, and reserve.

2. As the congee still cooks, prepare the lobster. Remove the lobster meat from the shell, devein, and wash. Cut into 1-inch pieces. Combine the marinade ingredients in a bowl and place the lobster meat in the marinade for no more than 5 minutes.

3. At this point, when the congee is done, raise the heat to medium and return to a boil. Add the lobster and marinade and stir well. Raise the heat and bring to a boil. Stir to prevent sticking. Boil for 2 minutes or until the lobster turns white. Drizzle in the beaten egg and stir. Turn off the heat. Remove the congee to a heated tureen. Transfer the deep-fried noodles to a dish and serve along with the other condiments.

MAKES 4 TO 6 SERVINGS

RED RICE SOUP WITH SHRIMP

Fuzhou Hung Jo Har Tong

*T*his soup, made with fermented red
rice, is a specialty of the Southern city
of Fuzhou. It is pleasantly, slightly sweet
from the rice. This dish is so localized that it
would be rare indeed to find it anywhere
else, and the chefs of Fuzhou generally will
not share their knowledge. But through tast-
ings I have solved the small mystery of their
soup.

1½ tablespoons White Peppercorn Oil
   (page 85) or peanut oil
¼ cup minced shallot
One ½-inch-thick slice fresh ginger,
   lightly smashed

5 scallions, trimmed and cut into
   2-inch pieces, white and green parts
   separated, and whites lightly
   smashed
½ cup Red Wine Rice (page 70)
½ cup Red Wine Rice liquid
3 cups Seafood Stock (page 76)
½ pound shrimp (about 24) washed,
   shells cut along backs with shears,
   veins removed, and shells left on
2 ounces bean thread noodles
   (1½ cups), soaked in hot water for
   20 minutes, drained, and cut into
   2-inch pieces

1. Heat a large pot over high heat. Add the oil. When a wisp of white smoke appears, add
   the shallot and ginger, stir, and cook for 30 seconds. Add the white parts of scallions
   and cook, stirring, for 1 minute or until their fragrance is released. Add the red rice,
   rice liquid, and stock to the pot and stir well. Bring to a boil, reduce the heat, and simmer for 3 minutes.

2. Raise the heat back to high. Add the shrimp and stir well. Cook until the shrimp turn
   pink and curl. Add the bean thread noodles and return to a boil. Turn off the heat.
   Add the green parts of scallions and stir to mix. Transfer the soup to a heated tureen
   and serve. This must be served immediately, for it thickens quickly and the bean
   threads tend to lose their texture.

MAKES 4 TO 6 SERVINGS

SIZZLING RICE SOUP WITH CRAB

Hai Yuk Guor Bah Tong

The concept of hot, crisp rice with soup poured over to provide taste and texture as well as theatrical sizzle is concentrated along China's coast from Shanghai south to Fuzhou and Canton and on the island of Taiwan.

¼ pound crabmeat
2 tablespoons Chinese white rice wine or gin
1 tablespoon Coriander Oil (page 86) or peanut oil
1 tablespoon minced fresh ginger

5 Chinese black mushrooms, soaked in hot water for 30 minutes until softened, washed, stems removed, and cut into ½-inch dice (½ cup)
1 teaspoon salt
1 pound hairy melon, peeled and cut into ½-inch dice
4¼ cups Milk Stock (page 78) or Chicken Stock (page 75)
1¼ cups cold water
6 ounces boneless chicken cutlet, cut into ½-inch dice
1 cup fresh or defrosted frozen green peas
½ recipe Guo Bah (page 73)
1 scallion, trimmed and finely sliced

1. In a bowl, gently toss the crabmeat with 1 tablespoon of the rice wine to combine. Reserve.

2. Heat a large pot over high heat for 20 seconds and add the coriander oil. When a wisp of white smoke appears, add the ginger and stir briefly. Add the mushrooms, stir, and cook for 1 minute. Add the salt and stir. Add the hairy melon and stir. Add the stock and cold water and mix well. Bring to a boil. Reduce the heat to low and simmer for 5 minutes or until the melon is tender. Add the chicken and stir well into the mixture. Add the peas and stir in. Raise the heat to high and return to a boil. Add the remaining rice wine and mix. When the chicken is cooked, add the crabmeat mixture and stir well. Return to a boil, then reduce the heat immediately, cover the pot, and reduce the heat to low to keep the soup hot.

3. As the soup cooks, deep-fry the *guo bah*. When hot and crisp, place at the bottom of a heated tureen, pour in the hot soup, and allow to sizzle. Serve the soup individually in bowls, with pieces of the *guo bah*, and sprinkle each bowl with scallion to taste.

MAKES 8 SERVINGS

BABY SHRIMP
SIZZLING RICE SOUP

Har Yun Guor Bah Tong

*T*his guor bah *soup is a specialty of Taiwan. Taiwan is famous for its tiny
baby shrimp,* har yun, *which are quite sweet,
similar to the rock shrimp familiar to us. I
specify the rock shrimp for this recipe, which
are usually sold shelled, ready for use. If
unavailable, you may buy baby shrimp,
frozen, in 5-pound packages; use what is
needed and save the rest. Or use medium
shrimp, washed, shelled, deveined, and cut
in half lengthwise. The combination of these
sweet small shrimp, the tart tomatoes, and
the texture of the fried* guor *is quite marvelous.*

*2 tablespoons Sichuan Peppercorn Oil
  (page 86) or peanut oil*
1 tablespoon minced fresh ginger
1 tablespoon minced garlic

1 cup minced shallot
*2 pounds fresh tomatoes, cut into
  ½-inch dice (4 cups)*
*1 tablespoon Chinese white rice wine
  or gin*
5 cups Seafood Stock (page 76)
1 teaspoon salt
2 teaspoons sugar
⅛ teaspoon freshly ground white pepper
2 teaspoons soy sauce
½ recipe Guo Bah (page 73)
*¾ pound rock shrimp (30 to 40), tossed
  with 1 tablespoon Chinese white rice
  wine or gin*
*¼ cup finely sliced green part of
  scallion*
*2 tablespoons finely sliced fresh
  coriander (cilantro)*

1. Heat a large pot over high heat for 30 seconds and add the oil. When a wisp of white
   smoke appears, add the ginger, stir briefly, add the garlic, and stir. When the garlic
   turns light brown, add the shallot and stir to mix. Reduce the heat to medium and
   cook for 5 minutes, stirring occasionally. Turn the heat back to high, add the tomatoes
   and wine, and cook, stirring, for 2 minutes. Add the stock, salt, sugar, white pepper,
   and soy sauce, stir well, and return the soup to a boil. Then reduce the heat and cover,
   leaving the lid cracked. Cook for 20 minutes.

2. Halfway through the cooking of the soup, deep-fry the *guo bah*. When done, raise the
   heat under the soup to high, add the shrimp and wine mix, stir well, and return the
   soup to a boil. Turn off the heat.

3. Place the hot, crisp *guo bah* at the bottom of a heated tureen and pour hot soup over it
   to a sizzle. Serve the soup in bowls, with pieces of *guo bah,* and sprinkle the bowls with
   scallions and coriander to taste.

MAKES 6 SERVINGS

TUNG KUAN LOTUS LEAF RICE

Tung Kuan Hor Yip Fan

Wrapping rice in lotus or bamboo leaves for steaming is not unusual in China, particularly in the tropical South, where such leaves are plentiful. But this recipe, peculiar to the small area of Tung Kuan, about halfway between Canton and Hong Kong, is special because of its special use of eggs and red rice vinegar. I have added my own piquant touches, pickled pears and white peppercorn–infused oil, to it to complement the fragrance and taste imparted by the lotus leaves.

¼ cup White Peppercorn Oil (page 85) or peanut oil
6 extra-large eggs, beaten with ¼ teaspoon salt and a pinch freshly ground white pepper

1 cup Chicken Stock (page 75)
10 ounces small rock shrimp, defrosted frozen baby shrimp, or medium shrimp, shelled, deveined, and cut in half lengthwise
6 cups Basic Cooked Rice (page 68)
½ pound Barbecued Pork (page 124), julienned (1½ cups)
½ cup minced Pickled Pears (page 101) in ⅛-inch dice
3 tablespoons soy sauce
3½ tablespoons oyster sauce
1 teaspoon salt
3 tablespoons sugar
2 tablespoons Chinese red rice vinegar
2 large lotus leaves, soaked in hot water for 20 minutes, washed, and patted dry

1. Heat a wok over high heat for 20 seconds. Add ½ tablespoon of the peppercorn oil and coat the wok with it using a spatula. When a wisp of white smoke appears, add half the beaten eggs. Tip the wok from side to side to make a thin pancake. Reduce the heat to low and cook for 2 minutes or until the pancake begins to come away from the wok surface and there is no more liquid. Turn off the heat. Transfer to a cutting board. Repeat with the remaining eggs. When cooled, roll the pancakes into sausage shapes. Slice across at ⅛-inch intervals. Reserve.

2. Place the stock in the wok and bring to a boil over high heat. Add the shrimp, stir, and cook for 45 seconds or until the shrimp turn pink. Turn off the heat, remove the shrimp, and drain. Discard the liquid.

3. Place the cooked rice in a large bowl. Add the pork, pickled pear, shrimp, eggs, remaining peppercorn oil, soy sauce, oyster sauce, salt, sugar, and vinegar. Mix together thoroughly.

4. Place the lotus leaves overlapping on a work surface. Mound the rice mixture in the center of the leaves. Fold the sides over the rice, overlapping. Repeat with the other ends to create a square bundle about 9 inches on a side. Place the bundle in a bamboo steamer, folded side down, cover, and steam for 30 minutes (see steaming, page 64). Turn off the heat and place the steamer on a large platter. With shears, cut a round hole, about 4 to 5 inches in diameter, in the leaves. Serve the rice by spooning it into individual bowls.

N O T E :   *If your wok is not well seasoned, the egg pancake may stick to its sides. Alternately, use a nonstick skillet to cook the pancakes, though the wok would be better. The recipe can be made a day ahead up to the steaming and refrigerated. Return it to room temperature before steaming.*

M A K E S   1 0   S E R V I N G S

Sun Tak, the Cooking of My Girlhood

顺德，我的女童時期

順德，我的女童時期

IN SUN TAK, WHERE I WAS BORN AND SPENT THE FIRST TWELVE YEARS OF MY LIFE, MY MOST VIVID MEMORIES ARE THOSE CONCERNING FOOD AND THE TABLE. TALK OF PROPOSED MARRIAGES WAS ALWAYS ACCOMPANIED BY DISCUSSIONS OF HOW MUCH, AND OF WHAT QUALITY, BIRD'S NESTS, SHARK'S FINS, AND ABALONE WERE TO BE OFFERED IN DOWRIES, NOT TO MENTION DRIED SCALLOPS AND DRIED MUSHROOMS. Upcoming birthdays always revolved around which festive, traditional foods were to be served. The Lunar New Year was a time of many symbolic foods, to be displayed, to be offered to gods and ancestors, to be given as gifts, proffered to guests, and eaten. All of our important family matters, and those of passing daily interest, were discussed at the table.

In those days Sun Tak Yeun, or the Sun Tak District, was a significant area of Guangdong province, situated on a direct line between Canton to the north and Macau to the south. Canton was, to be sure, a major city, Macau, an exotic Portuguese colony filled with people like us but governed by the *guei lo*, or foreign devils. Close by, near Fos-

han, was Chung Shan, the birthplace of Sun Yat-sen. Sun Tak, which these days is called Shun-Te, in Shun-Te Hsien, was a busy crossroad, a fairly prosperous farming suburb of Canton, known as well for its proximity to nearby Shek-ki, where to this day it is believed the best pigeons in all of China are raised.

My home was, and is, famous throughout China, to an extent that belies its size. There is a saying, repeated often: "*Sun Tak yan ho lah sau, ho sik jiu yeh,*" which translates as "The people of Sun Tak are highly skilled and have great knowledge of food," but which is understood to be a slogan: "If you were born in Sun Tak, you were born to cook." Wherever I go in China, when I am asked where I was born, and I respond, "Sun Tak," eyebrows are raised and I am told that of course I must be a fine cook. In most of the finer restaurants of China, chefs who were born in Sun Tak are to be found.

In our region rice was plentiful, as were vegetables and all manner of fruit. Pigs were slaughtered regularly for the benefit of all, and chickens and ducks abounded. Fish and all varieties of shrimp, prawns, and shellfish were

199

available to us without limit. I remember it as a happy time for my family, as landholders, and for me, as a little girl, even though World War II and the invasion of the Japanese swirled about us. We were sufficiently away from Canton and Hong Kong, both occupied and governed by the Japanese invaders, and the only time the war touched us directly was when some Japanese soldiers passed through our district, remaining for a few days en route to Canton. Some of the houses in our town were affected. Some were invaded. In some, women were assaulted. In some, food and drink were confiscated. But our home was spared. We always believed it was because of the dreams and communications between my mother, Miu Hau—her full name was Lo Chan Miu Hau—and my dead grandfather, Ah Yeh, my father's father. My mother had been his favorite daughter-in-law, and she always prayed to him for guidance. She would dream of him, see him in her dreams, and based on these she would abruptly take herself and us off to Canton to be with relatives or to the house of my grandmother, Ah Paw, her mother, to avoid trouble. She had prayed to Ah Yeh to help in keeping the Japanese soldiers from our door. They did not come to our house, and my mother believed Ah Yeh had accomplished this. I did too.

We knew our foods, which of course we considered the best, but we were familiar as well with the foods of Canton city; of Hong Kong, where my brother, Lo Ching Mo, had spent time; of Fujian, because our cousin had married a man from that nearby region; of Shanghai, from cookbooks that showed us how to make Tea-Smoked Duck and Drunken Chicken, and from an aunt who had married a Shanghai man. My mother had been to Shanghai to have her wedding dresses made. Another cousin had been to university in Beijing and told about its people and their food. They were taller than we were, he said; they ate lots of bread and noodles, and to them rice was a great delicacy. The only far voyager in our family was my father, Lo Pak Wan, who before I was born had sailed to South Africa to explore the gold fields. He had brought back with him what our family believed to be a large chunk of gold, which somehow disappeared when it was given to a friend of my brother who was to have a fine ring made from it. Except for that exploration, my father stayed close to the lands and the orchards he owned.

My kitchen memories are mostly those of the times I spent with Ah Paw, my grandmother, my mother's mother. She was an autocratic woman, an independent thinker, who taught me most of what I knew about cooking. She could barely walk, because of her bound feet, but she knew everything about food and cooking, despite the fact that she never, ever ventured into her kitchen. She would order, direct her cooks and servants to do as she asked, and I never knew her to be wrong. Whether her food knowledge was purely instinctive or the heritage from her early life, I never knew. What I did know was she, and my parents, urged me to cook, to learn all there was to know about the kitchen, to cook familiar and unfamiliar foods.

Ah Paw had an encyclopedic knowledge of foods and continually preached to me, telling me that I must be filled with knowledge and not be a *bun tung soi*, a "half-filled bucket." I learned how to kill and dress a chicken and a duck; how to chop *choi sum* properly, the right way to soak black mushrooms, how to salt a fish, the correct way to prepare an abalone, and how to tend the oranges, persimmons, pomelos, and tangerines that grew on the trees in her courtyard. She would tell me, precisely, as she would her cooks, which seasonal vegetables and fruits should be prepared and in what manner. She would consult her *tung sing* book of calendar days and declare which were *hoy wok,* or "open wok" days, the best days to prepare special dishes. She taught me to stir the fish mixtures we stuffed into bean curd in one direction only so they would be cohesive; how to season this food or that just right. If I listened, did as she dictated, I was rewarded with premeal tastes and on special occasions was allowed to *chuk san,* or "make the animals." These were sweet snacks of popped rice held together with sugar syrup and covered with a layer of glutinous rice dough molded into animal shapes, an edible zoo.

Much of what I do in the kitchen to this day I learned from my Ah Paw. If there was no school I would race off to her house to be in her kitchen. She would pet me and say, "Yin-Fei, do you know what your name means?" And though I did indeed know that it meant "Flying Swallow," I would say no, so she would tell me. "It means you fly. You are smart. Your name matches your personality.

You are pretty." Of course I wanted to hear that.

Another vivid memory I have is of the guava tree that grew in the courtyard of our house. My mother loved this tree, not only because of its fruit but because she believed that the crop of tree ears, the flowerlike fungus that grew at its base, was sweeter than any other because of the guava. She would use these tree ears and the tiger lily buds that grew in our garden for a variety of dishes, with chicken, with pork, steamed with pork liver or with snakehead fish, in soups, and in vegetarian dishes she would make for Ah Paw, when, as a practicing Buddhist, she refrained from eating meat. My mother was not a fine cook, principally because she did not have to cook in a house with three servants. But she nevertheless insisted that I learn to cook. My father, a meticulous man, enjoyed cooking as an occasional pastime. From them, as well as from my Ah Paw, I received encouragement to become a cook, not the least of the reasons offered that if I was a fine and expert cook, I would easily find a husband, no matter whatever else my circumstances. I assume they are looking down upon me, along with Ah Paw, and are happy for me. After all, they raised me and taught me in Sun Tak, and I have not forgotten that.

EGGPLANT STUFFED WITH SHRIMP

Yeung Ngai Guah

*T*his was a special dish in my home, made special because so much care and effort was expended on a vegetable that was so common and inexpensive in Sun Tak. We loved this dish, and I would ask so often that it be made that Ah Paw simply taught me to make it. This is one of those dishes that require stirring in one direction, as she ordered.

For the filling

2 fresh water chestnuts, peeled and cut
  into ⅛-inch dice
¼ cup minced white part of scallion
½ pound shrimp, shelled, deveined,
  washed, dried thoroughly with paper
  towels, and chopped into a paste
2 teaspoons sesame oil
½ teaspoon ginger juice, mixed with
  1 tablespoon Chinese white rice wine
  or gin

1¼ teaspoons sugar
½ teaspoon salt
1 tablespoon beaten egg white
1 tablespoon tapioca flour

For the sauce

2 tablespoons oyster sauce
2 teaspoons double dark soy sauce
2 teaspoons Chinese white rice wine
  or gin
1 teaspoon sugar
Pinch freshly ground white pepper
¾ cup Superior Stock (page 74) or
  Chicken Stock (page 75)

2 thin Chinese eggplants, about
  8 inches long
2½ tablespoons tapioca flour
¼ cup peanut oil
3 tablespoons trimmed and finely
  sliced scallion

1. Place all filling ingredients in a bowl and mix thoroughly, stirring in one direction, until well blended. Refrigerate, covered, for 4 hours.

2. Combine the sauce ingredients in a bowl and reserve.

3. Prepare the eggplant. Do not peel. Slice each eggplant diagonally along its length in this manner: On a diagonal, slice through to cut off an end and discard. Then continue to slice diagonally, at ⅓-inch intervals. The next slice will be two thirds of the way through, the next, all the way through, and so on. What you will have is a series of pieces, with pockets. Continue until you have 16 pieces.

4. Sprinkle each pocket with some tapioca flour. Stir the filling ingredients and place 1 tablespoon of the filling into each pocket. Pack and smooth with your fingers or with a butter knife. Repeat with the remaining 15.

5. Place 3 tablespoons of the peanut oil in a nonstick skillet and heat over medium heat until the oil is hot. Place 8 of the stuffed eggplant pieces, flat side down, in the oil and fry until brown, 4 to 5 minutes. Turn over and fry until brown on the other side, 4 to 5 minutes more. Remove to a serving platter and place in a warm oven. Add the remaining tablespoon of peanut oil to the skillet and repeat the process with the remaining 8 pieces.

6. Stir the sauce and add to the skillet. Cook, stirring constantly, until it bubbles, 3 to 4 minutes. Turn the heat off. Remove the platter of eggplant from the oven, pour the sauce over, sprinkle with sliced scallion, and serve with cooked rice.

NOTE: *In Sun Tak we also steamed this dish, out of deference to the digestion of our elders, who preferred steamed rather than fried foods. If you wish, steam the eggplant in a steamproof dish (see steaming, page 64) for 15 minutes, until the eggplant is soft, top with the sauce and scallion, and serve.*

MAKES 4 SERVINGS

STEAMED SPARERIBS
WITH PRESERVED PLUMS

Mui Ji Pai Kwat

A version of this dish, more familiar, is a staple of the dim sum *kitchen, where it is made with fermented black beans. In Sun Tak we made it this way. These were the only spareribs I knew until I moved to Hong Kong.*

1 pound lean spareribs, cut across meat
   and bone into 30 pieces, each
   1½ inches thick—have the butcher do
   this (2 cups)
½ teaspoon baking soda
5 preserved plums, pitted and mashed

5 garlic cloves, minced
4 teaspoons bean sauce
1 tablespoon oyster sauce
2 teaspoons dark soy sauce
1 tablespoon Chinese white rice wine
   or gin
1½ teaspoons minced fresh ginger
1½ tablespoons sugar
1½ tablespoons Chinese white rice
   vinegar or distilled vinegar
1 tablespoon cornstarch
Pinch freshly ground white pepper

1. Wash and dry the spareribs, place in a large mixing bowl, add the baking soda, and mix well. Allow to rest, covered, in the refrigerator for 2 hours.

2. Place the mashed plums and minced garlic in a small bowl and blend together.

3. Place the spareribs and all other ingredients, including the plum-garlic mixture, in a steamproof dish, mix well, and marinate in the refrigerator for at least 8 hours or overnight. Before cooking, return to room temperature.

4. Place the steamproof dish with spareribs and marinade in a steamer. Cover and steam for 45 minutes (see steaming, page 64), until the spareribs are tender. Turn off the heat. Serve the spareribs directly from the steamproof dish, accompanied by cooked rice.

MAKES 4 TO 6 SERVINGS

STIR-FRIED MILK

Dai Leung Chau Ngau Nai

*V*ery, very rarely did we have milk in Sun Tak—cow's milk, that is. A special treat we enjoyed occasionally was a drink made from sweetened milk powder from America that occasionally found its way to our market. But in a neighboring village, Dai Leung, restaurants were famous for their use of cow's milk in cooking. Only occasionally could milk be found in our market, but when it did we would cook this dish in the manner of Dai Leung.

4 jumbo egg whites (about ⅔ cup)
½ cup whole milk
¼ teaspoon salt
½ teaspoon sugar
Pinch freshly ground white pepper
2 tablespoons cornstarch
⅓ cup prepared Smithfield Ham
    (page 79), cut into ¼-inch dice
¼ pound crabmeat
1 cup peanut oil
2 tablespoons pine nuts
2½ tablespoons Shallot Oil (page 84) or
    peanut oil

1. Place the egg whites, milk, salt, sugar, white pepper, and cornstarch in a bowl. Beat well to blend. Add the ham and crabmeat and mix well. Set aside.

2. Heat a wok over high heat for 40 seconds, add the peanut oil, and heat to 350°F. Add the pine nuts and fry for 45 to 60 seconds or until the pine nuts turn golden. Turn off the heat, remove the pine nuts with a strainer, and drain on paper towels. Discard the oil or reserve for future use. Wash and dry the wok.

3. Heat the wok over high heat for 30 seconds, add the shallot oil, and coat the wok with it using a spatula. When a wisp of white smoke appears, stir the egg white mixture gently and pour in. Reduce the heat to medium and stir to make a soft scramble. Turn off the heat, transfer to a heated dish, sprinkle with the pine nuts, and serve.

MAKES 4 SERVINGS

FISH CONGEE

Yue Jook

*W*e ate this very often at home. We had
an abundance of fresh fish, particularly grass carp, which were farmed in the
countryside near Sun Tak. For us the best
time to eat this congee was autumn and
early winter, when the carp were fattest.
It is more work to steam a fish and extract
its flesh than to use fillets, but it is also
tastier. Carp is readily available in markets; request grass carp, which is farmed in
the American Midwest. If unavailable, use
sole, sea bass, or snapper, with sole preferred.

1 recipe Basic Congee (page 189)

For the marinade
2 tablespoons Chinese white rice wine
    or gin
1 teaspoon Chinese white rice vinegar
    or distilled vinegar

2 teaspoons soy sauce
2 teaspoons sesame oil
2 tablespoons Scallion Oil (page 82) or
    peanut oil
1 teaspoon salt
Pinch freshly ground white pepper

One 3-pound carp (1½ pounds after
    steaming), bones removed
6 thin slices fresh ginger, julienned
2 scallions, trimmed and cut into
    1½-inch pieces
1 tablespoon Scallion Oil (page 82)
⅛ teaspoon freshly ground white pepper
1 teaspoon soy sauce
3 scallions, trimmed and finely sliced,
    for garnish
1 tablespoon finely sliced fresh
    coriander (cilantro)

1. As the congee cooks, combine the marinade ingredients in a bowl. Place the fish in a
   steamproof dish and pour the marinade over it. Place the ginger and scallions beneath
   the fish, in its cavity, and on top of it. Cover and steam the fish for 15 minutes (see
   steaming, page 64). Turn off the heat. Remove the fish from the steamer and cool to
   room temperature. Discard the skin, bones, ginger, and scallions and break the fish
   flesh into very small pieces.

2. Place the fish in a bowl. Add the scallion oil, white pepper, and soy sauce. Mix lightly.
   When the congee is done, add the fish to it. Mix together and allow the congee to
   come to a boil. Immediately turn off the heat, pour the congee into a heated tureen,
   and serve, with scallions and fresh coriander sprinkled on top. Or, slice 1½ pounds carp
   fillet thinly. Place in the marinade. When the congee is cooked, add the raw fish slices
   and marinade and allow the congee to come to a boil. The fish will cook instantly. Turn
   off the heat immediately, pour the congee into a heated tureen, garnish, and serve.

MAKES 10 SERVINGS

MY MOTHER'S STEAMED PORK

Ma Ma Sum Oy Dik Ching Yuk

This is one of the recipes made with those tree ears that grew on the wood of the guava tree my mother loved so much, and included the tiger lily buds from her garden. The translation of the name I have given it, Ma Ma Sum Oy, is "Mother loved from the heart," and so she was.

¾ pound lean pork filet, cut into slices 2 inches long and 1 inch wide

3 tablespoons tree ears (cloud ears), soaked in hot water for 30 minutes, washed 3 times, and drained (1 cup tightly packed)

50 tiger lily buds, soaked in hot water for 30 minutes, ends cut off, rinsed, drained, and cut in half

1 teaspoon ginger juice mixed with 2 tablespoons Shao-Hsing wine or sherry

1½ tablespoons oyster sauce

1 tablespoon soy sauce

1 tablespoon peanut oil

1 teaspoon sesame oil

¼ teaspoon salt

1 teaspoon sugar

1 tablespoon cornstarch

6 tablespoons cold water

Pinch freshly ground white pepper

8 sprigs fresh coriander (cilantro)

1. Combine all the ingredients except the coriander in a large bowl and mix thoroughly. Allow to rest and marinate for 30 minutes. Place the mixture in a cake pan. Place the pan in a steamer, cover, and steam for 10 to 12 minutes (see steaming, page 64). Halfway through the steaming, turn the pork. It is done when the pork changes color.

2. Turn off the heat, transfer the pork to a heated dish, garnish with fresh coriander, and serve with cooked rice. My mother loved her dish with plain cooked congee. Try it.

MAKES 4 SERVINGS

ANCESTRAL PORK

Tai Gung Fun Ji Yuk

*T*his preparation is named for an administrative process in Sun Tak. Its Chinese characters translate as "ancestor distribute pork." Land, deemed to be community owned, thus the property of ancestors long gone, was customarily administered by local officials. Before each Lunar New Year this land was leased for farming by these officials on the basis of bids. The money taken in was used to buy pigs, which were slaughtered, their meat boiled, cut up, and distributed to the male members only of each family. The more males in a family, the more pork the family would receive. After the pork was distributed, a large, males-only banquet was held in the local government hall. We thought nothing of such discrimination in those times, because our family,

nation in those times, because our family, with my father, my brother, and all of my uncles and male cousins, managed to receive a large allotment of pork. After receiving the pork, we would salt it heavily, in crocks, for at least a month, to preserve it, and because of this heavy salting our ancestral pork would last us for a month of meals.

3½ pounds boneless fresh ham, skin on
2 quarts cold water, or enough to
*   cover pork*
One 1-inch-thick slice fresh ginger,
*   lightly smashed*
4 garlic cloves, peeled
6 scallions, white parts only
3 tablespoons salt

1. Place all ingredients except the salt in a large pot. Cover, bring to a boil over high heat, reduce the heat, leave the lid cracked, and simmer for 45 minutes to 1 hour. Halfway through the cooking, turn the pork.

2. Turn off the heat. Remove the pork from the pot and place in a large bowl of ice water. Allow to rest in ice water for 30 minutes, adding ice as necessary.

3. Remove the pork from the water. Remove the skin and discard. Place the pork in a shallow dish. Sprinkle the salt over it and rub in thoroughly. Cover the pork and allow it to rest in the refrigerator for 1 day.

    It is now ready for use. This salted pork will keep refrigerated for at least a week. In China, as I have noted, the heavy salting permitted us to keep the pork for a month. The pork should not be frozen. Its fiber will soften, and any defrosting will cause the salting to run off.

    We used this salted pork in many ways, in many combinations. Our family ate it with congee. We steamed it with fish and stir-fried it with various vegetables. We made soups with it. We even steamed this salted pork with fresh pork. A most versatile dish. Following are two of the ways we ate ancestral pork in Sun Tak.

SALTED PORK WITH CABBAGE

Ham Ji Yuk Chau Yeh Choy

咸肉炒椰菜

2 tablespoons Onion Oil (page 83) or
    peanut oil
2 teaspoons minced fresh ginger
1 pound green cabbage, quartered,
    cored, and julienned
1 tablespoon Chinese white rice wine
    or gin

4 to 6 tablespoons Superior Stock
    (page 74) or Chicken Stock (page 75)
¾ cup Ancestral Pork (preceding
    recipe), cut into pieces 1½ inches
    long and ⅓ inch thick
¼ teaspoon salt

Heat a wok over high heat for 30 seconds. Add the oil and coat the wok with it using a spatula. When a wisp of white smoke appears, add the ginger and stir for 20 seconds. Add the cabbage, stir, and cook for 1 minute. Drizzle the wine down into the mixture along the edges of the wok. Stir. At this point the cabbage should be dry. Add 1 tablespoon of the stock, mix well, and cook for 2 minutes. Add the pork and 2 more tablespoons of stock and stir well. Cook for 5 minutes. If the mixture is dry, add the remaining stock (from 1 to 3 tablespoons). Taste the cabbage and add salt only if needed. Cook the mixture for 1 minute more or until the cabbage is tender. Turn off the heat, transfer to a heated dish, and serve.

MAKES 4 TO 6 SERVINGS

SALTED PORK WITH MUSTARD GREENS SOUP

Ham Ji Yuk Gai Choy Tong

1 quart Chicken Stock (page 75)
One ½-inch-thick slice fresh ginger,
*   lightly smashed*
1 cup Ancestral Pork (page 208), cut
*   into very thin, 2½-inch-long slices*

1 pound fresh mustard greens, well
*   washed, drained, cut into ¾-inch*
*   pieces on a diagonal, and stalks and*
*   leaves separated*

Place the chicken stock and ginger in a large pot. Cover and bring to a boil over high heat. Add the pork, stir, and bring back to a boil. Add the mustard green stalks, stir well, and return again to a boil. Reduce the heat to medium, cook for 1½ minutes, raise the heat to high, and return to a boil. Add the mustard green leaves and stir well. Cook for 2 minutes or until tender. Turn off the heat. Transfer to a heated tureen and serve.

MAKES 4 SERVINGS

CHIVES STIR-FRIED WITH SHRIMP

Gau Choi Chau Har

As a little girl I always wanted to do what the boys did, what I was not supposed to do. Girls did not, for example, catch shrimp, certainly not the way the boys did it. I would run a shallow woven basket near the shore of the river near our house—one of the many tributaries of the Pearl River—and catch tiny baby shrimp. As I caught them, I would put them in my mouth to save until I had half a dozen. Then I would use them to bait the hook I had made from a bent needle and fish for larger shrimp. That's the way the boys did it. When I had caught enough to feed my family, I would take them home and insist I had the right to cook them. What I made, most often, was this dish. Not only does it taste good, but the colors of the pink shrimp and green chives are beautiful.

2 tablespoons peanut oil
½ teaspoon salt
¾ teaspoon sugar
2 teaspoons minced fresh ginger
¼ pound garlic chives, well washed, dried, hard stems cut into ¼-inch pieces, green parts cut into ½-inch pieces and stems and green parts separated
¾ pound medium shrimp (28 to 30), shelled and deveined
1 tablespoon Chinese white rice wine or gin
2 tablespoons Seafood Stock (page 76) mixed with 1½ teaspoons cornstarch

Heat a wok over high heat for 30 seconds, add the peanut oil, and coat the wok with it using a spatula. Add the salt and sugar and stir briefly. When a wisp of white smoke appears, add the ginger and hard ends of garlic chives, stir, and cook for 30 seconds, until the fragrance of the chives is released. Add the shrimp and spread in a thin layer. Add the wine, lower the heat to medium, and turn the shrimp over. Add the green chives, mix well, and cook for 1½ to 2 minutes or until the chives turn bright green and the shrimp turn pink and curl. Stir the stock-cornstarch mixture, add to the wok, stir, and cook until it thickens, about 1 minute. Turn off the heat, transfer to a heated plate, and serve.

MAKES 4 SERVINGS

SUN TAK FRIED RICE

Sun Tak Chau Fan

*V*ersions of fried rice exist throughout China. This is a fried rice preparation unique to my home, made with fish we salted and preserved. We used a gray, meaty fish, the "toothed croaker." It would be cleaned, rid of its scales and gills, dried, and salted thoroughly inside its cavity and out, then placed in a low, open crock. It would be covered with a straw mat, and a weight or large rock would be placed on it to press out the moisture. After several days it would be hung by its tail in the sun to dry. It then became hom yue, or salted fish, a food we enjoyed in many ways. We ate it steamed, or deep-fried to bring out its fragrance, and in our own fried rice.

Hom yue *is available in Chinese groceries, salted, in plastic-wrapped packages labeled either "toothed croaker" or, inexplicably,* han yee. *Be certain to use this dried fish; others could disappoint you. If this fish is unavailable, the closest to it is the dried codfish sold in many markets, though it too is but a barely satisfactory substitute.*

Another different aspect of this dish is that the rice is steamed before it is stir-fried, quite different from usual fried rice recipes.

1½ cups extra-long-grain rice
1½ cups cold water
2 Chinese sausages (lop cheung)
2 cups plus 2 tablespoons peanut oil
1 ounce salted, preserved fish

For the sauce
2 tablespoons Chicken Stock
* (page 75)*
1 tablespoon oyster sauce
1½ teaspoons soy sauce
¼ teaspoon salt
½ teaspoon sugar
½ teaspoon sesame oil
Pinch freshly ground white pepper

2 large eggs, beaten
1½ teaspoons minced fresh ginger
1½ teaspoons minced garlic

1. Place the rice in a bowl with water to cover. Wash it 3 times by rubbing it between your palms and drain well. Place in a cake pan and add the 1½ cups cold water. Place the Chinese sausages on top of the rice. Place the cake pan in a steamer, cover, and steam for 40 minutes (see steaming, page 64).

2. As the rice steams, prepare the fish. Place 2 cups of the peanut oil in a wok and heat to 350°F. Add the fish and fry until very crisp, 4 to 5 minutes. Turn off the heat, remove the fish, drain, and cool. Remove the bone, mince the fish to make 1 tablespoon, and reserve. The remainder may be kept for future use.

3. Combine the sauce ingredients and reserve.

4. When the rice is done, remove from the steamer and cool. Remove the sausages, cut them into quarters, then into ¼-inch pieces, and reserve. Loosen the rice and set aside.

5. Heat a wok over high heat for 1 minute, add 1 tablespoon of the remaining peanut oil, and coat the wok with it using a spatula. Beat the eggs lightly once again, then pour into the wok. Soft-scramble the eggs, then remove from the wok and cut coarsely with a knife and reserve.

6. Heat the wok over high heat, add the remaining tablespoon of peanut oil, and coat the wok with it using a spatula. When a wisp of white smoke appears, add the ginger, stir briefly, add the garlic, and stir. When the garlic turns light brown, add the fish and cook, stirring, for 30 seconds. Add the sausages and cook, stirring, for 1 minute. Add the rice and stir all ingredients thoroughly until the rice is hot. If the heat is too high, lower it to prevent burning. Stir the sauce ingredients, pour into the rice, and stir. Raise the heat to high again. When the rice has become an even brown color and is well coated, add the cooked eggs and stir well. Turn off the heat, add the scallion, and stir until well mixed. Remove the fried rice to a heated platter and serve.

MAKES 4 TO 6 SERVINGS

BONELESS STUFFED CHICKEN
Choi Pei Nor Mai Gai

*T*his was a holiday feast dish in Sun Tak, one we enjoyed on family occasions such as birthdays and often as the center of our Lunar New Year meal. It takes some time to prepare, but it is worth the effort. My parents and my Ah Paw impressed on me that to offer this preparation to a guest was to offer great respect. This stuffed chicken was also known in greater Guangdong province, around us, but unfortunately it has virtually vanished from restaurants in China. So, to enjoy it, make it yourself, as we did in Sun Tak.

1½ cups glutinous rice
1½ cups cold water
One 3¼- to 3½-pound chicken
Salt

For the sauce
3½ teaspoons Chinese white rice wine
   or gin
1½ teaspoons grated fresh ginger

¾ teaspoon salt
3 teaspoons sugar
3½ teaspoons oyster sauce
2 teaspoons sesame oil
2 teaspoons soy sauce
2 tablespoons cornstarch
¼ teaspoon freshly ground white pepper

3½ tablespoons peanut oil,
   for stir-frying
2 teaspoons minced garlic
2 teaspoons minced fresh ginger
¼ pound boneless lean pork, cut into
   ¼-inch dice
6 ounces shrimp, shelled, deveined, and
   diced
4 Steamed Black Mushrooms
   (page 81), cut into ⅛-inch dice
4 fresh water chestnuts, peeled and cut
   into ⅛-inch dice
4 scallions, trimmed and finely sliced
5 cups peanut oil, for deep-frying

1. Place the glutinous rice in a bowl with water to cover, wash 3 times by rubbing between your palms, rinse, and drain. Place the rice in a cake pan, add the 1½ cups cold water, place the pan in a steamer, and steam for 30 to 45 minutes (see steaming, page 64), until the rice tastes cooked through and sticks together. Reserve.

2. Meanwhile, clean the chicken thoroughly and remove the fat and membranes. Wash under cold running water and rinse. Sprinkle the outside with salt and rub in well. Rinse the chicken, drain, and reserve.

3. Bone the chicken, being careful not to puncture or tear the skin. For detailed instructions and photographs, see the color section. Remove the meat from the breasts, thighs, and drumsticks and cut into ¼-inch dice.

    To prepare the chicken for stuffing, sew the neck cavity closed. Check the skin for any holes or tears and sew them closed.

4. Stir together the sauce ingredients and reserve.

5. Heat a wok over high heat for 40 seconds, add the 3½ tablespoons peanut oil, and coat the wok with it using a spatula. When a wisp of white smoke appears, add the garlic and ginger and stir until the garlic turns light brown. Add the diced chicken meat, stir, and mix well for 2 minutes. Add the pork and cook, stirring, until it turns white, 2½ minutes. Add the shrimp, stir, and cook for 1½ minutes or until the shrimp turn pink. Make a well in the center of the mixture, stir the sauce, and pour it in. Mix thoroughly until the sauce bubbles. Turn off the heat and remove to a shallow dish to cool.

6. Place the cooked rice in a large bowl. Add the cooked mixture. Add the mushrooms, water chestnuts, and scallions. Mix well to combine evenly.

7. Stuff the chicken. Spoon the rice mixture into the skin, packing it loosely. Sew up the skin. Shape the stuffed chicken so that it looks like the chicken before it was boned.

8. Heat the oven to 325°F for 20 minutes. Place the chicken on a rack in a roasting pan and roast for 45 minutes. Turn the chicken over and roast for 45 minutes more, until the chicken is brown. Remove from the oven and cool for 5 hours so that the skin will become crisp when fried.

9. Heat a wok over high heat for 1 minute. Add the 5 cups peanut oil and heat to 375°F. When a wisp of white smoke appears, place the chicken in a large Chinese strainer and lower into the boiling oil. Deep-fry until the skin becomes golden brown and crisp, 7 to 10 minutes. If the entire chicken cannot be submerged in oil, then ladle the oil over it until it becomes crisp.

10. Turn the heat off, remove the chicken from the wok, and drain for at least 7 minutes. Place it on a platter, slice it across, and serve it as you would a terrine.

NOTE: *The boning may be done a day ahead. After the chicken has been roasted and cooled, it can be frozen. To complete the cooking, defrost, place in a 350°F oven for 30 minutes, then deep-fry. I have done this successfully many times.*

MAKES 8 SERVINGS

All Foods
in Harmony

和順食品

和順食品

THE OBJECT OF PREPARING AND COOKING FOOD IN CHINA IS TO GIVE PLEASURE TO OTHERS AND TO EXPERIENCE PERSONAL SATISFACTION. YET EQUALLY IMPORTANT AMONG THE CHINESE IS THE CREATION OF HARMONY AND BALANCE AMONG FLAVORS AND IN APPEARANCE, IN ACCORDANCE WITH OUR BELIEF THAT ALL FOODS SHOULD IMPROVE OR MAINTAIN BODILY HEALTH. Which food is compatible with or enhances another, to the ultimate benefit of the body, is always a consideration, and food is cooked accordingly. To the Chinese, devoting thousands of years to food as medicine has made this instinctive.

Within this context, whatever their region, most Chinese believe strongly that certain foods are beneficial when eaten in combination with others, that ideally such combinations bring balance to the body as natural medicines, curatives, restoratives. We believe that most foods are to be considered either yin or yang, representations of Lao-tze's two complementary forces that govern life. Foods considered in the Tao way are either yin, or cool, and should be eaten to reduce the body's heat or yang, or hot, and should counteract bodily coldness. This balance we seek not only in our food but in our lives and with our environments.

Over the years many foods in the Chinese kitchen have been classified by physicians and herbalists as inherently hot or cool. Vegetables such as asparagus, cucumbers, lotus root, water chestnuts, celery, lettuce, mushrooms, bean sprouts, spinach, boxthorn seeds, watercress, and some cabbages, among others, are understood to be cooling. Few vegetables are warming. Only leeks, onions, shallots, carrots, chives, and scallions are hot. Most fish and seafood are deemed to be cool, most meats warming. Fruits such as oranges, lemons, pears, watermelons, grapefruit, bananas, and coconuts are cool; cherries, litchis, longans, mangoes, apricots, strawberries, and blackberries are warm.

While observing these properties, the Chinese believe that dietary balance is enhanced by moderation. One should leave the table satisfied but not satiated, and we regard overindulgence in either food or drink as harmful. The amounts of food we eat, as well as the kinds, are relevant to our health. Further, we believe that many foods have innate characters and should not be consumed without consideration of that character. One food may be regarded as yin, or cool, but if cooked in a certain way, will become yang, or hot. Thus, we believe, if for example, yang foods are eaten largely by a yang person, his or her health could be harmed. What we select and eat should be based on balance and harmony, on the seasons, and surely on each individual.

Our beliefs that health can be the result of proper diet and disease of improper diet are embedded in our culture. Sun Simao, a court physician of the Tang dynasty, has written, "Treat an illness first with food. Only if this fails should medicines be prescribed." More than 2,000 years before him, an emperor known as Shen Nong was revered for his studies of herbs and health-giving foods, and by the time of the Zhou dynasty, from 1122 to 770 B.C., the imperial families were attended to by court dietitians. During the Han dynasty, which lasted from 200 B.C. to A.D. 200, *Emperor's Classic of Corporal Medicine* was published, along with a codification of Shen Nong's herbal studies. *Emperor's Classic* cautioned in part that salty flavors hardened the blood vessels, that pungency toughened the flesh, that too much sweetness harmed the bones.

By the time of the Yuan dynasty, in the thirteenth century, a court dietitian, Hu Su-hui, had set down the *Principles of a Correct Diet,* and under the Ming, who followed, came Chia Ming's *Essential Knowledge for Eating and Drinking.* It is said that when, as a one-hundred-year-old, he was asked by his emperor what the secret of his long life was,

he replied, "To be most cautious about what one eats or drinks."

Over the centuries much folklore has evolved regarding specific foods. Apricots were thought to be good for easing heart disorders, mung beans for cooling the stomach, lotus root juice for relieving skin rashes, chicken eggs for increasing blood flow, ginger and garlic for aiding digestion. Eggplant was said to be an age retardant. A double-boiled ginseng soup was thought to increase sexual potency, whereas a watercress soup was regarded as most cooling to the body. A mixture of pork with a green vegetable was a perfect balance of cool and hot. Bean curd and orange peel were said to relieve chest congestion. Turtle jelly, that essence in aspic of steamed turtle, was believed to be a circulation aid; chicken baked with eight herbs, four yin and four yang, would increase one's energy immensely.

Chicken cooked with ginkgo nuts could relieve coughs and asthma, it was said. And even today the leaves of the ginkgo tree are said to stem the pace of Alzheimer's disease. If one ate fried scorpions, it was said (as I have), it would stop hair from graying; and eating fried black ants in combination with potatoes (as I have) would help battle rheumatism and hepatitis . . . perhaps. Cassia tea would lower cholesterol, and poached pears with ovaries of snow frog would clear the lungs as well as the skin.

Fanciful tales of various foods, often in combination, surround pregnancy. Crabs should not be eaten. Why? Because crabs move sideways, and an expectant mother would rather her child be straightforward. Duck and goose are considered too hot and thus could damage the skin of the fetus. Lamb should be avoided because it increases the danger of epilepsy. Black sesame seeds, however, made into a soup and drunk near the end of a pregnancy, would, it is believed, shorten the period of labor and ensure that one's baby would have bright, shiny eyes and hair. It is believed widely in China that the first food that should be eaten by a woman after childbirth is plain rice stir-fried with julienned ginger. It is thought that during birth a woman's body becomes filled with air and that rice and ginger, ginger particularly, will dissipate this interior air and wind. This devotion to ginger continues further; the first time a woman washes her hair after giving birth, it is with ginger water.

There is a mixture—a food, a tonic, a soup; call it what you will—that is a tradition in my family, one all of us have adhered to for generations, from my grandmother to my mother to all of my aunts and cousins. It is what we make to eat following the birth of a child, a preparation that is said to replenish blood loss and to rejuvenate the body. Does it work? Indeed it does. I have given birth to three children, and after each I have cooked and eaten this food. I call it Sweet Birth Vinegar.

SWEET BIRTH VINEGAR

Tim Ding Tim Cho

2½ pounds young ginger, peeled, cut into 2½-inch pieces, and lightly smashed
Four 28-ounce bottles Chinese sweet rice vinegar (black colored)

4 pounds pig's feet, cut into 2-inch pieces
½ to ¾ pound sugarcane sugar or dark brown sugar
18 eggs, hard-boiled and peeled

1. Place the ginger, sweet vinegar, and pig's feet in a large pot. Cover and bring to a boil over high heat. Reduce the heat to a simmer, leaving the lid cracked, and simmer for 2 hours. Stir from time to time with a wooden spoon. The pig's feet should be tender.

2. Taste the vinegar. It should taste sweet and sour, balanced. Variations will occur because of differences in batches of rice vinegar. Add the sugar to taste. Cook until the sugar is melted and blended. Add the hard-boiled eggs, stir, and make certain the eggs are completely immersed in the vinegar. Simmer for another 30 minutes. Turn off the heat and serve with cooked rice.

The recipe above is for three days, three meals each day, two eggs per meal. In China it is usually prepared in vast amounts, and is eaten three times a day for one month, by a woman who has just given birth, to build her blood and strength. During this month the woman will eat only small amounts of pork or fish, with vegetables and nothing more. This recipe is extremely strong, and although it is meant to be eaten by females only, males in our family have been known to love it and to sneak into the kitchen to eat it when they were not supposed to. In fact, one of my teenage cousins, a boy, did just that. His sister had given birth, and the Sweet Birth Vinegar had been made for her. He began to

nip at it and came down with a fever.

Initially it was not understood why, but when what he had done was discovered, the reason was simple, my aunt, his mother, said. Her verdict, "Too much yang." Customarily the dish was also kept on hand so that when neighbors and friends came with "lucky money" envelopes for the newborn baby, the envelopes in bowls, the envelopes would be accepted and the bowls filled with this Sweet Birth Vinegar.

Many of these special, traditional, remedial foods are acknowledged as cures for specific ailments; others are believed to be; still others are rooted in myth and folktales. But they abound. Before one leaps headlong into the realm of food as medicine, however, I suggest a good deal of study. Much is fact, but just as much is fancy.

A pear, for example, is regarded as yin. But put it into a batter and fry it as a dessert, and it becomes yang. For a yin person, whose system is generally regarded as weak, yang foods can be helpful and healthful. A yang person, because of his or her inherent strength, is constantly striving for the balance that yin foods can bring. Walnuts, we were told early in our lives, are perfect for the health of our kidneys, regardless of our inner natures. Similarly, almonds are beneficial to the lungs. Each food will have medicinal qualities, but only in combination with other foods, other drink, and with careful bodily study can the balance we seek be attained, the cures we seek be effective.

These concepts are instilled in us at an early age, and we consider the effect that foods will have on our systems as a matter of course. Our continual effort to balance can be aided by Chinese herbal medicines. It is true that often foods are prescribed, usually by an herbalist, or a physician, following an examination. This can be as simple as a study of one's pulse, tongue, and eyes or as complex as a set of physical tests. A tea of powdered herbs may rightly be prescribed as an invigorating tonic or as a soup.

Yet there are restaurants that purport to be able to prescribe entire menus following a simple taking of a pulse. In most cases I regard such practices as mere marketing. I question them, for the concept of food as medicine in China is based on many factors, not simply a cursory placing of forefinger on wrist. Such consideration of the pulse is, to be sure,

important, but it cannot be complete. Responsible doctors and herbalists with whom I have spoken contend that to simply go into an establishment that claims to be preparing health-giving foods for the general populace could do more harm than good. They caution that before eating in this manner one should know his or her body and should understand the concept of eating for balance and harmony.

The Chinese believe, traditionally, that in the world surrounding us there are five dominant elements: wood, fire, earth, gold, and water. These elements refer to seasons, to climate, directions, colors, tastes, bodily organs and tissues, as well as other parts, the senses and temperament. The chart that Chinese doctors use as their reference is on pages 222–223.

Belief in these relationships carries with it the idea that each element begets the next, in a continuing cycle. Wood gives birth to fire. Fire and its ashes give birth to earth. Earth gives birth to gold. Gold gives birth to water. Water gives birth to wood. No element stands alone. None is innately good or bad. There are no absolutes. When, however, one is in excess, disorder and darkness may occur. Similarly, if there is a deficiency, disorder may result. When I was a girl, my grandmother, my Ah Paw, would reel off dozens of health combinations based on these principles. I remember she would look into my eyes and at my tongue and tell me what my nature was that particular day. Was I wet and cold? A simple tea of chrysanthemum flowers and sugar would soothe and balance me. Had I a tight cough, a symptom that my body was hot? She would give me winter

The Chinese Physician's Chart of the Five Elements, Their Relationship to Food Properties, and the Parts of the Body They Affect ◆

Elements	Seasons	Climate	Direction	Species Development	Colors	
Wood	Spring	Wind	East	Birth	Green	
Fire	Summer	Heat	South	Growth	Red	
Earth	Long Summer	Humidity	Central	Transition	Yellow	
Gold	Autumn	Dryness	West	Harvesting	White	
Water	Winter	Coolness	North	Storage	Black	

melon tea and fresh water chestnuts to eat, perfect coolers.

If anyone in the family was recovering from a long, debilitating illness, Ah Paw and my mother, Miu Hau, would have made a whole chicken, double-boiled with red dates and boxthorn seeds. This preparation was neither entirely hot nor entirely cold, but the combination was a restorative. In winter when it was cooler, we ate snake soup, a hot food, to build our blood and thus our resistance. But snake was too hot by far to eat in summer. If my body was too cool, I was given *mui choy*, preserved mustard, steamed with beef and served with rice, a dish of great energy. As was double-boiled black chicken, a fowl the meat of which is never eaten but which provides a deep, warming broth. These were not, quite obviously, the foods of folklore, but rather food remedies rooted in common sense.

If one ate heavily, then the following meal should be light. In our home, virtually every meal consisted of a soup, a stir-fried

	Taste	Organs	Organs II	Senses	Tissues	Temperament	
	Sour	Liver	Gall-bladder	Eyes	Tendons	Rage	
	Bitter	Heart	Small Intestine	Tongue	Pulse	Happiness	
	Sweet	Pancreas	Stomach	Mouth	Flesh	When One Thinks Too Much	
	Spicy	Lungs	Large Intestine	Nose	Hair	Sorrow	
	Salty	Kidneys	Bladder	Ears	Bones	Fear	

dish, and one steamed, these served always with cooked rice, a perfect balancing agent. It was always a meal of balance, in the best sense, prepared and cooked within the context of that instinctive, cultural knowledge. It was important, I recall my mother and grandmother saying, that at each meal we eat a steamed food. Ah Paw considered steaming the ultimate cooking process. Food that was fried or roasted became yang, or hot, no matter its nature. Steaming, essentially neutral, allowed yin and yang foods to retain their natures. Steaming was life-giving, she would say, and not just because of her age. The harmony of our meals was enhanced always with fresh fruit to finish, to balance.

Harmony and balance are what I seek always to achieve when I cook. Much of this is innate, some of it planned. In all of the preparations that follow I preach taste and texture, aroma and color, balance and harmony, the essentials of the Chinese kitchen. Ah Paw would say often, and I echo her, *"Sik tak fook,"* or "When you can eat, life is good."

Pork
and Other Meats

猪肉和其它肉类

猪肉和其它肉類

TRADITIONALLY, IN CHINA, MEAT IS PORK. PIGS, WILD IN PREHISTORIC TIMES, WERE THE FIRST ANIMALS TO BE DOMESTICATED FOR FOOD ON A LARGE SCALE. PARTICULARLY IN THE SOUTH, PORK IS A DIETARY NECESSITY, NOT TO OBSERVANT BUDDHISTS TO BE SURE, OR TO THOSE MOSLEM CHINESE, BUT TO THE LARGER POPULATION. Pork is eaten in many forms—steamed, braised, fried, roasted, baked. Pork is an ingredient in various *dim sum* dumplings. The skin of the suckling pig is a delicacy. The organs of pigs provide the bases for stocks and broths, and their livers go into those fine sausages, *lop cheung*. When "meat" is written of in those cookbooks of 2,000 years ago, pork is meant. When Confucius details the procedures for meticulous cutting of meat into morsels, pork is meant. The Chinese regard pork as not only a fine, versatile food but as health-giving. Pork lubricates one's interior, it is believed, and is thus a favored meat for the elderly. Soups are made with large chunks of pork cooked in them, preparations deemed perfect for the young, perfect for the aged.

In the North of China lamb was, and to some extent still is, the meat of choice, and by lamb I mean mutton. In the northern regions and extending west, sheep are raised widely for food, and their meat is cooked in quite the same ways as pork. In China's history the Mongols, for example, roasted whole sheep over fires, while people in other parts of China braised lamb, stewed it, and, classically, stir-fried it with a favorite vegetable, leek.

Beef, though ubiquitous in China, is the meat least likely to be eaten by traditional Chinese. Cattle were deemed too important as draft animals and were thus killed for food only when they had outlasted their usefulness. Then, it can be imagined, their meat would be tough and stringy and most useful as bases for stocks and soups. Nevertheless beef was and is eaten in China, more so in cities and regions that over the centuries have been in contact with Western habits and foods. Beef has been, for example, important for a long time in the West of China, down into Sichuan, a broad region encompassing the Silk Road. Throughout history the Chinese have regarded beef as a "strong" meat, a "hot" food, often with aromas they thought not pleasant. This has changed in later years, and in such essentially modern cities as Hong Kong, Guangzhou, and Shanghai beef is common, with veal becoming more common as well. Still, to the traditionally minded Chinese, meat is pork.

SHREDDED PORK
WITH SWEET BEAN SAUCE

Jeung Bau Yuk See

*T*his is a traditional dish of Beijing, where sweet bean sauce and the sweetness of sugar are to be found in much of the cooking. Jeung bau *translates as "with sauce to sear with high heat" and in Beijing is used to describe any meat with a marinade that is seared.*

For the marinade
1 medium egg white, beaten
½ teaspoon salt
¾ teaspoon sugar
2½ teaspoons tapioca flour

¾ pound boneless pork loin, cut into 2- by ¼-inch julienne

For the sauce
2 teaspoons Shao-Hsing wine or dry sherry

2 teaspoons double dark soy sauce, regular dark soy sauce, or mushroom soy sauce
1 teaspoon Chinese white rice vinegar or distilled vinegar
1 teaspoon sugar
¼ teaspoon salt
1 teaspoon sesame oil
½ teaspoon tapioca flour

2 cups peanut oil
1½ teaspoons minced fresh ginger
3 tablespoons trimmed and finely sliced scallions
2½ tablespoons sweet bean sauce
¼ cup julienned white part of scallion, for garnish

1. In a large bowl, combine the marinade ingredients. Add the pork and allow to rest for at least 20 minutes. In another bowl, combine the sauce ingredients and reserve.

2. Heat a wok over high heat for 45 seconds and add the peanut oil. When a wisp of white smoke appears, reduce the heat to low and add the pork and marinade. Loosen the pork with chopsticks or tongs and cook until the pork turns white, about 1 minute. Turn off the heat, remove the pork with a strainer, and drain. Pour off the oil into a bowl and reserve. Wipe off the wok with paper towels.

3. Heat the wok over high heat for 20 seconds, add 1 tablespoon of the reserved peanut oil, and coat the wok with it using a spatula. When a wisp of white smoke appears, add the minced ginger and sliced scallion and cook, stirring, for 20 seconds. Add the bean sauce and cook, stirring, for 20 seconds. Add the pork and cook, stirring, for 1½ minutes. Make a well in the center of the mixture, stir the sauce mixture, pour in, and mix well. Cook, stirring, for 1 minute or until the sauce bubbles. Turn off the heat, transfer to a heated dish, sprinkle with the julienned scallion, and serve.

MAKES 4 SERVINGS

SLICED WHITE PORK

Bok Yuk Pin

*T*his Beijing pork dish, with its condiments, is a tradition at banquets, particularly at weddings. The "white" in this
preparation refers to the plain water in
which the pork is boiled, usually in a clay
pot. Its name translates as "pork sliced like
paper," and it is customarily served sliced
almost tissue-thin, with a selection of 4 specific condiments. This dish is famous indeed
in Beijing, where it is said to have originated in 1741 in the Sah Wor Geui Fan
Jon, or Clay Pot Rice Shop, a restaurant so

well regarded that it is said the emperor
himself would travel out of the Forbidden
City for some sliced white pork. Often the
dish would be sold out before noon. In the
North there is a saying that this dish can be
made only by northerners and is beyond the
skill of Chinese from the South. Nonsense.
Here it is.

10 cups water
3 pounds fresh ham in 1 piece with
skin

1. Bring the water to a boil in a sand clay pot, if available. If not, use a large pot. Add the
   pork, lower the heat, and simmer for 2 hours, leaving the lid cracked. During the cooking, turn the pork 4 or 5 times.

2. Turn off the heat, remove the pork from the pot, and cool for 10 to 15 minutes.
   Remove and discard the skin. Slice very thinly, arrange on a platter, and serve with
   Steamed Bread Loaf (page 364) and the following 4 condiments, each in its own dish.

Red Wet Bean Curd Sauce
4 cakes red wet bean curd, mashed with
*   2 tablespoons bean curd liquid*
1½ tablespoons sugar

1 teaspoon Hot Pepper Oil (page 87) or
*   other hot chili oil*

Mix the ingredients together to blend thoroughly.

Chive Flower Paste
2 teaspoons peanut oil
¼ teaspoon crushed Sichuan
*   peppercorns*
¼ teaspoon salt

¾ teaspoon sugar
½ cup chive flowers (long lengths of
*   chives with buds attached), finely*
*   sliced, or ⅔ cup tightly packed*
*   Chinese chives*

Heat a wok over high heat for 30 seconds. Add the peanut oil and coat the wok with it using
   a spatula. When a wisp of white smoke appears, add the peppercorns, salt, and sugar

and stir for 5 seconds. Add the chive flowers, stir, and cook 4 to 5 minutes, until the flowers soften. (If chives are used, cook for 2 to 3 minutes.) Turn off the heat and transfer to a dish.

Soy and Chili Sauce
3 tablespoons soy sauce
4 fresh Thai chilies, minced

3 tablespoons Chicken Stock (page 75)

Mix the ingredients together well and place in a serving dish.

Double Garlic Sauce
2 tablespoons finely minced garlic

1 tablespoon Garlic Oil (page 84)
or peanut oil

Mix the ingredients together well and place in a serving dish.

MAKES 10 TO 12 SERVINGS

SLICED PORK WITH SPICY SAUCE

Jeung Bau Yuk

The origin of this preparation, depending on which chef you speak to, is either Beijing, Sichuan, or Shanghai. And they are all correct, for the dish exists in all of these regions, with only minor variations imposed by individual chefs. This version is from Sichuan.

7 cups cold water
1 pound lean fresh ham in 1 piece
2 celery stalks, each cut into 3 pieces
2 medium onions, peeled and quartered
3 scallions, trimmed and cut into
* 3 pieces*
Two ½-inch-thick slices fresh ginger,
* lightly smashed*
1 teaspoon sugar

¼ teaspoon baking soda
3 large stalks mustard greens, cut into
* ¼-inch diagonal pieces (1¾ cups)*

For the sauce
2½ teaspoons double dark soy sauce,
* regular dark soy sauce, or mushroom*
* soy sauce*
2½ teaspoons sugar
1 tablespoon Shao-Hsing wine or dry
* sherry*
1 tablespoon Chicken Stock (page 75)

2 tablespoons Shallot Oil (page 84) or
* peanut oil*
1 tablespoon julienned fresh ginger
2 tablespoons sweet bean sauce

*1 tablespoon preserved horse beans
with chili or Chili Sauce
(page 88)*

*1½ tablespoons Shao-Hsing wine or dry
sherry*
½ cup julienned white part of scallion

1. Place 5 cups of the water, the ham, celery, onions, scallions, and 1 slice of the ginger in a pot. Cover and bring to a boil over high heat. Lower the heat and simmer, leaving the lid cracked, for 30 minutes. Turn off the heat, remove the pork to a bowl of ice water, and allow to rest for 30 minutes. Either reserve the cooking liquid for future use or discard.

2. To blanch the mustard greens, place the remaining 2 cups water in a pot along with the other slice of ginger, the sugar, and the baking soda. Bring to a boil over high heat. Add the mustard greens and blanch for 10 seconds. Turn off the heat, run cold water into the pot, and drain. Repeat. Reserve the mustard greens.

3. In a bowl, mix the sauce ingredients and reserve. Cut the pork into thin slices, 2 inches by 1½ inches.

4. Heat a wok over high heat. Add the shallot oil and coat the wok with it using a spatula. When a wisp of white smoke appears, add the ginger, stir, and mix for 10 seconds. Add the bean sauce and horse beans with chili and stir to mix. Add the pork and stir to mix. Add the wine and mix well. Add the reserved mustard greens, stir to mix, and cook for 1½ minutes. Make a well in the center of the mixture, stir the sauce mixture, pour in, and stir to mix. Add the scallion and mix well. When the sauce thickens, turn off the heat, transfer to a heated dish, and serve.

MAKES 6 SERVINGS

STIR-FRIED THREE SHREDS

Chau Sam See

The characters of this Cantonese preparation, chau sam see, *translate as "stir-fried three shreds," and illustrate a popular aspect of Guangzhou's quick-cooking technique. The 3 shreds in this instance are the pork, the bean curd, and the snow peas. Among the Cantonese, other 3-shred stir-fries are possible as well.*

For the marinade
1 tablespoon egg white, beaten
1 teaspoon cornstarch
1 teaspoon sesame oil
½ teaspoon Chinese white rice vinegar
  or distilled vinegar
½ teaspoon Shao-Hsing wine or dry
  sherry
½ teaspoon soy sauce
½ teaspoon sugar
⅛ teaspoon salt
Pinch freshly ground white pepper

6 ounces lean pork loin, cut into
  ¼-inch julienne

For the sauce
2 teaspoons soy sauce
1 tablespoon oyster sauce
1½ teaspoons sugar
2 teaspoons cornstarch
Pinch freshly ground white pepper
½ cup Superior Stock (page 74) or
  Chicken Stock (page 75)

2½ tablespoons peanut oil
2 teaspoons minced fresh ginger
2 teaspoons minced garlic
3 bean curd cakes (brown colored),
  julienned
¼ pound snow peas, strings removed
  and julienned
1 tablespoon Shao-Hsing wine or dry
  sherry

1. Combine the marinade ingredients in a large bowl. Add the pork and allow to rest for 30 minutes. In another bowl, mix together the sauce ingredients and reserve.

2. Heat a wok over high heat for 30 seconds. Add 1 tablespoon of the peanut oil and coat the wok with it using a spatula. When a wisp of white smoke appears, add 1 teaspoon each of minced ginger and garlic and stir briefly. Add the bean curd cakes and snow peas, and cook, stirring, for 1 minute. Turn off the heat, remove the ingredients from the wok, and reserve. Wipe off the wok and spatula with paper towels.

3. Heat the wok over high heat for 20 seconds. Add the remaining peanut oil and coat the wok with it using a spatula. When a wisp of white smoke appears, add the remaining teaspoons of minced ginger and garlic and stir briefly. Add the pork and marinade.

Spread the pork in a thin layer, cook for 1 minute, turn over, add the wine, and cook, stirring, for 1 minute or until the pork changes color. Add the reserved bean curd cakes and snow peas and cook, stirring, for 2 minutes. Make a well in the center of the mixture, stir the sauce mixture, pour in, and mix well. When the sauce thickens, turn off the heat. Transfer to a heated dish and serve.

MAKES 6 SERVINGS

PORK WITH PICKLED MUSTARD GREENS

Seun Choi Chau Yuk Pin

This is a dish of the Chiu Chow people of southern China. It is a masterpiece of adaptation. The Chiu Chow, though using Cantonese ingredients, have created their own dish. As a matter of fact, you will find this dish in the Chiu Chow restaurants of Hong Kong but rarely in any Cantonese restaurant.

For the marinade
1 teaspoon ginger juice mixed with
*   2 teaspoons Chinese white rice wine or*
*   gin*
1 tablespoon oyster sauce
1 teaspoon soy sauce
1 teaspoon sesame oil
1 teaspoon sugar
⅛ teaspoon salt
½ tablespoon cornstarch

½ pound boneless lean pork loin, cut
*   across the grain into slices 2 inches*
*   by 1 inch*

For the sauce
¼ cup Superior Stock (page 74) or
*   Chicken Stock (page 75)*
1 tablespoon oyster sauce
1½ teaspoons dark soy sauce
2 teaspoons sugar
2 tablespoons cornstarch

2 tablespoons peanut oil
One ½-inch-thick slice fresh ginger,
*   lightly smashed*
½ pound Pickled Mustard Greens
*   (page 103), cut across into ¼-inch*
*   slices*
3 large fresh water chestnuts, peeled,
*   washed, cut in half, then thinly*
*   sliced (½ cup)*
¼ pound snow peas, strings removed
*   and cut into ½-inch pieces on a*
*   diagonal*
1 small red bell pepper, julienned
2 teaspoons minced garlic

continued

1. In a large bowl, combine the marinade ingredients. Add the pork and allow to rest for 30 minutes. In another bowl, mix together the sauce and reserve.

2. Heat a wok over high heat for 40 seconds. Add 1 tablespoon of the peanut oil and coat the wok with it using a spatula. When a wisp of white smoke appears, add the ginger and cook for 10 seconds. Add the mustard greens and cook, stirring, for 1½ minutes. Add the water chestnuts and cook, stirring, for 1 minute. Add the snow peas and pepper, stir, and cook for 1 minute more. Turn off the heat, remove the mixture from the wok, and reserve.

3. Wipe off the wok and spatula with paper towels. Turn the heat under the wok back to high for 30 seconds. Add the remaining tablespoon of peanut oil and coat the wok with it using a spatula. When a wisp of white smoke appears, add the garlic. When the garlic turns light brown, add the pork and marinade. Spread the pork in a thin layer, cook for 30 seconds, turn over, stir well, and cook for 30 seconds more or until the pork changes color. Add the reserved vegetables and cook well, stirring, for 1½ minutes. Make a well in the center of the mixture, stir the sauce mixture, and pour in. When the sauce thickens, turn off the heat, remove to a heated dish, and serve with cooked rice.

MAKES 6 SERVINGS

BRAISED FRESH BACON

Hangzhou Kau Yuk

This intensely flavored fresh pork dish is from Hangzhou, southwest of Shanghai. Kau yuk *translates as "long-cooked meat," and there are versions of it throughout China. Most often the meat is braised in soy sauce, sugar, and wine, and on occasion, depending on the regional taste, spices such as cinnamon, anise, fennel, cloves, or Sichuan peppercorns are added. This version, a tradition in Hangzhou, relies solely on the soy, sugar, and wine.*

3 pounds fresh, uncured bacon (pork belly), skin and meat, including short ribs

¼ pound sugarcane sugar or dark brown sugar

7 cups cold water

½ cup Shao-Hsing wine or dry sherry

One 1-inch-thick slice fresh ginger, lightly smashed

6 scallions, trimmed and cut into 3 pieces

⅔ cup double dark soy sauce, regular dark soy sauce, or mushroom soy

1. Cut the bacon into strip lengths 2½ inches wide. They will be 2 to 2½ inches thick. Cut along these lengths at 2-inch intervals, including the bones, to create pieces about 2 by 2½ inches. The yield will be 8 almost-square pieces.

2. Tie each piece of bacon with string around and across very tightly so that the bones will not fall away from the meat or otherwise fall apart.

3. Place the bacon pieces, sugar, water, 6 tablespoons of the wine, the ginger, and the scallions in a large pot. Cover and bring to a boil over high heat. Add the soy sauce and return to a boil. Lower the heat and simmer slowly, leaving the lid cracked, for 3 hours. Turn the meat from time to time. After 3 hours the liquid should be reduced by about one third. Cover the pot completely and cook for 1 hour more, turning the meat from time to time. The meat will become very tender and the liquid will be reduced by half.

4. Return the heat to high, add the remaining 2 tablespoons of wine, and mix thoroughly. Return again to a boil and turn the heat off immediately. Transfer the bacon pieces from the pot to a heated dish. Serve with cooked rice, over which the sauce from the pot has been spooned.

    Because of its richness, this dish is best served accompanied by a simply cooked green vegetable, a perfect balance. Fresh *choi sum* (recipe follows) is ideal.

MAKES 8 SERVINGS

CHOI SUM

2 quarts cold water

One ½-inch-thick slice fresh ginger, lightly smashed

2 teaspoons salt

2 pounds fresh choi sum, *tough outer leaves and tough ends of stalks removed (1½ pounds)*

Place the water, ginger, and salt in a large pot. Bring to a boil over high heat. Add the *choi sum* and return to a boil. This should cook the *choi sum* perfectly. However, another minute in the boiling water may be necessary for tenderness. Test. Turn off the heat and drain. While hot, transfer to a heated platter, cut into bite-sized pieces, and serve with the braised fresh bacon and rice.

MAKES 8 SERVINGS

FRESH BACON WRAPPED IN LOTUS LEAF

Hor Yip Fan Jing Yuk

*I*n Yunnan, when this dish is prepared, the pork is characteristically cooked in bak yim soi, or "white salt water," which indicates that no sauces or colorings are used. However, a stock is used, as are such spices as cinnamon, eight-star anise, anise seed, nutmeg, and Sichuan peppercorns— "white" but pungent.

One 1-inch cinnamon stick

1 piece eight-star anise

½ nutmeg

¼ teaspoon anise seed

¼ teaspoon Sichuan peppercorns

1 quart Milk Stock (page 78) or Chicken Stock (page 75)

2 cups water

One ¼-inch-thick slice fresh ginger

1½ teaspoons salt

2 tablespoons Mei Kuei Lu Chiew or gin

2 scallions, white parts only

For the coating sauce

3 tablespoons Cinnamon Roasted Rice Powder (page 72)

2 tablespoons double dark soy sauce, regular dark soy sauce, or mushroom soy sauce

2 tablespoons Shao-Hsing wine or dry
sherry

2 tablespoons sugar

1½ tablespoons preserved horse beans
with chili or Chili Sauce (page 88)

1½ tablespoons sweet bean sauce

1 cake red wet bean curd, mashed

1½ tablespoons julienned fresh ginger

3½ tablespoons julienned shallot

½ cup Chicken Stock (page 75)

1¾ pounds fresh, uncured bacon (pork
belly) with bone, whole (1¼ pounds
with bone removed)

1 large lotus leaf, soaked in hot water
for 20 minutes until softened,
washed, drained, and cut into
6 equal pieces

1. Wrap the cinnamon, anise, nutmeg, anise seed, and peppercorns into a cheesecloth bundle. Place the stock, water, spice bundle, ginger, salt, Mei Kuei Lu Chiew, and scallions in a pot. Cover and bring to a boil over high heat. Lower the heat and simmer, leaving the lid cracked, for 30 minutes. Turn off the heat. Strain the liquid and discard all other ingredients. You now have your "white salt water."

2. Combine the coating sauce in a bowl and reserve.

3. Place the "white salt water" in a pot and bring to a boil over high heat. Add the bacon and return to a boil. Lower the heat and simmer, leaving the lid cracked, for 1½ hours, until the bacon is quite soft. Turn off the heat, remove the bacon, and cool until it can be handled. Cut into 6 equal portions. Mix the coating sauce. Add the bacon pieces to the sauce and coat thoroughly.

4. Place one piece of bacon in the center of a piece of lotus leaf and add a bit of coating sauce. Wrap the bacon by folding the leaf over it in fours. Repeat with the remaining 5 pieces.

5. Place the wrapped bacon, folded sides down, in a steamer. Cover and steam for 1 hour (see steaming, page 64). Turn off the heat and transfer the lotus leave wraps to individual dishes. Unfold each and eat out of the leaves.

MAKES 6 SERVINGS

SICHUAN MUSTARD PICKLE SOUP WITH PORK

Jah Choi Yuk Pin Tong

*T*his rich soup is from Guangzhou, where the Cantonese have happily borrowed Sichuan mustard pickle from their western neighbors to give this pork soup its distinctive flavor. In Canton the use of this mustard pickle from Sichuan is widespread, not only in soups but in steamed and stir-fried dishes as well. I remember this soup as a favorite of our family during my childhood.

5½ cups Superior Stock (page 74) or Chicken Stock (page 75)
One 1-inch-thick slice fresh ginger, lightly smashed

¼ cup Sichuan mustard pickle (page 34), thinly sliced into pieces 2 inches by ½ inch
½ cup thinly sliced fresh bamboo shoots in pieces 2 inches by ½ inch
¾ cup straw mushrooms
½ cup baby corn, sliced lengthwise into quarters
⅛ teaspoon freshly ground white pepper
¼ pound lean boneless pork loin, thinly sliced
2 tablespoons Shao-Hsing wine or dry sherry
½ teaspoon salt (optional)
1½ teaspoons sesame oil
2 tablespoons finely sliced fresh coriander (cilantro)

Place the stock, ginger, and Sichuan mustard pickle in a pot, cover, and bring to a boil over high heat. Lower the heat and simmer, leaving the lid cracked, for 5 minutes. Raise the heat and return to a boil. Add the bamboo shoots, mushrooms, corn, and white pepper, stir well, and return to a boil. Lower the heat and simmer, leaving the lid cracked, for 5 minutes more. Raise the heat and return to a boil. Add the pork and wine, stir, and mix well. Return to a boil and boil for 1 minute. Taste to see if the salt is needed. Turn off the heat. Add the sesame oil and stir in thoroughly. Transfer to a heated tureen, sprinkle with the coriander, and serve.

MAKES 6 TO 8 SERVINGS

SALTED PORK
WITH BOK CHOY SOUP

Ham Jee Yuk Bok Choy Tong

*T*his is another of those dishes we made with our "Ancestral Pork." Our elders believed that salted pork, with bok choy, acted to reduce the heat of their bodies. My mother particularly loved this soup, and she was most inventive with the goodly amounts of salted pork we had each year.

4½ cups Chicken Stock (page 75)
¾ cup Ancestral Pork (page 208), thinly sliced

1 tablespoon minced fresh ginger
1¼ pounds bok choy, *stalks separated, stems and leaves cut crosswise into ½-inch pieces and reserved separately*
1 tablespoon Chinese white rice wine or gin
¼ teaspoon salt (optional)
2 tablespoons Scallion Oil (page 82) or peanut oil

Place the stock, pork, and ginger in a pot. Cover and bring to a boil over high heat. Add the *bok choy* stems, stir, and return to a boil. Lower the heat to medium and cook for 5 minutes, uncovered. Raise the heat to high, add the *bok choy* leaves, stir, and mix well. Return to a boil. Add the wine and stir in. Lower the heat to medium and cook for another 5 minutes. Test the stems for tenderness. Taste for salt. Add the scallion oil and stir in thoroughly. Turn off the heat, transfer the soup to a heated tureen, and serve.

MAKES 4 SERVINGS

HAM AND TIANJIN BOK CHOY SOUP

For Tui Jin Bok Tong

This traditional soup of Shanghai contains that fine cured ham of the Shanghai region, Jin Hua. As with Yunnan ham, which Jin Hua resembles, I substitute Smithfield ham, an admirable stand-in. In Shanghai this soup is called bok tong, or "white soup," because it is based on Milk Stock. For added vigor, the people of Shanghai, who like direct, straightforward tastes, add salted pork to the mix.

5 cups Milk Stock (page 78) or Chicken Stock (page 75)

1 cup Ancestral Pork (page 208), cut into ½-inch dice

One 1-inch-thick slice fresh ginger, lightly smashed

½ cup prepared diced Smithfield Ham (page 79) in ½-inch pieces

2 pounds Tianjin bok choy, individual stalks separated, washed, drained, cut in half lengthwise, then cut crosswise into ½-inch slices

1 tablespoon Onion Oil (page 83) or peanut oil

Place the stock, pork, and ginger in a large pot. Cover and bring to a boil over high heat. Reduce the heat to low, leave the lid cracked, and cook for 10 minutes. Add the ham and cook for another 10 minutes. Raise the heat and return to a boil. Add the *bok choy,* stir to make certain it is completely immersed, and return to a boil. Lower the heat, leave the lid cracked, and cook for 10 to 15 minutes more or until the vegetable is tender. Add the onion oil and stir in thoroughly. Turn off the heat, transfer to a heated tureen, and serve.

MAKES 6 SERVINGS

BARBECUED SPARERIBS

Siu Pai Guat

This familiar Cantonese preparation has probably been eaten as widely as any other dish. The ribs, roasted or broiled, are often referred to as barbecued. *The word* siu *means to roast by suspending over a fire. This recipe will make perfect ribs every time.*

1 rack spareribs (3 to 3½ pounds, 12 to 14 ribs)

For the marinade
2 tablespoons oyster sauce
2 tablespoons hoisin sauce
2 tablespoons soy sauce
2 tablespoons dark soy sauce
¼ cup honey
2 tablespoons Mei Kuei Lu Chiew
　or gin
½ teaspoon salt
Pinch freshly ground white pepper

1. Remove the flap from the rack and any extra fat from the ribs, then with a sharp knife score the rack all over so the meat is tenderized and absorbs the marinade.

2. In a bowl, combine the marinade ingredients.

3. Line a baking pan with foil and lay the rack in the pan. Using your hands, rub the marinade well into the rack. Marinate for at least 4 hours. The ribs may be prepared a day ahead and refrigerated, covered, overnight, but they must be brought to room temperature for cooking.

4. Preheat the broiler for 20 minutes. Place the pan with the ribs in the oven and broil for 30 to 50 minutes. Some boiling water may have to be added to the pan if the sauce begins to evaporate. During the broiling process, baste the ribs several times with the pan sauce and turn the rack over several times as well. To test the rack for doneness, make a cut in the thickest part of the meat with a sharp knife.

5. Remove the ribs from the broiler and allow to cool 5 to 7 minutes. Place on a cutting board and cut individual ribs along the meat between the bones. Serve with cooked rice, over which the pan sauce has been spooned.

MAKES 4 SERVINGS

DRUNKEN SPARERIBS
Joi Pai Guat

This original dish from Fujian incorporates many tastes of southern China, including wines and vinegars, spices, pastes, and sauces. It is a varied, exotic preparation, and the reason the people of Fujian call it "drunken" is not because of any alcoholic content, but because its tastes and fragrances excite the senses. Is it not a happy circumstance that the Chinese word for such sensual excitement is joi?

For the marinade
2 teaspoons Shao-Hsing wine or dry
    sherry
1/8 teaspoon salt
3 tablespoons tapioca flour
1 1/2 tablespoons egg white, beaten

1 pound spareribs, flap and fat
    removed and ribs cut into 1-inch
    pieces by the butcher (thirty 1-inch
    pieces)

For the sauce
1 tablespoon Colman's mustard
    powder

2 1/2 tablespoons sugar
2 tablespoons Chinkiang vinegar or
    red wine vinegar
1 tablespoon soy sauce
2 teaspoons chili paste
1 tablespoon sesame seed paste (tahini)
1/2 cup canned tomato sauce
2 teaspoons Shao-Hsing wine or dry
    sherry
Pinch freshly ground white pepper

1 quart peanut oil
One 1-inch-thick slice fresh ginger,
    peeled
2 large garlic cloves, peeled
2 teaspoons minced garlic
1 tablespoon curry powder mixed with
    1 tablespoon Chicken Stock
    (page 75)
1/4 cup Chicken Stock (page 75)
4 scallions, white parts only, thinly
    sliced (1/4 cup)

1. In a large bowl, combine the marinade ingredients. Place the chopped sparerib pieces in the marinade and allow to rest for 30 minutes. In another bowl, mix the sauce ingredients and reserve.

2. Heat a wok over high heat for 40 seconds, add the peanut oil, and heat to 375°F. When a wisp of white smoke appears, add the ginger and garlic cloves. Place the

spareribs in a single layer in a Chinese strainer and lower into the oil. Fry for 7 minutes or until the ribs turn golden. Turn off the heat, remove the spareribs, drain, then reserve on a heated platter. Transfer the oil to a bowl.

3. Heat a wok over high heat for 10 seconds and return 2 tablespoons of the reserved oil to the wok. Add the minced garlic and stir. When it turns light brown, add the curry mixture, stir, and cook for 1 minute. Add the stock, stir, and cook for 2 minutes. Stir the sauce mixture, pour into the wok, and stir to mix. Add the scallions, stir, and cook for 3 minutes. All the ingredients should blend well and release their fragrances. At this point you will have a varied, rich, thick sauce.

4. Turn off the heat. Pour the sauce over the spareribs on the platter and serve.

MAKES 6 SERVINGS

SPARERIBS WITH RED WINE RICE

Bau Cho Pai Guat

This is another preparation from those wonderfully inventive cooks from Fujian. In this recipe they have taken their own fermented red wine rice and made it the basis for another sparerib dish. This is most famous in Fuzhou, and people, it is said, will travel miles and days just to taste it. In Fujian province this dish would be batter fried, with red wine rice in the batter. My version emphasizes the taste of the red wine rice rather than any batter and, if I may be immodest, tastes better. Sometimes traditions can be improved on.

5 cups peanut oil
One 1-inch-thick slice fresh ginger, peeled
2 garlic cloves, peeled
1 pound spareribs, flap and fat removed and ribs cut crosswise into 1-inch pieces by the butcher (thirty 1-inch pieces)
2 teaspoons minced fresh ginger
2 teaspoons minced garlic
½ cup Red Wine Rice (page 70)
2 cups Red Wine Rice liquid
1 tablespoon soy sauce
2 tablespoons sugar
1 cup Chicken Stock (page 75)

1. Heat a wok over high heat for 40 seconds, add the peanut oil, slice of ginger, and garlic cloves, and heat to 350°F. Add the spareribs, stir to separate, and cook for 2 minutes, until their color is whitened. Turn off the heat, remove the ribs from the oil with a Chinese strainer, and drain. Transfer the oil to a bowl.

2. Heat the wok over high heat for 10 seconds and return 1 tablespoon of the reserved oil to the wok. Add the minced ginger and stir briefly. Add the minced garlic and stir. When the garlic turns light brown, add the spareribs and stir. Add the red wine rice and liquid and cook well, stirring, making certain the ribs are well coated. Lower the heat, add the soy sauce, and stir briefly. Add the sugar and stir well to mix. Add the stock, cover the wok, lower the heat, and simmer for 30 minutes or until the ribs are tender, stirring occasionally. About ½ cup of sauce should be left in the bottom of the wok. Turn off the heat, transfer the ribs and sauce to a heated platter, and serve with cooked rice.

MAKES 6 SERVINGS

PORK MEATBALLS FILLED WITH SOUP

Kun Tong Yuk Yeun

This imaginative dish is from Shanghai, the home of the soup-filled dumpling and the soup-filled bun. The cooks of Shanghai are always finding new ways to do things. This invention of the Shanghai kitchen is elegant, beautiful to look at, sumptuous to eat, and easy to make. All of China has meatballs of one sort or another, but only Shanghai puts soup in them. Their name, kun tong, *translates as "inject soup." The nature of this dish requires that most of the preparation work be done a day early, yet it is simple.*

For the meatballs
1 pound ground pork with some fat
2 jumbo eggs

2 tablespoons Shao-Hsing wine or dry sherry
½ teaspoon salt
1 teaspoon sugar
1½ teaspoons soy sauce
3 scallions, trimmed and finely sliced
1 tablespoon minced fresh ginger
⅛ teaspoon freshly ground white pepper
4½ tablespoons tapioca flour

For the soup filling
¾ envelope unflavored gelatin
⅔ cup Superior Stock (page 74) or Chicken Stock (page 75)

8 square slices white bread, frozen
6 cups peanut oil

1. Prepare the meatballs a day ahead. Place all the meatball ingredients in a bowl and mix thoroughly, stirring in one direction, until well blended. Place the bowl, covered with plastic wrap, in the refrigerator. Punch several holes in the plastic wrap cover and allow to rest overnight.

2. Also prepare the soup filling a day ahead. Place the gelatin in a bowl. Place the stock in a saucepan and bring to a boil. Pour the boiling stock over the gelatin. Stir until the gelatin is dissolved. Allow to cool. Cover and place in the refrigerator overnight to gel.

3. Also prepare the bread a day ahead. Cut the frozen bread into ¼-inch square croutons. Place the croutons on a cookie sheet. Heat the oven to 375°F for 20 minutes. Turn off the oven. Place the cookie sheet in the oven and toast the croutons for 18 to 20 minutes, until hard and crusted. Remove, cool, and reserve overnight at room temperature.

4. Sift the croutons, discard any fine powder, and return to the cookie sheet. Cut the set gelatin into twenty-four ¾-inch cubes.

continued

5. To prepare the soup meatballs, place a heaped tablespoon of pork in your hand and make a small well in the center. Place a soup gelatin cube in the well and close the pork around it completely. Because some meat will adhere to your hands, make 8 meatballs at a time, then rinse your hands. After the meatballs are formed, place them on the cookie sheet with the croutons and pat and roll them until the meatballs are well coated with croutons. Repeat in 2 more batches until 24 meatballs are made. Keep the meatballs refrigerated until ready for frying.

6. Heat a wok over high heat for 1 minute. Add the peanut oil and heat to 375°F. Place the meatballs, 8 at a time, in the oil and fry for 3 minutes, moving them about so they brown evenly. The oil temperature will drop when meatballs are added, so maintain a temperature of 325°F at all times. The meatballs should be crisp and deep reddish brown in color. Remove with a Chinese strainer and drain. Repeat until all 24 meatballs are cooked.

7. Serve in the traditional manner, with Chinese spoons in bowls. You bite into the top of the meatball, revealing the soup, then eat the meatball and soup accompanied by the following dip, the way it is done in Shanghai.

   These are usually served one to a person as part of a larger meal. However, be your own judge, depending on your own craving. A good individual portion is 3 or 4 meatballs.

Vinegar Ginger Dip
5 tablespoons Chinese red rice vinegar
  or distilled vinegar

3½ tablespoons finely julienned fresh
  ginger

Combine the ingredients in a bowl and serve with the meatballs.

MAKES 24 MEATBALLS

FIVE-SPICE BEEF

Ng Heung Ngau Yuk

This Beijing preparation, always served cold, is usually an appetizer or a first course. It is this beef preparation, thinly and artfully sliced, that often is used in those sculpted food dishes served at banquets in China.

2 quarts cold water
4 pounds shin of beef
7 ounces sugarcane sugar or dark
   brown sugar

½ cup Shao-Hsing wine or dry sherry
4 garlic cloves, peeled
Two ½-inch-thick slices fresh ginger
Three 3-inch-long cinnamon sticks
4 pieces eight-star anise
½ teaspoon Sichuan peppercorns
1 teaspoon salt
1 cup double dark soy sauce, regular
   dark soy sauce, or mushroom soy
   sauce

1. Place the water in a large pot. Add all the other ingredients except the soy sauce and stir. Cover the pot and bring to a boil over high heat. Add the soy sauce and return to a boil. Lower the heat and simmer the beef for 4 hours. Remove the pot cover to check, and if the liquid appears to be evaporating quickly, partially cover the pot, leaving space for the steam to escape. Test the beef with a chopstick. If it goes into the beef easily, it is done. About 2½ cups of cooking liquid should be left in the pot. Turn off the heat, cover the pot, and allow the beef to come to room temperature in the liquid.

2. Transfer the beef to a shallow dish. Reserve the cooking liquid for storing the meat. Cover the meat with plastic wrap and refrigerate. When it is cooled, slice thinly and serve or refrigerate for up to 7 days or freeze for up to 6 weeks, stored in a container with 1½ cups of cooking liquid. Defrost before slicing.

MAKES 10 TO 12 SERVINGS

BEEF WITH PICKLED PEARS

Ngau Lau Chau Seun Lei

This is my recipe, designed to demonstrate how the best of cuts fit comfortably in the Chinese larder, which rarely includes filet of beef. Cooking it in combination with my pickled pears gives it an unusual piquancy.

For the marinade
2 teaspoons egg white, beaten
¼ teaspoon salt
½ teaspoon sugar
2 teaspoons cornstarch

1 pound filet mignon, cut into pieces 1½ inches long by ½ inch thick

For the sauce
1½ tablespoons oyster sauce
2 teaspoons double dark soy sauce, regular dark soy sauce, or mushroom soy sauce
2 teaspoons Shao-Hsing wine or dry sherry

1½ teaspoons sugar
Pinch freshly ground white pepper
1 teaspoon sesame oil
1 tablespoon cornstarch
¼ cup Chicken Stock (page 75)

2 cups peanut oil
1 tablespoon minced fresh ginger
⅓ cup julienned Pickled Pears (page 101)
3 ounces snow peas, strings removed and cut in half
¼ cup fresh bamboo shoots, cut into julienne
½ cup red bell pepper, cut into julienne
½ cup sliced white parts of scallions, in ¼-inch diagonal pieces
1 tablespoon Shao-Hsing wine or dry sherry

1. In a large bowl, combine the marinade ingredients. Place the beef in the marinade and allow to rest for 20 minutes. In another bowl, mix together the sauce ingredients and reserve.

2. To blanch the beef, heat a wok over high heat for 1 minute, add the peanut oil, and heat to 350°F. Add the beef and marinade. Immediately turn off the heat. Loosen the beef with a spatula and cook for 1 minute or until the slices brown slightly. Remove the beef from the oil with a Chinese strainer and drain. Transfer the oil to a bowl.

3. Return 1 tablespoon of the reserved oil to the wok and heat over high heat for 20 seconds. Add the ginger and stir briefly. Add the pickled pear and vegetables and cook,

stirring, for 1½ minutes, until the snow peas turn bright green. Add the beef and stir. Add the wine and mix well. Cook, stirring, for 2 minutes, until the mixture is very hot. Make a well in the center, stir the sauce mixture, pour in, and mix well. When the sauce thickens, turn off the heat, transfer to a heated dish, and serve.

MAKES 4 SERVINGS

BEEF WITH EGGPLANT

Keh Gua Jiu Ngau Yuk

This is the essence of Cantonese home cooking. In much of China the egg-plant, though plentiful, does not usually find its way into restaurants, simply because it is quite common. It will be cooked, upon request. On the other hand, it is eaten widely in the home. In our house in Sun Tak we grew eggplants of various kinds, from white to purple, round to those small finger-length eggplants.

For the marinade
½ *teaspoon ginger juice*
½ *teaspoon Chinese white rice wine or gin*
¼ *teaspoon salt*

1½ *teaspoons peanut oil*
1 *tablespoon cornstarch*

½ *pound London broil, cut into pieces 2 by 1½ inches and ⅛ inch thick*
1¼ *pounds Chinese eggplant*
3½ *cups peanut oil*
2 *teaspoons minced fresh ginger*
2 *teaspoons minced garlic*
1 *tablespoon bean sauce*
½ *cup Superior Stock (page 74) or Chicken Stock (page 75)*
2 *teaspoons sugar*
2 *tablespoons oyster sauce*
1 *teaspoon double dark soy sauce, regular dark soy sauce, or mushroom soy sauce*

1. In a large bowl, combine the marinade ingredients. Place the beef in the marinade and allow to rest for at least 15 minutes.

2. Meanwhile, roll-cut the eggplants. Beginning at one end, cut diagonally into approximately ¾-inch slices. Turn the eggplant a quarter turn between cuts. The shape will be a kind of rounded, edged triangle the Chinese call *fu tau,* or the "ax."

continued

3. To blanch the beef, heat the wok over high heat for 1 minute, add the peanut oil, and heat to 325°F. Add the beef and marinade and loosen the beef with a spatula. Turn the heat off immediately. Let sit to blanch for 10 to 12 seconds; the beef should still be a little red. Remove with a Chinese strainer and drain.

4. To blanch the eggplant, heat the oil to 350°F. Add the eggplant and stir. Blanch for 1 minute. Turn off the heat, remove the eggplant with a Chinese strainer, and drain. Transfer the oil from the wok to a bowl.

5. Return 1 tablespoon of the reserved oil to the wok and heat over high heat for 20 seconds. Add the ginger and garlic and stir briefly. Add the bean sauce and stir. Add the eggplant, stir, and cook for 45 seconds. Add the stock and stir well. Add the sugar, oyster sauce, and soy sauce and stir. Cook for 1½ minutes or until the eggplant is very soft and the liquid bubbles. Add the beef and cook, stirring, for 45 seconds. Turn off the heat, transfer to a heated dish, and serve.

MAKES 4 TO 6 SERVINGS

SICHUAN DRY SHREDDED BEEF

Gawn Chau Ngau Yuk

Many and inventive are the ways of Sichuan when it comes to preparing beef. Marinades and cooking techniques are used to create different textures as well as tastes. Beef can be soft, crisp, even hard in the many versions from that region. Following are 2 examples of the best of Sichuan's beef preparations. The first is gawn chau, or "dry-fried," which connotes no stock, broth, or water used in its cooking. The second, the name of which translates as "twice deep-fried, once stir-fried," is my secret weapon. When I wish my daughter to visit me, I tempt her, always successfully, with this triple-fried Sichuan beef.

1½ tablespoons sweet bean sauce
1 tablespoon preserved horse beans with chili or Chili Sauce (page 88)
2½ teaspoons sugar
⅛ teaspoon cayenne pepper
¼ teaspoon Hot Pepper Oil (page 87) or other hot chili oil
¼ teaspoon salt
2 tablespoons peanut oil
1¼ teaspoons minced fresh ginger
1¼ teaspoons minced garlic
1 tablespoon Sichuan Peppercorn Paste (page 90)
2 medium carrots, julienned (1 cup)
¾ pound flank steak, julienned across the grain
1 tablespoon Shao-Hsing wine or dry sherry
½ cup julienned white part of scallions

1. In a bowl, combine the sweet bean sauce, preserved horse beans with chili, sugar, cayenne pepper, hot pepper oil, and salt. Set aside.

2. Heat a wok over high heat for 40 seconds. Add the peanut oil and coat the wok with it using a spatula. When a wisp of white smoke appears, add the ginger and garlic and stir briefly. Add the Sichuan peppercorn paste, stir, and cook for 30 seconds, until it releases its fragrance. Add the carrots, stir, and cook for 1 minute. Add the beef and stir. Add the wine and cook, stirring, for 1 minute or until the beef changes color. Add the reserved combined ingredients and cook, stirring, for 1 minute. Turn off the heat, add the scallions, and mix well. Transfer to a heated dish and serve.

MAKES 4 TO 6 SERVINGS

TRIPLE-FRIED
CRISP BEEF SICHUAN

Yee Jah Yut Chau

¾ pound flank steak, cut across grain
 in a precise julienne, each 3 inches
 long by ¼ inch thick
½ teaspoon baking soda
¼ teaspoon salt
¾ teaspoon sugar
1 tablespoon egg white, beaten
2 tablespoons cornstarch
3½ cups peanut oil
1½ teaspoons minced fresh ginger
2 teaspoons minced garlic
1 tablespoon Sichuan Peppercorn Paste
 (page 90)

½ cup julienned carrot
½ cup julienned white part of scallions
1 tablespoon preserved horse beans with
 chili
1 tablespoon sweet bean sauce
2 teaspoons sugar
½ teaspoon Hot Pepper Oil (page 87)
 or other hot chili oil
2 tablespoons finely sliced green part
 of scallion

1. Place the beef in a bowl with the baking soda, salt, and sugar, stir together, and allow to rest for 2 hours in the refrigerator. Add the egg white and cornstarch, mix, and allow to rest for at least 10 minutes.

2. Heat a wok over high heat for 1 minute, add the peanut oil, and heat to 375°F. Add the beef and marinade and loosen the beef with chopsticks. Fry for 3 minutes, keeping the beef slices separated. Turn off the heat, remove the beef with a Chinese strainer, drain, and cool to room temperature.

3. Heat the oil again to 375°F. Place the beef back in the wok and fry for 3 minutes, until crisp. Turn off the heat. Remove the beef with a Chinese strainer and drain.

4. Pour off all but 1 tablespoon of oil from the wok. Heat over high heat for 15 seconds. Add the ginger, garlic, and peppercorn paste and cook, stirring, until the paste releases its fragrance. Add the carrot and cook, stirring, for 30 seconds. Add the white part of the scallions and cook, stirring, for 30 seconds. Add the beef, stir to mix, and cook for 1 minute. Add the preserved horse beans, sweet bean sauce, sugar, and hot pepper oil. Stir well and cook for 1½ minutes or until all ingredients are well combined and hot. Turn off the heat, transfer to a heated platter, sprinkle with the green part of scallion, and serve.

MAKES 4 TO 6 SERVINGS

BEEF SOUP WITH PICKLED MUSTARD GREENS AND BEAN CURD

Seun Choi Ngau Yuk Dau Fu Tong

This soup, my own concoction, is a pleasant soup that I make often for my family. I find that it always stimulates their appetites further, which of course is what I intend.

For the marinade
1 teaspoon ginger juice
2 teaspoons Chinese white rice wine or gin
1 tablespoon oyster sauce
2 teaspoons soy sauce
1 teaspoon sugar
1 teaspoon sesame oil
Pinch freshly ground white pepper
1 tablespoon cornstarch

½ pound London broil, julienned across the grain
6 cups Chicken Stock (page 75)
One ½-inch-thick slice fresh ginger, lightly smashed
6 ounces Pickled Mustard Greens (page 103), cut into 1- by ¼-inch pieces (1 cup tightly packed)
2 tablespoons Chinese white rice vinegar or distilled vinegar
¾ pound fresh bean curd (medium-firm tofu), cut into ¾- by ¼-inch pieces
3 tablespoons trimmed and finely sliced scallion
3 tablespoons finely sliced fresh coriander (cilantro)

1. In a large bowl, combine the marinade ingredients. Place the beef in the marinade and allow to rest for at least 20 minutes.

2. In a large pot, place the stock, ginger, and pickled mustard greens, cover, and bring to a boil over high heat. Lower the heat and simmer, leaving the lid cracked, for 15 minutes. Raise the heat back to high, add the vinegar, and stir well. Add the bean curd and return to a boil. Add the beef and marinade, loosening the beef with a wooden spoon. Lower the heat to medium and return to a boil. Turn off the heat, transfer to a heated tureen, and serve in individual bowls, sprinkled with scallion and coriander to individual tastes.

MAKES 8 SERVINGS

STEAMED BRISKET WITH
CINNAMON ROASTED RICE

Fan Jing Ngau Yuk

*T*his beef preparation is claimed jointly by Beijing and Sichuan and, to be sure, is found in the traditions of both regions. There is little difference in the versions. Both, however, use the cinnamon roasted rice that originated in Beijing, so perhaps Beijing has more of a claim to the dish's provenance. As far as I am concerned, each can claim it equally, making it the most diplomatic of dishes.

For the marinade
2 teaspoons Chinese white rice vinegar
    or distilled vinegar
1 tablespoon oyster sauce
¾ teaspoon hot pepper flakes (page 87)
1 teaspoon sesame oil
½ tablespoon Scallion Oil (page 82)
    or peanut oil

1 tablespoon double dark soy sauce,
    regular dark soy sauce, or mushroom
    soy sauce
2 tablespoons hoisin sauce
1½ tablespoons Shao-Hsing wine or dry
    sherry
1½ teaspoons sugar
2 teaspoons minced fresh ginger
2 teaspoons minced garlic
Pinch freshly ground white pepper

¾ pound lean beef brisket, cut into
    2½- by 1-inch pieces
3 tablespoons Cinnamon Roasted Rice
    Powder (page 72)
⅔ cup Chicken Stock (page 75)
½ cup chopped white parts of scallions
    in ¼-inch diagonal pieces
⅓ cup finely sliced green part of
    scallions

1. In a bowl, combine the marinade ingredients.

2. Place the brisket slices in a steamproof dish, add the marinade, and mix well. Add the cinnamon roasted rice powder and mix thoroughly. Add the stock and mix well. Add the white parts of scallions and mix well. The meat should be well coated. Marinate in the refrigerator for at least 2 hours.

3. To steam the brisket, place 2 quarts of boiling water in a wok. Place a steamproof dish with the brisket and marinade in a steamer. Cover and steam for 40 minutes, until the brisket slices are tender (see steaming, page 64). Turn off the heat, sprinkle the green part of scallions over the brisket, and serve in the steamproof dish with cooked rice.

MAKES 4 SERVINGS

STIR-FRIED LAMB WITH LEEKS

Seun Bau Yung Yuk

T*his particular dish crosses the boundaries between Sichuan and Beijing
and uses the leeks so loved in China's North
and West. In those regions of China, lamb
traditionally has been the meat of choice—
roasted, boiled, fried, braised, stewed. The
words* seun bau *translate as "leeks seared,"
which indicates what happens with* yung
yuk, *or "lamb meat," which is how lamb is
described.*

For the marinade
2 teaspoons sesame oil
2½ teaspoons double dark soy sauce,
    regular dark soy sauce, or mushroom
    soy sauce
1½ teaspoons Shao-Hsing wine or dry
    sherry
1 teaspoon Chinese white rice vinegar
    or distilled vinegar

1½ teaspoons sugar
¼ teaspoon salt
1½ teaspoons cornstarch
Pinch freshly ground white pepper

½ pound lean lamb fillet, cut into
    slices 2 by 1½ inches
3 tablespoons peanut oil
¼ teaspoon salt
¾ pound leeks, washed thoroughly,
    trimmed, and cut into pieces
    1½ inches long by ¼ inch wide
4 teaspoons minced fresh ginger
1 tablespoon Shao-Hsing wine or dry
    sherry
1 teaspoon cornstarch mixed with
    3 tablespoons Chicken Stock
    (page 75)
½ teaspoon sesame oil

1. In a large bowl, combine the marinade ingredients. Place the lamb in the marinade and allow to rest for 1 hour.

2. Heat a wok over high heat for 1 minute. Add 1½ tablespoons of the peanut oil and coat the wok with it using a spatula. When a wisp of white smoke appears, add the salt and leeks and cook, stirring, for 1 minute. Turn off the heat, remove the leeks from the wok, and reserve.

3. Wipe off the wok and spatula with paper towels. Heat the wok over high heat for 40 seconds, add the remaining 1½ tablespoons peanut oil, and coat the wok with it using a spatula. When a wisp of white smoke appears, add the ginger, stir briefly, and add the lamb and marinade. Spread in a thin layer, cook for 1 minute, and turn over. Add the wine and stir. Add the reserved leeks and cook, stirring, for 1 minute. Make a well in the center, stir the cornstarch-stock mixture, pour in, and mix thoroughly. Cook, stirring, for 1 minute. Turn off the heat. Add the sesame oil and mix well. Transfer to a heated platter and serve.

MAKES 4 TO 6 SERVINGS

LAMB BRAISED WITH RED WINE RICE

Kung Cho Yung Yuk

*T*raditionally, in this Fujian recipe, an entire piece of lamb, with its bone, is water-blanched, then cut up and prepared. I have simplified this dish by having the lamb butchered simply and eliminating the blanching process. The flavor and texture, however, are true to their Fujian origin. This dish uses the richness of that wonderful Red Wine Rice so beloved, and widely eaten, throughout Fujian.

3 pounds butt end of leg of lamb, cut
  into 3 equal slices across the bone by
  the butcher

For the marinade
1 tablespoon ginger juice mixed with
  2 tablespoons Shao-Hsing wine or
  dry sherry
1½ teaspoons salt
1½ teaspoons sugar
Pinch freshly ground white pepper

2 tablespoons peanut oil
Four ½-inch-thick slices fresh ginger
5 tablespoons Red Wine Rice
  (page 70)
16 small Chinese black mushrooms,
  soaked in hot water for 30 minutes,
  washed, and stems removed
1½ cups diced bamboo shoots, cut into
  1-inch cubes
6 scallions, trimmed and cut into
  1½-inch pieces
2 cups Chicken Stock (page 75)
½ cup Red Wine Rice liquid
  (page 70)
Six 1- by 2-inch pieces dried tangerine
  peel, soaked in hot water for
  20 minutes, until softened
¼ cup Shao-Hsing wine or dry sherry
2 tablespoons soy sauce
1 teaspoon sugar

1. Prepare the lamb. Separate the meat from the bone. Trim the fat and discard. You should now have 1⅓ pounds of meat. Cut the meat into 1½-inch cubes. In a large bowl, combine the marinade ingredients. Place the lamb cubes and the bone in the marinade and allow to rest in the refrigerator for at least 2 hours. Separate the lamb and bones from the marinade and reserve separately.

2. Heat a wok over high heat for 1 minute, add the peanut oil, and coat the wok with it using a spatula. When a wisp of white smoke appears, add the ginger and cook, stirring, for 30 seconds. Add the red wine rice, stir, and cook for 1 minute, until its fragrance is

released. Add the reserved lamb and bone, stir well, and cook for 2 minutes. Add the marinade and mix well. Add the mushrooms and cook, stirring, until they are coated. Add the bamboo shoots and stir. Add the scallions and stir. Cook for 1 minute. Turn off the heat and transfer the contents of the wok to a large pot.

3. Set the pot over medium heat. Add the stock and mix well. Add the red wine rice liquid and stir in well. Add the tangerine peel and mix. Cover the pot and bring to a boil. Add the wine, stir well, and return to a boil. Add the soy sauce and mix well. Add the sugar and stir. Lower the heat and simmer, leaving the lid cracked, for 1½ hours, until the lamb is tender. Stir the pot frequently during cooking to prevent sticking. Turn off the heat, transfer the contents to a heated tureen, and serve. Traditionally this is served as one would a soup, in bowls, and accompanied by cooked rice.

MAKES 8 SERVINGS

LAMB STEW IN CLAY POT

Sah Wor Yung Yuk

*T*his slow-cooked lamb is a representa-
tive dish from Xi'an. This beautiful
city and region of China, which has yielded
from its archaeological sites that vast terra-
cotta army, is justly famed throughout
China for its lamb cookery. The initial
preparation of this particular recipe is quite
similar to the preceding recipe from Fujian,
another demonstration of how lamb is prepared in much of China. What makes this
dish distinctly from Xi'an follows and
includes the flavorings of fresh sugarcane
and lemon leaves. This stew is usually
cooked in a sand clay pot, a sah wor. If you
have one, by all means use it. If not, a large
pot will suffice. If you can't find bean curd
sticks, you could deep-fry fresh bean curd
until crispy, as a substitute.

3 pounds butt end of leg of lamb, cut
   into 3 equal slices across the bone by
   the butcher

For the marinade
1 tablespoon ginger juice mixed with
   2 tablespoons Chinese white rice wine
   or gin
1½ teaspoons salt
1½ teaspoons sugar
Pinch freshly ground white pepper

2 tablespoons peanut oil
Six ½-inch-thick slices ginger
   (3½ ounces)
2 tablespoons bean sauce
½ pound leeks, white parts only, well
   washed and cut into 1½-inch
   julienne
½ cup Chinese white rice wine or gin
2½ cups Chicken Stock (page 75), or
   more if needed
20 small Chinese black mushrooms,
   soaked in hot water for 30 minutes,
   washed, and stems removed
3 tablespoons oyster sauce
Eight 1- by 2-inch pieces dried
   tangerine peel, soaked in hot water
   for 30 minutes, until softened
¼ pound fresh water chestnuts or
   jicama, peeled and cut into ¼-inch
   slices
3 bean curd sticks, soaked in hot water
   for 1 hour, drained, and cut into
   1½-inch pieces
2 cups bamboo shoots in 1-inch cubes
One 9-inch-long stalk fresh sugarcane,
   hard skin peeled, cut into 3 equal
   pieces, and each piece quartered
   lengthwise
4 lemon leaves or Kaffir lime leaves
½ teaspoon salt

1. To prepare the lamb, separate the meat from the bone. Trim the fat and discard. You
should now have 1⅓ pounds of meat. Cut the meat into 1½-inch cubes. In a large
bowl, combine the marinade ingredients. Place the cubed lamb and bone in the mari-

nade and allow to rest at room temperature for at least 2 hours. Strain off the marinade. Separate the lamb and bone from the marinade and reserve separately.

2. Heat a wok over high heat for 1 minute. Add the peanut oil and coat the wok with it using a spatula. When a wisp of white smoke appears, add the ginger, stir, and cook for 30 seconds. Add the bean sauce and leeks and cook, stirring, for 1 minute. Add the lamb and bone, stir, and cook for 1 minute. Add the wine, stir, and cook for another minute. Turn off the heat and transfer the contents to a clay pot or a large pot.

3. Add the stock, mushrooms, oyster sauce, tangerine peel, water chestnuts, bean curd sticks, bamboo shoots, sugarcane, lemon leaves, and marinade. Mix together thoroughly. All ingredients should be covered by liquid; if not, add stock to cover. Cover and, over medium heat, bring to a boil. Lower the heat and simmer, in a clay pot for 1¼ hours or in a regular pot with the lid cracked for 1½ hours. Stir the contents frequently during cooking. The meat should be tender. Taste to see if salt is needed. If so, add, mix well, and cook for another 5 minutes. Turn off the heat. If using a clay pot, serve it at the table. Otherwise, transfer the contents to a heated tureen and serve, as a stew, in individual bowls.

This intensely flavored stew is traditionally served with a green vegetable (see following recipe) to complement its richness.

MAKES 10 SERVINGS

CHINESE BROCCOLI

2 quarts cold water
One 1-inch-thick slice fresh ginger,
    lightly smashed
1½ tablespoons sugar

2 pounds Chinese broccoli, old leaves
    and hard ends of stems removed
2 tablespoons fried onions (page 83)

Place the water, ginger, and sugar in a pot and bring to a boil over high heat. Add the Chinese broccoli, making certain it is completely immersed. Allow the water to return to a boil and cook for 2 minutes, uncovered. Drain off the water, transfer to a heated serving platter, cut the stalks into bite-sized pieces, and toss with fried onions. Serve with the preceding lamb stew.

MAKES 10 SERVINGS

Gifts
from the Water

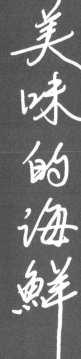

美味的海鲜

FISH, IN CHINA, SYMBOLIZE PLENTY, SIMPLY BECAUSE IT IS FELT THAT THE SUPPLY OF FISH IS ENDLESS AND THEY ARE PRIZED FOR FRESHNESS AND PURITY OF TASTE AS WELL AS FOR THEIR SYMBOLISM. ALONG THE COUNTRY'S EASTERN COAST FROM THE NORTH, FAR BEYOND SHANGHAI, DOWN TO THE SOUTHERN EDGES OF GUANGDONG PROVINCE, FRESH FISH IS VALUED, AS ARE ALL OTHER FOODS FROM THE WATER—CRABS, LOBSTERS, OYSTERS, AND CLAMS. Even in the West, much of it landlocked, fish from lakes are special, particularly those sweetest of freshwater shrimp.

To this day the Chinese will go to their markets twice daily for fresh, live fish and other seafood, for if a fish is on ice, it is not regarded as fresh, even if it has been out of the water only for a few hours. Fresh is live. For a Chinese housewife only a swimming fish is fresh, and in such markets as Yau Ma Tei and Sam Sui Po in Hong Kong, in the winding alleys of the Ching Ping market in Canton, and the vast markets of Hangzhou and Shanghai, the range, variety, and choice of live, fresh seafood is virtually limitless.

This has always been the case in China. Fish has always been with us, naturally, and always held in high regard. It has been written that in the Tang dynasty, more than 1,500 years ago, there were 98 functionaries at the imperial court whose jobs were to handle and preserve meats; yet at the same time there were 366 who cared for, cooked, and preserved fish. During those times when food became art, the roe of grass carp was "sown" in rice paddies to create fish farms. Mullet, whitebait, pomfret, char, and shark were well-known foods and used by court fish handlers. They were so talented as they minced fish for cooking that it was said fancifully that what they prepared was so light it often turned into butterflies; it was so light that it was called "snow."

Sturgeon was a fish considered so special that it was offered as court tributes. Its roe, caviar, was said to give one's face the glow of health after it had been eaten. There were, and are, those special hairy crabs from Shanghai, the fat crabs with their yellow oiled flesh from the South China Sea waters; clams from Shandong to Fujian, mussels and squid, and sheets of seaweed. So it remains today. In the Chinese kitchen fish and seafood are almost always enhanced with marinades and eaten with dips or sauces, and though fish preparations are known widely throughout China, the Cantonese way with fish and seafood is acknowledged to be the finest and most inventive.

Hoi sin, which translates as "deep water fresh," will be asked as a question by a buyer in a fish market, and given as an answer as well. Then one need only watch the interplay of fish buyer and seller. Shallow, galvanized metal vats are scattered about the markets; in them swim fish. When a buyer sees a fish she or he fancies, a finger is pointed. The fish is scooped from the vat with a net, then held so it can be inspected. A buyer will look over the body of the fish carefully, as it is held by the fish peddler, to see if there are hook or barb marks in its skin and that its gills are deep red. If the buyer is satisfied, she or he will nod. The fish seller will strike the fish on its head with a wood mallet, then while it still breathes will gut and scale it, drop it into a water-filled pail or plastic sack, and it will be taken home to cook.

The fish buyers in our family were our cooks, who took their orders often from my mother, father, or Ah Paw, my grandmother, who was very precise about her fish likes and dislikes. In our family we ate fish virtually every day, along with vegetables. Meat, pork, we had about twice a week; chicken perhaps twice a month, because these fowl were too valuable as egg layers to eat. The fish we ate most often was carp, green or grass carp, silver carp, and, on occasion, huge goldfish carp. These we would eat when Ah Paw was not around, for she refused to eat this fish that she referred to as a good Samaritan fish.

I would ask her why and she would tell me that it had to do with Kuan Yin, the Goddess of Mercy. Once, long ago, Ah Paw would tell me, Kuan Yin was unable to cross a swiftly flowing river. It was the golden carp, she said, who offered its back to the goddess and took her across the river. Because Kuan Yin was of utmost importance in the Buddhist religion, and because Ah Paw was an observant Buddhist she believed it was not right to eat this good fish. I have to say that we did eat golden carp, steamed, pan-fried, cooked with red

beans, or with tomatoes the way our family liked it particularly, but we never told Ah Paw.

We ate all of these carp and the fish we called *snakehead* and *big head,* and these we often caught ourselves. My brother would make two mud and branch dams, *gei wei,* across our small river, and pump the water out from between them with a chain-driven hand pump, a *soi cheh,* or "water car." Once the water was out we would collect fish to eat, to give to our relatives, and to preserve in salt. What we caught most in our small river was snakehead. This, Ah Paw said, could be eaten, also because of Kuan Yin.

Again, Kuan Yin found herself at a river, with only a straw basket to ferry herself across, a circumstance that would have seen her drown, according to Ah Paw. So all of the fish in the water came to her and gave her their scales, which she used to coat her basket and thus make it watertight. All the fish except the snakehead. In punishment the fish was given too many scales, so many that it covered its head. Ah Paw ate snakehead, with watercress, which she said cooled her body.

We ate river eel and catfish and fat, fleshy dace, the latter collected at the outset of cooler weather. The fish in the cold water would float up to the surface of the water, their bellies up, and we would collect them in nets before they were dead. Under Ah Paw's tutelage, I learned to kill, clean, and scale fish when I was six years old. These days I buy only live fish when possible, and I continue to be my own fishmonger.

Our family eats fish often, by choice, and when I plan a banquet or an extended festive meal, the final course is always, as it was when I was a child, a fresh fish.

POACHED LAKE FISH

Ching Soi Jeuh Yue

This fish preparation is from Suzhou, just west of Shanghai, where, it is said, the fish from Tai Hu Lake are so sweet they require no assertive flavorings when cooked. In Suzhou, a fish called ching yue, or "green fish," a lake carp, is cooked in ching soi, or "colorless water." Traditionally a sauce is added later. Grass carp, which is quite similar, is widely available, but its drawback is its great number of small bones. A lovely fat trout is a perfect substitute.

For poaching
3 quarts cold water
10 sprigs fresh coriander (cilantro), torn
One 1-inch-thick slice fresh ginger, lightly smashed
2 garlic cloves, peeled
3 scallions, trimmed and cut into thirds
3 tablespoons Scallion Oil (page 82) or peanut oil

2 teaspoons salt
3 teaspoons sugar
2 tablespoons Chinese white rice wine or gin
1 whole fresh trout (1½ to 1¾ pounds), washed, cleaned inside and out, all membranes and scales removed

For the sauce
2½ tablespoons soy sauce
1½ teaspoons sugar
1 tablespoon Shao-Hsing wine or dry sherry
1½ teaspoons Chinese white rice vinegar or distilled vinegar
Pinch freshly ground white pepper
2 tablespoons Superior Stock (page 74) or Chicken Stock (page 75)

2 tablespoons peanut oil
2 tablespoons julienned fresh ginger
2 scallions, white parts only, cut into 1½-inch julienne

1. In a fish poacher or an oval Dutch oven, bring the water to a boil and add all other poaching ingredients except the fish. Boil for 5 minutes. Place the fish in the liquid, cover, and turn off the heat immediately. Allow the fish to rest for 10 minutes. (If a well-done fish is desired, allow the fish to poach in the boiling liquid for 2 minutes. Turn off the heat and allow to rest for 10 minutes.) Transfer the fish from the pot to a heated serving platter. Discard all other ingredients.

2. As the fish poaches, combine the sauce ingredients in a bowl and set aside.

3. Heat a wok over high heat, add the peanut oil, and coat the wok with it using a spatula. When a wisp of white smoke appears, add the julienned ginger and scallions. Cook, stirring, for 1 minute. Stir the sauce mixture, pour into the wok, and bring to a boil. Turn off the heat, pour the sauce over the fish, and serve.

MAKES 4 SERVINGS

FRIED POMFRET

Jah Chong Yue

*T*his is a favorite of the fish-loving Chiu Chow people of southern China, who eat fish in many combinations and with many different, distinctive sauces. The pomfret is a meaty fish with few bones found off the Southern Chinese coast. The best is the silver pomfret, a big, round, wide fish known as *bak chong,* or the "white fish." When fried, the Chiu Chow especially like to eat the soft, fleshy lower fin and tail. The closest fish to it in texture is turbot.

1 whole pomfret (1¼ to 1½ pounds), intestines, gills, and scales removed, cleaned inside and out

For the marinade
2 tablespoons Shao-Hsing wine or dry sherry
2 teaspoons Chinese white rice vinegar or distilled vinegar
1½ teaspoons salt
1 teaspoon sugar
Pinch freshly ground white pepper

6 cups peanut oil
1 large egg, beaten
⅔ cup flour
2 tablespoons finely sliced fresh coriander (cilantro)

1. Dry the fish thoroughly with paper towels. Place in a large dish and set aside. In a bowl, combine the marinade ingredients and pour over the fish. Rub the marinade well into the fish, coating it well. Allow to rest for at least 15 minutes.

2. Pat the fish dry with paper towels. Heat a wok over high heat for 45 seconds. Add the peanut oil. As the oil heats, coat the fish with the beaten egg. Spread the flour on a sheet of wax paper and place the fish on it. Coat the fish well with the flour, shake off the excess, and place in a Chinese strainer.

3. The oil should be heated to 375°F. Lower the fish into the oil and deep-fry for 2 minutes. Reduce the heat and allow the oil temperature to lower to 350°F. Fry the fish for another 2 minutes, until it turns light brown. Turn off the heat, remove the fish with a strainer, drain, and allow to come to room temperature.

4. Reheat the oil to 350°F. Place the fish back in the oil and deep-fry for another 5 minutes or until the fish is golden brown and crisp. Turn off the heat. Remove the fish with the strainer and drain for at least a minute. Transfer to a heated platter, sprinkle with the coriander, and serve in the traditional Chiu Chow way, with the following dipping sauce.

Black Vinegar Dip
1½ tablespoons Chinkiang vinegar
¼ cup Chicken Stock (page 75)
2 tablespoons fish sauce
1½ teaspoons sesame oil

2 tablespoons trimmed and finely
  sliced scallion
2 teaspoons julienned fresh ginger
1 tablespoon sugar
Pinch freshly ground white pepper

Combine the ingredients and serve with the fried pomfret.

MAKES 4 SERVINGS

ROLLED FISH WITH OYSTERS

Jing Long Lei Tong

*T*he actual name for this Cantonese dish is chongsan jing long lei tong, *or "steamed dragon's tongue of Chang-shan." Chung Shan is the birthplace of Dr. Sun Yat-sen, regarded, certainly by the South, as the founder of modern China. Chung Shan is famed for its fish and its oysters.*

Three ¾-pound fresh sole, 2 fillets from each fish, or 6 fresh sole fillets

For the marinade
4 large garlic cloves, minced
2 tablespoons Shao-Hsing wine or dry sherry
1 tablespoon oyster sauce
2 tablespoons soy sauce
1½ tablespoons White Peppercorn Oil (page 85) or peanut oil

¼ cup trimmed and finely sliced scallion
1 teaspoon sesame oil
2 teaspoons Chinese white rice vinegar or distilled vinegar
⅛ teaspoon salt
2 teaspoons sugar
Pinch freshly ground white pepper

6 large fresh oysters, shucked and drained
3½ tablespoons julienned scallion (1-inch pieces)
1 tablespoon julienned ginger
1½ tablespoons White Peppercorn Oil (page 85) or peanut oil
1½ teaspoons finely chopped fresh coriander (cilantro)

1. Trim each fillet into a piece 5½ inches long by 3 inches wide. In a large bowl, combine the marinade ingredients. Place the fillets in the marinade briefly, remove, and reserve the remainder of the marinade.

2. Lay a sole fillet on a dish. Place an oyster, a sixth of the scallions, and a sixth of the ginger about 1 inch from the end. Roll the fillet into a cylinder. Repeat until all 6 fillets are rolled.

3. Place the rolls in a steamproof dish, with the end of the roll down, the smooth side facing up. Pour the reserved marinade over the fillets. Place the dish in a steamer, cover, and steam for 8 minutes (see steaming, page 64), until the fish is white and firm. If you use a metal dish to steam, the time will be 4 minutes. Turn off the heat, drizzle white peppercorn oil over the fillets, sprinkle with coriander, and serve in the steamproof dish.

MAKES 6 SERVINGS

FISH WRAPPED IN
BEAN CURD SHEETS

Wu Pei Bau Yue

In this recipe, from Shanghai, the fish is not the wrapper but what is wrapped. Its distinction rests on its combination of textures, the soft fish and the crisp bean curd wrappers.

1 pound thick sea bass or red snapper fillet

For the marinade
1 tablespoon Chinese white rice vinegar or distilled vinegar

1 tablespoon Shao-Hsing wine or dry sherry
1½ teaspoons soy sauce
1½ teaspoons sugar
1 tablespoon julienned fresh ginger
1 teaspoon sesame oil
¾ teaspoon salt
Pinch freshly ground white pepper

¼ cup cornstarch
One sheet fresh bean curd, cut into four 6-inch squares
5 cups peanut oil

1. Cut the fillet into 4 equal portions. In a large bowl, combine the marinade ingredients. Place the fish in the marinade and allow to rest for at least 10 minutes.

2. Remove the fish from the marinade and dust with cornstarch. Wrap each piece of fish in a bean curd sheet by placing the fish at one end of the sheet and rolling into a cylinder-shaped bundle.

3. Heat a wok over high heat for 1 minute. Add the peanut oil and heat to 350°F. Cook one rolled fish bundle at a time. Hold each bundle with tongs or chopsticks and place it in the oil. Continue to hold until the bean curd seals. The fish rolls are ready when the bean curd turns golden brown, about 2 minutes. Repeat until all 4 are fried.

    Serve as they would be served in Shanghai, with Shanghai Lima Beans (page 94).

MAKES 4 SERVINGS

SILK SQUASH SOUP WITH SEA BASS

Sze Gua Tong

This is a favorite soup in Guangzhou, especially because of the silk squash. This odd vegetable, shaped like a cucumber, but with ridges along its length, once was available only from late spring into early summer and was a treat I always anticipated when I was young. It is widely available now. I suggest that young, small silk squashes be used for this soup.

For the marinade
1 teaspoon ginger juice mixed with
   2 teaspoons Chinese white rice wine
   or gin
1 teaspoon White Peppercorn Oil
   (page 85) or peanut oil
2 teaspoons soy sauce

¾ teaspoon salt
1½ teaspoons sugar
1 tablespoon cornstarch
Pinch freshly ground white pepper

½ pound sea bass fillet, cut into
   2½-inch slices
2 pounds silk squash
2 tablespoons White Peppercorn Oil
   (page 85) or peanut oil
½ teaspoon salt
One ½-inch-thick slice fresh ginger
3½ cups Superior Stock (page 74) or
   Chicken Stock (page 75)
1½ cups cold water
¼ teaspoon baking soda

1. In a large bowl, combine the marinade ingredients. Place the fish in the marinade and allow to rest for at least 10 minutes.

2. To prepare the silk squash, wash it and peel it, but retain some of the green. To roll-cut it, starting at one end, cut diagonally into approximately ¾-inch slices. Turn the squash a quarter turn between cuts. The shape will be a rounded triangle that the Chinese call an "ax" shape.

3. Heat the wok over high heat, add the peppercorn oil, and coat the wok with it using a spatula. When a wisp of white smoke appears, add the salt and ginger. When the ginger browns, add the silk squash and cook, stirring, until it turns bright green, about 1 minute. Remove from the wok and place in a pot.

4. Add the stock, water, and baking soda to the pot and bring to a boil over high heat, uncovered. Lower the heat and cook for 4 minutes, until the silk squash is soft. The baking soda preserves the bright green color of the squash. Raise the heat back to high, add the fish and marinade, and return to a boil. Immediately turn off the heat, transfer to a heated tureen, and serve.

MAKES 4 SERVINGS

BLACK DRAGON PEARL

Wo Lung Toh Jiu

黑龍珠

*T*his braised preparation from Beijing, an imperial banquet dish, contains 2 exotics of the Chinese kitchen, sea cucumbers and quail eggs. In times past, sea cucumbers would have been dried before being transported to Beijing, then processed for cooking. The name of this dish translates as "black dragon spits out the pearl," the sea cucumber being the black dragon, the eggs the pearls. Eat as the dowager empress might have.

4 dried sea cucumbers, about 5 inches long, soaked in cold water for 8 hours until softened
6 cups cold water

Two 1-inch-thick slices fresh ginger, lightly smashed
4 scallions, trimmed, cut into thirds, and white parts lightly smashed
3 tablespoons Shao-Hsing wine or dry sherry
3 tablespoons peanut oil
½ teaspoon salt
1½ cups Chicken Stock (page 75)
2 tablespoons double dark soy sauce, regular dark soy sauce, or mushroom soy sauce
1½ teaspoons sugar
12 quail eggs, hard-boiled, shells removed
2 teaspoons cornstarch mixed with 1 tablespoon cold water

1. Prepare the sea cucumbers. After soaking they will be about 2 inches longer. Cut each partially along its length, remove the insides, discard, and wash thoroughly. (Sea cucumbers already soaked and cleaned are available in markets, usually stored in containers of water.) Cut each sea cucumber crosswise into 3 equal pieces.

2. Place the water, 1 slice of ginger, half of the scallions, and 1 tablespoon of the wine in a pot, cover, and bring to a boil over high heat. Add the sea cucumbers and return to a boil. Turn off the heat, remove the sea cucumbers, drain, and discard all the other ingredients.

3. Heat a wok over high heat for 40 seconds. Add the peanut oil, coat the wok with it using a spatula, and add the salt. When a wisp of white smoke appears, add the remaining ginger and scallions, stir, and cook for 1 minute, until the scallions release their fragrance. Add the sea cucumber and cook, stirring, for 1½ minutes. Add the remaining wine and stir. Add the stock and bring to a boil. Add the soy sauce and stir well. Add the sugar and mix. Lower the heat, cover the wok, and braise the sea cucumbers for 30 minutes. Stir frequently to prevent sticking or burning. *continued*

4. Uncover the wok, remove the ginger and scallions, and discard. Add the quail eggs and stir well into the mixture. Stir the cornstarch mixture, pour in, and stir quickly to mix. When the sauce thickens and bubbles, turn off the heat, transfer to a heated platter, and serve.

MAKES 6 SERVINGS

STIR-FRIED SHRIMP WITH CAVIAR

Sin Har Seung Hok Yu Don

I ate this truly luxurious preparation first in the lovely pagodalike restaurant in Taipei, Fu Yuen. It incorporates sturgeon roe, what the Chinese call hok yu don, *or "black fish eggs," and shrimp into a fine, unusual, elegant dish. I leave the grade of caviar to individual tastes and pocketbooks. I prefer the deep gray osetra.*

1 pound medium-large shrimp (about 24), shelled and deveined

For the marinade
2 teaspoons Mei Kuei Lu Chiew or gin
1 teaspoon soy sauce
¾ teaspoon salt
1¼ teaspoons sugar
1 teaspoon sesame oil
Pinch freshly ground white pepper

2 tablespoons peanut oil
6 teaspoons caviar

1. Dry the shrimp thoroughly with paper towels. Quarter each shrimp lengthwise, then cut each piece into 3 pieces. In a bowl, combine the marinade ingredients. Place the shrimp in the marinade and allow to rest for at least 20 minutes.

2. Heat a wok over high heat for 30 seconds, add the peanut oil, and coat the wok with it using a spatula. When a wisp of white smoke appears, add the shrimp and marinade. Spread in a thin layer, cook for 20 seconds, turn over, and stir. At this point the shrimp should be pink and curled. Turn off the heat and remove the shrimp. Divide the shrimp equally into 6 Chinese teacups or demitasse cups, top with a teaspoon of caviar, and serve.

MAKES 6 SERVINGS

DRUNKEN SHRIMP

Joi Har

This dish is found all along the eastern coast of China, in Guangzhou, in Hong Kong, Shanghai, and as far afield as Taiwan and Singapore. This is a very special preparation of live shrimp, with that potent rose wine, Mei Kuei Lu Chiew, poured over them to marinate them, make them "drunk," and then ignited chiew ladled through them to cook them. Once quite rare in some parts of the West, live shrimp are widely available not only in Chinese markets but in many large supermarkets as well.

¾ pound medium shrimp (about 24), preferably live

10 tablespoons Mei Kuei Lu Chiew or gin

For the dipping sauce
2 tablespoons soy sauce
3 fresh Thai chilies, minced
2 tablespoons Chinese white rice vinegar or distilled vinegar
2 teaspoons sesame oil
1 tablespoon Superior Stock (page 74) or Chicken Stock (page 75)
1 teaspoon sugar
1½ tablespoons finely sliced green part of scallion

1. Run cold water over the shrimp to clean them. Drain, pat dry with paper towels, and place in a bowl. Pour in 6 tablespoons of Mei Kuei Lu Chiew and allow the shrimp to become "drunk" as they ingest the rose wine, about 15 to 20 minutes. Initially the shrimp will flip about, so cover the bowl. Later they will be still after absorbing the wine. (If live shrimp are not used, cut the shrimp shells along the back vein from end to just before the tail, leaving the shell and tail on. Remove the veins under cold running water. Drain and dry thoroughly with paper towels. Place 6 tablespoons of rose wine in a bowl, add the shrimp, mix together well until the shrimp are coated, and marinate for 20 minutes.)

2. Meanwhile, combine the sauce ingredients in a bowl and set aside.

3. Heat a wok over high heat for 1 minute. Add the remaining ¼ cup of rose wine and coat the wok with it using a spatula. When quite hot, light a match and ignite the wine. Add the shrimp and wine marinade and cook, stirring, until the shrimp turn pink, about 4 to 6 minutes. Turn off the heat, transfer to a heated dish, and serve with individual small dishes of dipping sauce.

MAKES 4 SERVINGS

FANTAIL SHRIMPS

Fung Mei Har

This dish too is found along China's eastern seacoast. Its name, fung mei, translates as "phoenix tail," which is what it is known as in China. Elsewhere it has become known as fantail shrimp, perhaps because the shrimp, when butterflied, resemble an opened fan.

For the batter
1 cup flour
1 cup cornstarch

2¼ tablespoons baking powder
¾ teaspoon salt
11½ ounces cold water
1½ tablespoons peanut oil

6 cups peanut oil
1 pound shrimp (about 24), shelled but
   tails left on, deveined, butterflied,
   and dried with paper towels
3 tablespoons cornstarch for dusting

1. To make the batter, place the flour, cornstarch, baking powder, and salt in a bowl. Pour in the cold water gradually, stirring clockwise with chopsticks until the mixture is smooth. Add the 1½ tablespoons peanut oil and blend well. Reserve. The batter should have the consistency of pancake batter. If too thick, add a bit of water; if too thin, add a bit of flour.

2. Heat a wok over high heat for 1 minute, add the 6 cups oil, and heat to 350°F. Dust the shrimp with cornstarch, dip into the batter, holding each by its tail, then lower gently into the oil. Cook for 30 seconds, then turn over with tongs or chopsticks. Continue turning until golden brown. Fry 4 shrimp at a time. Regulate the heat to maintain the oil temperature at 350°F. As the shrimp turn brown, remove from the oil with a Chinese strainer and drain. Continue until all are fried. Serve with Pickled Peach Sauce.

Pickled Peach Sauce

Most would be familiar with that so-called duck sauce with which fried shrimp are often served. Enjoy the following instead.

½ Pickled Peach (page 101)
1 cup pickling liquid

Place the peach and pickling liquid in a blender and puree. Stir before serving, since the peaches tend to separate from the liquid when allowed to stand.

MAKES 6 SERVINGS, INCLUDING 1⅓ CUPS SAUCE

KUNG PAO SHRIMP

Kung Pao Ming Har

*T*he name of this traditional Shanghai preparation translates as "crown prince." There is also a recipe for Kung Pao chicken, cooked quite similarly. A tale told of both dishes in Shanghai is that once long ago a crown prince, while traveling through the Shanghai region, was presented with these dishes in his honor. He was so happy, it is said, that he brought them back to the imperial court. From that time the dishes have been named for his title.

½ pound medium shrimp (about 16), shelled and deveined
1 tablespoon egg white, beaten

For the sauce
2½ teaspoons preserved horse beans with chili or Chili Sauce (page 88)
1 teaspoon soy sauce
2 teaspoons sugar
1 teaspoon Chinkiang vinegar
3 tablespoons ketchup
⅛ teaspoon Sichuan peppercorns, crushed

3 cups peanut oil
½ cup fresh peanuts, skins removed
2 fresh Thai chilies, minced
½ cup chopped white parts of scallions (in diagonal ½-inch pieces)

1. Place the shrimp in a bowl, add the egg white, mix well, and reserve. Combine the sauce ingredients in a bowl and reserve.

2. Heat a wok over high heat for 1 minute. Add the peanut oil and heat to 350°F. Add the peanuts and fry for 1½ to 2 minutes or until they turn golden brown. Turn off the heat, remove with a Chinese strainer, and drain. Transfer the oil to a bowl.

3. Return 1 tablespoon of peanut oil to the wok. Heat the wok over high heat for 20 seconds and add the chilies. Stir and cook for 30 seconds. Add the scallions, stir, and cook for 1 minute. Add the shrimp and stir well to mix. Cook for 1½ minutes. Make a well in the mixture, stir the sauce mixture, pour in, mix well, and cook for 45 seconds, until very hot. Add the peanuts and stir to mix. Turn off the heat, transfer to a heated platter, and serve.

MAKES 4 SERVINGS

SALT-BAKED SHRIMP

Jiu Yim Har

*T*he provenance of this southern dish is shared by the Hakka and the Cantonese. The historic popularity of salt-baked chicken over the years led to various foods being called "salt-baked" even though they were not. The process of water-blanching, coating, and oil-blanching approximates baking to the Hakka taste. To the Cantonese the dish is simply jiu yim, or "pepper salt," to denote its primary flavors.

½ pound medium-large shrimp (about 12), feelers removed, shell slit along vein, and deveined
½ teaspoon baking soda
3 cups water
1 tablespoon plus ½ teaspoon salt
2 tablespoons cornstarch
1 quart peanut oil
1 tablespoon minced fresh Thai chilies

1. Place the shrimp and baking soda in a bowl and mix well to coat. Allow to rest for at least 20 minutes.

2. Place the water and 1 tablespoon salt in a pot, cover, and bring to a boil over high heat. Add the shrimp and water-blanch for 10 seconds. Remove the shrimp with a strainer and run cold water through them to cool. The water-blanching removes all of the liquid from the shrimp.

3. Place the shrimp in a dish, sprinkle with cornstarch to coat them lightly, and shake off excess. Heat a wok over high heat for 1 minute, add the peanut oil, and heat to 350°F. Place the shrimp in a Chinese strainer, lower into the oil, and oil-blanch for 1 minute. Turn off the heat, remove with the strainer, and drain. Transfer the oil from the wok to a bowl.

4. Return 1 tablespoon of the reserved oil to the wok and heat over high heat for 20 seconds. Add the remaining ½ teaspoon salt and the chilies and cook, stirring, for 45 seconds. Add the shrimp and cook, stirring, making certain they are well coated, for 1 minute. They should be dry and crusted. Turn off the heat, transfer to a heated platter, and serve.

MAKES 4 SERVINGS

SHRIMP STIR-FRIED WITH TIANJIN *BOK CHOY*

Tianjin Bok Choy *Chau Har*

This is a dish of my own, devised after discussions with an herbal doctor I consult with in Hong Kong. It is a perfectly balanced yin and yang dish, cooling and warming. Tianjin bok choy is a constant when vegetables are recommended for their health-giving properties. Shrimp, aquatic creatures, are cooling, and so is the bok choy. But the cooking process is yang, or warming, as are the ginger and garlic. A dish of harmony, when food is considered as medicine.

2 quarts cold water
1 pound Tianjin bok choy, *cut crosswise
    into ½-inch slices, stalks separated
    from leaves*

½ *pound medium shrimp (about 16),
    shelled and deveined*

For the sauce
1 tablespoon double dark soy sauce,
    regular dark soy sauce, or mushroom
    soy sauce
¾ teaspoon sesame oil
1½ tablespoons cornstarch
4½ tablespoons Chicken Stock
    (page 75)
Pinch freshly ground white pepper

2 teaspoons peanut oil
2 teaspoons minced fresh ginger
1½ teaspoons minced garlic
2 tablespoons julienned red bell pepper

1. Place the cold water in a pot, cover, and bring to a boil over high heat. Add the *bok choy* stalks, stir, and cook for 10 seconds. Add the leaves, stir well, and cook for another 20 seconds. Turn off the heat, run cold water into the pot, and drain well, using chopsticks or tongs to loosen the vegetable.

2. In a bowl, combine the sauce ingredients and set aside.

3. Heat a wok over high heat for 45 seconds. Add the peanut oil and coat the wok with it using a spatula. When a wisp of white smoke appears, add the ginger and garlic, stir, and cook for 10 seconds. Add the shrimp, spread in a single layer, and cook for 15 seconds. Turn over and cook for another 15 seconds, until the shrimp begin to turn pink and curl. Add the reserved *bok choy* and cook, stirring, for 2½ minutes. The shrimp should turn completely pink. Make a well in the center of the mixture, stir the sauce mixture, and pour in. Stir well and cook for 1½ minutes or until the sauce turns dark and thickens. Turn off the heat, transfer to a heated platter, sprinkle with red pepper, and serve with cooked rice.

MAKES 4 TO 6 SERVINGS

SHRIMP BALLS

Har Yeun

*T*his is another dish of blurred origins. Shrimp balls exist in the Cantonese kitchen as well as those of the Chiu Chow and Hakka people, and since the region of southern China is home to them all, all have a claim. The use of finely minced shrimp is perhaps used more imaginatively by the Cantonese, who, in addition to making balls of it, use the mix in dim sum dumplings, deep-fry it, wrap it around crab claws, and wrap bacon around it. The Chiu Chow usually add their shrimp balls to soups, but in combination with rice noodles and egg noodles. The Hakka eat the balls themselves or in soups with vegetables. One important aspect of this preparation is that raw gray (tiger) shrimp be used rather than pink. Gray shrimp, when minced, tends to stay together; the others tend rather to fall apart, even with binders.

½ pound tiger shrimp (gray colored), shelled and deveined
3 tablespoons trimmed and finely sliced scallion
2 tablespoons egg white, beaten
¾ teaspoon sugar
Pinch freshly ground white pepper
½ teaspoon soy sauce
1½ teaspoons oyster sauce
2 teaspoons Coriander Oil (page 86) or peanut oil
1½ teaspoons Chinese white rice wine or gin
2 quarts cold water

1. Place the shrimp on a chopping board. Cut each into 4 pieces, then with a cleaver chop into a paste. Place in a bowl and add all the other ingredients except the water. Mix either with an electric mixer or by hand. If using a mixer, mix for 4 to 5 minutes, using the flat paddle, until the mixture is firm. If by hand, mix, then pick up the shrimp mixture and throw with some force against the side of the bowl. Do this about 5 times.

2. Keep a small bowl of water at hand to keep your hands moist. Wet your hands and form a shrimp ball about 1 inch in diameter. Repeat, wetting your hands each time, until 20 balls are formed. Place the cold water in a pot and bring to a boil over high heat. Add the shrimp balls and return to a boil. Cook for 3 to 4 minutes, until the shrimp balls are firm but not hard. Turn off the heat, run cold water into the pot, and drain. Remove the shrimp balls to a heated platter and serve with the following dipping sauce.

Ginger Soy Sauce
1 teaspoon sugar
1 tablespoon dark soy sauce
1 tablespoon soy sauce
2½ teaspoons White Peppercorn Oil
    (page 85) or peanut oil

3 tablespoons Chicken Stock (page 75)
1½ tablespoons julienned fresh ginger
1½ tablespoons trimmed and julienned
    white part of scallion

Combine all ingredients, mix, and allow to rest for 30 minutes. Serve in small soy sauce
    dishes.

MAKES 4 SERVINGS, INCLUDING ½ CUP SAUCE

WATERCRESS SOUP WITH SHRIMP BALLS

Sai Yeung Choi Har Yeun Tong

This Hakka dish is a fine example of how shrimp balls are used in this distinctive kitchen. The Chinese believe that this particular dish is a perfect marriage of 2 cool foods, shrimp and watercress, combined to create a dish that will cool and balance one's system.

3 cups Chicken Stock (page 75)
1 cup cold water
¼ teaspoon baking soda
1½ tablespoons minced fresh ginger
2 large bunches watercress, washed
    thoroughly, each bunch broken into
    3 equal parts
1 recipe Shrimp Balls (preceding
    recipe)

Place the stock and water in a pot, add the baking soda and ginger, and bring to a boil, uncovered, over high heat. Add the watercress and return the soup to a boil. Add the shrimp balls and return to a boil again. Boil for 1 minute, turn off the heat, transfer to a heated tureen, and serve.

NOTE: *Watercress, it should be noted, must always be cooked in boiling liquid; if the water isn't boiling, the watercress becomes excessively bitter.*

MAKES 4 SERVINGS

SHRIMP WITH GREEN TEA LEAVES

Ching Cha Chau Har

This elegant dish has its origins in the imperial court of Beijing, where Long Jing tea, or "Dragon Well," from the Hangzhou region, was the most prized tea in China. Usually it was cooked with fresh tea leaves, newly picked, and rushed to court. What follows is my adaptation, using dried Dragon Well tea leaves. The coolness of this tea on one's tongue is quite evident in this recipe.

½ tablespoon Dragon Well green tea
   leaves
¼ cup water

For the sauce
1 tablespoon oyster sauce
2 tablespoons brewed tea
½ tablespoon soy sauce
1¼ teaspoons sugar
¼ teaspoon salt
½ teaspoon sesame oil

1 teaspoon Shao-Hsing wine or dry
   sherry
Pinch freshly ground white pepper
1¾ teaspoons tapioca flour
2 tablespoons Chicken Stock (page 75)

2½ cups peanut oil
One ¼-inch-thick slice fresh ginger,
   peeled
¾ pound medium shrimp (about 24),
   shelled and deveined
1 teaspoon minced fresh ginger
¼ cup chopped white parts of scallion
   in ¼-inch diagonal pieces
¼ cup diced red bell pepper in
   ¼-inch pieces
¼ cup diced green bell pepper in
   ¼-inch pieces
1 orange, cut thinly into rounds, then
   half moons, for garnish

1. To brew the tea, place the tea leaves in a bowl. Boil the water and pour over the leaves. Cover the bowl and steep for 10 minutes. Strain the tea. Reserve the tea leaves and 2 tablespoons of brewed tea for the sauce.

2. In a bowl, mix the sauce ingredients and reserve.

3. To blanch the shrimp, heat a wok over high heat for 1 minute. Add the peanut oil and slice of ginger and heat to 350°F. Place the shrimp in the oil, stir, and loosen. When the shrimp begin to turn pink, about 5 seconds, turn off the heat. Remove the shrimp with a Chinese strainer and drain. Transfer the oil to a bowl and discard the ginger slice.

4. Return 1 tablespoon of the reserved peanut oil to the wok. Heat over high heat for 20 seconds. When a wisp of white smoke appears, add the minced ginger and stir briefly. Add the scallion and cook, stirring, until its fragrance is released, about 15 seconds. Add the shrimp and reserved tea leaves and cook, stirring, for 20 seconds. Add the peppers and cook, stirring, until all ingredients are coated, about 20 seconds. Make a

well in the center of the mixture, stir the sauce mixture, pour in, and stir well. When the sauce bubbles and thickens, turn off the heat, remove to a heated platter, garnish around the edges with orange half moons, and serve.

LOBSTER STEAMED WITH LEMON

Ling Mung Jing Lung Har

This simple yet elegant preparation is from Shanghai. The lobster, lung har, translates as "dragon shrimp," a description of the large, clawless lobsters to be found in the waters off Shanghai. In Shanghai, lobster is almost always steamed, often traditionally with lemon, occasionally in combination with scallops. The large clawless lobsters are meaty and as sweet as those from Maine or Canada, but we shall use the latter for this recipe.

One 2-pound lobster

For the marinade
1 whole fresh lemon, ends cut off, sliced into thin rounds
2 tablespoons Chinese white rice wine or gin
1 tablespoon soy sauce
2 tablespoons Sichuan Peppercorn Oil (page 86) or peanut oil
½ teaspoon salt
1 tablespoon sugar
Pinch freshly ground white pepper
1 teaspoon ginger juice

2 tablespoons finely julienned fresh ginger
2 scallions, white parts only, cut into 1½-inch lengths and julienned
6 sprigs fresh coriander (cilantro), for garnish

1. Have your fishmonger kill the lobster or kill it yourself: Hold the lobster head, and with your other hand plunge a boning knife into the chest cavity and cut back to the tail. Pull apart firmly. Remove the vein and inedible interior black pouch. Then, with a cleaver, cut the body in half lengthwise. Cut the head and claws off. Cut the tail section into bite-sized pieces and cut the claws and head into pieces.

2. Combine the marinade ingredients and reserve.

3. Place the lobster and marinade in a steamproof dish and mix together. Sprinkle with the ginger and scallions, cover, and steam for 20 minutes (see steaming, page 64) or until the lobster shells turn red and the lobster meat turns white. Turn off the heat, garnish with coriander, and serve in the steamproof dish.

MAKES 4 SERVINGS

GRATED WINTER MELON WITH LOBSTER

Lung Har Tung Gua Yung

*T*his is a most unusual preparation that is said to have originated in imperial Beijing. That makes sense, for it is the kind of dish that would have been made to titillate the court. The winter melon is grated into a softened mass. Prepared in this manner, it is referred to as yung, which defies translation. It is not a soup, not a puree; it is yung. To the Chinese this means "melted," and it is essential that it be smooth to the tongue.

For the marinade
1 teaspoon ginger juice, mixed with
    1 tablespoon Chinese white rice wine
    or gin
1 tablespoon oyster sauce
1 tablespoon White Peppercorn Oil
    (page 85) or peanut oil
½ teaspoon salt
1 teaspoon sugar
4 teaspoons cornstarch

Pinch freshly ground white pepper

Three ½-pound lobster tails, frozen or
    fresh, meat removed from shells,
    deveined, and cut into ¼-inch pieces

For steaming
1 tablespoon Chinese white rice wine
    or gin
3½ cups Superior Stock (page 74) or
    Chicken Stock (page 75)
½ teaspoon salt
Pinch freshly ground white pepper
One 1-inch-thick slice fresh ginger,
    lightly smashed
1 teaspoon sugar
2¼ pounds winter melon, peeled and
    hand-grated
3 extra-large egg whites, beaten
3 tablespoons finely sliced green parts
    of scallion
2 tablespoons finely sliced fresh
    coriander (cilantro)

1. In a large bowl, combine the marinade ingredients. Place the lobster pieces in the marinade and allow to rest for at least 20 minutes.

2. In a bowl, combine the steaming ingredients. Place the grated winter melon and steaming ingredients in a steamproof dish. Cover and steam for 30 minutes (see steaming, page 64).

3. Place the stock, steamed grated melon, and its steaming liquid in a pot, cover, and bring to a boil over high heat. Add the lobster and marinade, stir well, and return to a boil. Fold in the beaten egg whites and stir. Turn off the heat, transfer to a heated tureen, and serve in individual bowls sprinkled with scallion and coriander to taste.

MAKES 6 SERVINGS

LOBSTER CANTONESE

Guangzhou Chau Lung Har

*T*his traditional preparation from
Guangzhou has not changed in hun-
dreds of years. I have seen it altered, by technique and with added flavors, but it should
not be. Why meddle with perfection?

For the marinade
1¾ teaspoons soy sauce
1½ tablespoons oyster sauce
¾ teaspoon salt
1½ teaspoons sugar
Pinch freshly ground white pepper
2 teaspoons sesame oil

One 2-pound lobster, cut in half
   lengthwise and into 1½-inch pieces

¼ **pound lean ground pork**
¼ **teaspoon salt**
¾ **teaspoon sugar**
¼ **cup peanut oil**
2 **teaspoons minced garlic**
3 **large eggs, beaten**
2 **teaspoons minced fresh ginger**
2 **tablespoons Chinese white rice wine**
   or gin
2 **scallions, trimmed and finely sliced**
1 **small cucumber, cut thinly into**
   rounds, then into half moons, for
   garnish

1. In a large bowl, combine the marinade ingredients. Place the lobster in the marinade and allow to rest 30 minutes. After 30 minutes, remove the lobster from the marinade and reserve both separately. As the lobster marinates, mix the ground pork with the salt and sugar thoroughly; reserve.

2. Heat a wok over high heat for 1 minute. Add 1 tablespoon of the peanut oil and coat the wok with it using a spatula. When a wisp of white smoke appears, add 1 teaspoon of the minced garlic and stir. When it browns, add the pork mixture. Stir to separate and cook for 3 minutes. When the pork changes color, add the eggs and mix into a soft scramble. Turn off the heat, remove all the ingredients from the wok, and reserve.

3. Wash and dry the wok and spatula. Heat the wok over high heat for 1 minute. Add the remaining peanut oil and coat the wok with it using a spatula. When a wisp of white smoke appears, add the minced ginger and stir briefly. Add the remaining teaspoon minced garlic and stir. When the garlic browns, add the lobster pieces. Spread in a thin layer, turning the wok from side to side to spread the heat evenly. Turn the lobster pieces. Add the wine at the edge of the wok and mix thoroughly. When the lobster meat reddens, add the pork-egg mixture and mix all ingredients thoroughly. Add the reserved marinade and stir. Add the scallions and mix well. Turn off the heat, transfer to a heated platter, garnish with cucumber half moons around the edges, and serve.

MAKES 4 TO 6 SERVINGS

CURRIED CRAB
WITH BEAN THREAD NOODLES

Gah Lei Sah Wor Hai

This curried crab dish, a Cantonese specialty traditionally cooked in a sand clay pot, carries with it the influences of Southeast Asia and India. Curry came east to China, initially along the Silk Road, but now it is well entrenched, particularly in Guangdong and Hong Kong.

1¾ pounds live blue crabs (4 or 5),
    placed in the freezer in a bag for at
    least 1 hour, until they are still
3 tablespoons cornstarch

For the curry paste
2½ tablespoons hot curry powder
½ teaspoon cayenne pepper
2½ tablespoons cold water

3½ cups peanut oil
1 tablespoon minced garlic
½ cup cold water
3 beef bouillon cubes, cut into small
    pieces
12 scallions, trimmed, white parts
    lightly smashed, and cut into 2-inch
    pieces
Four ¼-inch-thick slices fresh ginger
2 cups Chicken Stock (page 75)
2 teaspoons sugar
2 bundles bean thread noodles, soaked
    in cold water for 10 minutes,
    drained, and cut into 3-inch pieces

1. To prepare the crabs, place the frozen crabs in a large bowl and run cold water over them several times until clean. Pat dry. Break off the claws and crack with the flat of a cleaver blade. Remove the stomach flaps. Separate the top shell from the bottom and discard the gills and inedible interior. Cut the body in half so that there are 2 pieces, each with feelers attached. Repeat with all crabs. Coat the crab pieces, including the shells, with cornstarch and reserve.

2. In a bowl, mix together the curry paste ingredients and reserve.

3. Heat a wok over high heat for 1 minute. Add the peanut oil and heat to 350°F. Place the crabs in a Chinese strainer and lower into the oil. Cook for 1 minute, turn off the heat, remove the crabs with a strainer, and drain. Transfer the oil to a bowl.

4. Wipe off the wok and spatula with paper towels. Return 1½ tablespoons of the reserved peanut oil to the wok. Heat over high heat for 20 seconds. When a wisp of white smoke appears, add the minced garlic and stir briefly. Add the curry paste and cook, stirring continually, for 1 minute. Add half of the cold water and stir. Add the bouillon cubes, stir, and cook for 3 minutes. Add the scallions and sliced ginger, stir

well, and cook for 1 minute. If the mixture is dry, add the remaining water and stir well. Add the crabs, stir well, and cook for 2 minutes, making sure the crabs are well coated with the curry mixture.

5. Transfer to a sand clay pot or casserole. Add the stock and sugar and bring to a boil over high heat. Stir well and allow to cook for 2 minutes. Add the bean threads, stir well, and cook for 2 minutes or until the mixture begins to bubble. Turn off the heat and serve in the sand clay pot or casserole.

MAKES 6 SERVINGS

CRABS WITH BLACK BEANS
See Jiu Chau Hai

This, like its predecessor, is a classic of the Cantonese kitchen. I will say, immodestly, that nowhere else in China are crabs, or for that matter scallops and clams, prepared with as much inventiveness and flavor as in Guangdong.

1¾ pounds live blue crabs (4 or 5), placed in the freezer in a bag for at least 1 hour until they are still
3 tablespoons cornstarch
4 garlic cloves, peeled
2 tablespoons fermented black beans, washed 3 times and drained

For the sauce
1½ tablespoons oyster sauce
1½ teaspoons soy sauce

2 teaspoons sugar
½ teaspoon sesame oil
1½ teaspoons Chinese white rice wine or gin
Pinch freshly ground white pepper
1 tablespoon cornstarch
½ cup Seafood Stock (page 76)

3½ cups peanut oil
Four ¼-inch-thick slices fresh ginger
2 fresh Thai chilies, minced
1 small red bell pepper, cut into ¼-inch julienne
1½ tablespoons Chinese white rice wine or gin
3 tablespoons Seafood Stock (page 76)
1½ tablespoons minced fresh coriander (cilantro)

1. Prepare the crabs as in step 1 of the preceding recipe and reserve.
2. Mash the garlic and fermented black beans into a paste, in a mortar and pestle or with the handle of a cleaver, and reserve. In a bowl, mix together the sauce ingredients and reserve.

continued

3. Heat a wok over high heat for 1 minute. Add the peanut oil and heat to 350°F. Place the crabs and ginger slices in a Chinese strainer and lower them into the oil. Cook the crabs for 2 minutes, until the shells are red and the meat white. Turn off the heat, remove with the strainer, drain, and reserve. Empty the oil into a bowl.

4. Wipe off the wok and spatula with paper towels. Return 1½ tablespoons oil to the wok. Heat over high heat for 20 seconds. Add the reserved garlic–black bean paste and stir, loosening with the spatula. When the garlic turns light brown, add the chilies and bell pepper and stir. Add the crabs, stir well, and cook for 30 seconds. Add the wine, stir, and cook for 1 minute. Add the stock, stir, and cook for 2 minutes. Make a well in the center of the mixture, stir the sauce mixture, pour in, stir well, and cook for 1½ minutes. When the sauce thickens and bubbles, turn off the heat, transfer to a heated platter, sprinkle with coriander, and serve with cooked rice.

MAKES 4 SERVINGS

POACHED CRABMEAT WITH CAULIFLOWER

Fu Guai Bok Tau

Such a mundane name for a dish of such significance. This, another Cantonese classic, is the creation of an anonymous chef half a century ago. Its name, fu guai bok tau, *translates as "rich and noble, white head,"* to mean that the preparation itself is to be considered rich and noble, and that as one ages gracefully, with white hair, the dish will always be a favorite. The "white head" also refers to the whiteness of the ingredients—cauliflower, milk stock, and crab. It is traditionally eaten when a child is one month old and is the guest of honor at a celebratory feast given by his or her parents.

6 cups cold water
One ½-inch-thick slice fresh ginger, lightly smashed
1 teaspoon salt
¾ pound cauliflower florets

For the sauce
¾ cup Milk Stock (page 78) or Chicken Stock (page 75)
1 teaspoon White Peppercorn Oil (page 85) or peanut oil
⅛ teaspoon freshly ground white pepper
1 teaspoon Mei Kuei Lu Chiew or gin
3½ teaspoons tapioca flour

2¼ cups Milk Stock (page 78) or Chicken Stock (page 75)
¼ teaspoon salt
2 garlic cloves, peeled
3 ounces crabmeat
2 jumbo egg whites, beaten

1. Place the cold water, ginger, and 1 teaspoon salt in a large pot. Cover and bring to a boil over high heat. Add the cauliflower, stir, and cook for 45 seconds. Turn off the heat, run cold water into the pot, and drain. Repeat and reserve.

2. In a bowl, combine the sauce ingredients and reserve.

3. Add the stock to the pot with ¼ teaspoon salt and the garlic cloves. Cover and bring to a boil over medium heat. Add the cauliflower and poach for 2½ minutes or until tender. Turn off the heat and drain. Transfer the cauliflower to a heated platter. Discard the ginger and garlic and reserve the stock for another use.

4. Mix the sauce and pour into a wok over medium heat. Stir continually and bring to a boil. Add the crabmeat, stir in, and return to a boil. Lower the heat and slowly add the egg whites, stirring until opaque. Add the cauliflower, immediately turn off the heat, and mix well, making certain all ingredients are well coated. Remove to the heated platter and serve.

MAKES 4 SERVINGS

CORN SOUP WITH CRABMEAT

Suk Mai Hai Yuk Gung

This thick, pureelike soup, or gung, *is my adaptation of a Hong Kong version of a soup from southeastern China. It is a recipe of the city, because traditionally it has been made with canned corn and water. My soup is a* gung, *more like a chowder than a* tong, *or thinner soup.*

1¼ pounds fresh or frozen corn kernels
6 cups Chicken Stock (page 75)
1 teaspoon grated fresh ginger
⅛ teaspoon freshly ground white pepper
½ teaspoon salt
¼ pound crabmeat
5 large egg whites, lightly beaten
⅓ cup trimmed and finely sliced
   scallion

1. Place ¾ pound of the corn kernels and ¾ cup of the stock in a blender and process to a coarse puree. Reserve.

2. Place the remaining stock in a pot with the ginger, white pepper, and salt, cover, and bring to a boil over high heat. Add the remaining corn kernels and return to a boil. Cover the pot, lower the heat, and simmer, leaving the lid cracked, for 5 minutes. Raise the heat back to high, add the pureed corn, and mix well. Return to a boil and cook for 3 minutes, stirring frequently to prevent sticking. Add the crabmeat, stir well, and return to a boil. Fold in the egg whites. Turn off the heat, transfer to a heated tureen, sprinkle with the scallion, and serve.

MAKES 8 SERVINGS

SHANGHAI CHILI CLAMS

Hoi Dai Gua Jee

*T*his very special clam dish duplicates as closely as possible a classic preparation from Shanghai, which I first tasted in the exclusive confines of the Shanghai Club in Hong Kong years ago. The Shanghai original is called hoi dai gua jee, *which translates as "bottom of the sea watermelon seeds," to indicate that the clams used are as tiny as those melon seeds. Such clams are rarely available outside of Shanghai waters, or off Taiwan, where they also grow. So I have made this version with small clams, but with a sauce that perfectly duplicates its tastes.*

For the chili sauce
4 teaspoons Chili Sauce (page 88)
1 tablespoon double dark soy sauce, regular dark soy sauce, or mushroom soy sauce

1½ teaspoons Chinese white rice vinegar or distilled vinegar
2 tablespoons Shao-Hsing wine or dry sherry
¼ teaspoon salt
1 tablespoon sugar
Pinch freshly ground white pepper

2 pounds Manila clams (about 48), well washed under cold running water until very clean
½ cup cold water
1½ tablespoons peanut oil
1½ teaspoons minced fresh ginger
1½ teaspoons minced garlic
½ cup minced onion
½ pound ripe tomato, cut into ½-inch pieces
⅛ teaspoon salt
3 scallions, trimmed and cut into ¼-inch pieces on a diagonal

1. In a bowl, mix together the sauce ingredients and reserve.

2. Place the clams and water in a 10- to 12-inch skillet. Bring to a boil over high heat. When the clams begin to open, there will be the sound of soft pops. As they open, one by one, transfer to a bowl until all are opened. Discard the liquid from the skillet. Reserve the clams and their liquid in the bowl.

3. Heat a wok over high heat, add the peanut oil, and coat the wok with it using a spatula. When a wisp of white smoke appears, add the ginger and stir briefly. Add the garlic, stir, and cook for 30 seconds. Add the onion, stir, and cook for 1 minute. Lower the heat and cook the mixture, stirring, for 5 minutes. Raise the heat back to high, add the tomato and salt, and stir well. Lower the heat to medium and cook for 7 minutes or until the tomato and onion become like a puree. *continued*

4. Turn the heat back to high, stir the sauce mixture, pour it into the wok, and stir well. When the mixture comes to a boil, cook for 1 minute. Add the reserved clams and their liquid, stir well, making certain the clams are coated evenly, and cook for 2 minutes. Add the scallions and stir well. Turn off the heat, transfer to a heated platter, and serve with cooked rice.

MAKES 4 SERVINGS

CLAMS WITH GINGER AND SCALLIONS

Geung Chung Chau Hin

This is one of the most popular of dishes in Guangdong. There is not a Cantonese restaurant in existence without this dish, so long as fresh clams are available. When I was growing up in Sun Tak, we ate these clams regularly, always with great enjoyment. Particularly, I must admit, I liked the sauce very much, and I would eat so much of it with rice that my mother would have to take away my bowl.

For the sauce
1½ tablespoons oyster sauce
1 teaspoon double dark soy sauce, regular dark soy sauce, or mushroom soy sauce
2 tablespoons Chinese white rice wine or gin
1½ teaspoons Chinese white rice vinegar or distilled vinegar

2½ teaspoons sugar
1 teaspoon sesame oil
Pinch freshly ground white pepper
1 tablespoon cornstarch
¾ cup Seafood Stock (page 76)

2 pounds Manila clams (about 48), well washed under cold running water until very clean
½ cup cold water
1½ tablespoons peanut oil
2 tablespoons julienned fresh ginger
2 tablespoons minced garlic
1½ tablespoons hoisin sauce
½ tablespoon bean sauce
8 scallions, trimmed, cut into 1½-inch pieces, and white parts lightly smashed
2 tablespoons Seafood Stock (page 76)
2 tablespoons minced fresh coriander (cilantro)

1. In a bowl, combine the sauce ingredients and reserve.

2. Prepare the clams as in step 2 of the preceding recipe and reserve the clams and their liquid.

3. Heat a wok over high heat for 30 seconds. Add the peanut oil and coat the wok with it using a spatula. When a wisp of white smoke appears, add the ginger and stir briefly. Add the garlic, stir, and when the garlic turns brown add the hoisin sauce and bean sauce. Stir well and add the scallions. Stir and cook for 1½ minutes. Add the stock, stir, and cook for 1 minute or until the green parts of scallions turn bright green. Stir the sauce mixture, pour in, and continue to cook, stirring, until the sauce thickens and bubbles. Add the clams and their liquid and stir well, making certain the clams are coated evenly. Cook for 2 minutes, turn off the heat, transfer the clams to a heated platter, sprinkle with the coriander, and serve with cooked rice.

MAKES 4 SERVINGS

JELLYFISH
Hoi Jit Pei

This ocean creature, a gelatinous mass with tentacles, is to be found in the South China Sea all along the Chinese coast. Its top is round and grows larger and thinner as it ages. When caught, the tentacles and inner mass are discarded, and only the top, a thin sheet, is boiled, then preserved in salt. It comes in these pliable sheets wrapped in plastic. This way of cooking and serving jellyfish is the art of Shanghai. Everywhere in China where it is eaten, it is prepared in the manner of Shanghai. Jellyfish is served usually as a first course at a banquet, or it can be one of those "small dishes," appetizers before a meal proper.

10 cups cold water
1 pound jellyfish, cut into ¼-inch-wide
   slices

For the sauce
1 teaspoon soy sauce
2 teaspoons Shao-Hsing wine or dry
   sherry
¼ teaspoon salt
1 teaspoon sugar
1¼ teaspoons Chinese white rice
   vinegar or distilled vinegar
1½ teaspoons sesame oil
1 tablespoon trimmed and finely sliced
   scallion
Pinch freshly ground white pepper

1. To prepare the jellyfish, bring the cold water to a boil over high heat. Add the jellyfish slices and cook for 45 seconds to 1 minute. The jellyfish will shrink to about half their volume. Remove from the pot, strain, and wash with cold water 4 times to remove all of the salt. Place the slices in a bowl, cover with cold water, and allow to rest overnight, refrigerated.

2. Drain the jellyfish and dry thoroughly. In a bowl, combine the sauce ingredients, then add to the dried jellyfish and toss well to coat completely. Serve cool, not cold.

MAKES 4 TO 6 SERVINGS
AS AN APPETIZER

STEAMED SCALLOPS WITH BLACK BEANS

See Jup Jing Dai Jee

*S*callops are plentiful along China's eastern coast, and like other shelled creatures are cooked in a variety of ways. Though dry scallops are expensive and considered rare delicacies, traditionally they have been eaten in far greater numbers than fresh scallops. This is a custom that has been with us for many centuries, and to this day, conpoy, *the dry variety, are important enough to be the occasional centerpiece of a feast or banquet. Where I lived in Sun Tak, we rarely saw fresh scallops, although we were so close to the sea. They were treats to be eaten when we visited the city of Canton, now Guangzhou, where they were most often steamed, on the half shell, with black beans.*

For steaming
1 tablespoon fermented black beans, washed and drained

1½ teaspoons minced fresh ginger
1½ teaspoons minced garlic
1½ tablespoons oyster sauce
2 teaspoons soy sauce
1 tablespoon Chinese white rice wine or gin
1½ teaspoons Chinese white rice vinegar or distilled vinegar
1½ teaspoons sugar
½ teaspoon salt
2 teaspoons Garlic Oil (page 84) or peanut oil
Pinch freshly ground white pepper

1 pound large fresh sea scallops (about 24), excess liquid drained
1½ tablespoons fried garlic (page 84)

In a bowl, mix the steaming ingredients well. Place the scallops in a steamproof dish. Pour the steaming ingredients over them and mix well to coat them. Allow to rest for 30 minutes. Place the dish in a steamer, cover, and steam for 5 minutes (see steaming, page 64), until the scallops are white and opaque. Do not oversteam, or the scallops will become tough. If steaming in a metal dish, steam for 3 minutes. Turn off the heat and serve in the steamproof dish (still in the bamboo steamer) with fried garlic sprinkled on top. Serve with rice.

MAKES 4 TO 6 SERVINGS

HOT HENG YANG SCALLOPS

Lot Heng Yang Dai Jee

*F*resh scallops did, and do, make their way inland. In this case, by rail, through the famous market and transportation city of Heng Yang in the middle of Hunan province. This preparation was created there, it is said, by a visiting chef from Shanghai.

For the sauce
1 tablespoon soy sauce
⅛ teaspoon freshly ground white pepper
2 teaspoons sugar
½ teaspoon salt
2 tablespoons Shao-Hsing wine or dry sherry
½ teaspoon Chinese white rice vinegar or distilled vinegar
⅓ cup Chicken Stock (page 75)
1 teaspoon Hot Pepper Oil (page 87) or other hot chili oil
1½ teaspoons hot pepper flakes (page 87)

1 tablespoon hoisin sauce
1 teaspoon sesame oil
1 tablespoon cornstarch

2 cups peanut oil
1 pound large fresh sea scallops (about 24), drained and cut across the width to make 48 rounds
1 teaspoon minced fresh ginger
1 teaspoon minced garlic
1½ teaspoons cloud ears, soaked in hot water for 30 minutes, washed, and hard ends discarded
½ cup diced red bell pepper in ½-inch pieces
½ cup diced green bell pepper in ½-inch pieces
6 fresh water chestnuts, peeled, washed, and sliced into ¼-inch rounds
3 tablespoons trimmed and finely sliced scallion

1. In a bowl, combine the sauce ingredients and reserve.

2. Heat a wok over high heat for 1 minute. Add the peanut oil and heat to 350°F. Place the scallops in a Chinese strainer, lower into the oil, and cook for 1½ minutes. Turn off the heat, remove with the strainer, drain, and reserve.

3. Drain off all but 1½ tablespoons of the oil from the wok. Heat over high heat for 20 seconds. When a wisp of white smoke appears, add the ginger and stir briefly. Add the garlic and stir. Add the cloud ears and stir briefly. Add the red and green peppers and water chestnuts and cook, stirring, for 2 minutes. Add the scallops, mix, and cook, stirring, for 1½ minutes. Make a well in the mixture, stir the sauce mixture, pour in, and stir well. When the sauce thickens and bubbles, turn off the heat, transfer to a heated platter, sprinkle with the scallion, and serve.

MAKES 4 TO 6 SERVINGS

BOK CHOY AND BEAN CURD SOUP WITH SCALLOPS

Bok Choy *Dau Fu Yue Chiu*

*T*his very unusual soup, with ingredients put together after a visit to my market, is my invention. The bok choy was fresh, sweet, and green. The dry scallops I had steamed 2 days earlier. The plump bean curd cakes had been fashioned that morning by my supplier in his small Chinatown factory. I put all of these together, and how pleasant it was. I wish to share it.

1 pound bok choy, *stalks separated from leaves, washed well, and drained*

5 cups Superior Stock (page 74) or Chicken Stock (page 75)
One 1-inch-thick slice fresh ginger, lightly smashed
2 Steamed Dry Scallops (page 80), julienned (¼ cup)
1 tablespoon Mei Kuei Lu Chiew or gin
½ pound fresh bean curd (medium-firm tofu), cut into ⅓-inch dice
1 tablespoon Shallot Oil (page 84) or peanut oil
Pinch freshly ground white pepper
½ teaspoon salt (optional)

1. Cut the *bok choy* stalks into ½-inch dice. Tear the leaves into 2-inch-wide pieces, then cut into ½-inch pieces.

2. Place the stock and ginger slice in a large pot, cover, and bring to a boil over high heat. Add the *bok choy* stalks and julienned scallops and return to a boil. Lower the heat to medium and cook for 5 minutes. Turn the heat back to high, add the Mei Kuei Lu Chiew, stir well, and cook for 1 minute. Add the *bok choy* leaves, mix well, return to a boil, and cook for 2 minutes. Add the bean curd, stir and mix well, return to a boil, and cook for 1 minute. Add the shallot oil and white pepper, stir, and mix well. Taste, add salt if necessary or to taste, and mix well. Turn off the heat, transfer to a heated tureen, and serve.

MAKES 6 SERVINGS

TAI PONG BAY NOODLES

Tai Pong Mai Fon

*T*ai Pong Bay is a small but famous body of water, just north of Hong Kong. In its waters, it is said, live the sweetest of scallops and shrimp, as well as squid, and those caught in this bay are often shipped to Hong Kong and other cities in China's South. This traditional dish from the region around this small bay combines its fresh seafood with fine rice noodles. The several blending steps make this a grand seafood dish indeed.

½ pound fine rice noodles

For the sauce
2½ tablespoons oyster sauce
2 tablespoons Chinese white rice wine or gin
2 tablespoons soy sauce
2 teaspoons sugar
Pinch freshly ground white pepper

1 cup Chicken Stock (page 75)
One ½-inch-thick slice fresh ginger, lightly smashed
6 ounces fresh sea scallops (about 10), cut across the width to make 20 rounds, drained well
6 medium Chinese mushrooms, soaked in hot water for 30 minutes, washed, stems removed, and julienned (1 cup)
3 tablespoons Coriander Oil (page 86) or peanut oil
6 ounces Chinese chives, cut into 1½-inch pieces, stems separated from flat leaves
2 teaspoons minced garlic
6 ounces medium shrimp (about 12), shelled, deveined, and quartered lengthwise
½ teaspoon salt
¼ cup Pickled Ginger (page 102)
5 ounces mung bean sprouts, both ends removed

1. Soak the rice noodles in hot water for 20 minutes. Drain well and loosen the strands with chopsticks. Dry completely for 1½ hours, turning the noodles 3 times. As the rice noodles dry, in a bowl, mix together the sauce ingredients and reserve.

2. Place the stock and ginger in a wok and bring to a boil over high heat. Add the scallops, stir, cook for 1 minute, remove with a Chinese strainer, and drain. Return the stock to a boil, add the mushrooms, stir and mix, return to a boil, and cook for 3 minutes. Turn off the heat and ladle the mushrooms into the Chinese strainer next to the scallops. Let both drain. Remove the stock from the wok and discard. Wash the wok and spatula and dry with paper towels.

3. Heat the wok over high heat for 40 seconds, add 1 tablespoon of the coriander oil, and coat the wok with it using a spatula. When a wisp of white smoke appears, add the chive stems and cook for 30 seconds. Add the garlic and mix briefly. Add the shrimp, stir, and cook for 30 seconds. Add the scallops and mushrooms, stir, and cook for 1 minute. Stir the sauce mixture, pour in, and cook, stirring, for 1½ minutes. Turn off the heat, transfer the mixture to a bowl, and reserve.

4. Wash and dry the wok and spatula. Heat the wok over high heat for 1 minute. Add the remaining oil and coat the wok with it using the spatula. Add the salt and stir. Add the noodles and stir well, loosening the strands. Lower the heat to medium and cook for 1 minute. Add the pickled ginger and stir well. Add the chive leaves, stir well, and cook for 2 minutes. Add the bean sprouts, stir, and cook for 3 minutes. Add the scallop-mushroom-shrimp mixture and cook, stirring vigorously to make certain the ingredients are well blended. Raise the heat back to high and continue to cook, stirring, until the noodles are very hot, 1 to 2 minutes. Turn off the heat, transfer to a heated platter, and serve.

MAKES 6 TO 8 SERVINGS

Poultry
and Other Fowl

鷄和家禽類

POULTRY, FOWL, AND CHICKEN IN PARTICULAR HAVE ALWAYS BEEN MOST SIGNIFICANT IN THE CHINESE KITCHEN, HISTORICALLY, NUTRITIONALLY, AND SYMBOLICALLY. CHICKEN WERE THE FIRST CREATURES, ALONG WITH PIGS, TO BE DOMESTICATED BY PREHISTORIC CHINESE, THOUSANDS OF YEARS BEFORE DYNASTIES BEGAN TO BE COUNTED. It is known that domesticated chickens, as well as wild fowl of all sorts, were important foods for the P'ei-li-kaang, a prehistoric people who lived about 9,000 years ago in what is today the fertile central river valley of the Yangtze. It was the people of China's South and center who brought the chicken to the North.

Throughout its history, the chicken has been a symbol of rebirth, and of the female, to the Chinese, who equate it with the phoenix and pair it with the dragon, to represent the female and the male, a recurring image. This symbolic belief is reflected in the dietary belief we hold that chicken is our most nutritious food, food that helps promote longevity and has recuperative powers. And we Chinese never tire of chicken, never weary of cooking it in a variety of ways. We steam chickens, double-boil them, roast, stew and braise them, bake and fry them, wrap them in leaves, doughs, and salt to cook them, cook them in stocks, and make stocks, broths, and sauces from them. They are sliced, julienned, minced, and ground, made into salads and cooked in wine or soys. The combinations are endless.

In some parts of China, and at different periods, chickens, though plentiful, were eaten only occasionally, because it was felt that the chicken was too valuable as a recurring source for its eggs to be killed for one simple meal. This was not widespread, however. But always it was considered a delicacy, and in many parts of the country careful note was taken of the ages of chickens, hens and roosters, for when they reached the optimal older age they were killed for the richness of the broth they would make. Old chickens make the best soup, we believed, and it happens to be true. Chickens, when young, are only slightly yang, or warming, but as they become older they become more yang and thus provide a stronger, heat-giving soup.

In our family, when I was growing up, we always thought of chicken as a food for special occasions. We marked birthdays, engagements, and weddings with chicken. Chicken was the phoenix, the bride, at weddings. Chicken, as a symbol of rebirth, was important in the dinners we had on the eve of the Lunar New Year and on the second day after the New Year, when we would cook a chicken to mark *hoi lin*, the "opening of the year." At the traditional feast given in honor of a baby one month after its birth, chicken was always its most important component. Not the least of its attributes was that it was valued for its role in waking humans up each morning.

Though to a lesser degree, the cousins to the chicken are important as well. Ducks and geese, squabs and pigeons, are important to the Chinese diet, as are game birds such as quail, partridge, and pheasant. Evidence of preparations of various fowl has been found in the Shang dynasty, which extended from 1766 to 1122 B.C., and in the ensuing Zhou dynasty, which continued to 770 B.C. Chickens as well as geese, quail, pheasant, partridge, and sparrows are known to have been foods both common and festive. The wall rubbings of those unearthed Han tombs depict chickens as abundant sources of food, and there is evidence that the chicken was regarded as a perfect food to offer a guest.

Chickens were also offered not only to the emperors but by them, to gods and ancestors. The Ming, who ruled China from the fourteenth to the seventeenth century, and were not known for gastronomic reticence, appear to have regarded chickens as quite special indeed. More than 6,000 cooks labored in the imperial kitchens, a number that grew to more than 9,000 by the middle of the fif-teenth century. Among them were a group designated as functionaries for the court of imperial sacrifice. Each year, we know from anthropological studies, this group sacrificed 200,000 animals a year, among them 18,000 pigs, but most of them, 138,000, chickens.

While we did not sacrifice chickens, our family offered food, including chickens, as offerings, a practice overseen by my Ah Paw, my grandmother. We would offer whole cooked chickens at our family ancestral altar and in the temples we visited. Our family, including me, would take our food to the temple, and there we would light incense sticks and candles. We would kneel, place our hands together, and pray to our ancestors, offer them our food, particularly those chickens, in *bai jo sin*, to give us their blessings for a good harvest, for good business. Then we would take our chickens home, poach them in a stock, then cut them up to eat as "white cut chicken." It was our way of sharing in this ancestral offering.

Such offerings were an important ritual in another way. A scholar, a candidate for the civil service, would of course pray for the blessings of an ancestor. If he was successful, he would have a banquet in celebration of having secured a position. He would offer food, including a chicken, in the temple. He would make a similar offering at his family's ancestral altar, all of these in a grateful gesture, a *wan sun*, a "return to gods," a way of saying thank you. This practice was followed in my family.

We also offered chickens at the graves of our ancestors during the Ching Ming festival, which was celebrated each spring with a visit to these graves and a general tidying up of the gravesites.

It is worth setting down, simply to illustrate the high regard for chickens as food, portions of a 1754 menu from the court of Emperor Ch'ien-lung, an eighteenth-century ruler of the Ching dynasty that ruled China for the last 300 years of the dynastic eras, until 1911. This is recounted in *Food in Chinese Culture*. The extensive meal included "fat chicken with pot-boiled duck," "swallow's nests and julienned smoked duck," "julienned pot-boiled chicken," "smoked fat chicken," "salted duck and pork," and "court-styled fried chicken."

Chickens, I remember, were always live, always freshly killed. We never had such things as chicken parts. We bought a whole chicken, prepared it, cooked it, ate it. There is no taste quite like that of a well-prepared, freshly killed chicken. If possible, seek out fresh chickens and avoid processed birds. In these times of packaged chickens, packaged parts, one should check the dates on these packages. Never buy a chicken whose date has passed. Often frozen chickens are permitted to defrost in the refrigerated compartments of markets. It is best to avoid frozen chickens if possible. Test them. Press them. The flesh might still be hard, partially frozen, or there could be traces of crystallization.

If a chicken has been in a refrigerated case too long, the package may contain an excessive amount of red, blood-colored liquid. I suggest that if you are buying whole chicken breasts, have your butcher cut them from a fresh chicken; if chicken cutlets, the same. When buying other small birds, such as squab and quail, it is best to order them fresh and to the size you wish. This is not difficult; most markets will oblige, and the birds are widely available, certainly in Chinese markets. I suggest the same for ducks. Ducks are frozen more frequently than chickens. Avoid them if possible. Freshly killed ducks of the domesticated Pekin variety are relatively easy to obtain, usually on order. They are large-breasted and ideal for roasting or for such as Peking Duck. The Long Island duckling is an admirable substitute. Always, however, buy your fowl as Ah Paw would stress to me, her finger wagging, fresh, fresh, fresh.

In another context involving Ah Paw, chicken is memorable to me. On Ah Paw's birthday, every year, her cooks would prepare for her raw fish dishes. These were deemed too strong for childish stomachs, so as a child I was not permitted to eat them. But in its place, Ah Paw would have had made for us young people a thick, rich chicken congee, something I always looked forward to at her birthday dinners.

Quite a bit of significance for those feathered creatures that strut about and cluck.

CHICKEN WITH GARLIC SHOOTS

Gai See Chau Seun Miu

In Sichuan province it is common practice to stir-fry different foods with a generous amount of fresh garlic shoots. These are the shoots that flower out of the tops of garlic bulbs. They are picked just as they begin to form buds. They are widely available in Chinese and other Asian markets; just ask for garlic shoots, or seun miu, *stems. They are crisp and sweet, a perfect accompaniment to chicken. Usually when mention of Sichuan is made, the association* hot *springs to mind. This is not always so. This preparation is a delicate taste of Sichuan.*

¾ *pound skinless, boneless chicken breasts, thinly sliced into pieces 2 inches long by ½ inch wide (1¼ cups)*
1½ *tablespoons egg white, beaten*
1½ *tablespoons tapioca flour*

For the sauce
6 *tablespoons Milk Stock (page 78) or Chicken Stock (page 75)*
1 *tablespoon tapioca flour*
½ *teaspoon sugar*
¼ *teaspoon salt*

1 *quart peanut oil*
One 1-inch-thick slice fresh ginger, peeled
2 *garlic cloves, peeled*
1½ *teaspoons minced fresh ginger*
¼ *teaspoon salt*
½ *pound garlic shoots, cut into 2-inch pieces*
2 *tablespoons Milk Stock (page 78) or Chicken Stock (page 75)*

1. Place the chicken slices in a bowl, add the egg white and tapioca flour, mix together well, and allow to rest for at least 10 minutes. In another bowl, combine the sauce ingredients and reserve.

2. Heat a wok over high heat for 1 minute. Add the peanut oil, ginger slice, and garlic cloves and heat to 300°F. Add the chicken mixture, lower the heat to medium, and separate the chicken slices with chopsticks. Cook for 1 minute or until the slices are completely separated. Raise the heat back to high and cook for 1½ minutes or until the chicken turns white. Turn off the heat, remove the chicken with a Chinese strainer, and drain. Empty all but 2 tablespoons of the oil from the wok.

3. Heat the wok over high heat for 10 seconds, add the minced ginger and salt, stir, and cook for 30 seconds. Add the garlic shoots and stir for 1 minute. Add the stock, stir, and cook for 2 minutes, until the shoots are tender. Add the chicken, stir well, and cook for 1 minute. Make a well in the mixture, stir the sauce mixture and pour in, and cook, stirring, for 2 minutes or until the sauce turns white and transparent. Turn off the heat, transfer to a heated platter, and serve.

MAKES 8 SERVINGS

CHICKEN WITH STRANGE TASTE

Guai Mei Gai

This is another unusual recipe from Sichuan. It has some spice and a "strange taste" as well, provided by that "secret ingredient" from the regional Sichuan kitchen, Sichuan Peppercorn Paste. The dish itself is prepared to be eaten cool, either as a small appetizer or as an initial course of a banquet.

3 cups cold water
2 scallions, trimmed and cut
   into thirds
1 large onion, peeled and quartered
One ½-inch-thick slice fresh ginger,
   lightly smashed
1 teaspoon salt
1 teaspoon sugar
¾ pound skinless, boneless whole chicken
   breast

For the sauce
1 tablespoon dark soy sauce
1½ tablespoons sesame paste (tahini)
1½ tablespoons Chinkiang vinegar
1 tablespoon Sichuan Peppercorn Paste
   (page 90)
1 teaspoon Hot Pepper Oil (page 87) or
   other hot chili oil
1½ tablespoons sugar
2 tablespoons trimmed and finely
   sliced scallion
1 teaspoon minced fresh ginger
1 teaspoon minced garlic
1 teaspoon sesame oil
¼ teaspoon salt
3 tablespoons Chicken Stock (page 75)
1 tablespoon Shao-Hsing wine or dry
   sherry

2 cups Iceberg lettuce, julienned

1. Place the water, scallions, onion, ginger, salt, and sugar in a pot, cover, and bring to a boil over high heat. Lower the heat and simmer for 15 minutes, leaving the lid cracked. Raise the heat back to high, add the chicken, lower the heat, and simmer for 7 minutes, leaving the lid cracked. Turn off the heat and allow the chicken to rest in the liquid and come to room temperature. Remove the chicken to a chopping board, pound with the flat of a cleaver blade to break its fibers, then shred the chicken by hand. Reserve. Reserve the cooking liquid for another use.

2. As the chicken cooks, mix the sauce ingredients in a large bowl. Add the shredded chicken to the sauce and mix to combine and coat well. Refrigerate for at least 2 hours before serving. Place julienned lettuce around the edges of a platter, mound the chicken into the platter, and serve.

MAKES 6 SERVINGS

JADE TREE CHICKEN WITH HAM

Jinhua Yuk Seuh Gai

*T*his is a well-known, in fact famous, preparation from Shanghai. In its original form it uses that fine, cured, salty Jinhua ham from the Shanghai region and combines it very poetically with Chinese broccoli called yuk seuh, or "jade tree." Smithfield ham substitutes quite well for the Jinhua ham, as it does for Yunnan ham. This steamed preparation is found at virtually every important Shanghai banquet.

One 4½-pound chicken, fat and membranes removed, rubbed well with 4 tablespoons salt, then rinsed, drained, and dried

3 tablespoons Mei Kuei Lu Chiew or gin

2 teaspoons salt

3 teaspoons sugar

One 2-inch-thick slice fresh ginger, cut into 5 pieces

6 cups cold water

1 tablespoon sugar

1 teaspoon baking soda

12 stalks Chinese broccoli, all leaves and tough ends of stems removed

½ pound prepared Smithfield Ham (page 79)

1. Place the chicken in a steamproof dish, drizzle with Mei Kuei Lu Chiew, and rub into the skin and cavity. Sprinkle the chicken with the salt and 3 teaspoons sugar, outside and in the cavity; rub it in. Place 2 pieces of ginger in the cavity, 3 outside in the dish. Place the dish in a steamer, cover, and steam for 1 hour (see steaming, page 64) or until the chicken is cooked. Turn off the heat, remove the chicken from the dish, and cool to room temperature. Reserve the liquid. Pull the meat of the whole breast from the breastbones and cut across into ¼-inch slices about 2 inches long. Reserve. Reserve the thigh and leg meat and the carcass, to be used in the recipe that follows.

2. As the chicken steams, prepare the Chinese broccoli: Place 6 cups water, 1 tablespoon sugar, and the baking soda in a pot. Cover and bring to a boil over high heat. Add the broccoli and blanch for 15 to 20 seconds. Turn off the heat, run cold water into the pot, and drain. Repeat and drain well.

3. Cut the ham into slices similar to those of chicken.

4. Place the broccoli stalks in parallel lines along the length of a platter. Between them, alternate chicken and ham slices, overlapping them slightly. The broccoli will border and frame the slices.

5. Mix 1 cup of the reserved steaming liquid with the tapioca flour in a saucepan. Heat over medium heat, stirring continuously, until the liquid boils. It is now a sauce. Turn off the heat, pour in a drizzle over the platter of chicken, ham, and broccoli to cover well, and serve.

MAKES 6 SERVINGS

SHANGHAI CHICKEN SALAD

Gai See Sah Lud

*T*his recipe uses the thigh and leg meat of the chicken steamed in the previous recipe. In China, chicken never comes in parts; one always buys a whole chicken. However, this may be made with suitable parts. The recipe is my invention. I call it Shanghai Chicken Salad simply because I use the chicken remaining from the previous Shanghai recipe. It demonstrates how far one chicken can go. Perhaps it may go even further, because the wings of the chicken, its bones, and its skin can certainly be added to any stock mixture.

1¼ cups julienned cooked chicken thigh and leg meat (preceding recipe)

1 cup peeled and julienned cucumber
3 tablespoons thinly sliced Shallot Pickles (page 102)
1 cup julienned red bell pepper
¾ cup julienned celery
3 tablespoons Pickled Ginger (page 102)
¼ teaspoon salt
1 tablespoon soy sauce
1½ tablespoons Chinese white rice vinegar or distilled vinegar
2 teaspoons sugar
1 teaspoon sesame oil
⅛ teaspoon freshly ground white pepper
5 cups peanut oil
2 ounces dry rice noodles

1. Place all the ingredients except the peanut oil and rice noodles in a large bowl. Mix thoroughly to combine and coat. Refrigerate, uncovered, for at least 1 hour before serving.

2. As the salad cools, prepare the rice noodles: Heat a wok over high heat for 1 minute. Add the peanut oil and heat to 375°F. Add the rice noodles, stir to loosen them, and fry for about 30 seconds. The rice noodles will cook almost instantly, expanding,

quickly becoming crisp and white. Turn off the heat, remove the noodles, and drain well.

3. Place the noodles around the edges of a serving platter. Mound the chicken salad into the platter and serve.

MAKES 6 SERVINGS

CHICKEN SMOKED WITH RICE AND TEA

Mai Fun Gai

*T*his is quite an unusual smoked chicken from Sichuan, where smoking is an art, whether with tea or camphor. What makes this preparation so different is that cooking processes are reversed. Usually a chicken or duck is first smoked, then deep-fried just before serving. This recipe, which utilizes 3 methods of cooking with the wok, changes the order. The chicken is first deep-fried, then steamed, and finally smoked before serving. Cooking the chicken in this order removes virtually all of the cooking oil from the chicken, as well as its fat.

One 4½-pound chicken, fat and membranes removed, rubbed well with 4 tablespoons salt, rinsed, and drained
2½ teaspoons salt
6 cups peanut oil
2 scallions, trimmed and cut into thirds
Three ½-inch-thick slices ginger
¼ cup uncooked rice
3 tablespoons Chinese black tea

1. Place the chicken in a large dish and dry well with paper towels, inside the cavity and out. Sprinkle 2½ teaspoons salt in the cavity and between the skin and breast meat until all the salt is used. Allow to rest for 30 minutes, refrigerated.

2. Remove from the refrigerator and dry again with paper towels. Make a foil ball, place in the tail cavity, and close the cavity with skewers. (The foil ball prevents oil from entering the cavity while it cooks.)

3. Heat a wok over high heat for 1 minute. Add the peanut oil and heat to 375°F. Place the chicken, breast side up, in a Chinese strainer, lower it into the oil, and fry for 5 minutes. As the chicken fries, ladle hot oil over the breast to ensure even cooking. Turn the chicken over and fry for another 5 minutes, ladling oil. Turn off the heat, remove the chicken, and drain. Empty the oil from the wok into a bowl. Wash and dry the wok. When the chicken cools, remove the foil ball from the tail cavity.

4. Place the chicken in a steamproof dish. Place the scallions and ginger in the cavity. Place the dish on a rack in a wok over boiling water, cover, and steam for 1 hour (see steaming, page 64). Turn off the heat, remove the chicken from the wok, and cool until it can be handled. Place on a rack.

5. Heat the wok over high heat for 30 seconds. Add the rice to the dry wok, stir, and cook for 30 seconds. Add the tea leaves, stir to mix with the rice, and cook for 1½ minutes, or until the rice turns brown, smoke appears, and the tea leaves release their fragrance. Place the chicken on the rack on the rice and tea mixture, cover with the wok lid, and seal around the edge with wet paper towels. Lower the heat to medium and allow the chicken to smoke for 7 minutes. Turn off the heat and allow the chicken to rest in the wok for 4 minutes. Discard the rice and tea leaves, remove the chicken, cut into bite-sized pieces, and serve with Lotus Leaf Bread (page 366).

MAKES 8 SERVINGS

CHICKEN BRAISED
WITH ONIONS AND SHALLOTS

Chung Yau Gai

This is a very old traditional recipe from Guangzhou. Rarely can it be found in restaurants these days. It requires 2 cooking processes, an initial braising and a second to blend all of its flavors. Many such dishes as this have vanished from restaurant menus, even in China, simply because of the time necessary to prepare them properly. But in the cooking lies the enjoyment, and the taste is unique.

One 4¼-pound chicken, fat and membranes removed, rubbed well with 4 tablespoons salt, rinsed, and placed in a sitting position in a strainer to drain

3 tablespoons double dark soy sauce, regular dark soy sauce, or mushroom soy sauce

2 tablespoons peanut oil

1 tablespoon minced fresh ginger

1 tablespoon minced garlic

2 ounces shallots, peeled and cut into ¼-inch dice

1 small onion, peeled and cut into ¼-inch dice

1½ tablespoons bean sauce

3 tablespoons oyster sauce

¼ cup Shao-Hsing wine or dry sherry

1½ cups Chicken Stock (page 75)

2 teaspoons soy sauce

2½ tablespoons sugar

8 sprigs fresh coriander (cilantro)

1. Place the drained chicken on a large platter and rub with 1½ tablespoons of the dark soy sauce, making certain the chicken is well coated. Tie the chicken legs together with string.

2. Heat a wok over high heat for 40 seconds. Add the peanut oil and coat the wok with it using a spatula. When a wisp of white smoke appears, add the ginger and garlic and stir. When the garlic turns light brown, add the shallots and onion, stir to mix, and cook for 1½ minutes. Add the bean sauce, stir and mix, and cook for 1 minute. Add the oyster sauce and stir well. Add the wine and stir in. When the mixture begins to boil, add the stock and return to a boil. Add the remaining dark soy sauce, the regular soy, and the sugar, mix well, and return to a boil. Place the chicken in the wok, breast side down, and with a spatula coat the chicken well. Cook for 2 minutes. Turn the chicken over and repeat until all 4 sides are sealed. Care should be taken that the heat is not too high, or the chicken skin can burn.

3. Turn off the heat. Transfer the chicken and sauce to a Dutch oven, breast side up. Cover and bring to a boil over medium heat. Lower the heat and simmer for 30 minutes, covered. Use a wooden spoon to move the chicken about several times to prevent sticking. Turn the chicken over and simmer for another 45 minutes, moving the chicken with a wooden spoon. Turn off the heat and allow the chicken to rest in the pot for 20 minutes. The sauce should reduce to 1¼ cups.

4. Remove the chicken to a cutting board, tail up, breast out. With a cleaver, cut from the tail down the backbone, until the chicken is cut in half. Remove the skin and bones. Cut into bite-sized pieces, place on a serving platter, pour the sauce over the chicken, sprinkle with coriander, and serve with cooked rice.

MAKES 6 TO 8 SERVINGS

DOUBLE-BOILED CHICKEN
WITH HONEY DATES

Mut Jo Dun Gai

A perfect example of home cooking. All one needs is a chicken and a large pot in which to cook it. Variations of this preparation exist throughout China. Quite often this is made with "black chicken," a species that is all black, flesh and skin, and the chicken is discarded. Only its broth is drunk. This is a custom among women who have given birth, and older people drink this intense broth twice each month for its perceived regenerative powers. In terms of food-as-medicine properties, it is a most yang, or warming, dish. A final note: You need not discard the chicken; enjoy it with the broth.

One 3½-pound chicken, fat and membranes removed, rubbed well with 4 tablespoons salt, rinsed under cold water, and placed in a strainer in a sitting position to drain
8 dried dates (the "honey dates" sold in Chinese groceries or customary dates)
2 tablespoons boxthorn seeds, soaked in warm water for 15 minutes, until softened

1. Wash the chicken neck and giblets well and drain. Reserve the liver for another use. Place the chicken, again in a sitting position, in a ceramic pot or casserole. Add the neck and giblets. Add the dates and boxthorn seeds. Cover the ceramic pot.

2. Place 3 quarts boiling water in the bottom tier of a clam steamer. Place the ceramic pot with the chicken in the top tier, set it atop the bottom tier, cover, and double-boil over high heat for 4 hours. During this time, keep boiling water at hand to replenish any that evaporates.

3. Turn off the heat. Transfer the ceramic pot to the table and serve. There will be about 2 to 2½ cups of broth in the pot with the chicken. Divide among individual bowls. The chicken will be soft and falling off the bone. Serve with the broth. You may also serve, if desired, with small individual dishes of soy sauce as a dip.

MAKES 4 TO 6 SERVINGS

JADE FLOWER CHICKEN

Yuk Lan Gai Fai

The image of jade recurs in the Chinese kitchen. The words for broccoli, yuk lan, translate as "green flower" to symbolize imperial jade. The antecedents of this dish reside in the Beijing imperial court, where the dish would have been served as a first course at a banquet. The whiteness of the chicken breast contrasts with the green to create "jade" on a plate.

One 2¾-pound chicken breast, rib bones and skin intact, large-breasted oven roaster preferred
2 tablespoons Mei Kuei Lu Chiew or gin
1½ teaspoons plus ⅛ teaspoon salt
2 teaspoons sugar
3 scallions, trimmed and cut into 3-inch pieces
One 1-inch-thick slice fresh ginger, cut into 4 slices

¾ pound broccoli florets, cut into pieces 2¼ inches long and 1½ inches wide
6 cups cold water
One ½-inch-thick slice fresh ginger, lightly smashed
½ teaspoon baking soda
1 tablespoon Scallion Oil (page 82) or peanut oil
½ teaspoon ginger juice (page 23) mixed with 2 teaspoons Mei Kuei Lu Chiew or gin
½ teaspoon sesame oil

For the sauce
½ tablespoon soy sauce
1 tablespoon tapioca flour
Pinch freshly ground white pepper
1 cup steaming liquid

1. Wash the chicken breast well, remove the fat and membranes, drain, and dry. Cut in half lengthwise, place in a cake pan, rub with the wine, sprinkle with 1½ teaspoons salt and the sugar, and rub in. Put half the scallions and 2 of the ginger slices underneath the chicken, the remaining scallions and the other 2 ginger slices under the skin. Place the cake pan in a steamer, cover, and steam for 30 minutes (see steaming, page 64).

2. As the chicken steams, blanch the broccoli. Place the cold water, the ½-inch ginger slice, and the baking soda in a pot and bring to a boil over high heat. Add the broccoli and stir well until the broccoli turns bright green, about 5 seconds. Turn off the heat, run cold water into the pot, drain, and reserve.

3. Heat a wok over high heat for 30 seconds, add the scallion oil and remaining ⅛ teaspoon salt, and coat the wok with it using a spatula. When a wisp of white smoke appears, add the broccoli, stir well, and cook for 1 minute. Add the ginger juice–wine mixture around the edge of the wok and stir-fry for 2 minutes, making certain the

broccoli is well coated. Add the sesame oil and stir well. Turn off the heat, transfer the broccoli to a heated platter, and arrange as a border.

4. Remove the skin and bone from the chicken and cut into ⅓-inch slices across. Arrange the chicken slices on a platter with the broccoli surrounding them.

5. Mix the sauce ingredients. Heat the wok over high heat and add the sauce. Stir continually until it thickens and bubbles. Turn off the heat, ladle the sauce over the chicken, and serve.

MAKES 6 TO 8 SERVINGS

VIRGIN CHICKEN

Lot Jee Gai Ding

*T*his is an oddly and humorously named preparation from Sichuan. Lot jee gai translates as "peppery male virgin chicken." This special, festive dish is traditionally made with the breast of a young male chicken. Old male chickens, roosters, are considered too tough and produce too much bodily heat to eat, so the breasts of young male chickens are used. In China it is easy to buy a whole young male chicken. However, if you are buying chicken breasts, it is rather difficult to know if you are getting a male. I suppose you must trust your butcher.

For the marinade
1 medium egg white, beaten
½ teaspoon salt
1 teaspoon sugar
2 teaspoons tapioca flour

10 ounces lean skinless, boneless chicken breasts, cut into ½-inch cubes

For the sauce
2½ teaspoons double dark soy sauce, regular dark soy sauce, or mushroom soy sauce
2 teaspoons Shao-Hsing wine or dry sherry
1 tablespoon Chinkiang vinegar
1 teaspoon sugar
¼ teaspoon salt
1 teaspoon tapioca flour

2 cups peanut oil
⅓ cup raw skinless peanuts
1½ teaspoons minced fresh ginger
1½ tablespoons minced Sichuan Pepper Pickle (page 99)
4 fresh water chestnuts, peeled and cut into ¼-inch dice
1 tablespoon Shao-Hsing wine or dry sherry
3 tablespoons trimmed and finely sliced scallion

1. In a large bowl, combine the marinade ingredients. Add the chicken and allow to rest at least 20 minutes. In another bowl, combine the sauce ingredients and reserve.

2. To prepare the peanuts, heat a wok over high heat for 45 seconds. Add the peanut oil and heat to 350°F. Place the peanuts in a Chinese strainer, lower into the oil, and fry until they are golden, 1 to 1½ minutes. Turn off the heat. Remove the peanuts with a strainer to drain on paper towels. Allow the peanuts to cool to room temperature and reserve.

3. Turn the heat back to high and heat the oil to 350°F again. When a wisp of white smoke appears, reduce the heat to low. Add the chicken and marinade and spread the chicken with chopsticks or tongs. Cook for 1 to 1½ minutes, until the chicken turns white. Turn off the heat, remove the chicken with a Chinese strainer, drain well, and reserve. Pour off all but 1 tablespoon of the oil from the wok.

4. Heat the wok over high heat for 20 seconds. Add the ginger and stir for 10 seconds. Add the pickle and water chestnuts, stir, and cook for 30 seconds. Add the reserved chicken and cook, stirring, for 1½ minutes. Add the wine, mix well, and cook for 30 seconds. Make a well in the center of the mixture, stir the sauce mixture, and pour in. Stir until the chicken is completely coated and the sauce thickens. Turn off the heat and transfer to a heated platter. Sprinkle with the roasted peanuts and sliced scallions and serve.

MAKES 4 SERVINGS

BOK CHOY CHICKEN SOUP

Bok Choy *Gai See Tong*

This is one of my recipes, one I devised and have been making for my family for many years. My 3 children grew up with this soup, and my husband never tires of it. The complementary tastes—sweet bok choy and the marinated chicken—as well as the textures of crisp bok choy and chewy chicken make this a perfectly balanced yin and yang dish—the cooling vegetable, the warming chicken.

For the marinade
2 teaspoons soy sauce
2 teaspoons oyster sauce
1 teaspoon ginger juice (page 23) mixed
    with 2 teaspoons Chinese white rice
    wine or gin
1 teaspoon sesame oil

1¼ teaspoons sugar
1 teaspoon salt
Pinch freshly ground white pepper
1 tablespoon cornstarch

¾ pound lean skinless, boneless chicken
    breasts, cut into slices 2 inches by
    ½ inch
5 cups Chicken Stock (page 75)
One 1-inch-thick slice fresh ginger,
    lightly smashed
1 pound bok choy, stalks and leaves
    separated and cut into ¼-inch slices
1 tablespoon Chinese white rice wine
    or gin
2 teaspoons Shallot Oil (page 84) or
    peanut oil

1. In a large bowl, combine the marinade ingredients. Add the chicken and allow to rest for at least 15 minutes.

2. Place the stock and ginger in a large pot, cover, and bring to a boil over high heat. Add the *bok choy* stalks, stir, and return to a boil. Lower the heat to medium and cook for 5 minutes or until the stalks become tender. Turn the heat back to high, add the leaves, stir, return to a boil, and cook for 2 minutes. Add the chicken and marinade and stir well to separate the chicken slices. Return to a boil, add the wine, and stir well. Add the shallot oil and stir well. Turn off the heat, transfer to a heated tureen, and serve.

MAKES 6 SERVINGS

SHREDDED CHICKEN
WITH TWO PEPPERS

Seung Jiu Chau Gai See

This stir-fry is my invention, an effort at cross-regionalization if you will. I have taken the basic elements of an Eastern stir-fry and added those pepper pickles from Sichuan. What emerges is an example of what I preach, harmony and a good balance of tastes and textures.

For the marinade
1 teaspoon ginger juice (page 23)
  mixed with 2 teaspoons Chinese white
  rice wine or gin
1½ tablespoons oyster sauce
1 teaspoon sesame oil
1½ teaspoons sugar
¾ teaspoon salt
Pinch freshly ground white pepper
2 teaspoons tapioca flour

¾ pound skinless, boneless chicken
  breasts, julienned
3 tablespoons Garlic Oil (page 84) or
  peanut oil
2 teaspoons minced fresh ginger
¾ pound green bell peppers, cut into
  julienne (about 1½ cups)
1 tablespoon Sichuan Pepper Pickle
  (page 99)
2½ tablespoons Chicken Stock
  (page 75)
2 teaspoons minced garlic
½ cup julienned white part of scallion
2 teaspoons Chinese white rice wine
  or gin
2 teaspoons tapioca flour mixed with
  ¼ cup Chicken Stock (page 75)

1. In a large bowl, combine the marinade ingredients. Add the chicken and allow to rest for at least 20 minutes.

2. Heat a wok over high heat for 40 seconds. Add 1 tablespoon garlic oil and coat the wok with it using a spatula. When a wisp of white smoke appears, add the ginger, stir, and cook for 10 seconds. Add the bell peppers and stir briefly. Add the Sichuan pepper pickle, stir, and cook for 1 to 1½ minutes or until the bell pepper turns bright green. If the bell pepper is too dry, add 1 tablespoon of stock. This will create steam, and the pepper will cook immediately. (This is offered because bell peppers occasionally release quite a bit of liquid, though not in all cases.) Turn off the heat, remove the peppers, and reserve. Wipe off the wok and spatula with paper towels.

3. Heat a wok over high heat for 30 seconds. Add the remaining garlic oil and coat the wok with it using a spatula. When a wisp of white smoke appears, add the garlic and cook, stirring. When the garlic turns light brown, add the chicken and marinade,

spread in a thin layer, and cook for 1 minute. Turn over, mix well, add the scallion, and stir in. Add the wine around the edge of the wok and stir well. Add 1½ tablespoons stock and stir in. Add the reserved peppers and cook, stirring, for 2 minutes. Make a well in the center of the mixture, stir the tapioca flour–stock mixture, and pour in. Stir together for 1½ minutes or until the sauce thickens and bubbles. Turn off the heat, transfer to a heated platter, and serve.

MAKES 6 SERVINGS

CHICKEN STIR-FRIED WITH BOSC PEARS

Gai Pin Chau Lei Gua

*I*n Guangzhou it is not uncommon to eat fruit stir-fried with chicken, duck, or other meats as well as with vegetables. It was something commonly eaten in our family when I was growing up. Later, when I went to live in Hong Kong, I saw and ate many other food combinations with various fruits. It was in Hong Kong that I ate my first dishes cooked with the crisp, round pears called sah leh, or "sand pears," which are very much like Bosc pears. Here is my version of this Hong Kong dish, with Bosc pears in combination with macadamia nuts.

For the marinade
2 teaspoons beaten egg white
1 teaspoon Chinese white rice wine
    or gin
2 teaspoons cornstarch
¼ teaspoon salt
½ teaspoon sugar

½ pound skinless, boneless chicken
    breasts, cut into thin slices 1½ inches
    long by 1 inch wide

For the sauce
1½ tablespoons oyster sauce
2 teaspoons Chinese white rice wine
    or gin
¼ teaspoon salt
1 teaspoon sugar
Pinch freshly ground white pepper
1 tablespoon cornstarch
¼ cup Chicken Stock (page 75)
1 teaspoon sesame oil

3 tablespoons peanut oil
1 tablespoon sliced fresh ginger, in
    tissue-thin half moons
5 ounces asparagus, tough ends cut off,
    cut into ¼-inch pieces on a diagonal
    (¾ cup)
1 celery stalk, cut into ¼-inch pieces on
    a diagonal (½ cup)

½ cup red bell pepper cut into 1- by ¼-inch-thick pieces

1 Bosc pear, peeled, quartered, cored, and cut into ¼-inch pieces on a diagonal (¾ cup)

2 large shallots, thinly sliced

1 teaspoon minced garlic

2 teaspoons Chinese white rice wine or gin

½ cup macadamia nuts

1. In a large bowl, combine the marinade ingredients. Add the chicken and allow to rest for at least 20 minutes. In another bowl, combine the sauce ingredients and reserve.

2. Heat a wok over high heat for 45 seconds. Add 1½ tablespoons of the peanut oil and coat the wok with it using a spatula. When a wisp of white smoke appears, add the ginger slices, stir, and cook for 15 seconds. Add the asparagus and cook, stirring, for 1 minute. Add the celery and bell pepper and cook, stirring, for another minute. Add the pear and cook, stirring, for 30 seconds. Turn off the heat, remove the contents of the wok, and reserve. Wipe off the wok and spatula with paper towels.

3. Heat the wok over high heat for 30 seconds. Add the remaining 1½ tablespoons of oil and coat the wok with it using a spatula. When a wisp of white smoke appears, add the shallots, stir, and cook for 20 seconds. Add the garlic and stir briefly. Add the chicken and marinade, spread in a thin layer, and cook for 45 seconds. Turn over and cook for 1 minute. Add the wine and stir to mix. Add the reserved vegetable-fruit mixture and cook, stirring, for 2 minutes. Make a well in the center of the mixture, stir the sauce mixture, pour in, and stir to mix until the sauce thickens, about 1½ minutes. Turn off the heat, add the macadamia nuts, mix well, transfer to a heated platter, and serve.

MAKES 4 TO 6 SERVINGS

ORANGE CHICKEN
Chun Pei Gai Pin

Traditionally this Hunan recipe contained what is called chun pei, or "old skin," to describe the dried citrus peel used in its preparation. In my adaptation of it, I use fresh orange peel, which makes for, I believe, a fresher, more intense taste.

½ pound skinless, boneless chicken
   breast, thick oven roaster preferred,
   cut into slices 2½ inches long by
   1 inch wide by ¼ inch thick

For the coating
1 tablespoon beaten egg white
¼ teaspoon Mei Kuei Lu Chiew or gin
Pinch freshly ground white pepper
1 tablespoon peanut oil
2½ tablespoons cornstarch

For the sauce
1 tablespoon double dark soy sauce,
   regular dark soy sauce, or mushroom
   soy sauce

4½ teaspoons sugar
¼ teaspoon salt
½ teaspoon Mei Kuei Lu Chiew or gin
1 teaspoon sesame oil
1 teaspoon Chinese white rice vinegar
   or distilled vinegar
Pinch freshly ground white pepper
2 tablespoons Chicken Stock (page 75)

3½ cups peanut oil
7 small whole dried chilies
2 teaspoons minced fresh ginger
1 teaspoon minced garlic
2 scallions, trimmed and cut into
   ½-inch pieces
1½ tablespoons chopped fresh orange
   zest in ½- by ⅛-inch pieces
2 tablespoons diced red bell pepper in
   ¼-inch pieces
6 slices fresh orange, cut into half
   moons

1. Place the chicken in a large bowl and add the chicken coating ingredients one at a time, mixing by hand. There should be no residue.

2. In another bowl, mix the sauce ingredients and reserve.

3. Heat a wok over high heat for 1 minute. Add the peanut oil and heat to 400°F. Turn off the heat. Place the chicken pieces, one by one, into the hot oil. They will cook quickly. Turn the slices over. Turn the heat back to high and cook for 1½ minutes. Loosen the chicken pieces as they cook. Turn off the heat, remove the chicken with a Chinese strainer, and drain.

4. Heat the oil again to 400°F. Place the chicken again into the oil and cook for 2 minutes, until the chicken turns golden. Turn off the heat, remove the chicken with the strainer, and drain. Remove all but 1 tablespoon of the oil from the wok.

5. Heat the wok over high heat. Add the dried chilies, stir, and cook until darkened, 45 seconds to a minute. Add the ginger, garlic, scallions, orange zest, and bell pepper and cook, stirring, for 1½ minutes. Add the chicken, stir, and cook for 45 seconds. Make a well in the mixture, stir the reserved sauce, and pour in. Stir and cook for 2 minutes, until the sauce is absorbed. Turn off the heat, transfer to a heated platter, garnish around the edges with orange slices, and serve.

STEAMED CHICKEN
WITH SICHUAN ROASTED RICE

Fun Jing Gai

This is a classic way of preparing chicken, as well as other fowl and meats, in Sichuan. At its core is Sichuan roasted rice, which gives this steamed dish its special flavor.

½ pound skinless, boneless chicken breast, thick oven roaster preferred, cut into 2-inch-long by ¼-inch-thick pieces
3 tablespoons Sichuan Roasted Rice (page 71)
1 tablespoon sweet bean sauce
3½ tablespoons Sweet Wine Rice liquid (page 69)

1½ teaspoons sugar
1 teaspoon soy sauce
1 teaspoon sesame oil
1 teaspoon minced fresh ginger
3 tablespoons finely minced scallions
2 teaspoons Shao-Hsing wine or dry sherry
⅛ teaspoon salt
1 tablespoon preserved horse beans with chili
Pinch freshly ground white pepper
1½ teaspoons peanut oil
6 tablespoons Chicken Stock (page 75)
3 tablespoons trimmed and finely sliced green parts of scallion

1. Place the chicken and all other ingredients except scallion in a bowl and mix thoroughly to combine. Place the contents of the bowl in a steamproof dish and the dish in a bamboo steamer, cover, and steam for 15 minutes (see steaming, page 64).

2. Turn off the heat and sprinkle with the scallion. Serve in the steamproof dish accompanied by cooked rice.

CHICKEN STIR-FRIED WITH CAULIFLOWER

Yeh Choi Far Chau Gai Pin

Years ago cauliflower was not grown widely in China. It was virtually an unknown vegetable except in the restaurants of major cities and was regarded as exotic. Only in recent years, fewer than two decades, has cauliflower become commonplace. Now it is grown extensively and enjoyed. I pickle it, for example, and it can be a major ingredient in a stir-fry, as this recipe demonstrates. This is another stir-fry that illustrates that cooking process so well. Its success lies in the preparation of all of its elements.

For the sauce
2 tablespoons oyster sauce
1½ teaspoons soy sauce
1 teaspoon sesame oil
1¼ teaspoons sugar
Pinch freshly ground white pepper
1 tablespoon water chestnut powder
5 tablespoons Chicken Stock (page 75)

6 Steamed Black Mushrooms
* (page 81)*
1 quart cold water
One ½-inch-thick slice fresh ginger,
* lightly smashed*
2 garlic cloves, peeled
2⅛ teaspoons salt
¾ pound cauliflower florets, cut
* 2 inches long by 1 inch*
½ pound skinless, boneless chicken
* breast, cut into pieces 2½ inches long*
* by 1½ inches wide by ¼ inch thick*
2 teaspoons water chestnut powder
1½ cups peanut oil
2 teaspoons minced fresh ginger
1½ teaspoons minced garlic
3 scallions, trimmed and cut into
* ½-inch pieces on a diagonal, white*
* and green parts separated*
2 tablespoons Chicken Stock (page 75)
½ cup diced red bell pepper in ¼-inch
* pieces*

1. Combine the sauce ingredients and reserve. Cut the steamed mushrooms into ½-inch pieces and reserve.

2. Blanch the cauliflower: Place the water, ginger, garlic, and 2 teaspoons salt in a pot. Cover and bring to a boil over high heat. Add the cauliflower and blanch for 1½ minutes. Turn off the heat, run cold water into the pot, drain, and reserve.

3. Place the chicken slices in a bowl. Add ⅛ teaspoon salt and the water chestnut powder and mix well to coat the chicken. Allow to rest for at least 20 minutes. To blanch the chicken, heat the wok over high heat for 1 minute. Add the peanut oil and heat to

350°F. Add the chicken to the oil and loosen with chopsticks. Blanch for 1 minute, until the chicken turns white. Turn off the heat. Remove with a Chinese strainer and drain. Empty all but 1½ tablespoons of the oil from the wok.

4. Heat the wok over high heat for 20 seconds. Add the minced ginger, minced garlic, and white parts of the scallion, stir, and cook for 30 seconds. Add the cauliflower, stir, and cook for 1 minute. Add the stock and reserved mushrooms and cook, stirring, for 1 minute. Add the bell pepper and cook, stirring, for another minute. Add the chicken and cook, stirring well, for 1 minute. Make a well in the mixture, stir the sauce mixture, pour in, and stir until the sauce thickens. Turn off the heat, transfer to a heated platter, sprinkle with the green parts of the scallion, and serve.

MAKES 6 SERVINGS

POACHED CHICKEN IN WINE SAUCE

Jau Yeung Gai

*T*his is a traditional dish from Suzhou, the neighbor of Shanghai and Hangzhou that is famed for its family-style cooking. The influence of Shanghai is evident in many of Suzhou's dishes, as can be seen with the inclusion of the sweet wine rice from Shanghai in this dish. Suzhou is also known for the use of various Shao-Hsing wines in its cooking. This dish, served cold, is eaten either as an appetizer or as a first course at a banquet.

6 cups cold water
3 celery stalks, cut in half
3 scallions, trimmed and cut in half
One 1-inch-thick slice fresh ginger, lightly smashed
2 teaspoons salt
2 teaspoons sugar
One 3½-pound chicken, fat and membranes removed, rubbed with ¼ cup salt, rinsed with cold water, and drained

For the wine sauce

1 cup Superior Stock (page 74) or Chicken Stock (page 75)
3 tablespoons Sweet Wine Rice and liquid (page 69)
4 scallions, white parts only, julienned
2 tablespoons julienned fresh ginger
1 teaspoon salt
¼ teaspoon whole Sichuan peppercorns
1½ teaspoons sugar
5 tablespoons Shao-Hsing wine or dry sherry

1. Place the water, celery, scallions, ginger, salt, and sugar in a large pot. Add the chicken to the pot, cover, and bring to a boil over high heat. Lower the heat and simmer, covered, for 15 minutes. Turn the chicken over and simmer for another 15 minutes, covered. Turn off the heat and allow the chicken to rest in the pot until cool enough to handle. Remove from the pot, cut into bite-sized pieces, place in a deep plate, and reserve.

2. As the chicken simmers, make the wine sauce. Place the stock, sweet wine rice and its liquid, scallions, ginger, salt, peppercorns, and sugar in a saucepan and bring to a boil over medium heat. Lower the heat and allow to cook at a slow boil for 10 minutes. Turn off the heat, strain the liquid, and allow to cool to room temperature. Add the Shao-Hsing wine and stir well to combine.

3. Pour the sauce over the chicken pieces. Cover the chicken with plastic wrap and refrigerate for at least 2 hours. Serve cold.

MAKES 8 TO 10 SERVINGS

WHITE CUT CHICKEN

Bok Chit Gai

白切雞

This is a dish of tradition, not limited to any particular region of China. It exists everywhere and is prepared virtually the same way, whichever the region. It is this chicken that is most often prepared after the whole chicken has been offered symbolically to one's ancestors on the Lunar New Year, on remembrances of birthdays, and on anniversaries.

2 quarts cold water
One 1-inch-thick slice fresh ginger, lightly smashed

6 scallions, trimmed and cut into thirds
½ cup fresh coriander (cilantro), stalks cut in half
¼ cup Chinese white rice wine or gin
1 tablespoon salt
3 tablespoons sugar
One 3½-pound chicken, washed, fat and membranes removed, rubbed with ¼ cup salt, rinsed under cold water, and drained well

1. In an oval Dutch oven or large pot, place the water and all ingredients except the chicken. Cover and bring to a boil over high heat. Boil for 5 minutes. Lower the heat, place the chicken, breast up, in the liquid, and return to a boil. Reduce the heat and simmer, covered, for 15 minutes.

2. Turn the chicken over and simmer for another 15 minutes. Turn off the heat and allow the chicken to rest in the liquid for 10 minutes. Remove and allow to come to room temperature. Place in a dish, cover with plastic wrap, and refrigerate for 2 hours.

3. Cut into bite-sized pieces and serve in the traditional way, with small, individual dishes of soy sauce as a dip.

MAKES 4 TO 6 SERVINGS

STEAMED LEMON CHICKEN

Ling Mung Jing Gai

This is a recipe I learned from aunt number six, Luk Gu Cheh, my father's younger sister, with whom I lived for a decade in Hong Kong. She created it. I have never seen it anywhere else except in her kitchen and, of course, mine. What customarily goes by the name of lemon chicken is usually fried chicken pieces doused with a thick, sweetish lemon sauce that is, in my view, an absolutely awful presentation, which honors neither the chicken nor the lemon. My aunt's lemon chicken is fresh, vibrant, flavorful, and natural, a perfect dish of great harmony.

One 4-pound chicken, washed, fat and membranes removed, rubbed with ¼ cup salt, rinsed under cold water, drained, and dried thoroughly with paper towels cut into bite-sized pieces
1¼ fresh lemons (5 quarters)

For the marinade
1 tablespoon Chinese white rice wine or gin mixed with 1 teaspoon ginger juice (page 23)
1½ tablespoons soy sauce
1½ tablespoons oyster sauce
2 teaspoons sesame oil
1 tablespoon peanut oil
2 teaspoons salt
2 teaspoons sugar
⅛ teaspoon freshly ground white pepper
3½ tablespoons cornstarch

2 tablespoons trimmed and finely sliced scallion

1. Place the chicken in a bowl, squeeze the 5 lemon quarters over, then place the quarters in the bowl. Add all the marinade ingredients and mix thoroughly to combine. Allow to rest 30 for minutes.

2. Place the chicken in a steamproof dish, spread out, and pour the marinade over it. Place the dish in a bamboo steamer, cover, and steam for 40 to 50 minutes (see steaming, page 64). Turn the chicken 2 or 3 times during steaming. The chicken is cooked when it turns white. (If steaming in a metal plate, reduce the time to 30 minutes.)

3. Turn off the heat, remove the bamboo steamer, and serve the chicken in the dish in the steamer, sprinkled with the sliced scallion, with cooked rice.

MAKES 6 TO 8 SERVINGS

DUCK WITH FRESH BAMBOO SHOOTS

Juk Sun Chau Op Pin

Most often, throughout China, the duck is cooked whole, braised, roasted, stuffed, or smoked. Long cooking makes duck meat more tender. Occasionally it is cut up for stews or for steaming and braising. Rarely is duck meat stir-fried—a most notable exception is as part of the presentation of Peking Duck—because it tends to be not as tender as chicken. Nevertheless it can be stir-fried to advantage, when properly prepared. I have devised several recipes for stir-fried duck including this, which pairs it with bamboo shoots, utterly marvelous when fresh.

For the marinade
1 tablespoon egg white, beaten
½ teaspoon sesame oil
½ teaspoon baking soda
¼ teaspoon salt
½ teaspoon sugar
2 teaspoons Mei Kuei Lu Chiew or gin
2 teaspoons tapioca flour

½ pound duck breast, cut into ⅛-inch slices across the grain
½ cup fresh bamboo shoots
6 cups water

For the sauce
1½ tablespoons oyster sauce
2 teaspoons double dark soy sauce, regular dark soy sauce, or mushroom soy sauce
1 teaspoon sugar
¼ teaspoon sesame oil
Pinch freshly ground white pepper
2½ teaspoons tapioca flour
6 tablespoons Chicken Stock (page 75)

2 cups peanut oil
2 teaspoons minced fresh ginger
1 tablespoon minced garlic
⅓ cup white part of scallion, cut into ¼-inch diagonal pieces
¼ pound snow peas, strings removed and cut into thirds on a diagonal
1 tablespoon Mei Kuei Lu Chiew or gin

1. In a large bowl, combine the marinade ingredients. Place the duck in the marinade and allow to rest for at least 2 hours, refrigerated.

2. To prepare the bamboo shoots, peel off the outer layers and cut off the hard end. Place in a pot with the water, cover, and bring to a boil over high heat. Lower the heat and simmer for 20 minutes or until tender. A good test: press a fingernail into the bamboo shoot; it will give when tender. Turn off the heat, run cold water into the pot, and drain. Repeat. Cut the bamboo shoots in half lengthwise, then across into thin half

moons. Reserve. (Canned bamboo shoots may be used, but there is no comparison in taste and texture with those fresh.)

3. In a bowl, combine the sauce ingredients and reserve.

4. To prepare the duck, heat a wok over high heat for 1 minute. Add the peanut oil and heat to 325°F. Turn off the heat, add the duck and marinade, loosen the duck meat with chopsticks, and cook for 1 minute, making sure the duck pieces are separated. Remove the duck with a Chinese strainer, and drain over a bowl. Empty all but 1 table-spoon of the oil from the wok.

5. Heat the wok over high heat for 20 seconds. Add the minced ginger and stir briefly. Add the minced garlic and stir until the garlic turns light brown. Add the white parts of the scallion, stir, and cook for 30 seconds. Add the bamboo shoots, stir, and cook for 1 minute. Add the snow peas, stir, and cook for 1 minute. Add the duck meat and cook, stirring, for 30 seconds. Add the Chinese wine, mix well, and cook, stirring, for 1½ minutes. Make a well in the mixture, stir the sauce mixture, pour in, and stir until the sauce thickens. Turn off the heat, transfer to a heated platter, and serve.

MAKES 4 SERVINGS

DUCK WITH LILY BULBS

Bok Hop Chau Op Yuk

This is another stir-fry with a fresh, once rare ingredient, lily bulbs. These pure white bulbs, which peel off in crisp petals, have always been highly prized in the Chinese kitchen but rare elsewhere. These days they are widely available, usually flown in from China. They, like fresh bamboo shoots, are worth seeking out, for they are sweet, crisp, and fine. They are also available in plastic sacks, never the whole bulb but rather a mass of dried petals, but they cannot compare to fresh lily buds. The Chinese call them bok hop, *which means that hundreds of things will go smoothly, and thus lily bulbs are always served at weddings.*

For the marinade
1 tablespoon egg white, beaten
½ teaspoon sesame oil
½ teaspoon baking soda
¼ teaspoon salt
½ teaspoon sugar

¾ pound skinless, boneless duck breast, cut into ½-inch dice

For the sauce
1½ tablespoons oyster sauce
2 teaspoons double dark soy sauce, regular dark soy sauce, or mushroom soy sauce
1 tablespoon hoisin sauce
½ teaspoon sesame oil
2 teaspoons Shao-Hsing wine or dry sherry
1 teaspoon sugar
1 tablespoon tapioca flour
Pinch freshly ground white pepper
6½ tablespoons Chicken Stock (page 75)

2 cups peanut oil
1 tablespoon minced fresh ginger
2 teaspoons minced garlic
⅔ cup chopped celery in ⅓-inch dice
⅓ cup peeled and chopped fresh water chestnuts in ¼-inch dice
½ cup chopped red bell pepper in ⅓-inch dice
½ cup chopped green bell pepper in ⅓-inch dice
1 tablespoon Shao-Hsing wine or dry sherry
½ cup fresh lily bulb petals, washed, drained, and dried

1. In a large bowl, combine the marinade ingredients. Place the duck in the marinade and allow to rest for at least 2 hours, refrigerated. In another bowl, mix the sauce and reserve.

2. Heat a wok over high heat for 1 minute. Add the peanut oil and heat to 350°F. Add the duck meat and marinade, separating the pieces, and cook for 1 minute. Turn off the

heat, remove the duck with a Chinese strainer, and drain over a bowl. Empty all but 1 tablespoon of the oil from the wok.

3. Heat the wok over high heat for 20 seconds, add the ginger, and stir briefly. Add the garlic, stir, and when the garlic turns light brown, add the celery, stir, and cook for 30 seconds. Add the water chestnuts, stir, and cook 45 seconds. Add the red and green peppers, stir, and cook for 1 minute. Add the duck meat and cook, stirring well, for 1 minute. Add the Shao-Hsing wine, stir, and cook for 1 minute. Make a well in the mixture, stir the sauce mixture, pour in, and stir. When the sauce thickens, after 1 to 1½ minutes, turn off the heat, transfer to a heated platter, sprinkle with the fresh lily bulbs, and serve.

MAKES 4 SERVINGS

BRAISED DUCK WITH CHESTNUTS

Leut Ji Mun Op

This seasonal Cantonese classic is centered on the fresh chestnuts that abound each fall. When braised with the duck, they take on its flavors and those of the added spices. My grandmother, Ah Paw, had a beautiful, thick spreading chestnut tree in her garden, and we would enjoy the chestnuts from it. When it began to yield fewer and fewer chestnuts, she lost patience with it and ordered it uprooted so that her other fruit trees would have more sun and more space. But even when we had to buy our chestnuts in the fall, we enjoyed them, fresh.

2 tablespoons peanut oil
One 1-inch-thick slice fresh ginger, lightly smashed
1 tablespoon minced garlic
2 tablespoons bean sauce

One 4½-pound duck, washed, fat and membranes removed, fatty skin around neck cut away and removed, duck rubbed with ¼ cup salt, rinsed well under cold water, drained well, and the meat with bones cut into bite-sized pieces
3 tablespoons Mei Kuei Lu Chiew or gin
12 Chinese black mushrooms, soaked in warm water for 30 minutes, stems removed, and cut into quarters
2½ tablespoons oyster sauce
1½ tablespoons double dark soy sauce, regular dark soy sauce, or mushroom soy sauce
1½ pounds fresh chestnuts, peeled (see Note)
3 ounces sugarcane sugar or 5 tablespoons dark brown sugar
3½ cups Chicken Stock (page 75)

1. Heat a wok over high heat for 40 seconds. Add the peanut oil and coat the wok with it using a spatula. When a wisp of white smoke appears, add the ginger and cook for 20 seconds. Add the garlic and stir briefly. Add the bean sauce and mix well. Add the duck pieces, stir to mix well, and cook for 2 minutes. Add the Chinese wine, stir to mix well, and cook for 2 minutes. Add the mushrooms and stir to mix. Add the oyster sauce and soy sauce and mix well, making certain the mushrooms and the duck are coated evenly. Cook, stirring, for 1 minute. Turn off the heat.

2. Transfer the contents of the wok to a large pot. Add the chestnuts, sugar, and 3 cups of the stock, mix well, cover, and bring to a boil over medium heat. Lower the heat and simmer, partially covered, for 1 hour and 15 minutes, stirring frequently to prevent sticking. If the stock is completely absorbed, add the remaining stock. The duck and chestnuts will be tender. Turn off the heat, transfer to a heated platter, and serve with cooked rice.

N O T E :   *To peel chestnuts, cut an X in them and roast in a 350°F oven for 45 minutes or until the shells pop open. Peel the nuts as soon as they are cool enough to handle.*

M A K E S   8   S E R V I N G S

CURRIED DUCK

Gah Lei Op

*T*his is a dish from my early memories of Hong Kong. When I was growing up in China, our family had never heard of, much less eaten, curried food. It was not until I went to Hong Kong to live with my aunt that I discovered curries, brought there by the sizable Indian and Pakistani population. For it is in Hong Kong that all of the flavors and techniques of Asia are to be found and adapted. I remember eating curried duck prepared in a Chinese manner, and I have re-created it.

3½ tablespoons peanut oil
1¼ cups chopped onion in ¼-inch dice
¾ pound fresh tomatoes, cut into
    ½-inch cubes (about 1½ cups)

For the curry paste
3½ tablespoons hot curry powder
1¼ teaspoons cayenne pepper
¼ cup cold water

1 tablespoon minced fresh ginger
½ cup cold water
3 beef bouillon cubes, broken into
    small pieces
One 4½-pound duck, washed, fat and
    membranes removed, fatty skin from
    neck area removed and discarded,
    duck rubbed with ¼ cup salt, rinsed
    under cold water, dried with paper
    towels, and meat and bones cut into
    bite-sized pieces
1½ cups Chicken Stock (page 75)
1½ teaspoons salt
1 tablespoon sugar

1. Heat a wok over high heat for 45 seconds. Add 1½ tablespoons of the peanut oil and coat the wok with it using a spatula. When a wisp of white smoke appears, reduce the heat to medium, add the onion, stir, and cook for 5 minutes. Raise the heat back to high, add the tomatoes, and stir well. When the mixture begins to boil, lower the heat to medium and cook for 5 to 7 minutes. As the mixture thickens and resembles a puree, stir several times to prevent sticking. Turn off the heat, remove the mixture, and reserve. Wash and dry the wok and spatula.

2. As the mixture cooks, combine the curry paste ingredients and reserve.

3. Heat the wok over high heat for 45 seconds. Add the remaining 2 tablespoons peanut oil and coat the wok with it using a spatula. When a wisp of white smoke appears, add the minced ginger, stir, and cook 10 seconds. Add the curry paste, stir to mix well, and cook for 30 seconds. Add the cold water and stir well. Add the bouillon cubes, stir, and

reduce the heat to low. Use a spatula to help dissolve the bouillon cubes, about 3 minutes. Turn the heat back to high, add the duck, and stir well, making certain the duck is well coated with the curry mixture. Add the reserved onion-tomato mixture and cook, stirring continually, for 2 minutes. Turn off the heat and transfer the contents of the wok to a pot.

4. Add 1 cup of the stock, the salt, and the sugar to the pot and stir well. Cover and bring to a boil over high heat. Lower the heat and simmer for 1 hour and 15 minutes, leaving the lid cracked, until the duck is tender. During the cooking time, stir frequently, perhaps every 10 minutes, to prevent sticking. You may have to add the remaining ½ cup stock if the mixture is too thick. Turn off the heat. The duck has a tendency to be fatty. If a film of fat appears on the surface of the food in the pot, skim it off before serving. Transfer to a heated platter and serve with cooked rice.

MAKES 6 TO 8 SERVINGS

SQUAB
BOK GOP

Squabs, or small nestling pigeons, are a highly regarded delicacy throughout China, prized for the taste of their meat and the elegance of their preparation. They are always included in festive or formal banquets, always to show that great care and effort have been expended on such small birds. Squabs are eaten in many ways: braised, stewed in soy sauce, double-boiled, roasted, baked in salt, put into soup, but traditionally they are enjoyed fried crisply or minced and served wrapped in lettuce leaves. As with other foods of the Chinese kitchen, provenance is considered of great importance. The unfledged squabs of Shek-ki, a small corner of Guangdong, are considered the finest in all China, and menus will always specify them.

Squabs are small, weighing only about 1 pound. They are commonly available freshly killed in markets, usually by advance order. Customarily they will have had their interiors cleaned, and their heads will be on, true to custom, in Chinese poultry shops, off in Western markets. They are occasionally available frozen, often with their innards intact. I suggest these be avoided, for they require extra cleaning time.

The two recipes for squab that follow are elaborate banquet preparations, the reason I include them, for they demonstrate the regard bestowed, the effort expended, on special dishes. As the French might say, they are worth the effort. The first, Crisp Fried Squab, is quite like a miniature of the classic Cantonese Roast Chicken, coated and cooked so its skin is like a rich mahogany lacquer. The second, minced with vegetables and rolled in lettuce, is a delight of varied textures. When the Chinese say minced squab, they always mean squab wrapped in lettuce. Enjoy these birds.

CRISP FRIED SQUAB

Chui Pei Bok Gop

2 squabs, about 1 pound each
2 tablespoons plus 1 teaspooon salt
2 tablespoons Mei Kuei Lu Chiew
    or gin
1 tablespoon double dark soy sauce,
    regular dark soy sauce, or mushroom
    soy sauce
2 teaspoons sugar
Two 3-inch cinnamon sticks, broken
    in half
4 whole eight-star anise
Four ¼-inch-thick slices fresh ginger,
    peeled

For the coating
1 tablespoon honey mixed with
    2 tablespoons boiling water
1½ teaspoons Chinese white rice
    vinegar or distilled vinegar
½ teaspoon cornstarch

6 cups peanut oil
1 tablespoon Sichuan Peppercorn Salt
    (page 89)

1. To prepare the squabs, wash each squab inside and out under running water. Rub each with 1 tablespoon salt and rinse. Drain and dry with paper towels. Place both squabs in a steamproof dish. Rub each with Mei Kuei Lu Chiew, inside and out. Rub the outsides with the soy sauce. Sprinkle the remaining teaspoon of salt inside the cavities and on the outsides. Sprinkle the sugar inside the cavities and on the outsides. Spoon the liquid in the dish inside the cavities to coat well. Place 1 piece of cinnamon stick, 1 piece of star anise, and 1 slice of ginger in each cavity. Place the remaining cinnamon, anise, and ginger in the dish. Turn the birds breast sides up, place the dish in a steamer, cover, and steam (see steaming, page 64) for 50 minutes. Halfway through the steaming, turn the birds over. Turn off the heat, transfer the birds to a rack, and cool, at least 10 minutes.

2. As the squabs steam, combine the coating ingredients and reserve.

3. When the squabs are cooled, brush them thoroughly and repeatedly with the coating mixture until all the mixture is used. Tie strings around their necks and hang to dry for 8 to 10 hours. This time can be cut in half with the use of a fan.

4. Heat a wok over high heat for 1 minute, add the peanut oil, and heat to 350°F. Place both squabs in a Chinese strainer and lower into the oil. Lower the heat to medium and deep-fry for 2 minutes, ladling oil over the birds as they fry. Turn over and fry for another 2 minutes, ladling. Raise the heat back to high. Turn the squabs over again

and deep-fry for 1½ minutes, ladling oil. Turn again and fry for another 1½ minutes, ladling. The squabs should turn deep brown, their skins glistening. Turn off the heat and remove with a strainer to drain over a bowl for 5 minutes.

5. Remove to a chopping board. Chop off the necks with a cleaver. Cut in half along the backbones, then into bite-sized pieces. Serve with Sichuan peppercorn salt for dipping.

MAKES 4 SERVINGS

MINCED SQUAB

Bok Gop Sohn

*1 squab, about 1 pound (yielding
  ¼ pound minced meat)*
1 tablespoon salt

For the marinade
½ tablespoon egg white, beaten
½ tablespoon oyster sauce
½ teaspoon sugar
1 teaspoon soy sauce
½ teaspoon sesame oil
Pinch freshly ground white pepper
½ teaspoon cornstarch

2 tablespoons peanut oil
1 teaspoon minced fresh ginger
¼ cup minced white part of scallion
*¼ cup diced Chinese (or regular)
  celery in ⅛-inch pieces*
⅓ cup diced carrots in ⅛-inch pieces
*2 large fresh water chestnuts, peeled
  and cut into ⅛-inch dice (¼ cup)*

*3 medium Steamed Black Mushrooms
  (page 81), cut into ⅛-inch dice
  (¼ cup)*
½ tablespoon oyster sauce
½ teaspoon sugar
⅛ teaspoon salt
1 teaspoon minced garlic
1 teaspoon Mei Kuei Lu Chiew or gin

For the hoisin sauce mixture
3 tablespoons hoisin sauce
1 teaspoon sugar
*1½ tablespoons Shao-Hsing wine or dry
  sherry*
1 teaspoon sesame oil

*8 Iceberg lettuce leaves, trimmed to
  4-inch rounds*

1. To prepare the squab, wash under cold running water, inside and out. Drain. Rub with 1 tablespoon salt, rinse, and drain thoroughly. Place on a chopping board and cut off the feet at the joint (if not already removed by the poultry dealer). Chop off the neck and head (if not already removed). Place the squab, tail up, with the back facing you. With a knife straight along the backbone, fold the meat outward, butterfly fashion. Then cut through the breastbone. Cut the legs and wings off both sides. Remove the breast meat, leaving it intact, using a knife to loosen it from the breastbone. The 2 sides of breast will yield about ¼ pound of meat. (The carcass, legs, and wings should be frozen for later use in making stock.) Cut the meat into ⅛-inch dice. Combine the marinade ingredients in a large bowl and add the diced meat. Allow to rest for at least 30 minutes.

2. Heat a wok over high heat for 45 seconds. Add 1 tablespoon of the peanut oil and coat the wok with it using a spatula. When a wisp of white smoke appears, add the ginger and stir briefly. Add the scallions and celery, stir, and cook for 30 seconds. Add the carrots and water chestnuts, stir and mix, and cook for 30 seconds. Add the mushrooms and stir. Add the oyster sauce, sugar, and salt, mix, and cook for 2 minutes. Turn off the heat, transfer the contents of the wok to a plate, and reserve.

3. Wipe off the wok and spatula with paper towels. Heat the wok over high heat for 20 seconds. Add the remaining tablespoon of peanut oil and coat the wok with it using the spatula. When a wisp of white smoke appears, add the garlic and stir briefly. Add the minced squab, spread in a thin layer, cook for 45 seconds, turn over, and stir. Add the Mei Kuei Lu Chiew and stir well. Cook until the meat changes color. Add the reserved vegetables, mix well, and cook, stirring, for 2 minutes. Turn off the heat and transfer to a heated dish.

4. Serve in the traditional way. In a small bowl, combine the hoisin sauce ingredients. Coat the inside of a lettuce leaf with the hoisin sauce mixture, place 1½ tablespoons of the squab mixture in the leaf, fold closed, and serve.

MAKES 4 SERVINGS
OF 2 MINCED SQUAB ROLLS EACH

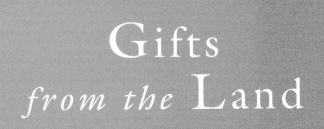

Gifts
from the Land

大地的美食

WHEN I WAS GROWING UP IN SUN TAK, IN SOUTHERN CHINA, IT WAS IMPRESSED ON ME THAT I EAT SPRING ONIONS AND LOTUS ROOT. WHY? THE STEM OF THE SPRING ONION WAS HOLLOW, AND THERE WERE HOLES IN THE LOTUS ROOT, BOTH OF WHICH SYMBOLIZED OPENNESS OF MIND AND WISDOM. I ate broccoli because it was as green as jade and lettuces because their name, *sahng choy,* meant liveliness and health. At the festival of the August Moon, I would offer boiled whole taro, moon cakes, and pomelo, along with incense, from the small altar in our garden because these would ensure that in my reincarnation I would be beautiful. Tangerines and oranges were sweet and represented good feelings, and pomegranates indicated that a number of sons were in my future, as did grapefruit. We often served fresh bean curd in whole cakes because they represented, in that form, blocks of land that our family hoped might be added. And bean curd dyed yellow symbolized gold, according to Ah Paw. Always, it seemed to me, the vegetables and fruits we ate were more than food. We were eating life.

Soybeans were cool foods, leeks warm; cabbages cool, carrots warm; bean curd cool, scallions warm; mushrooms cool, garlic warm. Cooling foods, my grandmother, my Ah Paw, taught me, were to be eaten in summer, warming foods in winter. Yet all vegetables, all fruits, provided they were fresh and prepared in harmoniously balanced ways, were deemed beneficial to the body, and my grandmother believed that vegetables were the easiest foods to digest.

Fresh vegetables and fruits, enhancing their growth and development, inventing methods of agriculture and tools for greater yields, have always been honored in China. The wheelbarrow was invented in China; the plow with concave blades was a Chinese invention of the ninth century that did not reach Europe until 800 years later. The method of, and devices for, drilling holes in the soil in which to plant seeds was Chinese. No matter which dynasty ruled China, no matter whether the rulers were Han, Tang, Mongol, or Ming, no matter whether the country was in political turmoil, ancient or modern, agriculture was its life-giving constant.

Nor did it matter whether China's capital was in the north, in Beijing, or whether the country was administered for brief times in other capitals such as Luoyang, Nanjing, Chang-an, Kaifeng, or Hangzhou, planting and growing foods was held sacred. Freshness was prized, in the South, where historically vegetables, fruits, and rices were grown in abundance, as well as in the North, which imported them at great cost and effort. Fresh foods from the land are prized to this day, particularly in the fertile plains around Guangzhou and extending throughout the South. In most of this region it is not at all unusual to grow and harvest two crops a year, and the changes of season always bring new fresh treasures. It was these crops that were so desirable in imperial times that they were ordered as taxes, as tithes, and picked, packed with huge slabs of ice, covered with thick layers of straw, and rushed by caravan and canal to the court in Beijing.

Southern China remains China's vegetable and fruit basket, and much of what is grown there is still sent north, not as offerings but to markets. The Chinese fruit and vegetable palate has always been varied, and tomb excavations of the Han dynasty dating to 200 B.C. prove that soybeans, taro, all manner of beans, gourds, turnips, leeks, spring onions, lettuces, cabbages, various roots, water chestnuts, various greens, garlic, and ginger were in common use in the Chinese kitchen and are today.

In Canton and the South vegetables are most significant because they comprise more than half of that region's diet. Vegetables and fish are commonplace, pork and poultry usual but eaten less often. It was in this atmosphere, with the added influence of my Ah Paw, who was an observant Buddhist and a more than occasional vegetarian, that I grew up. Summer meant *bok choy* and *choi sum*, winter Tianjin *bok choy* and winter melon, potatoes, and squashes. My grandmother demanded freshness and when her servants went to market what they brought back was inspected.

I was sent to the market by Ah Paw with Dai Kom Me, my mother's brother's first wife, to buy fresh foods not grown on her lands or to add to them. We would look for the best watercress with which to make snakehead fish, firm silk squash, which I loved in soup, big, fat mustard greens, which would be pickled, and Chinese spinach, *yin choi,* which I also liked a lot. We would buy boxthorn, its seeds, its leaves, even its twigs all bases for different, cooling soups.

One vegetable I did not care for, however, was the chard, *jiu choy,* very much like Swiss chard. It would be served at our family tables, both in my house and in Ah Paw's, because it was "good for me." I always thought of it as pig food, because the first character in its name, *jiu,* sounded like the word for pig, and I would say this. For my trouble I would sit at table and eat, stare, eat, stare, and eat until it was finished. Except for its iron, I never knew why else it was good for me, certainly not symbolically.

Ah Paw taught me about bean sprouts, how the ends of mung bean sprouts had to be broken off so the sprouts would become "silver needles" and how the yellow beans at the ends of soybean sprouts were to be left on because they connoted elegance. Vegetables were to be respected, she said, in the preparing, and her diet was a careful selection of those she regarded as special—ginkgo nuts and bean curd, Chinese celery and cloud ears, hair seaweed and bean threads, cakes of taro root and turnips, sweet dumplings filled with bean paste and peanuts and sesame seeds. From the first to the fifteenth of every month she was a strict Buddhist, eating only vegetables and fruit.

Because of her bound feet, she walked but little. She was a tiny lady, who asked her granddaughter to help her walk by supporting her shoulders. As we walked she talked about things that she thought important—my schooling, her religion, my obligations as an honorable daughter as well as my need to be independent, her observations about her family, her diet, and the nutritional importance and symbolism of food. We eat life, and we eat spirit, she would teach.

SILK SQUASH NOODLES

See Gua Mien

I first encountered this dish, simple,
imaginative, and tasty indeed, in Taiwan, at the Fu Yuan restaurant in Taipei.
The texture of the silk squash is crisp, and
when briefly blanched, it can easily be cut
into "noodles."

3 pounds silk squash
2 quarts cold water
½ teaspoon baking soda
1 tablespoon salt
1 whole cooked abalone, canned
    (a tin usually holds 2)
2 cups Chicken Stock (page 75)

1. To prepare the silk squash, peel off the outer skin and remove the ridges, but allow the
    green portions just under the skin to remain intact. With a knife, slice lengthwise pieces
    ¼ inch thick from all around the surface. Discard the interiors. Cut each length into
    2½-inch lengths, then finely julienne each length into "noodles."

2. To blanch the silk squash, bring the water, baking soda, and salt to a boil in a large pot.
    Add the silk squash "noodles" and blanch for 10 seconds, until bright green. Turn off
    the heat. Run cold water into the pot and drain. Repeat and reserve.

3. Slice the abalone paper-thin, then julienne and reserve.

4. Divide the julienned abalone equally among 6 bowls. Place portions of silk squash
    "noodles" on top. Bring the stock to a boil, pour into bowls atop the "noodles" and
    abalone, and serve.

MAKES 6 SERVINGS

Poaching is a popular method of preparing vegetables throughout China. Particular vegetables such as bok choy, Tianjin bok choy, choi sum, Chinese spinach, and snow pea shoots lend themselves perfectly to poaching. In the two recipes from Guangzhou that follow, I poach those round pale green bulbs of Shanghai bok choy and the bright green stalks of Chinese broccoli, but any of the other vegetables just mentioned, even the spinach that most of us are used to, broccoli, broccoli rabe, or chicory, is enhanced by poaching. ◆

SHANGHAI *BOK CHOY* POACHED IN SUPERIOR STOCK

Seung Tong Jum Shanghai Bok Choy

1¾ pounds Shanghai bok choy
6 cups cold water
One 1-inch-thick slice fresh ginger,
  lightly smashed
1½ teaspoons baking soda

2 teaspoons salt, for blanching
6 cups Superior Stock (page 74) or
  Chicken Stock (page 75)
1½ teaspoons salt (optional)

1. To prepare the *bok choy,* wash very well under cold running water to remove residual grit. Drain. Trim off the leaves and discard. Cut the *bok choy* bulbs in half lengthwise.

2. To blanch the *bok choy,* place the water, ginger, baking soda, and salt in a pot and bring to a boil over high heat. Add the *bok choy* and return to a boil. Immediately turn off the heat, run cold water into the pot, and drain.

3. Place the stock and salt in a pot, cover, and bring to a boil over high heat. Add the *bok choy* and return the stock to a boil, uncovered. Lower the heat and simmer for about 5 minutes or until the *bok choy* is tender. Turn off the heat, remove the *bok choy* with a slotted spoon to a heated platter, and serve. The stock may be served as a broth in individual bowls.

MAKES 4 SERVINGS

CHINESE BROCCOLI
POACHED IN CHICKEN STOCK

Gai Ton Jum Gai Lan

1½ to 1¾ pounds Chinese broccoli
6 cups cold water
1½ tablespoons sugar
One 1-inch-thick slice fresh ginger,
  lightly smashed

1½ teaspoons baking soda
5 cups Chicken Stock (page 75)
1¼ teaspoons salt (optional)

1. To prepare the broccoli, remove all the outer leaves and tough bottom edges of the broccoli stalks and discard. Wash the broccoli well.

2. To blanch the broccoli, in a pot place the water, sugar, ginger, and baking soda and bring to a boil over high heat. Add the broccoli and return to a boil. Turn off the heat, run cold water into the pot, and drain. Run cold water into the pot again, and drain.

3. Place the stock and salt in a pot, cover, and bring to a boil over high heat. Add the broccoli and return to a boil. Turn off the heat. Remove the broccoli with tongs to a heated platter and serve. The stock may be served as a broth in individual bowls.

MAKES 4 SERVINGS

BRAISED TIANJIN *BOK CHOY*

Mun Tianjin Bok Choy

Braising of stalked or bulbous vegetables is a common method of preparation throughout China. This dish, traditional to both Shanghai and Guangzhou, is also found in Beijing, proving that a good recipe can transcend regional boundaries.

6 cups Superior Stock (page 74) or
   Chicken Stock (page 75)
One 1-inch-thick slice fresh ginger,
   lightly smashed
1½ pounds Tianjin bok choy, *washed,*
   drained, and cut into quarters
¾ teaspoon salt
2 teaspoons tapioca flour mixed with
   2 teaspoons cold water

1. Heat a wok over high heat for 10 seconds, add the stock and ginger, and bring to a boil. Add the *bok choy,* immerse, and cook for 5 minutes, uncovered. Turn the *bok choy* 3 times during cooking. Turn off the heat.

2. Transfer the *bok choy* to a Chinese clay pot, a casserole, or a deep nonstick skillet that can be covered. Add 1½ cups of the cooking stock, cover, and bring to a boil over medium heat. Lower the heat and simmer for 30 minutes or until the *bok choy* is very soft. Remove the *bok choy* to a heated dish. Pour off all but ½ cup of the braising stock.

3. Add the salt to the pot. Turn the heat back on and bring to a boil over medium heat. Stir the tapioca flour–water mixture and pour slowly into the pot, stirring continuously until it comes to a boil. Turn off the heat, pour the sauce over the *bok choy,* and serve.

MAKES 4 SERVINGS

STIR-FRIED LOTUS ROOT

Chau Lin Ngau

This dish of lotus root, or lin ngau, *is a favorite for the Lunar New Year because of its symbolism and a play on words. Its name sounds very much like* lin yau, *which translates as "every year there will be abundance." No traditional New Year meal is without lotus root.*

1½ tablespoons Scallion Oil (page 82)
    or peanut oil
One ½-inch-thick slice fresh ginger,
    lightly smashed

½ teaspoon salt
¾ cup peeled and julienned fresh
    lotus root
¾ cup julienned carrot
½ cup julienned fresh bamboo shoot
½ cup Chinese celery in 2½-inch
    lengths
3 large peeled and julienned fresh
    water chestnuts (½ cup)
¼ cup Vegetable Stock (page 76)

Heat a wok over high heat for 30 seconds, add the scallion oil, and coat the wok with it using a spatula. Add the ginger and salt and stir briefly. When a wisp of white smoke appears, add all the vegetables and cook, stirring well, for 1 minute. Add 1 tablespoon of the stock and stir well. Stir and cook for 4 minutes. During the cooking, if the vegetable mixture is too dry, add the stock 1 tablespoon at a time if needed. Usually all of the stock will be needed. Occasionally the vegetables will release water during cooking, so less stock will be necessary. The vegetables will have absorbed all the liquid when cooked. Turn off the heat and transfer to a heated serving platter.

MAKES 4 SERVINGS

SNOW PEA SHOOTS
DAU MIU

These ends of the vines that bear snow peas have always been small, tender, and sweet, their best season late spring and early summer. A very special vegetable. Of late their quality has become varied. Recently "discovered" by chefs from the West, snow pea shoots are now in great demand, and are grown faster and in greater quantities. Shoots tend to be larger and less tender, even flowering. This is unfortunate. Shop carefully and try to obtain the small end tips. These days snow pea shoots, *dau miu,* are referred to often simply as "pea shoots."

If only larger and less tender pea shoots are available, those with thicker veins with as many as two or three leaves branching out of them, water-blanch them to ensure tenderness. I usually suggest that when vegetables are blanched in water a bit of baking soda be added. Some say that this removes most of the vitamins from the vegetables. A bit is lost, to be sure, but not all, not even most, and blanching ensures a bright green color. I might add that water-blanching is practiced in most Western kitchens as well, particularly in France. If you prefer not to use these tougher veins, then strip the leaves from the vine tendrils and use only them, a time-consuming process. Also, if you opt to do this, you will probably have to buy double the specified weight called for in the recipes. It's your choice.

The desired end is to have tender pea shoots, the younger, the more tender; the sweeter, the better. Though both of the following recipes are not strictly vegetarian, I include them in this portion of my book because crabmeat in the first instance, eggs in the second, are support ingredients to the sweet *dau miu.*

SNOW PEA SHOOTS WITH CRABMEAT

Hai Yuk Boon Dau Miu

6 cups cold water
1 teaspoon salt
½ teaspoon baking soda
½ pound snow pea shoots, tough vines removed, washed, and drained
2 tablespoons Garlic Oil (page 84) or peanut oil
¼ teaspoon salt
½ teaspoon sugar
1 tablespoon fried garlic (page 84)

For the sauce
2 teaspoons Chinese white rice wine or gin
½ tablespoon tapioca flour
5 tablespoons Milk Stock (page 78) or Chicken Stock (page 75)
Pinch freshly ground white pepper

2 tablespoons beaten egg white
2 ounces crabmeat, sprinkled with freshly ground white pepper

1. To blanch the snow pea shoots, place the water, salt, and baking soda in a pot, cover, and bring to a boil over high heat. Add the pea shoots and stir, making certain they are immersed. Cook for 1 minute or until the water returns to a boil. I specify this because of the differing toughness of the vines. If just leaves are used, blanch for 20 seconds only. Turn off the heat, run cold water into the pot, and drain. Repeat and drain thoroughly. Reserve.

2. Heat a wok over high heat for 30 seconds, add the garlic oil, and coat the wok with it using a spatula. When a wisp of white smoke appears, add the salt, sugar, fried garlic, and reserved pea shoots, stir well, and cook for 1½ minutes or until very hot. Turn off the heat and transfer to a heated serving dish.

3. In a small bowl, combine the sauce ingredients. Stir the sauce, pour it into the wok, and turn the heat back to high. Stir the sauce continuously until it comes to a boil. Drizzle the beaten egg white into the sauce, stirring continuously, until the egg turns white. Add the crabmeat and stir well. Turn off the heat, remove from the wok, top the snow pea shoots with the crabmeat mixture, and serve.

MAKES 4 SERVINGS

SNOW PEA SHOOT SOUP
WITH TWO EGGS

Pei Dan Gai Dan Dau Miu Tong

6 cups cold water

1 teaspoon salt

½ teaspoon baking soda

½ pound snow pea shoots, tough vines removed, washed, and drained

3 cups Superior Stock (page 74) or Chicken Stock (page 75)

One ½-inch-thick slice fresh ginger, lightly smashed

1 preserved egg, shelled and cut into ¼-inch dice

1 hard-boiled egg, shelled and cut into ¼-inch dice

1. To blanch the snow pea shoots, place the water, salt, and baking soda in a pot. Cover and bring to a boil over high heat. Add the pea shoots and stir, making certain they are immersed. Blanch for 1 minute if shoots, 20 seconds if using leaves only. Turn off the heat, run cold water into the pot, and drain. Repeat and drain thoroughly.

2. Place the stock and ginger in a pot. Cover and bring to a boil over high heat. Uncover, add the preserved egg, stir, and cook for 30 seconds. Add the pea shoots, stir, and return to a boil. Add the hard-boiled egg and stir well. Transfer to a heated tureen. Serve in individual bowls.

MAKES 4 SERVINGS

NOTE: *The traditional ingredients in this Hong Kong preparation are preserved eggs and salted duck eggs. However, the duck eggs available in Chinese and Asian groceries are not, I have found, of a consistent quality. So I use hard-boiled eggs instead, which are nicely suitable.*

VEGETARIAN OYSTERS

Jai Ho See

This preparation I first ate, and later learned to cook, in a Taoist monastery in Hong Kong. Vegetarian cookery, as practiced in Buddhist and Taoist temples, is designed to deceive the eye and satisfy the palate. In this case the "oysters" should look like oysters but should surprise and delight the tongue with entirely different tastes. They do indeed.

2 small Chinese eggplants

For the batter
1½ cups high-gluten flour
2 teaspoons baking powder
½ teaspoon salt
1¼ cups cold water
2 tablespoons peanut oil
¼ cup julienned Pickled Ginger (page 102)
¼ medium onion, thinly sliced
1 quart peanut oil, for frying

1. To prepare the eggplants, slice diagonally to create sandwich pockets in this manner, after discarding the first diagonal end cut: Cut the first slice all the way through, the next about three quarters of the way through, the next all the way through, to create a pocket. Do this until the eggplants are all sliced. You should have 20 pockets.

2. To make the batter, place the flour in a bowl and mix in the baking powder and salt. Add the water gradually, stirring until smooth. Add the 2 tablespoons peanut oil and blend until the batter is even and smooth.

3. Into each eggplant pocket, put 5 or 6 shreds of pickled ginger and an equal amount of sliced onion. Repeat until all the pockets are filled.

4. Place the quart of peanut oil in a wok and heat to 350°F. Dip each filled pocket into the batter, holding it tightly with chopsticks or tongs. Coat well and place in the oil, 4 to 5 at a time. As soon as they are in the oil, turn off the heat. When they brown on one side, turn them over. Turn the heat on again to bring the temperature up. As they fry they will resemble perfectly plump fried oysters. The oil should be a constant 325°F to 350°F, no higher, so that the "oysters" fry to a golden brown color. Remove and serve.

MAKES 4 TO 6 SERVINGS

BEAN CURD
WITH GARLIC CHIVES

Dai Mah Jom Choi

This is an old, storied Guangdong recipe. Dai Mah Jom is a district, part of Guangzhou, Guangdong's capital city, and before the age of motorized transportation was a regular stop for horse-drawn coaches into and out of the city. In a restaurant in Dai Mah Jom, this preparation was served in the autumn and winter, because it was considered a colder weather dish, in individual bubbling small clay pots. A story is told that an official from Mongolia was passing through and smelled this dish as it was cooking. When he arrived home, he told his cook about it and asked him to make it. The cook, a clever fellow, raced off to Dai Mah Jom, ate the dish, and later reproduced it for his employer's household and guests. It has come to be known by the name of the town. This is my rendition of Dai Mah Jom Choi.

2 tablespoons Garlic Oil (page 84) or peanut oil

½ pound Chinese chives (garlic chives), stems cut into ¼-inch pieces, leaves cut into ½-inch pieces, stems and leaves separated

2 teaspoons minced garlic

¾ of a cake (¾ ounce) red wet bean curd (soybean paste), mashed

¾ pound fresh bean curd (medium-firm tofu), cut into 1-inch cubes

2 tablespoons oyster sauce

1½ teaspoons sugar

3 tablespoons Vegetable Stock (page 76)

¼ teaspoon salt (optional)

Heat a wok over high heat for 40 seconds. Add the garlic oil and coat the wok with it using a spatula. When a wisp of white smoke appears, add the chive stems and minced garlic and stir. When the garlic turns light brown, add the wet bean curd, stir well, and cook for 1 minute. Add the fresh bean curd, stir, and cook for 1 minute. Add the oyster sauce and sugar, stir well, and cook for 1 minute more. Add the chive leaves and stir well. Add the stock and salt, stir, and cook for 3 minutes, until the mixture is well blended. Turn off the heat, transfer to a heated platter, and serve with cooked rice.

MAKES 4 SERVINGS

BEAN CURD
WITH STEAMED MUSHROOMS

Dong Gu Chau Dau Fu

*T*hough this is an invention of mine, I owe its inspiration to my grandmother, my Ah Paw. Wet bean curd, when added to particular dishes, whether stir-fried or braised, even steamed, tends to accentuate the flavors of other ingredients. This was a lesson I learned from Ah Paw, for whom wet bean curd was a constant food. She even would eat this bean curd, steamed, with a bit of sugar added. But her observation that the wet bean curd served to enhance other ingredients is absolutely accurate.

For the sauce
2 tablespoons oyster sauce
1 tablespoon Chinese white rice wine
   or gin
1 teaspoon sesame oil
1¼ teaspoons sugar

Pinch freshly ground white pepper
1 tablespoon cornstarch
¼ cup Vegetable Stock (page 76)

2 tablespoons peanut oil
1 teaspoon minced garlic
2 cakes (2 ounces) wet red bean curd
   (soybean paste), mashed
3 scallions, trimmed and cut into
   ½-inch pieces on a diagonal, green
   and white parts separated
10 Steamed Black Mushrooms
   (page 81), cut into ½-inch dice
1 pound fresh bean curd (medium-
   firm tofu), cut into 1-inch cubes
1 tablespoon Vegetable Stock
   (page 76)
½ cup chopped red bell pepper in
   ½-inch dice

1. In a bowl, combine the sauce ingredients and reserve.

2. Heat a wok over high heat for 30 seconds, add the peanut oil, and coat the wok with it using a spatula. When a wisp of white smoke appears, add the garlic and stir briefly. Add the wet bean curd, stir well, and cook for 40 seconds. Add the white parts of the scallions, stir well, and cook for 1 minute. Add the mushrooms, stir well, and cook for 30 seconds. Add the fresh bean curd and stir well. If the mixture is dry, add the tablespoon of stock and stir. Add the pepper, stir, and cook for 1½ minutes. Stir the sauce, make a well in the mixture, pour in, stir well, and cook for 2 minutes or until the sauce thickens and bubbles. Add the green parts of the scallions and stir. Turn off the heat, transfer to a heated serving platter, and serve with cooked rice.

MAKES 4 SERVINGS

BEAN CURD
WITH POACHED ASPARAGUS

Fung Seut Yat Fan Jung

*T*his is one of those dishes given a name with great flourish to entice one to eat. It was the creation of a certain Chef Chan Wing, a master, who founded the first cooking school in Hong Kong. He was a talented master chef, a dai see fu, *but it seems he was a poet as well. It is always a challenge, particularly in Guangdong and Hong Kong, for chefs to continue to come up with new dishes. This is pure fancy. Its complete name,* fung seut yat fan jung, *translates as "the monk sailing serenely through wind and snow." What is the wind? The snow? Sailing? I am not certain. I do know that bean curd is a recurring reminder of Buddhist and Taoist vegetarianism. Whatever, it is a lovely name for a dish of fine tastes.*

1½ cups Vegetable Stock (page 76)
One 1-inch-thick slice fresh ginger, lightly smashed
Ten 7½-inch-long asparagus spears, hard ends removed and cut into ½-inch diagonal pieces (1⅓ cups)
1 tablespoon cloud ears, soaked in hot water for 30 minutes and washed 3 times (⅓ cup, tightly packed)
1 tablespoon Onion Oil (page 83) or peanut oil
½ teaspoon salt
¾ teaspoon sugar
½ pound fresh bean curd (medium-firm tofu), minced

1. Heat a wok over high heat. Add the stock and ginger and bring to a boil. Add the asparagus, stir, and cook for 2 minutes. Remove the asparagus with a Chinese strainer and drain over a bowl. Bring the stock back to a boil, add the cloud ears, stir, and cook for 3 minutes. Turn off the heat and place the cloud ears in the strainer with the asparagus to drain. Pour off the stock and reserve for another use. Discard the ginger. Dry the wok and spatula.

2. Heat the wok over high heat for 20 seconds, add the onion oil, salt, and sugar, and coat the wok with the oil using the spatula. When a wisp of white smoke appears, add the bean curd, stir, and cook for 2 minutes. Add the asparagus and cloud ears, stir well, and cook for 2 minutes. Turn off the heat, transfer to a heated platter, and serve.

MAKES 4 SERVINGS

BAMBOO SHOOTS
WITH BEAN CURD AND BROCCOLI

Dong Yuk Jiu Dau Fu

*W*inter bamboo shoots, always the best, crisp and firm, when they can be obtained—and these days they are available in Chinese and Asian groceries, flown in from China, from November to May—are the core of this traditional recipe from Shanghai. This dish is best with fresh bamboo shoots, but even with the canned variety it is delightful.

1½ tablespoons Shallot Oil (page 84)
   or peanut oil
2 teaspoons minced fresh ginger
¼ cup minced shallot
⅓ cup prepared fresh bamboo shoots
   (page 15), cut into thin slices
    1 inch wide by 1½ inches long

¾ pound broccoli florets (about 2 cups)
1 tablespoon Chinese white rice wine
   or gin
½-inch piece hair seaweed, soaked in
   hot water for 30 minutes and
   drained
⅔ cup Vegetable Stock (page 76)
¼ teaspoon salt
2 teaspoons sugar
1 tablespoon oyster sauce
2 teaspoons double dark soy sauce, dark
   soy sauce, or mushroom soy sauce
½ pound fresh bean curd (medium-
   firm tofu), cut into ½-inch dice
1 tablespoon cornstarch mixed with
   2 tablespoons Vegetable Stock
   (page 76)

1. Heat a wok over high heat for 30 seconds. Add the shallot oil and coat the wok with it using a spatula. When a wisp of white smoke appears, add the ginger and shallot, stir well, and cook for 1 minute. Add the bamboo shoots and broccoli florets, stir, and cook for 1 minute. Add the wine and stir well. Add the seaweed, stir, and cook for 30 seconds. Add the stock and stir well. At this point, break up the hair seaweed, add the salt, sugar, oyster sauce, and soy sauce, and mix well. Cook for 7 minutes or until the broccoli is tender.

2. Add the bean curd, stir, and cook for 2 minutes. Make a well in the mixture, stir the cornstarch mixture, and pour in. Stir well and cook for 1 minute or until the liquid bubbles and thickens. Turn off the heat, transfer to a heated platter, and serve.

MAKES 4 TO 6 SERVINGS

MUSHROOMS WITH RED IN SNOW

Seut Choi Chau Mah Gu

Perhaps the most well-known, widely known food from Shandong is Tsing-Tao beer. But for traditionalists, red in snow, that ubiquitous pickled vegetable from Shanghai, is equally important. Red in snow, hseut loi hung, also known as Shanghai cabbage, snow cabbage, or pickled cabbage, is a favorite in Shandong, where it is usually prepared in combination with fresh vegetables.

2 tablespoons peanut oil
2 teaspoons minced fresh ginger

10 ounces fresh mushrooms, thinly sliced
¼ teaspoon salt
⅛ teaspoon crushed Sichuan peppercorns
⅓ cup chopped white part of scallion in ¼-inch diagonal pieces
2 teaspoons Shao-Hsing wine or dry sherry
½ cup chopped red bell pepper in ¼-inch dice
½ cup chopped red in snow in ¼-inch pieces

1. Heat a wok over high heat for 30 seconds. Add 1 tablespoon of the peanut oil and coat the wok with it using a spatula. When a wisp of white smoke appears, add 1 teaspoon of the minced fresh ginger and stir briefly. Add the mushrooms, stir, and cook for 2 to 3 minutes or until they begin to release their liquid. Turn off the heat, transfer the mushrooms to a strainer, and drain.

2. Wipe off the wok and spatula with paper towels. Heat the wok over high heat for 20 seconds. Add the remaining peanut oil and coat the wok with it using the spatula. When a wisp of white smoke appears, add the remaining ginger, the salt, and the peppercorns, and stir. Add the scallion and cook, stirring, for 1 minute. Add the reserved mushrooms and cook, stirring, for 30 seconds. Add the wine, stir thoroughly, and cook for 30 seconds. Add the bell pepper and cook, stirring, for 1½ minutes. Add the red in snow and cook for 2 minutes, stirring well. Turn off the heat, transfer to a heated dish, and serve.

MAKES 4 SERVINGS

HARMONIOUS VEGETABLE STIR-FRY

Wor Hop Saw Choi

*T*his preparation of mine is meant to illustrate how a combination of common vegetables can become a dish of harmony and balance, neither too yin nor too yang. The mung bean sprouts and cucumbers are essentially cooling, carrots are warming, and though garlic, like most spices, is warm, it is often added to other foods for its aroma and taste and as a digestive that tends to lower blood pressure and cholesterol. Stir-frying, as a cooking process, is considered warming, but peanut and sesame oils are neutral. The result is that this cooked dish is in perfect balance and will not disrupt one's yin or yang. Thus it is quite healthy.

6 cups cold water
One ¼-inch-thick slice fresh ginger, lightly smashed
10 ounces mung bean sprouts
1½ teaspoons peanut oil
½ teaspoon salt
1½ teaspoons minced garlic
¾ cup sliced carrots in pieces 2 inches long by ½ inch wide by ⅛ inch thick
⅔ cup peeled, seeded, and sliced cucumber in ¼-inch-thick half moons
½ teaspoon sesame oil

1. To blanch the mung bean sprouts, place the water and ginger in a pot, cover, and bring to a boil over high heat. Add the bean sprouts and blanch for 5 seconds only. Turn off the heat. Run cold water into the pot and drain. Repeat and drain well. Discard the ginger. Reserve the bean sprouts.

2. Heat the wok over high heat for 45 seconds. Add the peanut oil and coat the wok with it using a spatula. When a wisp of white smoke appears, add the salt and garlic, stir, and cook for 10 seconds, until the garlic fragrance is released. Add the carrots and cook, stirring, for 2½ minutes, until the carrots soften slightly. Add the cucumber and stir for 1 minute or until softened. Add the reserved sprouts and stir for 10 seconds. Turn off the heat and continue to stir for another 10 seconds. Add the sesame oil to the mixture and combine well. Transfer to a heated dish and serve.

MAKES 4 SERVINGS

SOYBEANS ANHUI STYLE

Anhui Wong Dau Gung

*A*nhui is a central province to the west of Shanghai and just over the border from the city of Nanjing. Most of it is a fertile plain, part of the Yangtze River valley, in which are grown much rice, often 2 crops a year, and soybeans, as well as wheat and vegetables. This dish, essentially a thickened soup of many flavors, is a tradition from that Anhui region.

½ pound dried soybeans
10 cups water
6 tablespoons peanut oil
1 tablespoon minced garlic
1½ tablespoons minced fresh ginger

¼ cup finely sliced white part of
   scallion
2 soybean cakes, cut into ¼-inch dice
2 tablespoons preserved horse beans
   with chili or Chili Sauce (page 88)
¾ cup red bell pepper in ¼-inch pieces
2 tablespoons double dark soy sauce,
   dark soy sauce, or mushroom soy
   sauce
6 tablespoons Shao-Hsing wine or dry
   sherry
1 tablespoon sesame oil
3 cups Vegetable Stock (page 76)
2 tablespoons finely sliced fresh
   coriander (cilantro)

1. Soak the soybeans in the water overnight.

2. Discard the water, drain the beans, and place in a food processor. Mix gently. What will result will be a mashed puree of soybeans and soybean milk. Reserve.

3. In a large pot, heat the peanut oil. Add the garlic, ginger, and scallion. When the garlic browns, add the soybean cakes and cook, stirring, for 1 minute. Add the preserved horse beans and bell pepper, stir, and cook for 30 seconds. Add the reserved soybean puree and mix together thoroughly.

4. Mix the soy sauce, wine, sesame oil, and stock in a bowl, then pour into the pot. Stir together until all ingredients are well mixed. Lower the heat and simmer for 30 minutes, covered, leaving the lid cracked. Stir frequently to prevent sticking. Turn off the heat. Add the coriander and stir well. Transfer to a heated tureen and serve in individual bowls.

MAKES 4 SERVINGS

MUNG BEAN SOUP
WITH CUSTARD AND ASPARAGUS

Lo Dau Fu Far Tong

This refreshing summer soup is a classic mixture of textures and tastes, my adaptation of a traditional Buddhist soup of mung bean sprouts and bean curd. Soft bean curd, glistening and custardlike, is not pressed into cakes as with fresh bean curd but is allowed to set in large containers. In China it is customarily eaten to refresh, served in scoops, with sweet sugar syrup poured over it, which is the way I remember eating it as a child. In this preparation I complement this softness with the crispness of the sprouts and fresh asparagus. To ensure crispness, both the sprouts and asparagus are water-blanched to rid them of residual water so that water will not be released into the soup and dilute it.

3 quarts cold water
1½ tablespoons salt
One 1-inch-thick slice fresh ginger, lightly smashed
10 ounces fresh mung bean sprouts, end beans left on, washed, and drained
¾ teaspoon baking soda
½ pound fresh asparagus, thick spears preferred
5 cups Vegetable Stock (page 76)
1 tablespoon minced fresh ginger
1 tablespoon White Peppercorn Oil (page 85) or peanut oil
½ teaspoon freshly ground white pepper
½ cup trimmed and finely sliced scallion
16 ounces soft bean curd

1. To blanch the mung bean sprouts, place the water, 1 tablespoon of the salt, and the slice of ginger in a pot, cover, and bring to a boil over high heat. Place the sprouts in a mesh strainer and lower into the boiling water for 5 seconds. Remove and place in a bowl of ice water for 5 minutes. Drain and reserve.

2. To blanch and prepare the asparagus, place the baking soda into the water, stir, and bring back to a boil. Add the asparagus, immerse, and blanch for 10 seconds or until the asparagus turns bright green. Turn off the heat, run cold water into the pot, and drain. Repeat twice more. Drain thoroughly. Cut the asparagus into 2-inch matchsticks and reserve.

3. Place the stock in a pot with the minced fresh ginger, peppercorn oil, 1½ teaspoons salt, and the white pepper. Cover and bring to a boil over high heat. Uncover the pot, add the reserved sprouts, mix, and return to a boil. Add the reserved asparagus, mix,

and return to a boil. Turn off the heat. Add the scallion and stir in well. With a large spoon, scoop out portions of the soft bean curd and add to the soup. Gently mix so as not to break up the custard. Transfer to a heated tureen and serve in individual bowls.

MAKES 4 TO 6 SERVINGS

GLUTEN
MIEN GUN

This sinewy component of wheat flour dough, which remains after the powdery flour has been rinsed away, is eaten occasionally by vegetarians in China and other parts of Asia, notably in Taiwan. Unlike the various aspects of the soybean, the curds, cakes, and sheets of which are often fashioned, prepared, and cooked to resemble meat, gluten usually is eaten on its own, as a defined vegetable product, only on rare occasions as a so-called meat substitute. Its name, *mien gun*, translates as "tendons of dough," to indicate its pliable nature. It is found both fresh and frozen, usually in the latter form outside of China.

In China it is often sold fried and ready for use or even fried, then braised in sauce as a ready-to-eat snack. I recall a preparation cooked by my father, gluten braised in oyster sauce and chicken stock, that he called *yue toh*, or "fish stomach," because of its spongy texture.

To give it texture and to make it more digestible, gluten is usually fried before becoming part of other dishes. After frying it is customarily braised or stewed so that it will absorb the flavors of what it is combined with. It has no flavor of its own. It should be noted that gluten is not only eaten by vegetarians. It can be, and is, cooked in chicken or superior stock as well. It can usually be found frozen in 1-pound plastic-wrapped packages containing nine irregular cakes in the frozen food sections of Chinese and Asian markets. The packages are usually labeled "Wheat Dough." These rough, sand-colored cakes expand when defrosted. They become hard when fried, then they soften and become chewy, occasionally spongelike, when cooked. Following are two traditional Chinese vegetarian methods of preparing gluten.

BRAISED GLUTEN WITH MIXED VEGETABLES

Hung Siu Mien Gun

5 cups peanut oil

6 ounces gluten, cut into ⅓-inch strips
(like French fried potatoes)

1 tablespoon minced fresh ginger

1 cup sliced white part of scallion in
½-inch diagonal pieces

2⅛ cups Vegetable Stock (page 76)

2 teaspoons double dark soy sauce, dark
soy sauce, or mushroom soy sauce

1 tablespoon Shao-Hsing wine or dry
sherry

¾ teaspoon salt

1¼ teaspoons sugar

6 ounces snow peas, strings removed
and cut lengthwise in half on a
diagonal

4 fresh water chestnuts, peeled, halved,
and thinly sliced

1 medium red bell pepper, cut into
¼-inch julienne (1 cup)

1. To prepare the gluten, heat a wok over high heat for 1 minute. Add the peanut oil and heat to 350°F. Place the gluten strips in the oil and deep-fry for 2½ minutes, until golden brown, turning so they will brown evenly. Turn off the heat, remove with a Chinese strainer, and drain over a bowl. Empty all but 1½ tablespoons of oil from the wok.

2. Heat the wok over high heat for 20 seconds. Add the ginger and stir briefly. Add the scallion, stir, and cook for 1 minute. Add the gluten strips, stir, and cook for another 1 minute. Add 1¾ cups of the stock, stir, and bring to a boil. Add the soy sauce, wine, salt, and sugar and stir well. Lower the heat, cover the wok, and cook for 20 minutes, stirring frequently to prevent sticking. If all the liquid is absorbed, add another ¼ cup. Raise the heat back to high, add the snow peas, and stir. Add the water chestnuts and stir. If the mixture is too dry, add a bit of remaining stock to moisten it. Add the bell pepper, stir, and cook for 1 minute. The mixture should be moist but without residual liquid. If too dry, add the remaining bit of stock. Turn off the heat, transfer to a heated platter, and serve.

MAKES 4 TO 6 SERVINGS

GLUTEN STEWED
WITH CHINESE MUSHROOMS

Dong Gu Mun Mien Gun

5 cups peanut oil

10 ounces gluten, cut into
 ¼-inch-thick slices

One ½-inch-thick slice ginger, lightly
 smashed

4 scallions, trimmed and cut into
 1-inch pieces

1¼ cups bamboo shoots, cut into pieces
 1 inch square and ¼ inch thick

1 cup carrots cut into ¼-inch-thick
 half moons

30 small Steamed Black Mushrooms
 (page 81)

2 tablespoons Shao-Hsing wine or dry
 sherry

2½ cups Vegetable Stock (page 76)

1 tablespoon double dark soy sauce,
 dark soy sauce, or mushroom soy
 sauce

1½ teaspoons sugar

¾ teaspoon salt

1. To prepare the gluten, heat a wok over high heat for 1 minute. Add the peanut oil and heat to 350°F. Add half of the gluten slices and deep-fry for 2 minutes, turning to prevent sticking, until golden brown. Remove with a Chinese strainer and drain over a bowl. Repeat with the second batch. Reserve. Empty all but 2 tablespoons of the oil from the wok.

2. Heat the wok for 20 seconds over high heat. Add the ginger slice, stir, and cook for 30 seconds. Add the scallions, stir, and cook for 45 seconds. Add the reserved gluten slices, stir, and cook for 30 seconds more. Add the bamboo shoots, carrots, and mushrooms and stir. Add the wine and mix well. Add 2 cups of the stock and bring to a boil. Add the soy sauce, sugar, and salt and stir well. Cover the wok, lower the heat, and simmer for 20 minutes. Stir frequently to prevent sticking. If the mixture is too dry, add more stock, ¼ cup at a time. The liquid should be absorbed, but the mixture should be moist. Turn off the heat, transfer to a heated platter, and serve.

MAKES 6 TO 8 SERVINGS

VEGETARIAN DUCK

Jai Siu Op

This tasty artifice is practiced in Shanghai and parts south. Once regarded as a vegetarian dish for the monks, it has evolved into a favorite that appears at most banquets, vegetarian or otherwise, in Shanghai and south into Fujian and Guangdong. The aim with vegetarian duck is to form and cook the bean curd skins so that they resemble the skin of roast duck in both color and texture, a delicious deception.

For the sauce
4 teaspoons dark soy sauce
1 tablespoon sesame oil
3 teaspoons sugar

Pinch freshly ground white pepper
¼ cup Vegetable Stock (page 76)

5 tablespoons peanut oil
8 Chinese dried black mushrooms, soaked in hot water for 30 minutes, washed, stems removed, and julienned
½ cup julienned bamboo shoots
½ cup julienned carrot
1 large sheet fresh bean curd skin
1 cup julienned Iceberg lettuce

1. In a small bowl, mix together the sauce ingredients and reserve.

2. To prepare the vegetable filling, heat a wok over high heat for 40 seconds. Add 1 tablespoon peanut oil and coat the wok with it using a spatula. When a wisp of white smoke appears, add the vegetables and cook, stirring, for 1 minute. Stir the sauce mixture, pour into the wok, and mix well. Lower the heat to medium, stir, and cook until the liquid is absorbed, about 3 minutes. Turn off the heat, transfer to a bowl, and reserve.

3. To prepare the bean curd sheet, place the sheet flat on a work surface. With kitchen shears, cut into 3 sections, each 6 by 4 inches. Wet the sheets lightly to help it stay pliable. Make a ridge of the vegetable mix across the long end, roll up, and press closed. As you work, keep the other sections of bean curd sheet covered with plastic wrap so that they do not dry out and become brittle.

4. To steam the vegetarian duck, place the rolls in a steamproof dish. Place the dish in a steamer, cover, and steam for 12 minutes (see steaming, page 64). Turn off the heat, remove, and reserve.

5. As the rolls steam, prepare a platter. Line with the julienned lettuce and set aside.

6. Pour the remaining ¼ cup peanut oil into a cast-iron skillet. Heat over high heat until a wisp of white smoke appears. Place the vegetarian duck rolls into the pan and fry for 6 minutes, rolling them so they brown evenly. Turn off the heat, transfer to a cutting board, and cut each vegetarian duck roll into 4 equal pieces. Place these in the platter on the bed of lettuce and serve.

MAKES 4 SERVINGS

VEGETARIAN CHICKEN

So Gai

*T*his is a peculiarity of the Chinese kitchen, a food fashioned for one purpose only, to imitate chicken. It is an oblong loaf, made from ground soybean flour, yeast, and baking powder that have been cooked, made into sheets, and rolled tightly into that oblong. This is then wrapped tightly in cheesecloth, tied, and boiled slowly in water for several hours until it becomes a firm loaf.

Shanghai is famous for its manufacture of this "vegetarian chicken" and ships it frozen in 1-pound loaves, wrapped in plastic, labeled "mock vegetarian chicken" or "frozen mock vegetarian chicken." It can be found in the frozen food sections of Chinese markets.

Defrosted, with its liquid squeezed out, it has a certain pliability. Usually it is sliced, as if it were a boneless chicken breast, then deep-fried. It can be eaten cooked that way or used as chicken in a stir-fry.

In Hong Kong, where I first encountered this mock chicken, it was sold fresh and unfrozen. As such it was often simply sliced and eaten as is, with no further preparation. It cannot be eaten that way once it has been frozen, because once defrosted it becomes spongelike. It is better cooked. Briefly deep-fried, the slices become rather crisp. Fried this way and lightly salted, they may be eaten as a snack, a chip, or as one of a selection of small appetizers before a dinner. But they are best in a stir-fry, combined with vegetables.

So gai *has a unique property. Even when crisp, once it is stir-fried, it softens, becomes pliable, its texture quite like that of slices of chicken breast. A note: When preparing this dish, make certain that vegetables that accompany this mock chicken are thoroughly dried.*

1 quart peanut oil
½ pound vegetarian chicken, defrosted, water squeezed out, cut crosswise into 24 round slices

For the sauce
1 tablespoon double dark soy sauce, dark soy sauce, or mushroom soy sauce
2 teaspoons Shao-Hsing wine or dry sherry
1¼ teaspoons Chinese white vinegar or distilled vinegar
1¾ teaspoons sugar
¼ teaspoon salt
Pinch freshly ground white pepper
1 tablespoon cornstarch
⅓ cup Vegetable Stock (page 76)

1 tablespoon minced fresh ginger
¾ cup julienned white part of scallion
1 cup julienned carrot
¼ pound snow peas, strings removed and halved lengthwise
1 cup julienned Chinese celery or regular celery
¼ cup Vegetable Stock (page 76)

1. Heat a wok over high heat for 1 minute. Add the peanut oil and heat to 350°F. Slide slices of mock chicken, a batch of 8 at a time, down the sides of the wok into the oil. Deep-fry, moving the slices about to prevent them from sticking together, for 1 minute. Turn over and fry for another minute. (This timing is for subsequent stir-frying. If the slices are to be eaten as chips or an appetizer, fry for another 1 to 1½ minutes, turning them over again.) Remove from the wok and drain over paper towels. Repeat with the other 2 batches until all slices are fried. Turn off the heat. Reserve the slices. Empty all but 2 tablespoons of the oil from the wok.

2. In a small bowl, combine the sauce ingredients and reserve.

3. Heat the wok over high heat for 20 seconds. Add the ginger and stir briefly. Add the scallion and cook, stirring, for 30 seconds. Add the carrot and cook, stirring, for 30 seconds. Add the snow peas and stir briefly. Add the celery and cook, stirring, for 30 seconds. Add 2 tablespoons of the stock and mix well. Add the reserved mock chicken slices and cook, stirring well. Add the remaining 2 tablespoons stock, stir, and cook for 1½ minutes. Make a well in the mixture, stir the sauce mixture, pour in, and mix well. Cook for 1½ minutes or until the sauce thickens and turns dark brown. Turn off the heat, transfer to a heated platter, and serve.

MAKES 4 TO 6 SERVINGS

Chinese Breads, Noodles, *and* Dim Sum

中國饅頭麵點心

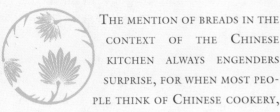THE MENTION OF BREADS IN THE CONTEXT OF THE CHINESE KITCHEN ALWAYS ENGENDERS SURPRISE, FOR WHEN MOST PEOPLE THINK OF CHINESE COOKERY, NO FOOD IS CONSIDERED MORE CENTRAL THAN RICE. It is, however, a fact that bread has been a staple and bread making an integral aspect of the Chinese kitchen for more than 2,000 years, as far back as the Chin and Han dynasties. It is also true that in Beijing and in other parts of China's North, wheat, millet, and barley were and are traditionally as important as is rice in the South. Breads from wheat have been a northern staple in Beijing and throughout Shandong ever since methods of flour milling passed into China through the routes established by the Silk Road.

China's first breads were, as might be expected, steamed, steamed and fried, later baked, and are usually referred to generically as *ping,* or foods made from flour, to include noodles. Before milling, the Chinese in the North ate their staple grains, as did the Southerners, boiled. But milling and flour changed that. Stone mills were found in Han excavations, and wall paintings depict the process of kneading flour and water into doughs. Steamed breads and noodle making preceded baked breads, which were rare and were baked like the *nan* breads of India, slapped to the sides of wood-burning clay ovens in the regions north of Beijing.

Once the practice of milling flour and adding water to it to make doughs took hold, the cooking of so-called noodle foods—breads, cakes, and noodles—quickly gained popularity not only in imperial Beijing but among the general populace. Steamed, baked, and fried breads, formed into decorative loaves and shapes, became common, and breads assumed so much importance that in the Yuan and Ming dynasties breads of all sorts were offered in temples as ancestral gifts, different offerings each day of a month.

Simply to illustrate the scope and variety of the breads of the Ming, it is worth listing a number of these temple offerings, as recorded by Kwang-chih Chang in *Food in Chinese Culture*: rolled fried cakes, sugared biscuits, steamed rolls with mutton, clover honey biscuits, steamed sugar biscuits, sugared date cakes, oven-baked breads, sugar-filled steamed breads, rice-flour cakes, fat-filled pastries, honey cakes, puff-paste baked breads, flaky filled pastries, marrow cakes, rolled cookies, scalded-dough baked breads, sesame-oil noodles, pepper and salt breads, sesame and sugar-filled baked breads, and thousand-layer baked breads. These included but were not limited to fried breads, sugared cruller-like breads, steamed breads filled with mutton, breads covered with honey, meat pastries, breads filled with marrow, breads covered with sesame seeds.

The first baked breads, it would appear,

originated in the region north of Tibet, where pitalike breads, layered breads, were baked in clay ovens, an indication of Persia's influence on that part of northern China. These were wheat breads. Throughout the rest of China, however, stoves burned wood, producing fires that burned under woks, thus producing steamed and fried foods, as well as breads.

Generally the breads steamed in Beijing and throughout the rest of the North were solid loaves or rolls, unfilled. They were enjoyed for their texture and sweetness and as accompaniments for such dishes as Peking Duck or duck smoked with green tea in Shanghai or with camphor in Sichuan, with salty Yunnan ham sweetened with sugar syrup as it is served in Hunan. Later, the Cantonese would adopt these steamed breads to eat with their traditional roasted chicken and roasted suckling pig.

Steamed breads, filled with meats, cut into small pieces and seasoned, or sweet pastes made from red beans, sesame seeds, dates, and lotus seeds, arrived at the Southern Chinese table later. As imports from the North they were always restaurant foods, rarely prepared in the home. Meat-filled breads, buns, and dumplings owe a bit of lineage as well to foreign traders and to immigrants. The inventive Cantonese filled steamed and baked buns with curried meats, another imported flavor.

The breads I remember from my childhood in Sun Tak were steamed in a big *dim sum* restaurant. My older brother, Ching Mo, would lift me onto his shoulders, and we would go off to the huge restaurant on the second floor of a huge building, the first floor of which was a honeycomb of various prepared foods and vegetable shops. The men who offered our steamed breads would weave their way through the tables, huge steamers in front of them, supported by straps around the backs of their necks, chanting, *"Har gau, siu mai, char siu bau. Har gau, siu mai, char siu bau."* These are the same shrimp dumplings, the same basket-shaped treats known as "cook and sell" dumplings, the same steamed buns with barbecued pork inside them so familiar to this day.

I was fascinated by the steam vapors seeping through the layered bamboo steamers, by the puff of steam that would rise when the top was removed from a steamer, and of course overjoyed when my *char siu bau* was set in front of me. I suppose I should refer to these as *jing char siu bau,* to denote that they were steamed, not baked, but they were always just pork buns to me, a recurring treat shared by me and my brother.

How marvelous they were, the bread soft, spongelike, faintly sweet, contrasting with the flavored pork or chicken inside, the meats peeking out from the tops of the buns, almost like a flower bud beginning to open. Just watching steamers was a treat for me, for in our house and that of my grandmother, my Ah Paw, the servants would steam our foods and the breads they had bought in big steamers set into woks over boiling water and covered. Because breads were not part of our everyday cooking, they were always special. On birthdays we would order breads shaped like peaches, to be steamed. The birth of a daughter into our extended family would have us, me, waiting impatiently for a month to pass from her birth, for we knew that this month would be celebrated with steamed breads dyed red in celebration.

Steamed wheat flour buns, dyed deep red, are also traditionally offered in great quantities in temples when a person pleads for a specific good fortune from a specific deity. Each year, in May, on the island of Cheung Chau, one of Hong Kong's outlying islands, the Bun Festival is held. This feast of many days includes parades, stilt-walking performances, opera, with the event centered about great towers of steamed buns, in effect an offering to placate heaven's deities. The festival's end calls for the towers of buns to be taken apart and the buns distributed. It is believed that the more buns one gathers, the greater the fortune to be realized.

When I came to live in Hong Kong, I discovered not only variations of these steamed breads and dumplings I loved but also fried and baked breads that had come south from Beijing and Shanghai. I had my first *guk char siu bau,* or baked pork bun, in Hong Kong. In Hong Kong and throughout Guangdong, the Cantonese integrated breads, steamed, baked, and fried, into their *dim sum* kitchen. And from the Shanghai kitchen, so open to and influenced by Europe, came other doughs and breads. Scallion pancakes, infused with scallions and *lop cheung,* Chinese sausages, are quite like flatbreads, fried on both sides and offered usually as a first course or as an accompaniment to meats. Shanghai produced sweet cakes and savories as well, a particular joy, deep-fried pastries filled with curried chicken, easily the equal of most Western savories. When made properly, it is impossible to believe that they have been fried, for their pastry is as flaky as a piecrust made from scratch.

I have written extensively on the *dim sum* kitchen, peculiar to southern China, and about noodles and breads. I have taught and continue to teach the art of the Chinese dumpling. A challenge to making Chinese breads and *dim sum* is the variation in doughs. Doughs vary in gluten content, and doughs react to climate, temperature, and humidity. It is not at all unusual for a bread maker or pastry cook to carry dough along. It is not unusual to use different doughs for the same preparation when climatic conditions must be considered. In China, restaurant kitchens order mixtures of flours, with differing gluten contents, to their specifications so that breads will rise but not crack or break when they are steamed. Chinese bread makers also insist on bleached flour, for whiteness in flour is desirable, aesthetically, in quite the same manner as whiteness in rice.

I continue to test flours for my breads and dumplings. I have combinations and brands, all accessible, which I believe closely approximate the mixes in the Chinese kitchen with which I am familiar. I have also added unbleached flour on occasion because I believed it necessary to keep bread shapes intact. The specific flours I suggest in the various dough mixtures seem, after much trial, to work well.

With virtually all Chinese breads, lard traditionally is the shortening of choice. I use it and prefer it. However, peanut oil may be used as well, as is the case with China's Buddhist nuns and monks, who do not eat animal fat. I have used it with breads and with various *dim sum* recipes and find it quite good, but I believe the taste of breads and of *dim sum* buns is finer when lard is used.

STEAMED BREAD LOAF

Man Tau

This is the basic steamed bread of Beijing but is eaten widely in Shanghai, as are variations of it in Sichuan and Hunan. The basic dough, with its bleached flour base, can be used for filled buns as well.

2 cups Pillsbury Best All-Purpose Flour
½ cup Pillsbury Best Bread Flour
½ cup sugar
4 teaspoons baking powder
½ cup lukewarm milk
¼ cup lukewarm water
2½ tablespoons lard or peanut oil

1. Mix the flours, sugar, and baking powder together on a work surface. Make a well in the middle and add the milk gradually, combining it with your fingers. After the milk has been absorbed, add the water and with your fingers continue to work the dough. Add the lard and again, with your fingers, continue to work the dough until well blended.

2. Using a dough scraper, gather the dough in one hand and begin kneading with the other. If the dough is dry and shows traces of flour, add another bit of water. Knead for 12 to 15 minutes. If the dough is still dry, add 1 teaspoon of water at a time and continue to knead until the dough becomes elastic. If the dough is too wet, sprinkle a bit of flour on the work surface and on your hands and continue to work the dough.

3. When the dough is elastic, cover with a damp cloth and allow to rest for 1 hour.

4. To make the loaves, divide the dough into 2 equal parts. Roll each into a cylinder 12 inches long, then divide each cylinder into 3 equal pieces. Dough that is not being worked on should be covered with a damp cloth. With wet hands, shape each piece to create a small loaf, pressing and rounding the ends. Place each loaf on a rectangular piece of parchment or wax paper, 5 inches by 2½ inches (the paper should be larger than the loaf). Repeat with 2 other cut pieces and with the 3 from the other cylinder. You will have 6 loaves.

5. Place the loaves into 2 bamboo steamers, 3 in each, tiered, cover, and steam for 20 to 25 minutes (see steaming, page 64). When done, the loaves become soft and sponge-like. Occasionally, because of flour and climate variations, the loaf will open in the top during steaming, a natural occurrence. Turn off the heat, remove from the steamer, slice, and serve.

MAKES 6 LOAVES

DECORATIVE STEAMED BREADS ◆

*T*hroughout China, particularly in the North, small, sculpted steamed breads are served as accompaniments to festive, classic dishes such as Peking Duck, Tea-Smoked Duck, Crisp Cantonese Chicken, and Roasted Suckling Pig. Here are two of the most popular. ◆

LOTUS LEAF BREAD

Haw Yip Ping

These small breads, shaped like rounded lotus leaves or perhaps like shells, are a favorite in Hunan, where they are eaten as tiny sandwiches filled with Honey Ham (recipe follows).

1 cup Pillsbury Best All-Purpose Flour
¼ cup Pillsbury Best Bread Flour
¼ cup sugar
2 teaspoons baking powder
¼ cup lukewarm milk
⅛ cup lukewarm water
1¼ tablespoons lard or peanut oil

1. Make the dough in the manner of Steamed Bread Loaf (page 364). Knead the dough into an elastic ball, cover, and allow to rest for 1 hour.

2. Divide the dough into 2 equal pieces. Roll each into a cylinder 15 inches long. Cut into equal 1-inch pieces. Work with one at a time and keep the others covered with a damp cloth. Roll each piece into a ball. Press it down on the work surface with your palm into a round 1½ inches in diameter. Retain a round shape, but pinch a small protrusion at the bottom.

3. After pressing, the shape will widen at the sides, which is the desired lotus leaf shape. Press a dinner fork into the dough to create fanlike lines and ridges. If the dough is too moist, dust with flour. Place each on a square of parchment or wax paper. Repeat until 30 small lotus leaf breads have been made.

4. Place in bamboo steamers, 10 to a steamer, cover, and steam (see steaming, page 64) for 5 to 6 minutes. Turn off the heat, remove the breads, and serve with honey ham.

MAKES 30 SMALL BREADS

NOTE: *These decorative breads can be kept, after steaming, covered with plastic wrap and refrigerated, for 3 days. They may also be frozen. To resteam, defrost and bring to room temperature.*

HONEY HAM

Mut Jop For Tui

*I*n Hunan this ham is made with salty, cured Hunan ham. Use Smithfield ham as a substitute. Serve it with Lotus Leaf Bread (preceding recipe).

1 thick slice Smithfield ham, boned
    (2 pounds after trimming)
1⅓ cups dark brown sugar
1½ cups cold water

1. Remove the black coating from the ham and trim, but leave a layer of fat on one side. After cleaning and trimming, the ham should weigh 2 pounds. Soak the ham, covered with water, for 8 hours or overnight. This removes much of the salt.

2. Place the ham in a steamproof dish. Sprinkle with 1 cup of the dark brown sugar to coat well. Add 1 cup of the water to the dish around the ham. Cover and steam over medium heat (see steaming, page 64) for 3 to 3½ hours. This will remove the residual salt and tenderize the ham.

3. As the ham steams, make a syrup. Place the remaining ½ cup water in a wok and bring to a boil. Add the remaining ⅓ cup dark brown sugar and stir until the sugar dissolves. Cook for 3 to 4 minutes, until the syrup thickens slightly, stirring occasionally. Turn off the heat.

4. Turn the heat off under the ham. Transfer to a work surface. Slice into pieces 2 inches square and ⅛ inch thick and place in a serving dish. Pour the syrup over the ham and serve, one piece with syrup, with each lotus leaf bread.

MAKES ENOUGH
FOR 10 SERVINGS

SILVER THREAD BREAD

Ngan See Geun

*L*ike all Chinese breads, these steamed breads may be enjoyed hot, as they are, from the steamer or with particular dishes. These "silver threads" complement crisp roast chicken and duck dishes.

1 cup Pillsbury Best All-Purpose Flour
¼ cup Pillsbury Best Bread Flour
¼ cup sugar
2 teaspoons baking powder
¼ cup lukewarm milk
⅛ cup lukewarm water
1¼ tablespoons lard or peanut oil

1. Make a dough in the manner of the preceding recipe. Knead into an elastic ball, cover, and allow to rest for 1 hour.

2. Roll the dough into a cylinder 10 inches long. Divide into 10 equal pieces. Working with one at a time, cover the remaining pieces with a damp cloth. Dust the work surface with flour and roll each dough section into a flat rectangle, 5½ inches by 2 inches. With the edge of a dough scraper, cut the rectangle lengthwise into 8 strips. Press the strips together gently and curl into a loose knot. Place on a square of parchment or wax paper. Repeat with the remaining dough pieces.

3. Place the rolls in a steamer, cover, and steam (see steaming, page 64) for 6 to 8 minutes, until done. Turn off the heat, remove from the steamer, and serve.

MAKES 10 BREADS

FRIED BREAD LOAF

Jah Man Tau

The ingredients and amounts for this bread are the same as for the Steamed Bread Loaf. When the loaves are deep-fried, as they are in Sichuan and Shanghai, they acquire a pale golden color, a glistening sheen, and an extraordinarily thin crust that is most pleasant indeed to bite into.

1 recipe Steamed Bread Loaf
 (page 364)
5 cups peanut oil

1. Make the loaves as in the recipe for Steamed Bread Loaf.

2. Heat a wok over high heat for 40 seconds, add the peanut oil, and heat to 350°F. Remove the paper from beneath the loaf, place in a Chinese strainer, and lower into the oil. Allow the loaf to brown, turning frequently, until it acquires an even pale golden color, about 3 to 4 minutes. Repeat with the remaining loaves.

3. Remove each bread from the wok and drain thoroughly on paper towels. Slice and serve. As noted, the bread will have a sheen and a thin crust, and the peanut oil confers on it a decidedly different flavor from that when it is steamed.

MAKES 6 LOAVES

STEAMED PORK BUNS

Jing Char Siu Bau

This is one of the first dim sum *that I ever remember eating when my brother took me to our teahouse in Sun Tak to* yum cha, *or "drink tea." It is a classic of the Cantonese* dim sum *kitchen. Its dough, with a bleached flour base, is ideal for other varieties of steamed* dim sum *as well. Once it has been cooked through, the dough becomes soft and spongelike and complements various fillings such as roast pork, sweet lotus seed and red bean pastes, and* lop cheung, *Chinese sausage. The dough is a special mix; it must be used within 1 to 2 hours from the time it is made, and it cannot be frozen.*

For the sauce
1 tablespoon oyster sauce
1½ teaspoons dark soy sauce
2 teaspoons ketchup
2¼ teaspoons sugar

Pinch freshly ground white pepper
2¼ teaspoons tapioca flour
5 tablespoons Chicken Stock (page 75)

1 tablespoon peanut oil
½ cup diced onion in ¼-inch pieces
¾ cup Barbecued Pork (page 124), cut thinly into ½-inch-square pieces
1½ teaspoons Chinese white rice wine or gin
½ teaspoon sesame oil

For the dough
2¼ cups Gold Medal All-Purpose Flour
3½ teaspoons baking powder
½ cup sugar
6 tablespoons milk
3 tablespoons water
2½ tablespoons lard or peanut oil

1. In a small bowl, combine the sauce ingredients and reserve.

2. Heat a wok over high heat for 40 seconds, add the peanut oil, and coat the wok with it using a spatula. When a wisp of white smoke appears, add the onion. Lower the heat to medium and cook for 5 minutes, until the onion turns light brown. Raise the heat, add the pork, and cook, stirring, for 2 minutes. Add the wine and mix well. Stir the sauce, pour into the wok, stir and mix, and cook for 1 to 1½ minutes, until the sauce thickens and turns brown. Add the sesame oil and mix well. Turn off the heat and transfer the filling mixture to a shallow dish. Cool to room temperature, then refrigerate, uncovered, for 4 hours or, covered, overnight.

3. To make the dough, mix the flour, baking powder, and sugar together on a work surface. Make a well in the center, add the milk gradually, and with your fingers combine with the flour mixture. When the milk is absorbed, add the water and work the dough with your fingers. Add the lard and continue to work the dough with your fingers.

Using a dough scraper, gather the dough in one hand and knead with the other. Knead for 12 to 15 minutes. If the dough is dry, add 1 teaspoon water at a time and continue to knead until the dough is elastic. If the dough is wet, sprinkle a bit of flour on the work surface and on your hands and continue working it. When the dough is elastic, cover with a damp cloth and allow to rest for 1 hour.

4. Prepare the pork buns: Roll the dough into a cylinder 16 inches long. Cut into 1-inch pieces. Roll each piece into a ball. Work with one piece at a time; cover those not being used with a damp cloth. Press a ball of dough down lightly, then, with your fingers, press into a well-like shape. Place 1½ tablespoons filling into the well, close, and pleat the dough with your fingers until the filling is completely enclosed. Repeat for all 16. Place the buns on 2½-inch squares of wax paper and place in a steamer at least 2 inches apart to allow for expansion. Cover the steamer and steam (see steaming, page 64) for 15 to 20 minutes. Turn off the heat, remove the buns, and serve.

NOTE: *These buns may be frozen after steaming and will keep for 2 months. To reheat, defrost thoroughly, bring to room temperature, and steam for 8 to 10 minutes.*

MAKES 16 PORK BUNS

BAKED PORK BUNS

Guk Char Siu Bau

This dim sum *bun is perhaps the most well known outside of China. People who are not even familiar with the term or concept of* dim sum *know "pork buns." I have over the years experimented with different fillings for this Cantonese classic baked bun, but the traditional pork filling remains my favorite.*

1 recipe Pork Bun filling (page 370)
One ¼-ounce envelope active dry yeast
⅓ cup sugar
½ cup hot water (110°F)
2 cups Pillsbury Best Bread Flour
½ large egg, beaten
5 tablespoons lard or peanut oil
1 large egg beaten with equal amount of water for egg wash
1½ tablespoons Scallion Oil (page 82) or peanut oil (optional)

continued

1. Prepare the filling.

2. To prepare the dough, in a large mixing bowl, dissolve the yeast and sugar in the hot water. Put in a warm place for 30 minutes to 1 hour, depending on the outside temperature. (In cooler weather, the longer time will be required.) When the yeast rises and brownish foam appears on top, add the flour, egg, and lard, stirring continuously with your hand. Begin kneading. When the mixture becomes cohesive, sprinkle the work surface with flour and place the dough on it. Continue kneading for about 15 minutes, picking up the dough with a scraper and flouring the work surface to prevent sticking. When smooth and elastic, place the dough in a large bowl. Cover with a damp cloth and put in a warm place to rise for 2 to 4 hours, depending on the temperature (longer in cold weather). The dough is ready when it has tripled in size.

3. To prepare the pork buns, heat the oven to 350°F. Cut parchment paper into 12 pieces, 3½ inches square. Remove the dough from the bowl, knead several times, then roll out into a cylinder 12 inches long. Divide into 1-inch pieces. Work with one piece at a time, keeping the others covered with a damp cloth. Roll each piece into a ball and press with your fingers to create a well. Place 1½ tablespoons of the filling into the well, hold a bun in one hand, and with the other turn the bun, pinching it closed. Press firmly to seal. Place the completed bun, sealed end down, on a square of wax paper. Repeat until 12 are done.

   Place all the buns on a cookie sheet, at least 2 inches apart to allow for expansion. Place the buns in a warm place to rise for 1 hour. Using an atomizer, spray each bun lightly with warm water. With a pastry brush, brush each with beaten egg. Bake for 15 to 20 minutes. Halfway through the baking time, turn the cookie sheet around. When the buns are golden brown, remove from the oven and serve. As the buns cool, their crusts will become slightly hard. If you wish them to remain soft, brush lightly with scallion oil immediately after baking.

N O T E :   *These buns can be frozen, after baking, for up to 2 months. To reheat, defrost, bring to room temperature, cover with foil, and place in a 350°F oven for 10 to 15 minutes or until hot.*

MAKES 12

BAKED PORK BUNS

SHRIMP DUMPLINGS

Har Gau

These tiny, pleated dumplings are surely the most famous dim sum *in China. There is no other dumpling in the Cantonese* dim sum *kitchen that is as popular or as ubiquitous. There is no teahouse that does not serve* har gau. *The dough for it and its filling are made in virtually the same way by every chef who fashions* har gau, *yet one finds minute differences. Sometimes the cooked dough covering is thick; sometimes it is like tissue. Sometimes the filling is thick and meaty, sometimes spongy, sometimes light with the crunch of water chestnuts. I expect these differences lie with the hands that fashion these* dim sum. *I make them in the traditional way—the only way—but at times with a minor variation. Occasionally I add extra egg white to the filling, as here, and the result is a lighter-textured filling.*

¼-*pound piece of pork fat*
1½ *cups boiling water*
½ *pound shrimp, shelled, deveined, and diced*

¾ *teaspoon salt*
1 *teaspoon sugar*
1 *medium egg white, beaten*
1½ *tablespoons tapioca flour*
1½ *teaspoons oyster sauce*
¾ *teaspoon sesame oil*
Pinch freshly ground white pepper
¼ *cup peeled and finely diced fresh water chestnuts*
¼ *cup finely sliced white part of scallion*
2 *tablespoons finely diced bamboo shoots*

For the har gau *dough*
1⅓ *cups wheat starch*
⅔ *cup tapioca flour*
¼ *teaspoon salt*
1 *cup plus 3 tablespoons boiling water*
2 *tablespoons liquefied pork fat or peanut oil*

1. To prepare the filling, place the pork fat in the boiling water and boil until fully cooked and translucent, about 30 minutes. Remove, place in a bowl, run cold water over it, and allow to stand for several minutes. Remove, dry with paper towels, and cut 2 tablespoons of fat into ⅛-inch dice. Reserve.

2. Place the shrimp in the bowl of an electric mixer. Start the mixer and add, mixing thoroughly after each ingredient, the salt, sugar, egg white, tapioca flour, oyster sauce, sesame oil, and white pepper. Add the pork fat, water chestnuts, scallion, and bamboo shoots. Combine evenly and thoroughly. Remove the mixture, place in a shallow dish, cover, and refrigerate for 4 hours or overnight.

continued

3. To make the dough, in the bowl of an electric mixer, place the wheat starch, tapioca flour, and salt. Start the mixer and add the boiling water. (If an electric mixer is unavailable, mix by hand in the same order, pouring water with one hand, mixing with a wooden spoon with the other.) Add the lard and mix thoroughly. If the dough is too dry, add 1 teaspoon boiling water. Continue to mix until a ball of dough is formed. Remove from the bowl, knead a few times, and divide into 4 equal pieces. Place each piece in a plastic bag to retain moisture.

4. To prepare the dumplings, before working the dough, oil the work surface. Soak a paper towel in melted pork fat or peanut oil and repeatedly run a cleaver blade across it so that the blade stays oiled. Roll each piece of dough into a cylinder 8 inches long and 1 inch in diameter. Cut into ½-inch pieces. Work with one and keep the others covered with plastic. Roll each into a small ball and press down with your palm to flatten it. Press flatter with the broad side of the oiled cleaver to create a round skin 2½ inches in diameter.

5. To form the dumplings, place 1½ teaspoons of the filling in the center of each round and fold in half, forming a crescent or half moon. Hold the dumpling securely in one hand, then begin to form pleats with the fingers of the other hand. Continue to form small pleats until the dumpling is completely closed. Press the top edge of the dumpling between your thumb and forefinger to seal tightly. Tap the sealed edge lightly with your knuckle to give the dumpling its final shape. Oil a steamer, place the *har gau* into a steamer, cover, and steam for 7 minutes (see steaming, page 64). Turn off the heat and serve.

N O T E : *This recipe will make about 60 skins. I allow for extras to account for initial mistakes when forming dumplings. Once steamed,* har gau *can be frozen for later use. They will keep for 4 to 6 weeks when piled neatly and wrapped in a double layer of plastic wrap and wrapped again in foil. If you intend to freeze them, steam them for only 4 minutes. To reheat, defrost, bring to room temperature, and steam for 3 to 5 minutes.*

M A K E S   A B O U T

4 5   D U M P L I N G S

CHIVE DUMPLINGS

Gau Choi Gau

These dumplings, filled with pungent garlic chives, are a variation from the traditional dim sum *kitchen concocted by the Chiu Chow people in and around Hong Kong. I first ate them one Sunday morning in an old Kowloon teahouse and brought them home to my kitchen.*

7 ounces shrimp, peeled, deveined, and diced

For the marinade
½ teaspoon soy sauce
¾ teaspoon sugar
1 teaspoon sesame oil
1½ teaspoons Chinese white rice wine or gin
1½ teaspoons oyster sauce
1½ teaspoons cornstarch
Pinch freshly ground white pepper

For the sauce
¾ teaspoon soy sauce
1 teaspoon Chinese white rice wine or gin
¾ teaspoon sugar
1½ tablespoons oyster sauce
5 teaspoons cornstarch
Pinch freshly ground white pepper
¼ cup Chicken Stock (page 75)

2 tablespoons White Peppercorn Oil (page 85) or peanut oil
¼ teaspoon salt
2 teaspoons minced fresh ginger
½ pound Chinese (garlic) chives, cut into ⅓-inch pieces
1 recipe Har Gau dough (preceding recipe)

1. Place the shrimp in a bowl with the combined marinade ingredients and allow to rest for 20 minutes. Combine the sauce ingredients and reserve.

2. Heat a wok over high heat for 30 seconds. Add the peppercorn oil, salt, and ginger and coat the wok with it using a spatula. When a wisp of white smoke appears, add the chives. Stir and cook until the chives turn bright green and their fragrance is released, about 1 minute. Add the shrimp and marinade, stir, and cook for 1 minute. Make a well in the mixture, stir the sauce mixture, pour in, and stir. When the sauce begins to thicken, turn off the heat, transfer to a shallow dish, cool, then refrigerate, uncovered, for 4 hours or, covered, overnight.

3. To prepare the dough, roll the *har gau* dough into 2 cylinders, each 12 inches. Cut each into 1-inch segments. Make the round dumpling skins 4 inches in diameter. Form 5 at a time. Dough not being worked should be kept under plastic wrap. Place 1 tablespoon of filling in the center of each skin. Gather the edges together to cover the filling

and squeeze shut, creating a round bundle. Twist the skin at the point of closure and break off the surplus dough. Place the dumpling, sealed side down, in a steamer. Repeat until all 24 dumplings are made. Place in a steamer, cover, and steam (see steaming, page 64) for 7 minutes. Turn off the heat and serve.

N O T E : *The dough will be sufficient to make about 30 skins. I allow this so that mistakes may be discarded. Chive dumplings may not be frozen.*

MAKES 24 DUMPLINGS

COOK AND SELL DUMPLINGS

Siu Mai

*T*hese dumplings, shaped like tiny ket-tles, bear the name "cook and sell," to indicate that once they are made, they are never left unsold. Like other classics of the dim sum *kitchen, they have their own par-ticular dough, a wheat flour–based dough. The dough requires effort and time, but for those who love to work with doughs, it is time well spent. However, those who do not care to knead or shape may use any of a number of ready-made wheat-flour wrappers available in Chinese and Asian markets.*

Since wrappers are used for many dumplings in the dim sum *kitchen, I offer the following: Ready-made dough squares can be bought in 1-pound packages of vary-ing thicknesses, 90 to 100 skins to the pack. I prefer the thinner sort, and commercial makers can manufacture skins thinner than one can make at home.*

Won ton skins come square, about 3½ inches to a side. They are labeled either "skins" or "wrappers." Water dumpling

skins are round, from 3¼ to 3½ inches in diameter. These may also be labeled "Hong Kong style." Dumpling skins are usually round, about 3½ inches in diameter. You may even see a label reading suey gow, *which is phonetic Cantonese for dumpling skins.*

What you need to know is that these are identical. They can be found in the refriger-ated sections of markets, and all brands are about equal in quality. Any left over after using them in recipes may be frozen. They will keep, double-wrapped in plastic, then in foil, for 2 months. To use, defrost and bring to room temperature. Or use the wheat flour dough recipe here.

10 Chinese black mushrooms, soaked in hot water for 30 minutes, rinsed, dried, stems discarded, and caps cut into ¼-inch dice
¾ pound coarsely ground pork

½ pound shrimp, shelled, deveined, and diced

¾ teaspoon salt

2 teaspoons sugar

1 tablespoon peanut butter

1 tablespoon peanut oil

1½ tablespoons oyster sauce

2 tablespoons cornstarch

1 teaspoon sesame oil

Pinch freshly ground white pepper

For the dough (or use 36 dumpling skins)

1¼ cups Pillsbury Best All-Purpose Flour

½ teaspoon baking soda

2 extra-large eggs

2 tablespoons water

⅓ cup cornstarch, for dusting

1. In a large bowl, combine all the ingredients except the the dough ingredients or skins and mix until the consistency is smooth and even. Place in a shallow dish and refrigerate, uncovered, for 4 hours or, covered, overnight.

2. To make the dough, combine the flour and baking soda on a work surface. Make a well in the mixture, add the eggs, and work with your fingers until the eggs have been absorbed. Slowly drizzle in the water, mixing as you do, until thoroughly mixed. Knead the dough for 5 minutes or until it becomes elastic. Set aside, covered with a damp cloth, for 4 hours.

3. When the dough is ready, dust the work surface with cornstarch. Roll out the dough with a rolling pin until you have a sheet ¼ inch thick. Pick up the sheet, dust the surface again with cornstarch, and roll again until the sheet is ⅛ inch thick. Roll the dough around a dowel or long broom handle to prevent tearing. Dust the surface again. Roll the dough again, as thinly as possible, then pick up by rolling again around a dowel. Dust the surface yet again, carefully roll out the sheet, and roll again until the sheet is about 21 inches square. With a dough scraper and a ruler, cut 3½-inch squares from the sheet. As you cut and stack them, sprinkle each with cornstarch to prevent sticking. (The dough is more elastic if made the night before and stored, covered with plastic, in the refrigerator.)

4. To make the dumplings, in the middle of each skin place 4 teaspoons filling. Hold the filling in place with your fingers and, holding the dumpling in the other hand, gradually turn the dumpling, flattening the filling on top. This will result in a basket shape. Pack down the filling, and smooth the top of the dumpling. This will ensure that the dumpling and filling will remain intact during steaming. Tap the dumpling bottom lightly on the work surface to flatten it so it will stand in the steamer. Place the dumplings in a steamer, cover, and steam (see steaming, page 64) for 7 minutes. Turn off the heat and serve.

continued

MAKES 36 DUMPLINGS

SHANGHAI POTSTICKER DUMPLINGS
Wor Tip

*I*t is difficult to say in which city these filled and fried dumplings are more famous, Shanghai or Beijing. In Shanghai, where they are said to have originated, the 2 characters that illustrate them, wor tip, translate as "pot stick." In Beijing they are called chiao-tzu, or "little dumplings"; in the dialect of Guangdong they are gau ji, which is translated as "little dumpling." A bit of folklore suggests that these dumplings were created by accident when one day an imperial chef, making dumplings, forgot them on his stove and they burned on one side. The chef, fearing punishment, admitted no mistake but said rather that he had created a new dish.

As with Siu Mai, these dumplings have their own dough, and for those who enjoy dough work, I suggest it. However, commercial dumpling skins exist for this particular dumpling. Two in particular are quite good, Twin Dragon and Twin Marquis Dumpling Wrappers, Shanghai Style. Both are round. The first brand is sold frozen, the second unfrozen. Both come in 1-pound packages and are made without eggs, which differentiates them from other dumpling skins. Twin Dragon skins, once defrosted, cannot be refrozen. Twin Marquis can be frozen and will keep, wrapped in plastic wrap and foil, for 2 months.

1 quart water
1 teaspoon salt
½ teaspoon baking soda
¾ pound bok choy, *cut into ½-inch pieces, stalks and leaves separated*
10 ounces lean ground pork
1 scallion, trimmed and finely sliced (⅓ cup)
2 teaspoons sugar
1½ teaspoons minced fresh ginger
1½ teaspoons Shao-Hsing wine or dry sherry
1 teaspoon soy sauce
2 teaspoons sesame oil
1 medium egg, beaten
1 tablespoon oyster sauce
2 tablespoons cornstarch
Pinch freshly ground white pepper

For the Shanghai dumpling dough
(or use 36 dumpling skins)
2 cups Gold Medal All-Purpose Flour
⅞ cup cold water

5 tablespoons peanut oil
1 cup cold water

1. To blanch the *bok choy,* place the water, salt, and the baking soda in a pot, cover, and bring to a boil over high heat. Add the *bok choy* stalks, stir, and cook for 1 minute. Add the leaves, stir, and cook for another minute. Turn off the heat, run cold water into the pot, and drain. Squeeze the *bok choy* in paper towels to dry thoroughly.

2. To make the filling, combine the *bok choy,* pork, and all other ingredients except the dough ingredients, peanut oil, and cold water. Mix thoroughly. Place in a shallow dish and refrigerate, uncovered, for 4 hours or, covered, overnight.

3. To make the dough, place the flour in a mixing bowl, make a well in the center, and gradually add the water. Stir with your fingers to make a firm dough. If the dough is too dry, add more water. Knead until smooth and set aside to rest, covered with a damp cloth, for 30 minutes.

4. To make the dumplings, dust the work surface with flour. Divide the dough into 3 equal pieces. Roll each into a cylinder shape 12 inches long. Cut each into 12 equal pieces. Work with 1 piece at a time, keeping the others covered with a damp cloth. With a rolling pin, roll each piece into a 3-inch round. Spread about 1½ teaspoons of filling in the center of the round and wet the edges. Fold into a half moon shape, pleating as you seal it. Press one side of the dumpling against the fleshy part of your hand to flatten it slightly and create the classic shape. Repeat until all the dumplings are made.

5. To pan-fry the dumplings, heat 3 tablespoons of the peanut oil in a large cast-iron skillet over high heat until a wisp of white smoke appears. Place the dumplings in the skillet in 3 rows of 6 dumplings each, touching lightly. Cook for 3 minutes, then pour ½ cup cold water into the skillet and cover. Cook until the water evaporates. Lower the heat and continue to fry until the dumplings are browned on the bottoms and somewhat translucent on top. (Move the skillet back and forth so that the dumplings will not stick and will brown evenly.) Remove from the pan and drain on paper towels. Repeat with the second batch. Turn off the heat, transfer to a heated dish, and serve with Vinegar Soy Sauce (recipe follows).

MAKES 36 DUMPLINGS

VINEGAR SOY SAUCE

See Cho Yau

1 tablespoon dark soy sauce
1 tablespoon soy sauce
1½ tablespoons Chinese white rice
    vinegar or distilled vinegar

1 tablespoon Hot Pepper Oil (page 87)
    or bottled chili oil
1 tablespoon trimmed and finely sliced
    scallion
¼ cup Chicken Stock (page 75)

Combine all the ingredients in a bowl. Mix well, allow to rest for 30 minutes, then place in small individual soy sauce dishes and serve with potstickers.

NOTE: *I prefer that potstickers not be frozen since dumplings containing leafy vegetables often tend to lose shape after defrosting. However, if you opt to freeze them, do so after they have been formed but not cooked. Dust liberally with cornstarch and double-wrap them in plastic wrap, then in foil. They will keep frozen for 2 months. To cook, defrost, bring to room temperature, then pan-fry as directed.*

SOUP DUMPLINGS

Gun Tong Gau

*T*he name of these dumplings from Shanghai translates as "soup inject" or "soup force," the words used to indicate that a child must be forced to take medicine. It is a humorous connotation, but it explains how soup in gelatinous form is placed into the dumplings and becomes liquid soup once they are steamed. When made perfectly, the soup virtually explodes in the mouth when the dumplings are bitten into.

1 cup Chicken Stock (page 75)
1 envelope unflavored gelatin

6 ounces lean ground pork
½ teaspoon salt
1 teaspoon grated fresh ginger
1½ teaspoons sesame oil
1 teaspoon soy sauce
1½ teaspoons Shao-Hsing wine or dry
    sherry
2 tablespoons beaten egg white
1 tablespoon cornstarch
Pinch freshly ground white pepper
3 ounces crabmeat
Lettuce leaves for lining steamers
20 square won ton skins

1. Place the stock in a pot, cover, and bring to a boil over medium heat. Place the gelatin in a bowl. Pour in the boiling stock, stir well, and cool to room temperature. Refrigerate until set, 3 to 4 hours. This may be done a day earlier.

2. To make the filling, in a bowl, combine all other ingredients except the crabmeat, lettuce leaves, and *won ton* skins. Mix thoroughly to blend evenly. Fold in the crabmeat and blend. Place in a shallow dish and refrigerate, uncovered, for 4 hours or, covered, overnight. This too may be done a day earlier.

3. Cut the gelatin into 1-inch square cubes and reserve.

4. To prepare the steamers, line them with washed and dried lettuce leaves and set aside.

5. To make the dumplings, work with one *won ton* wrapper at a time, keeping the others covered with a damp cloth. Keep a bowl of water at hand to moisten the skins. Place 1 heaped tablespoon of filling in the center of each skin. Make an indentation in the filling, place a gelatin cube in it, and cover completely with filling. Wet the edges of the wrapper with fingers dipped in water. Pick up the diagonal corners of the wrapper, bring together, and press. Repeat with the other 2 corners. Pinch along the seams to seal. You will have a plump, square bundle. Repeat until all the dumplings are made. As each is made, place in a prepared steamer to minimize handling of this delicate dumpling.

6. To steam the dumplings, place the steamers in tiers, cover, and steam (see steaming, page 64) for 12 minutes. Turn off the heat. Serve in the traditional way, in the steamer, then transferred with porcelain soupspoons to small bowls. Accompany with the following version of Shanghai's traditional vinegar ginger dip.

MAKES 20 DUMPLINGS

VINEGAR GINGER DIP

Geung See So Jop

5 tablespoons Chinese red rice distilled
  vinegar

3 tablespoons water
3½ tablespoons finely julienned ginger

In a small bowl, combine all the ingredients. It is ready for use immediately.

WATER DUMPLINGS

Soi Gau

This dumpling from the Cantonese tea-house can be served in many ways. Its name, soi gau, *translates as "water dumplings," because it is customarily boiled in water for serving. Often, however, the dumplings are served after steaming on small plates with a bowl of rich chicken soup as an accompaniment. Often, yellow chives find their way into this soup. These dumplings will be used with soup and other ingredients in a recipe to follow, but in this instance I offer them steamed with a dipping sauce.*

For the filling
½ pound lean ground pork
¼ pound shrimp, shelled, deveined, and diced

3 tablespoons diced bamboo shoots
3 tablespoons peeled and diced water chestnuts
1 teaspoon salt
1 teaspoon sugar
¼ cup finely chopped white parts of scallion
1¾ teaspoons sesame oil
Pinch freshly ground white pepper
1½ tablespoons tapioca flour

24 won ton skins
1 large egg, beaten
2 quarts cold water
1 teaspoon salt
1 tablespoon peanut oil

1. Combine all the filling ingredients and mix thoroughly to blend evenly. Place in a shallow dish and refrigerate for 4 hours, uncovered, or overnight, covered.

2. To prepare the skins, cut each into a round 3 inches in diameter. Cover with a damp cloth.

3. To make the dumplings, work with one skin at a time, keeping the others covered with a damp cloth. Place 1 heaped tablespoon of filling in the center of the skin. With a butter knife, brush the edges of the skin with egg. Fold over the filling into a half moon shape and press together along the curved edge with thumb and forefinger to seal. Continue until all the dumplings are made.

4. Place the water, salt, and peanut oil in a pot and bring to a boil over high heat. Place the water dumplings in the pot and cook for 5 to 7 minutes, depending on the intensity of your heat source, until the dumplings are translucent and the filling can be seen

through the skin. It is best, the first time, to remove one dumpling and cut it to see if the filling has cooked. Later you will not need to do this. Turn off the heat, transfer the dumplings to a bowl, and serve with Ginger Soy Sauce (recipe follows).

MAKES 24 DUMPLINGS

GINGER SOY SAUCE
Geung Chung Yau

1 tablespoon dark soy sauce or
    mushroom soy sauce
1 tablespoon soy sauce
1 teaspoon sugar
1 teaspoon Scallion Oil (page 82) or
    peanut oil
3 tablespoons Chicken Stock (page 75)

½ tablespoon sesame oil
1½ tablespoons trimmed and finely
    sliced fresh ginger
1½ tablespoons sliced white part of
    scallion in ½-inch pieces
Pinch freshly ground white pepper

Combine all the ingredients in a bowl and mix well. Allow to rest for 30 minutes, then serve in individual small soy sauce dishes.

A FEAST OF DUMPLINGS AND NOODLES

Soi Gau Dan Mien Dai Wui

*T*his is a rich collaboration of 2 aspects of the Chinese "noodle foods" tradition, dumplings and noodles. It is my creation. The name I give it, dai wui, *means a coming together of many great things or a large meeting. Noodles and dumplings are rarely, if ever, served in this manner. I serve it in a large, communal bowl, with the noodles as the bed, the water dumplings arranged on top, and wedges of Shanghai* bok choy *as the last topping ingredient. Much of the work is done a day in advance of the day it is to be served. The effect is worth the effort, for it is a grand noodle dish indeed.*

1 recipe Water Dumplings (page 382)
14 cups cold water
4 teaspoons salt
½ teaspoon baking soda
One ½-inch-thick slice fresh ginger, lightly smashed
1½ pounds Shanghai bok choy, washed thoroughly, dried, leaves trimmed at ends to a point like spears, then stalks cut in half lengthwise
6 cups Chicken Stock (page 75)
2 tablespoons Scallion Oil (page 82) or peanut oil
1½ pounds fresh Chinese egg noodles

1. Make the water dumplings and reserve at room temperature.

2. To blanch the *bok choy,* place 6 cups of the water, 2 teaspoons of the salt, the baking soda, and the slice of ginger in a pot, cover, and bring to a boil over high heat. Add the *bok choy,* immerse, and blanch for 1 minute. Turn off the heat, run cold water into the pot, and drain. Repeat, drain thoroughly, and reserve.

3. Boil the stock and noodles simultaneously in 2 separate pots. Place the stock in the first pot over high heat. Place the remaining 2 quarts water and remaining 2 teaspoons salt in the second over high heat. Cover the stock and, when it comes to a boil, add the *bok choy* and return to a boil. Add the scallion oil, stir in well, and return to a boil. Add the water dumplings, stir, and return to a boil. Turn off the heat.

4. The second pot should be boiling. Add the noodles, stir and separate, and cook for 1½ minutes, until al dente. Turn off the heat, run cold water into the pot, and drain the noodles.

5. Place the noodles in a large serving bowl. Add some soup and toss to loosen and separate them. Pour in the soup with the water dumplings. Arrange the *bok choy* on top of the dumplings and noodles and serve in the bowl.

MAKES 6 TO 8 SERVINGS

NOODLES
MIEN ◆

*A*t the risk of irking the spirit of Marco Polo, let me point out that noodles have been an important aspect of the Chinese kitchen for more than 2,000 years, specifically since the Han dynasty, which began in 206 B.C., about 1,500 years before Marco Polo journeyed through the China he knew as Cathay to what is today Beijing. Whether the Chinese invented tortellini, fettuccine, or ravioli I do not know, but they had been boiling, frying, and steaming noodles for many centuries before Marco Polo. There are various sorts of noodles in China, which I detail here, and with them I add corresponding Italian pasta numbers, not only to indicate the sizes but also to specify which pastas may be used as better-than-adequate substitutes for fresh Chinese noodles. ◆

EGG NOODLES ◆

*M*ade from wheat flour, eggs, water, and, occasionally, salt, they are available in several forms:

FRESH • These are found in the refrigerated compartments of Chinese groceries and markets, in plastic sacks, weighing either 12 or 16 ounces. They are pale yellow and come in various sizes, the most common resembling capellini #11, vermicelli #10, spaghetti #8, and linguine # 17. They will keep refrigerated for two days or frozen for a month.

PREBOILED • Though these are considered fresh, they are actually preboiled (the size of spaghetti #8) and are ready to use for cold noodle dishes. There are also very thin "fresh" egg noodles, the size of capellini #11, that have also been boiled and are specifically meant to be used in pan-fried noodle dishes. Both of these are labeled "precooked." These precooked noodles are usually coated lightly with vegetable oil to prevent sticking.

DRIED • These come in plastic or cellophane packages of 12 or 16 ounces and in boxes ranging from 2 to 5 pounds. Their sizes are similar to those of fresh noodles. Dried noodles will keep at room temperature, sealed, for three to six months.

PREFRIED • These egg noodles (about spaghetti #6 and #8 sizes) come packed in plastic, inside cardboard boxes—two 6-ounce packs per box. Although they appear dried, they have been fried for a few seconds and bent into the circular-shaped bundles before they stiffened. They must be boiled to soften before using. Generally regarded as the best quality, they are often referred to as "longevity noodles."

EGGLESS NOODLES ◆

Made from wheat flour and water only. Occasionally salt is added.

FRESH • These are usually soft, cream colored, and packaged in 1-pound plastic sacks. Made in two sizes, spaghetti #8 and linguine #17, they are found in refrigerated cases and are often labeled, in Chinese characters, "Shanghai noodles." They will keep refrigerated for two days or frozen for a month.

DRIED • Also of a creamy white color, these noodles come in 12-ounce packages. They range in sizes from very thin capellini #11 to linguine #17 and are often labeled "creamy Chinese-style noodles" or "Shanghai Chinese-style noodles." They will keep, sealed, at room temperature for three to six months.

RICE NOODLES ◆

Translucent, made from rice flour and water, they come in several forms:

FRESH • There are three kinds of fresh rice noodles. They come in wide sheets that may be cut to any size: in the size of spaghetti #8, packed in plastic; and as hand-rolled small tubular noodles. The latter are rarely seen in shops, usually being reserved by noodle manufacturers for restaurants only, but I did wish to note them.

DRIED • These come in various sizes, from as thin as capellini #11 in size through linguine #17 to fettuccine and even wider to as much as ½ inch.

CELLOPHANE NOODLES ◆

These are noodlelike bean threads made from the starch of mung beans. Although they are called noodles, in China they are rarely, if ever, used as the major component of any dish but rather are added to other dishes for texture and appearance.

WON TON

Won Ton

*O*f infinite variety is the *won ton.*
Though often looked on as a
dumpling, it is actually a filled noodle, very
much like Italian tortellini. Once made, it
can be boiled, fried, steamed, or put into
soup. It can be an hors d'oeuvre, a first
course, or an ingredient in a larger scheme.
Traditionally it is filled with a pork mix-
ture, but I have made it with veal with
great success.

For the filling
¾ pound lean ground pork
¼ pound shrimp, shelled, deveined, and
*   finely diced*
1½ cups trimmed and finely chopped
*   scallions*
1½ teaspoons minced garlic

4 fresh water chestnuts, peeled and
*   finely diced*
1 tablespoon Chinese white rice wine or
*   gin mixed with 1½ teaspoons ginger*
*   juice (page 23)*
1 teaspoon salt
1 teaspoon sugar
1 teaspoon soy sauce
1 teaspoon sesame oil
1 tablespoon oyster sauce
Pinch freshly ground white pepper
2½ tablespoons cornstarch

36 won ton skins
3 quarts water
1 tablespoon salt
1 tablespoon peanut oil

1. In a large bowl, mix together the filling ingredients thoroughly to blend evenly. Place in a shallow dish and refrigerate, uncovered, for 4 hours or, covered, overnight.

2. To make the *won ton*, the skins should be at room temperature. Work with one at a time, keeping the others under a damp towel. Keep a bowl of water at hand to wet the edges of the skins. Place 1 tablespoon of filling in the *won ton* skin, wet the edges, fold in half, and seal the edges. Wet the folded corners, not the sealed corners, and draw the ends together to create a bowlike dumpling, like a tortellini. Repeat until 36 *won ton* are made. As each is made, place on a cookie sheet dusted with cornstarch.

3. Place the water, salt, and peanut oil in a pot, cover, and bring to a boil over high heat. Add the *won ton*, stir, and cook for about 8 minutes, until the *won ton* are translucent and the filling can be seen through the skin. Turn off the heat, run cold water into the pot, and drain. Repeat and drain thoroughly. Place on wax paper to dry thoroughly.

   The *won ton* may be eaten exactly as they have been cooked, or try one of these variations:

PAN-FRIED WON TON (JIN WON TON) • Place 3 tablespoons peanut oil in a flat skillet and heat the oil until a wisp of white smoke appears. Place the *won ton* in the pan and fry until brown on both sides. Turn off the heat and transfer to paper towels to drain.

DEEP-FRIED WON TON (JAH WON TON) • Place 5 cups peanut oil in a wok, heat the oil to 350°F, and add a lightly smashed 1-inch slice of ginger and a peeled clove of garlic. Add the *won ton* and fry, turning, until the *won ton* are golden brown. Turn off the heat and transfer to paper towels to drain.

WON TON SOUP (WON TON TONG) • Bring 6 cups Chicken Stock (page 75) to a boil, add the *won ton*, 6 to a person, and return the soup to a boil. Add a sprinkling of 3 tablespoons Chinese (garlic) chives, turn off the heat, transfer to a heated tureen, and serve.

MAKES 4 SERVINGS

WON TON AND NOODLE SOUP

Won Ton *Mien*

*T*his is a classic Cantonese specialty. I remember as a young girl, when I was visiting my aunt in Guangzhou, every evening we would hear the noodle man coming through the streets, hitting bamboo sticks together. We knew from the clack of the bamboo who he was, and we would race down to order bowls of won ton *and noodles.*

2½ *cups Chicken Stock (page 75)*

6 *cups water*

16 **won ton** *(preceding recipe)*

1 *pound fresh Chinese egg noodles (size of #11 capellini)*

2 *tablespoons yellow chives*

1. Boil the stock and water in separate pots. Add the *won ton* to the boiling stock, return to a boil, and turn off the heat. Add the noodles to the boiling water, boil for 1 minute, stirring to loosen, and cook until al dente. Turn off the heat, run cold water into the pot, and drain thoroughly.

2. Divide the noodles into 4 individual bowls. Add the soup and 4 *won ton* to each bowl. Sprinkle with yellow chives and serve.

MAKES 4 SERVINGS

PAN-FRIED NOODLES
WITH CHICKEN

Gai See Chau Mien

*T*his traditional noodle dish from
Shanghai is often referred to as dou-
ble-fried noodles, *or* leung mien wong,
which translates as "yellow both sides,"
because they are fried to a golden brown on
both sides. They can be topped with a variety
of foods, beef, pork, and seafood mixtures.
There is a version of this dish in Guangzhou
in which noodles are fried but soft. In Hong
Kong it is made quite like the Shanghai
version. Outside of China the Shanghai version is the norm. I prefer making it with
chicken because of its lightness.

2 quarts water
½ pound fine fresh egg noodles
 (like #11 capellini)

For the marinade
1 teaspoon sesame oil
¾ teaspoon sugar
½ teaspoon salt
½ teaspoon Chinese white rice vinegar
 or distilled vinegar
1 teaspoon Shao-Hsing wine or dry
 sherry
¾ teaspoon cornstarch
½ teaspoon soy sauce
Pinch freshly ground white pepper

6 ounces chicken cutlet, julienned

For the sauce
2 teaspoons dark soy sauce
1 teaspoon sugar
1 teaspoon sesame oil
1 teaspoon Chinese white rice vinegar
 or distilled vinegar
1 teaspoon Shao-Hsing wine or dry
 sherry
Pinch freshly ground white pepper
1½ teaspoons cornstarch
1 cup Chicken Stock (page 75)

6 tablespoons peanut oil
1 teaspoon minced fresh ginger
1 teaspoon minced garlic
½ cup julienned snow peas, strings and
 ends removed and cut into diagonal
 julienne
3 fresh water chestnuts, peeled and cut
 into julienne
¼ cup julienned bamboo shoots
2 scallions, trimmed and cut into
 1½-inch pieces, and the white parts
 quartered lengthwise

1. Place the water in a pot, cover, and bring to a boil over high heat. Add the noodles, stir, and cook for 10 seconds. Turn off the heat, run cold water into the pot, and drain. Repeat the rinsing. Drain for 2 hours, turning occasionally, until completely dry.

2. In a large bowl, combine the marinade ingredients. Add the chicken and allow to rest for at least 30 minutes. In another bowl, combine the sauce ingredients and reserve.

3. Heat a cast-iron skillet over high heat for 40 seconds and add 3 tablespoons of the peanut oil. When a wisp of white smoke appears, place the noodles in the skillet in an even layer, covering the entire bottom. Fry for 2 minutes, moving the pan about on the burner to ensure that the noodles brown evenly. Slide the noodle mass onto a large dish and place another dish, inverted, over it. Turn the dishes over so the noodles are upside down and slide the noodles back into the skillet. (The uncooked side should now be at the bottom.) Fry for 2 minutes. If a bit more oil is needed, pour an additional tablespoon into the pan, but only if necessary.

4. As the noodles are cooking, heat a wok over high heat for 40 seconds. Add the remaining 2 tablespoons peanut oil and coat the wok with it using a spatula. When a wisp of white smoke appears, add the ginger and stir briefly. Add the garlic and stir. When the garlic browns, add the chicken and marinade, spread in a thin layer, and cook for 2 minutes. Turn over and mix well. Add all the vegetables and stir. When the vegetables have softened slightly, make a well in the mixture, stir the sauce mixture, and pour in. Stir well and cook until the sauce thickens. Turn off the heat.

5. Place the fried noodles on a heated platter. Pour the contents of the wok atop them. Cut the covered noodles into 4 equal pie-shaped wedges and serve.

MAKES 4 SERVINGS

BOILED NOODLES WITH GROUND PORK AND BEAN SAUCE

Jah Jeung Mien

These eggless noodles, made with only wheat flour and water, are a tradition of many centuries in Beijing, where the staple grain was wheat rather than rice. They are as popular in Shanghai. The preserved horse beans with chili with which they are combined impart the flavor of China's North as well.

For the sauce
⅓ cup Chicken Stock (page 75)
1 tablespoon double dark soy sauce, dark soy sauce, or mushroom soy sauce
1½ teaspoons sesame oil
1 tablespoon Shao-Hsing wine or dry sherry
1 teaspoon Chinese white rice vinegar or distilled vinegar

2½ teaspoons sugar
⅛ teaspoon salt
Pinch freshly ground white pepper

6 cups water
6 ounces mung bean sprouts, washed and drained
½ pound fresh eggless noodles (size of #17 linguine)
1½ tablespoons peanut oil
1 teaspoon minced garlic
¼ pound lean ground pork
1½ tablespoons preserved horse beans with chili or Chili Sauce (page 88)
1 teaspoon Chili Sauce
¼ cup trimmed and finely sliced scallion
1½ tablespoons minced red bell pepper

1. In a small bowl, mix together the sauce ingredients and reserve.

2. To blanch the bean sprouts, place the 6 cups water in a pot, cover, and bring to a boil over high heat. Place the sprouts in a mesh strainer and lower into the boiling water for 10 seconds. Transfer to a bowl of ice water.

3. Return the water to a boil. Add the noodles, stir, and separate with chopsticks. Cook until al dente, about 1 minute. Turn off the heat, run cold water into the pot, and drain. Repeat the rinsing and drain thoroughly.

4. Remove the sprouts from the ice water and drain thoroughly.

5. Heat the wok over high heat for 30 seconds. Add the peanut oil and coat the wok with it using a spatula. When a wisp of white smoke appears, add the garlic and stir until lightly browned, about 30 seconds. Add the pork and stir well to loosen. Add the horse beans, chili sauce, and scallion and cook, stirring, until the pork is no longer pink, 1 to 1½ minutes. Stir the sauce, pour in, mix well, and cook for 1 minute. Turn off the heat.

6. Arrange the bean sprouts around the edge of a platter. Place the noodles in the center of the platters and pour the pork mixture over the noodles. Sprinkle with the minced red pepper and serve.

MAKES 4 SERVINGS

SOFT-FRIED NOODLES WITH SCALLOPS

Yiu Cheuh Bon Mien

This dish of noodles is the creation of Master Chef Chan Wing in Hong Kong. A half century ago he traveled about China investigating its many regional styles of cooking, and he was as famous for taking various dishes and re-creating them in his Guangzhou restaurant as he was for inventing new ones. In his writings and recipes he does not specify the origin of this noodle dish, which leads me to believe that it was his, and it is a fact in recent years it began appearing on the menus of many Hong Kong restaurants. Here is his dish, offered in his honor.

6 cups cold water

1 teaspoon salt

¾ pound fresh fine egg noodles (size of #11 capellini)

3 tablespoons Shallot Oil (page 84) or peanut oil

2 Steamed Dry Scallops (page 80), shredded by hand

2 tablespoons julienned fresh ginger

2 tablespoons oyster sauce

⅓ cup julienned white part of scallion

1 teaspoon sugar

1 teaspoon soy sauce

½ cup mung bean sprouts, ends removed (3 ounces)

1. Place the water and salt in a pot, cover, and bring to a boil over high heat. Add the noodles, loosening with chopsticks, and cook for 20 seconds. Turn off the heat, run cold water into the pot, and drain. Repeat the rinsing. Drain for 1½ hours. With kitchen shears, cut the noodles into 1-inch-long pieces.

2. Heat a wok over high heat for 40 seconds. Add 2 tablespoons of the shallot oil and coat the wok with it using a spatula. When a wisp of white smoke appears, add the noodles and cook for 1 minute, stirring continuously. Lower the heat to medium and cook for

2 minutes, until very hot. Add the scallops, stir, and cook for 1 minute. Add the ginger, mix well, and cook for 2 minutes. Add the oyster sauce, stir, and cook for 1 minute. If the mixture is too dry, add the remaining tablespoon of shallot oil. Add the scallion and stir. Add the sugar and stir well. Add the soy sauce and mix well. Add the bean sprouts, stir, and cook for 2 minutes. Turn off the heat, transfer to a heated platter, and serve.

MAKES 4 SERVINGS

FRESH RICE NOODLES WITH BEEF AND BLACK BEANS

See Jiu Chau Hor

*T*his snow-white noodle, sold in sheets that have already been cooked by steam, is a favorite in the Cantonese dim sum *teahouses*, where it is eaten most often steamed to glistening white and folded around shrimp, pork, or beef. But fresh rice noodles need not be limited to steamed dim sum. *Cut into more recognizable noodle shapes, and stir-fried with those pungent, fermented black beans, for contrast, it is striking as well as fine tasting.*

For the marinade
½ *teaspoon salt*
1 *teaspoon sugar*
½ *teaspoon ginger juice (page 23) mixed with 2 teaspoons Chinese white rice wine or gin*
1½ *tablespoons oyster sauce*

½ *teaspoon dark soy sauce*
½ *teaspoon sesame oil*
1½ *teaspoons cornstarch*
Pinch freshly ground white pepper

6 *ounces London broil, thinly sliced across the grain*
2½ *tablespoons peanut oil*
One ½-*inch-thick slice fresh ginger, lightly smashed*
2 *teaspoons minced garlic*
2 *tablespoons fermented black beans, washed well 2 or 3 times and drained well*
¾ *cup thinly sliced red bell pepper*
¾ *cup thinly sliced green bell pepper*
1 *pound fresh rice noodle, cut into pieces 2 inches long by ¾ inch wide*

1. Combine the marinade ingredients in a large bowl. Add the beef and allow to rest for at least 30 minutes.

2. Heat a wok over high heat for 30 seconds. Add 1½ tablespoons of the peanut oil and coat the wok with it using a spatula. When a wisp of white smoke appears, add the ginger and stir briefly. Add the garlic and black beans, stir, and cook until their fragrance is released, about 1 minute. Add the beef and marinade, spread in a thin layer, cook for 30 seconds, and turn over. Add the peppers, stir, and cook for 30 seconds. Add the rice noodles and stir well. If too dry, add the remaining tablespoon of peanut oil. Cook for 3 to 4 minutes, until the mixture is very hot. Turn off the heat, transfer to a heated platter, and serve.

MAKES 4 SERVINGS

LONGEVITY NOODLES

Cheung Sau Jai Mien

The one constant reminder of long life in the Chinese diet is the noodle. The noodle is symbolic to such an extent that it often transcends its nutrition. Simply because of its length, the noodle represents longevity, and noodles are served at all occasions that relate to long life—birthdays, the Lunar New Year, anniversaries—and great care is taken at such feasts not to cut them. The longer the better. The Chinese even believe that noodles are easier to digest than bread, though both are warming foods. In fact, in winter, it is deemed more health-ful to eat a bowl of warming noodles than a cold sandwich. Wheat is a cool grain, a yin food, but once processed into noodles, partic-ularly with eggs, it becomes warm. Longevity noodles are essentially a warming preparation; stir-frying, a warming cook-ing process. This "warmth" is slightly leav-ened with three cooling vegetables and a neutral sauce to prevent it from becoming overly yang or too hot for the body. A plate of longevity.

10 cups cold water
5 ounces soybean sprouts, washed and
　drained
1½ teaspoons salt
½ pound egg noodles, prefried
　"longevity noodles"

For the sauce
3½ teaspoons soy sauce
½ teaspoon sesame oil
¼ cup Chicken Stock (page 75)

1 tablespoon peanut oil
One ¼-inch-thick slice fresh ginger,
　lightly smashed
¼ pound snow peas, strings removed
3 fresh large water chestnuts, peeled
　and cut into ⅛-inch slices

1. Place the water in a large pot, cover, and bring to a boil over high heat. Place the soy-bean sprouts in a mesh strainer and lower into the boiling water for 15 seconds. Remove the strainer, run cold water through the sprouts, drain, and reserve.

2. Add the salt to the pot and bring the water back to a boil. Add the noodles, loosening with chopsticks, and cook for 1 minute. Turn off the heat, run cold water into the pot, and drain. Repeat the rinsing and drain the noodles thoroughly, using chopsticks to loosen them. Reserve.

3. Combine the sauce ingredients in a small bowl and reserve.

4. Heat a wok over high heat for 45 seconds. Add the peanut oil and coat the wok with it using a spatula. When a wisp of white smoke appears, add the ginger and cook for 10 seconds. Add the snow peas, stir, and cook for 1 minute or until the snow peas turn bright green. Add the water chestnuts, stir, and cook for 30 seconds. Add the reserved sprouts, stir well, and cook for 1 minute. Stir the sauce mixture, pour into the wok, and bring to a boil. Add the noodles and cook, stirring well to combine all ingredients, until the sauce is absorbed, about 1½ minutes. Turn off the heat, transfer to a heated platter, and serve.

MAKES 4 SERVINGS

Transplanting Chinese Food
in the West

中國食品風行全球

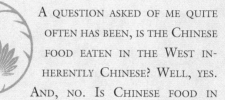

A QUESTION ASKED OF ME QUITE OFTEN HAS BEEN, IS THE CHINESE FOOD EATEN IN THE WEST INHERENTLY CHINESE? WELL, YES. AND, NO. IS CHINESE FOOD IN NEW YORK TRULY CHINESE? IN LONDON? IN PARIS? IN MOST WESTERN COUNTRIES, PARTICULARLY IN EUROPE, WHAT ARE OFFERED AS EXAMPLES OF CHINESE COOKING ARE HYBRIDS, THOUGH THEY ARE CALLED CHINESE. This is true as well in the United States, though often what is served is referred to as Chinese-American. As with other hyphenated foods in the larger Western culinary experience there is, to be sure, some relation to the original, though often that is tenuous. In far too many instances, unfortunately for the Chinese kitchen, many gastronomic offspring of what originally were forced marriages of economic and social circumstance have come to be considered Chinese through and through, though decidedly they are not.

Let me relate a personal experience, one I have recounted before but that nonetheless bears retelling. It concerns my first encounter with what often passes for Chinese food in the West but is not. It occurred shortly after I was married and came to the United States to live. My American in-laws, in an effort to please me, took me to their favorite neighborhood Chinese restaurant in New York, introduced me to its owner, and ordered what they had always ordered on Friday nights—shrimp *chow mein* and egg *foo yung*. The first was a thick gelatinous mound of white and pale green vegetable stalks and onions suspended in a white sauce that resembled mucilage; the second a large omelet, with the elastic consistency of an overdone pancake, folded over several times and covered with a viscous brown sauce.

My in-laws were pleased with the presentation. I was less so and called for the restaurant proprietor. When he arrived at our table, I told him that I had just arrived from Hong Kong, and I asked him, in Chinese, if he had anything to eat that was Chinese, truly Chinese. His eyes widened. What would I like? he wished to know. "*Char siu chau choi sum,*" I suggested, saying that a simple dish, in this case thinly sliced roasted pork quickly stir-fried with those tiny, leafy stalked vegetables, *choi sum,* or flowering cabbage, would be fine. And it was fine when he brought it. Cooked with just a touch of oil, the leaves and stalks were green and crisp, the pork faintly sweet, familiar to my palate. I was to discover over and over again that food thought to be Chinese by most Americans was not. What was served in those restaurants, identified often as Chinese-American, often went by names with which I was familiar and often approximated preparations I had known and eaten in China but actually were corruptions of traditional dishes. I tasted "*chow mein*" and wondered what I was eating, for it bore no relation to the noodle and vegetable preparations I knew as *chau mien.* I met the egg roll, a clumsy, overly large version of the elegant spring roll. I recall asking for *chop suey* and being presented with a dish of mixed vegetables, celery, cauliflower, and broccoli instead of the classic dish of pork innards, finely diced and stir-fried with vegetables. Another stranger. I ate what was called lemon chicken, breaded and fried with a thick, syruplike lemon sauce poured over it. I encountered the fortune cookie, unknown anywhere in China, and ice cream balls made "Chinese" by sticking tiny paper parasols in them.

Later I was to meet up with another aspect of cooking called "Chinese," cooking that did not and does not exist in China, though it is quite often labeled "Mandarin cuisine." Then along came restaurants calling themselves "Sichuan" or "Hunan," which doused what they had cooked with peppered oil or bottled hot sauces or sprinkled diced dried chilies on their food. Still later entrepreneurs termed themselves "Shanghai" or "Hakka," "Peking" or "Chiu Chow," yet cooked dishes that were in no way related to these important schools of the Chinese kitchen, fanciful dishes called by such names as "Hong Kong Steak" or "Sichuan *Won Tons*." To satisfy all American tastes and demands, these restaurants simply had new signs made from time to time. In all of these permutations the overriding taste was sweetness, sugary sweetness, which these restaurants believed was what the American palate desired. The so-called Chinese food I saw being eaten was flavored with sweet duck sauce, sopped with soy sauce, thickened with excessive cornstarch.

I found these false representations of Chinese dishes most depressing, yet at the same time I saw people eating them with apparent enjoyment. Why? How had such food evolved? I repeatedly asked myself these questions as I compared these dishes with the authentic foods of China. I believe wholeheartedly that few would argue with the premise that the food of China, no matter how it is presented, whether of doubtful authenticity, is widely accepted in the West. There is no city, no town, no village, it seems, that does not have a Chinese restaurant, eat in or take out, usually a narrow storefront eating place with booths along its walls. "Let's have Chinese tonight" has become part of America's lexicon.

The story of how the foods of China, most of them Cantonese, came to America is not complicated, nor is the evolution of these foods into the peculiar forms they have taken. America's first taste of the foods of China was brought by men from southern China who came to the West Coast a century and a half ago. They came either to dig for riches in those "mountains of gold" around San Francisco or to lay down the transcontinental railroad beds, ties, and rails. Similarly adventurous Chinese migrated afar to Europe and elsewhere in Asia, even to Africa, seeking fortunes. The vast majority of them were from Guangdong province, the region around Canton, or Guangzhou, and they came without women, from a society in which women did the family cooking. Initially their aim was to acquire wealth as quickly as possible and return to China, yet they stayed in great numbers, despite many decades of discrimination, including the government's shameful exclusionary acts.

Out of necessity, some of these men became cooks for their brother workers just as others became launderers. Out of such services arose two occupations through which Chinese immigrants traditionally gained footholds, and handholds, into American society—large consolidated laundries and restaurants in which transplanted Chinese could eat foods familiar to them and in which, early on, adventuresome Americans could try something new.

But the cooking of these men was secondhand and was further altered by the absence of familiar ingredients and the need to prepare large meals even more quickly than usual. Vegetables such as *bok choy,* fresh water chestnuts, long beans, taro, dark green Chinese broccoli, green and yellow chives, bean sprouts, Chinese celery, all commonplace in China, were not to be found. In China, meat had always meant pork. Chicken was a luxury, beef a rarity. Lamb was the meat of western China, virtually unknown to these Cantonese men, who in any event preferred fish.

So these male cooks had to improvise. Available were spinach and Swiss chard, carrots, scallions and onions, peppers, cucumbers, and squashes, all familiar. There were Iceberg lettuces that replace the romainelike lettuces of China. The more bland celery of California replaced the small stalks, with more flavor, that they had been used to. String beans replaced long beans; potatoes, a minor ingredient in the Chinese diet, became more important, often replacing taro.

These vegetables were rapidly stir-fried in great quantities for the workers. In Canton, where vegetables had been blanched quickly, there had been no need for vast amounts of cornstarch to bind foods together. These cooks had no time for such niceties as blanching, so vegetables became watery as they cooked, and to soak up that water while simultaneously giving bulk to the vegetables, they added more cornstarch.

Fine and delicate dishes such as *mah gu gai pin,* slices of chicken with fresh mushrooms, became the coarse and quickly tossed-together chicken pieces and mushrooms from cans, and even its pronunciation changed so that to the Western tongue trying to speak Chinese it became *moo goo gai pan.* Slim, fingerlike spring rolls became wrist-size egg rolls. Lightly scrambled eggs with baby shrimp, a dish known in China as *fu yung don,* became *egg foo yung.* And a masterpiece of a noodle dish, *yuk see chau mien,* a preparation in which a cake of crisply fried noodles is topped with stir-fried pork and vegetables, became the formless, and ubiquitous, *chow mein.*

Cornstarch added for bulk and viscosity. Excessive sugar and too much salt. Later monosodium glutamate, a cheap chemically derived salt used to temporarily heighten flavors. These became the norms, the bases for the heavier cooking devised out of necessity by this womanless society of Chinese immigrants, and it became the cooking in the first Chinese restaurants in America and elsewhere in the West to which Chinese men had migrated. In China's traditional cookery, sugar, salt, and cornstarch are used most sparingly, and among good chefs who prize their ingredients, no MSG is used at all. These traditions were discarded, and what the West came to regard as Chinese was this heavy kitchen without finesse or care. Even later Chinese immigrants who became restaurateurs and knew the true cooking of their homeland were affected. They presumed that this cooking was what Westerners wanted, so they adapted and cooked it.

Yet when the women came to join their fathers, husbands, brothers, and sons, cooking at home remained true to tradition and the practices of many centuries. And as more and more Chinese came to the West, and demanded the foods of their homeland, produce was cultivated for them. Chinese vegetables and ginger were grown, turtles were raised, carp and bass were farmed, and shrimp, squid, and abalone made their way into Chinese and Asian markets. Varieties of tea were imported as were all manner of pickled, preserved, and dried foods and spices, for to the Chinese immigrants food was essential if a group was to retain its unique authenticity. In China pork had been bred for leanness, but in the United States it was fatty and marbled. A demand for the meat to which they were accustomed led to changes in breeding. Today in places where large numbers of Chinese have settled, in New York and San Francisco, in Vancouver and Toronto, virtually anything that can be and is grown in China is also grown in North America.

The care taken in the home to cook true Chinese food did not, and to a great extent does not, apply to most Chinese restaurants, and this remains the case in those Chinese restaurants frequented by most Westerners. A dish of intensive flavors, fermented black beans and garlic, with peppers and a bit of beef, became pepper steak, a somewhat bland mixture of strips of beef and peppers. And sweet-and-sour pork is not the piquant dish of south China and Hong Kong, but rather fried pork chunks in a sweet sauce, heavy with cornstarch and even containing canned pineapple chunks, a preparation unknown in China. Light and airy egg drop soup became another victim of cornstarch. Spareribs and barbecued pork, restaurant offerings in China and rarely cooked in the home, were thought to be enhanced by the addition of red dyes.

Unfortunately, most Chinese cookery books published for Westerners were and are based on this poor restaurant cooking. Thus bad habits, second-rate recipes, and interpretations at variance with tradition have proliferated and have become dogma. It was perfectly fine, we were told, to add MSG to everything. It was equally fine, for example, to substitute cooking wine for Shao-Hsing. Never should this be done. A dry sherry may be substituted, but note that the perfume, the *ho heung* of a dish, will be different. In these cookery books we are told that prosciutto can replace salted Yunnan ham, that apples can be used instead of water chestnuts, that tortillas may be eaten instead of the traditional pancakes for Peking Duck. If an odd Chinese vegetable is not available, they say, simply add celery and more celery. To be sure, you may, but what you are cooking will essentially change.

Luckily these days virtually anything available to cooks in China is available in the West, due of course to the influx of Chinese and of ethnic Chinese from other Asian countries. To some extent this has helped restaurants become better and true. It is possible to eat authentic food, perfectly prepared in restaurants, particularly in cities and places to which large numbers of Chinese have migrated. You need no longer endure the poor, pseudo-Chinese food of the take-out counter.

What follows is a selection of recipes, the names of which will probably be familiar, the tastes of which may surprise you, for they are true Chinese originals, the pure ancestors of what became Western Chinese restaurant clichés.

EGG DROP SOUP

Don Far Tong

*I*n China this simple soup, don far tong, *which translates as "egg flowers soup," is made from the very freshest of ingredients— good stock, fresh eggs, freshly pulled scallions. Transplanted into the West, it has become dull, thick with cornstarch, often with eggs tossed in so that they become lumpy. What follows is the true* don far tong, *in which the beaten egg, poured slowly, becomes, as the name suggests, like flowers.*

6 cups Chicken Stock (page 75)
Salt to taste
6 eggs at room temperature, beaten
½ cup trimmed and thinly sliced
  scallion

Pour the stock into a large pot, cover, and bring to a boil over high heat. Add the salt to taste. Gradually pour in the beaten eggs, whisking constantly with a large cooking fork until soft, silken threads of egg form, about 1 minute. Turn off the heat, pour the soup into a heated tureen, softly mound the scallion in the center of the soup, and serve in individual bowls.

MAKES 6 SERVINGS

EGG ROLLS

Don Geun

*T*his is a true creation of Chinese cooking gone Western. There is no such
thing in China as the egg roll or, to give it a
name, don geun. There are, however,
spring rolls, more like fingers than wrists,
delicate rolls filled with bean sprouts and
scallions, shrimp and pork, encased in
paper-thin wrappers. Egg rolls are filled
usually with a bewildering mélange of
whatever is handy, though largely of julienned cabbage. It is possible, however, to create a fine egg roll. Here it is, and I follow it
with a recipe for a traditional, true-to-
China spring roll. In the West, egg rolls are
usually served with sweet duck sauce. These
rolls are better without a sauce.

One 1-inch-thick slice fresh ginger
1 large garlic clove, peeled
1½ tablespoons sugar
2½ teaspoons salt
¼ pound large shrimp, shelled and
    deveined
One 2-pound head green cabbage,
    tough outer leaves discarded, halved,
    cored, and finely chopped (6 cups)
1 medium onion, cut into ¼-inch dice
2 large celery stalks, cut into ¼-inch
    dice
¼ pound Barbecued Pork (page 124),
    cut into ¼-inch dice
12 egg roll wrappers
1 large egg, beaten
1 quart peanut oil

1. Fill a large saucepan with water, add the ginger, garlic, sugar, and salt, and bring to a
   boil over high heat. Add the shrimp and cook until they curl and turn pink, about 1
   minute. Turn off the heat, discard the ginger and garlic, and remove the shrimp to a
   strainer to drain. Cool slightly, then cut into ¼-inch dice and reserve.

2. Bring the water in the saucepan back to a boil over high heat. Add the cabbage, onion,
   and celery and cook until the cabbage turns bright green, about 1½ minutes. Turn off
   the heat, remove the vegetables, and drain in a colander. Cool and press the mixture
   down to remove excess water.

3. In a large bowl, combine the shrimp and barbecued pork. Add the vegetables and mix
   well to make the filling. Divide the filling into 12 equal portions.

4. To make the egg rolls, place a wrapper on a work surface with one corner facing you.
   Keep the remaining wrappers covered with plastic wrap. Place a portion of the filling in
   a horizontal line across the bottom third of the wrapper and fold the tip closest to you
   over the filling toward the center. Brush the side tips of the wrapper with beaten egg
   and fold into the center. Brush lightly with egg and roll up the wrapper from the bot-

tom. Brush the tip with egg and fold toward you to create a cylinder. Repeat with all the wrappers.

5. Heat a wok over high heat for 45 seconds. Add the peanut oil and heat to 350°F. Place 4 egg rolls in the oil and fry, turning frequently with chopsticks or tongs, until golden brown, 4 to 5 minutes. Remove with a Chinese strainer and drain over a bowl. Repeat until all 12 are fried. Serve immediately.

MAKES 12 EGG ROLLS

SPRING ROLLS

Chun Geun

These are the spring rolls found in southern China in the Sun Tak region where I grew up. We looked forward to them, particularly in the spring, when bean sprouts are at their best—thus their name, for chun *means "spring." Take note of what happened to the true spring roll when it was transplanted.*

For the shrimp marinade
⅛ teaspoon salt
⅛ teaspoon soy sauce
⅛ teaspoon sugar

For the pork marinade
½ teaspoon salt
¼ teaspoon soy sauce

3 ounces shrimp, shelled, deveined, and julienned
2 ounces lean boneless pork, cut into shreds
5 cups peanut oil
3 scallions, trimmed and cut into 1½-inch pieces, white parts julienned
1 pound mung bean sprouts, ends removed
12 spring roll wrappers
1 large egg, beaten

1. In 2 separate bowls, combine the ingredients for both marinades. Place the shrimp in its marinade and allow to rest for at least 30 minutes. Do the same for pork in its marinade.

2. To make the filling, heat the wok over high heat for 30 seconds. Add 1 tablespoon peanut oil and coat the wok with it using a spatula. When a wisp of white smoke appears, add the pork and its marinade. Stir and cook for 20 seconds. Add the shrimp and its marinade, stir, and cook for 10 seconds. Add the scallions, stir, and cook for 30

seconds. Add the bean sprouts, stir, and cook for 1 minute, until the sprouts wilt. Turn off the heat, transfer the mixture to a strainer, and drain well.

3. To make the spring rolls, work with one wrapper at a time, keeping the others covered with plastic wrap. Place a wrapper on the work surface with a corner facing you. Place 2 tablespoons filling in a line across one end of the wrapper. Dip your fingers in the beaten egg and wet the edges of the wrapper. Fold over the tip and continue to roll, folding in the sides as you do. Keep rubbing the beaten egg at the edges to ensure the spring roll will be sealed. Repeat until all the spring rolls are made.

4. Place the remaining oil in a wok and heat to 325°F. Place 4 spring rolls in the oil at a time and fry, turning, until they are golden brown, 3 to 4 minutes. Remove, drain on paper towels, and keep warm. Repeat until all 12 are done. Turn off the heat and serve immediately.

MAKES 12 SPRING ROLLS

FRESH MUSHROOMS WITH SLICED CHICKEN

Mah Gu Gai Pin

This delicate preparation is what became the somewhat coarse dish generally known as "moo goo gai pan." The names sound a bit alike, the changes due of course to the Westernization of unfamiliar Chinese words, yet even the latter name sounds heavier, less fine. Its name in Chinese translates simply as "fresh mushrooms cooked with sliced chicken."

For the marinade
1 tablespoon finely grated fresh ginger
1½ teaspoons sesame oil
1 teaspoon Chinese white rice wine or gin
½ teaspoon sugar

¼ teaspoon salt
1½ teaspoons oyster sauce
½ teaspoon soy sauce
1 teaspoon cornstarch
Pinch freshly ground white pepper

½ pound skinless, boneless chicken breast, cut into 2- by 1½-inch strips

For the sauce
2 teaspoons oyster sauce
½ teaspoon sugar
1 teaspoon soy sauce
½ teaspoon sesame oil
2 teaspoons cornstarch
Pinch freshly ground white pepper

5 tablespoons Chicken Stock (page 75)

3½ tablespoons peanut oil

1 tablespoon minced fresh ginger

¼ teaspoon salt

¼ pound small button mushrooms, stems removed and caps cut into ¼-inch slices

6 ounces snow peas, strings removed and cut into 1- by 1½-inch pieces

¼ cup bamboo shoots, cut into 1- by 1½-inch pieces

4 water chestnuts, peeled and cut into ¼-inch slices

1 tablespoon minced garlic

1 tablespoon Chinese white rice wine or gin

1. In a large bowl, combine the marinade ingredients. Add the chicken and allow to rest for at least 30 minutes. Reserve. In a small bowl, combine the sauce ingredients and reserve.

2. Heat a wok over high heat for 30 seconds. Add 2 tablespoons of the peanut oil and coat the wok with it using a spatula. When a wisp of white smoke appears, add the ginger and salt and stir for 10 seconds. Add the mushrooms and stir for 10 seconds. Add the snow peas, bamboo shoots, and water chestnuts and cook, stirring, for 2 minutes. Turn off the heat, transfer the mixture to a bowl, and reserve. Wipe off the wok and spatula with paper towels.

3. Heat the wok over high heat for 20 seconds. Add the remaining peanut oil and coat the wok with it using the spatula. When a wisp of white smoke appears, add the garlic. When it begins to brown, add the chicken and marinade. Spread in a thin layer and cook for 2 minutes. Turn the chicken over and cook for 1 more minute. Drizzle the wine down the sides of the wok, stir into the chicken, and cook until the chicken is cooked through, about 1 more minute. Add the reserved vegetables and cook, stirring, for 2 minutes. Make a well in the mixture, stir the sauce mixture, and pour in. Stir well and cook until the sauce bubbles and thickens, about 30 seconds. Turn off the heat, transfer to a heated platter, and serve.

MAKES 6 SERVINGS

CHAU MIEN
Fried Noodles

The dish that goes by the name of chow mein *bears no resemblance to true* chau mien, *which simply are pan-fried noodles with one's choice of stir-fried toppings of vegetables, meats, or seafood. My husband tells me the* chow mein *of his youth was eaten in this fashion: A layer of cooked rice was put onto a plate, crisp fried noodles were mounded on the rice, then a rather glutinous mixture of cooked vegetables, mostly celery and cabbage, went on the noodles. Then it was determined whether one wished chicken, pork, beef, or shrimp* chow mein, *and a sprinkling of whichever was chosen went on top of that, all of those covered with a liberal pouring of soy sauce. Even the dish's name was changed*—mien, *pronounced "mean," became* mein, *pronounced "main." My goodness! What follows is the true dish known in China as* chau mien.

For the marinade
1½ teaspoons oyster sauce
1 teaspoon sesame oil
½ teaspoon Chinese white rice wine
  or gin
1½ teaspoons finely grated
  fresh ginger
½ teaspoon soy sauce
½ teaspoon sugar
½ teaspoon cornstarch

⅛ teaspoon salt
Pinch freshly ground white pepper

¼ pound boneless pork loin, cut into
  julienne 2 inches by ¼ inch

For the sauce
1 cup Chicken Stock (page 75)
1½ tablespoons cornstarch
1 tablespoon oyster sauce
1 teaspoon sesame oil
½ teaspoon dark soy sauce
1 teaspoon sugar
⅛ teaspoon salt
Pinch freshly ground white pepper

6 cups cold water
½ pound fresh Chinese egg noodles
  (size of #11 capellini)
5 tablespoons peanut oil
1½ tablespoons minced fresh ginger
1½ teaspoons minced garlic
⅓ cup Chinese black mushrooms,
  soaked in hot water for 30 minutes,
  squeezed dry, stems discarded, and
  caps cut into thin strips
1½ cups yellow chives or garlic chives
  cut into ½-inch pieces
1 cup trimmed fresh mung bean
  sprouts

1. In a large bowl, combine the marinade ingredients. Add the pork strips, allow to rest for at least 30 minutes, and reserve. In a small bowl, combine the sauce ingredients and reserve.

2. Place the water in a pot, cover, and bring to a boil over high heat. Add the noodles, stirring with chopsticks to loosen. Cook for 20 seconds. Turn off the heat and drain the noodles under cold water through a colander. Allow to cool. Separate and allow to dry thoroughly for 2 hours, tossing occasionally.

3. Heat a large cast-iron skillet over high heat for at least 2 minutes. Add 2 tablespoons of the peanut oil. When a wisp of white smoke appears, place the noodles in the skillet and spread in an even layer. Cook until browned on the bottom, 3 to 4 minutes. Turn the noodles over by sliding them onto a plate and inverting them over the skillet. Add 1 more tablespoon of peanut oil to the skillet. Cook until brown on the other side, about 3 minutes. Turn off the heat, remove the browned noodles, cover, and keep warm.

4. Heat a wok over high heat for 40 seconds, add the remaining 2 tablespoons peanut oil, and coat the wok with it using a spatula. When a wisp of white smoke appears, add the ginger and stir briefly. Add the garlic and stir. Add the pork and marinade, spreading in an even layer, and cook for 30 seconds. Add the mushrooms and stir to mix. Make a well in the mixture, stir the sauce mixture, pour in, and bring to a boil. Stir in the chives and bean sprouts and cook, stirring, until hot, 2 to 3 minutes. Turn off the heat. Place the reserved noodles on a heated platter, spoon the pork mixture over them, and serve.

MAKES 6 SERVINGS

PEPPER STEAK

See Jiu Chau Ngau

This is another dish transformed when it made its way to the West. Traditionally in China it was known as see jiu chau ngau, *which not only describes it—black beans and peppers stir-fried with beef—but gives proper emphasis to the black beans and peppers, the dominant ingredients. In its transition the beef became the center of the dish, all other ingredients parts of a supporting cast. This is the true black beans and peppers stir-fried with beef.*

For the marinade
2 teaspoons oyster sauce
1 teaspoon sesame oil
½ teaspoon minced fresh ginger
1½ teaspoons Shao-Hsing wine or dry sherry
¾ teaspoon dark soy sauce or mushroom soy sauce
½ teaspoon salt
1 teaspoon sugar
1½ teaspoons cornstarch
Pinch freshly ground white pepper

¾ pound London broil

For the sauce
2 teaspoons oyster sauce
1 teaspoon sesame oil
1 teaspoon dark soy sauce
1 teaspoon sugar
2 teaspoons cornstarch
Pinch freshly ground white pepper
½ cup Chicken Stock (page 75)

2 large garlic cloves, smashed with the flat of a cleaver and skin removed
2 tablespoons fermented black beans, washed, rinsed, and drained
3 tablespoons peanut oil
One ½-inch-thick slice fresh ginger, peeled
1 medium green bell pepper, cut into 2- by 1-inch pieces
1 medium red bell pepper, cut into 2- by 1-inch pieces

1. In a large bowl, combine the marinade ingredients. Add the beef, allow to rest for at least 30 minutes, and reserve. In a small bowl, combine the sauce ingredients and reserve. Place the smashed garlic and black beans in a bowl and, with the handle of the cleaver, mash into a paste, or use a mortar and pestle. Reserve.

2. Heat a wok over high heat for 30 seconds. Add 1 tablespoon of the peanut oil and coat the wok with it using a spatula. When a wisp of white smoke appears, add the ginger and stir until the ginger turns light brown. Add the peppers and cook, stirring, for 1

minute. Turn off the heat, transfer the peppers to a small bowl, and set aside. Wipe off the wok and spatula with paper towels.

3. Heat the wok over high heat for 30 seconds. Add the remaining 2 tablespoons peanut oil and coat the wok with it using the spatula. When a wisp of white smoke appears, add the garlic–black bean paste and stir. When the garlic turns light brown, add the beef and marinade and spread in a thin layer. Cook for 1 minute, tipping the wok from side to side for even cooking. Turn the beef over and cook for 30 seconds, until the beef changes color. Add the reserved peppers and cook, stirring, for 2 minutes. Make a well in the mixture, stir the sauce mixture, and pour in. Stir and mix well until the sauce thickens and turns dark brown, about 1½ minutes. Turn off the heat, transfer to a heated platter, and serve with cooked rice.

MAKES 6 SERVINGS

STEAK KEW

Ngau Yuk Kau

*I*n China, when we ate beef in a stir-fry, it was usually thinly sliced. Never would we use chunks or cubes of beef. In fact, beef with bok choy *is called* bok choy chau ngau yuk, *which as is customary gives emphasis to the* bok choy. *This dish, Steak Kew, its name probably a mispronunciation of* steak cubed, *is a pure invention of the transplanted Chinese restaurant in America, created no doubt to make use of the good beef to be found in the United States. In fact, at its best, Steak Kew, during its most popular time three decades ago, was made only with filet mignon. The dish is rare these days, but as a good-tasting relic of this earlier Chinese restaurant cooking, it is worthy of note.*

For the sauce
2 tablespoons oyster sauce
2 teaspoons double dark soy sauce, dark soy sauce, or mushroom soy sauce
1 teaspoon sesame oil

1½ teaspoons Chinese white rice wine or gin
1½ teaspoons sugar
¼ teaspoon salt
1½ tablespoons cornstarch
Pinch freshly ground white pepper
⅓ cup Chicken Stock (page 75)

6 cups cold water
One ½-inch-thick slice fresh ginger, lightly smashed
2 teaspoons salt
½ teaspoon baking soda (optional)
1 pound bok choy, stalks and leaves separated and cut into ½-inch pieces
2 cups peanut oil
¾ pound lean filet mignon, cut into 1-inch cubes
2½ teaspoons minced fresh ginger
2 teaspoons minced garlic
1 tablespoon Chinese white rice wine or gin

1. In a small bowl, combine the sauce ingredients and reserve.

2. To water-blanch the *bok choy*, place the water, ginger, salt, and baking soda in a pot. Cover and bring to a boil over high heat. Add the *bok choy* stems, stir, and blanch for 30 seconds. Add the leaves, stir, and blanch for an additional 30 seconds. Turn off the heat, run cold water into the pot, and drain. Repeat the rinsing, drain thoroughly, and reserve.

3. To oil-blanch the beef, heat a wok over high heat for 1 minute. Add the peanut oil and heat to 325°F. Add the beef, stir to loosen, and blanch for 45 seconds to 1 minute or until the beef changes color. Turn off the heat, remove the beef cubes with a Chinese

strainer, and drain over a bowl. (If well-done beef is desired, blanch for another 30 seconds.) Pour off all but 1½ tablespoons of the oil from the wok.

4. Heat the wok over high heat for 20 seconds. When a wisp of white smoke appears, add the ginger and stir briefly. Add the garlic, stir, and cook until the garlic releases its fragrance, about 30 seconds. Add the beef and cook, stirring, for 1 minute. Drizzle the wine down the edges of the wok and mix well. Add the *bok choy* and cook, stirring, for 1½ minutes. Make a well in the mixture, stir the sauce mixture, pour in, stir, and cook until the sauce thickens, about 1 minute. Turn off the heat, transfer to a heated platter, and serve with cooked rice.

MAKES 4 TO 6 SERVINGS

EGG FU YUNG

Fu Yung Don

True egg fu yung *is a preparation of elegance. It is not the "egg* foo young*" found all too often in hyphenated Chinese restaurants, a somewhat flexible, hard egg omelet pancake, served folded over itself and doused with a viscous brown sauce. This is another salient example of how a dish, though bearing a similar name, has little or no relation to its antecedent. What follows is the classic egg* fu yung. *Baby shrimp is more traditional but is sold only in inconvenient,* very large bags. It's also not of the best quality, so I suggest using medium shrimp.

8 large fresh eggs at room temperature
1 cup peanut oil
¼ teaspoon salt
Pinch freshly ground white pepper
¼ cup finely sliced green part of scallion
½ pound medium shrimp, shelled, deveined, and cut in half

1. In a large bowl, whisk the eggs briskly with 1½ tablespoons of the peanut oil until frothy. Mix in the salt and white pepper and stir in the scallions. Reserve.

2. Heat a wok over high heat for 30 seconds, add the remaining oil, and heat to 350°F. Add the shrimp and fry, turning frequently, until they curl and turn pink, about 30 seconds. Turn off the heat, remove the shrimp with a Chinese strainer, and drain and cool slightly. Pour the oil from the wok into a bowl and wipe the wok clean with paper towels.

3. Add the shrimp to the beaten eggs and stir in gently. Heat the wok over high heat for 20 seconds, return 2 tablespoons of the peanut oil to the wok, and coat the wok with it using a spatula. When a wisp of white smoke appears, stir the eggs briefly once again and pour into the wok. Cook the eggs, stirring gently with the spatula until the eggs are softly scrambled but not runny, about 3 minutes. Turn off the heat, transfer the eggs to a heated platter, and serve, sprinkled with the scallions.

MAKES 4 SERVINGS

SWEET-AND-SOUR PORK
Wu Loh Yuk

*S*weet-and-sour pork is ubiquitous, found everywhere that transplanted Chinese restaurants are. It is, I have found, a particular favorite among Americans. But the sweet-and-sour pork they dote on is a coarse evolution of a dish with balance and complexity as it exists in China to a cloying, overly sweet dish, with a gluelike sauce in which canned pineapple is a prime ingredient. This is sweet-and-sour pork as it is traditionally prepared in China, at its best in Hong Kong.

For the batter
¾ cup all-purpose flour
¾ cup cornstarch
1½ tablespoons baking powder
¼ teaspoon salt
1 cup cold water
1½ teaspoons peanut oil

For the sauce
¾ cup Chinese white rice vinegar or distilled vinegar

½ teaspoon salt
6 tablespoons tomato sauce
1 tablespoon double dark soy sauce, dark soy sauce, or mushroom soy sauce
¾ cup sugar
1 tablespoon cornstarch

1 quart peanut oil, for deep-frying
¾ pound boneless pork loin, cut into 1-inch cubes
2 tablespoons all-purpose flour, for dusting
1 large garlic clove, minced
4 scallions, white parts only, sliced into ½-inch pieces on a diagonal
½ cup bamboo shoots cut into ¾- by 1-inch pieces
1 small red bell pepper, cut into ¾-inch cubes
½ cup Shallot Pickles (page 102)

1. To make the batter, in a large bowl, combine the flour, cornstarch, baking powder, and salt. Slowly add the cold water, stirring with a fork until the batter is smooth. Stir in the peanut oil until thoroughly combined. The batter should have the smooth consistency of pancake batter. If too thick, add up to 2 tablespoons of water, 1 tablespoon at a time. Set aside.

2. In a small bowl, combine the sauce ingredients and reserve.

3. Preheat the oven to 250°F. Heat a wok over high heat for 40 seconds. Add the peanut oil and heat to between 350°F and 375°F. Meanwhile, in a shallow dish, dust the pork cubes in the flour. Working with one third of the pork cubes at a time, place them in the batter, then with tongs place them in the oil. Fry for 5 seconds, then turn over. Fry for 3 minutes, turning several times, until light brown. With a slotted spoon, transfer the pork to a strainer to drain over a bowl. Skim off any bits of batter and residue in the oil. Repeat with the other cubes until all are fried.

4. Return the oil to 350°F. Place all the pork cubes back in the oil and fry until golden brown, about 3 minutes. Turn off the heat. With a slotted spoon, transfer the pork to a warm platter and place in the heated oven.

5. Pour off the oil from the wok and return to high heat. When a wisp of white smoke appears, add the garlic and stir briefly. Add the scallions and stir for 30 seconds. Add the bamboo shoots, red pepper, and shallot pickles and cook, stirring, for 30 seconds. Stir the sauce mixture, pour into the wok, and continue to stir. Bring the sauce to a boil and turn off the heat. Remove the pork from the oven, pour the sauce over the pork, and serve with cooked rice.

MAKES 6 SERVINGS

GENERAL TSO'S CHICKEN

Tso Chung Gai

*S*urely this is one of the most well known of all of the dishes of the transplanted Chinese restaurant. How it became the dish of a general is one of those questions with many answers. I have seen it referred to on menus not only as the chicken of one General Tso but of General Tsao, General Taso, General Toa, General Cho, General Gau, General Ching, General Kung, and General Tseng, not to forget General Ciao, who, it may be assumed, might have been an Italian general in the service of the emperor (a latter-day Marco Polo, perhaps?). Whichever the general, the dish is a constant, always some version of a classic recipe from Hunan known usually as jeung bau gai kau, *a simple description of the dish as boned chunks of chicken, customarily thigh and leg meat, cooked with sauce over high heat. It later became known as* chung tong gai, *which translates as "ancestor meeting place chicken." This, on transplanted restaurant menus, became either, in English, some general or, in Chinese characters,* Tso chung gai, *or* Tso chung tong gai, *which translate as "Tso ancestor meeting place chicken." The question of course is: Is or was there ever a General Tso? Well, apparently there was, in Hunan, in the nineteenth century, and he was by all reports a fine general with a good appetite. It is not certain whether the dish was actually named for him or simply evolved. As for myself, I see nothing wrong with naming a dish for a general. As a matter of fact, in* my family we had two illustrious generals, General Chan of the air force and General Yim of the army. As far as I know, there is no chicken named for them. Why not? As a matter of fact, why not name a chicken dish for the female General Mulan or, as she is known in China, General Far Mu Lan, who never, it is said, lost a battle or retreated? Perhaps because it would not, given its connotation, be proper to attach a general's name to chicken.

Unfortunately, the dish is quite often done poorly in hyphenated Chinese restaurants, most often with scrap or small leftover pieces of chicken reconstituted into chunks, or even ground chicken formed into chunks. What follows is the proper dish, as it is cooked in Hunan.

1 large egg, beaten
¼ teaspoon salt
Pinch freshly ground white pepper
2 tablespoons cornstarch
2 large chicken legs with thighs, each
*   ¾ pound, boned and skinned, fat*
*   and membranes removed, and cut*
*   into 1-inch cubes (1 pound)*

For the sauce
2½ tablespoons double dark soy sauce,
*   dark soy sauce, or mushroom soy*
*   sauce*
1 teaspoon minced garlic
1 tablespoon minced fresh ginger
2 tablespoons hoisin sauce

3 teaspoons sugar

3 teaspoons Chinese white rice vinegar or distilled vinegar

1½ teaspoons Shao-Hsing wine or dry sherry

3½ cups peanut oil

1 tablespoon cornstarch, for dusting

8 small dried hot chili peppers

¼ cup finely sliced scallion

1. In a bowl, mix together the egg, salt, white pepper, and 2 tablespoons cornstarch. Add the chicken cubes, mix to coat, and marinate for at least 15 minutes. In a small bowl, combine the sauce ingredients and reserve.

2. Heat a wok over high heat for 40 seconds. Add the peanut oil and heat to 350°F. With tongs, remove the chicken cubes individually, dust with 1 tablespoon cornstarch, and place in the oil. Deep-fry for 1½ to 2 minutes, until the chicken is browned and crisp. Turn off the heat. Remove the chicken with a Chinese strainer and drain over a bowl. Pour off all but 1½ tablespoons of the oil from the wok.

3. Heat the wok over high heat for 20 seconds. When a wisp of white smoke appears, add the chilies and stir for 15 seconds. Add the scallion and stir for 30 seconds. Add the chicken and cook, stirring, for 1 minute. Stir the sauce mixture, pour into the wok, stir well, and cook until the chicken cubes are completely coated with sauce, about 1½ minutes. Turn off the heat, transfer to a heated dish, and serve.

MAKES 4 TO 6 SERVINGS

Some Things Sweet

蜡味

THE DAYS LEADING UP TO THE LUNAR NEW YEAR WERE EXCITING TIMES FOR ME AS A YOUNG GIRL IN SUN TAK, FOR I WAS ALLOWED TO MAKE SOME OF THE SWEETS WITH WHICH OUR FAMILY TRADITIONALLY CELEBRATED THIS MOST IMPORTANT FESTIVAL OF ANY YEAR. At home with my mother, and at the house of Ah Paw, my grandmother, I was entrusted with fashioning *jin dui*, sweet popped rice dumplings, a happy task that I had begun to do when I was only six years old.

Jin dui were and are to this day made with rice kernels in their husks, popped by dry-roasting them in a wok. They are then glazed with a sugar syrup, wrapped in glutinous rice dough, and, while still pliable, shaped into balls or into animal or fruit shapes such as goldfish, ducks, and pomegranates (I was very good at the last two), then deep-fried. A proper day to make them would be chosen by my mother and by Ah Paw, after consulting her *tung sing*, her book of propitious days. At Ah Paw's house she would supervise the making of these special New Year sweets. Her cooks, my two aunts, her daughters-in-law, the two wives of my uncle, her son, and I prepared them in the salon, not in the kitchen.

I enjoyed going to Ah Paw's house to cook, and I would race there, but only if I had finished what I had to do at home, to be with her, with my aunts, and enjoy the company of my cousin, Jeung Yeun. Dai Cum Mo, the name by which I called my uncle's first wife, was a soft-spoken woman, quiet and retiring, as I remember, who had not managed to bear any children, thus giving way to Sai Cum Mo, the second wife, who had borne three boys. Two of them, sadly, had died in infancy, and the third, Jeung Yeun, was well known in our family for a special reason. He had, as a baby, been given a girl's name, Ah Mui, and he was dressed as a girl, because my grandmother's *feng shui* adviser had recommended that he be disguised so that the evil gods would not take him as they had the other two boys. Jeung Yeun was older than me by eight years, but I liked hearing the stories about him as a baby, and I loved to talk with him, because he was to me very much like another big brother, and I spent a lot of time with him at Ah Paw's house when I was not in the kitchen.

We would fashion the *jin dui*, fry them, and reserve them for New Year's Day. We would also make small cakes of yeast-fermented rice flour, water, and sugarcane sugar and steam them. These were called *lin goh* and were considered very lucky for New Year's because their name sounded like the phrase *lin ngao*, which translates as "every year there will be abundance." These were offered, along with *jin dui*, candied watermelon rind and coconut, sugar-glazed lotus seeds (or *lin jee*, or "every year there will be sons") and lotus root slices, and cups of tea, to all of our friends who would visit our houses on New Year's Day.

China has many other sweets, many of them, as those mentioned, connected to traditional feasts, many not. China has a long history of sweets, basically sweetened and candied foods, both vegetables and fruits, sweetened drinks and sweet candies, but no tradition of desserts as the West would understand the term. Sweets were to be enjoyed in tea shops, with tea, or at home, with cups of tea, a custom by which guests are welcomed. It is true that often special sweet soups or puddings are included in meals, often near the end of a meal, before the traditional conclusion of fresh fruit, but they are not to be considered desserts in the Western sense. It is only in recent years and because of the Western presence and influences in Shanghai, Canton, and Hong Kong that the concept of cakes and desserts has arisen, particularly in Shanghai, where, even years ago, it was not at all unusual for Western-style bakery shops to flourish to such an extent that huge multitiered wedding cakes became customary additions to traditional Chinese weddings.

China's first sweets were most probably foods sweetened with honey and sugarcane sugar. In the Han dynasty excavations that yielded so much information about the history of the Chinese kitchen, evidence of honey in this period 200 years B.C. was common, and in later writings honey is mentioned often, even to the extent of noting how superior the "white" honey of the North of China, including Tibet, was to the honey of the South. Perhaps China's first "cakes" were made in the North, mixtures of honey and milk, perhaps the milk of yaks, and were

referred to as *stone honey*. Sugarcane was known to be used widely in Han times as well, and these cakes were subsequently made with sugarcane sugar. Later foods were sweetened with maltose, or malt sugar. Yet it was in these Han times that the custom began of having fresh fruit at the end of a meal, a tradition that has continued for 2,500 years.

Fruit, so plentiful in the South, was regarded as a luxury in the North and at the imperial court and was carried up from the South, fresh when possible, dried when not, often preserved in honey or sugared. China's South was rich with fruits, generically known as *guoh*, and melons, called *guah*, and it was a sign of wealth or position in the North when one was able to have a selection of fruits with one's social meal, one's banquet. To have fruit preserved in honey was a custom in the North, one perhaps of necessity when fresh fruit could not be obtained. These fruits, all native to China, which later spread to the rest of the world, include oranges, tangerines, and the grapefruitlike pomelo; kumquats, loquats, and persimmons; pears, rough-skinned, known as *sha li*, or sand pears, quite familiar these days, and crisp, hard pears, *hseuh li*, or snow pears; peaches, apricots, plums, and the *mei* of Guangzhou, small plums, more like apricots; cherries, wild strawberries, and the Chinese dates called jujubes. In southern China longans, litchis, coconut palms, banana trees, and the fruit known as the kiwi, which the Chinese called *sheep peach* because of its fuzzy skin, all grew wild. Lemons and limes came into China from the West, as did guavas, papayas, avocados, and pineapples and were embraced into the great southern Chinese fruit orchard.

Thus there was a rich fruit harvest

indeed, and all of it was usually picked and served hard, commonly before the fruits were fully ripened, which is the way the Chinese preferred them. Thus they were more sour than Westerners would be used to and would be considered unripe. They were even salted and pickled while green and unripe and eaten as condiments. Sweet drinks were made from the branches of the raisin tree and from hawthorn bush berries.

Sugar beets came into China from the Near East during the Tang dynasty, and it was in the same period, during the seventh century, that Yangzhou became the sugar refining and manufacturing center of China. During the Song dynasty, 200 years later, Hangzhou became famous for its cakes and pastries. Cakes based on both wheat and rice flour doughs were of two sorts, steamed and fried, and included savories as well as sweets, all of which were served in Hangzhou's many restaurants and teahouses. In the South of China the custom arose of having moon cakes to celebrate the mid-autumn Moon Festival. These baked cakes, with sweetened fillings of lotus seed paste or red bean paste and ground nuts, and containing salted duck eggs, in addition to being eaten are often given as gifts. The more egg yolks a cake contains, the greater the honor. For four duck eggs to be encased in a moon cake is to have the best one can give. In the spring the annual Dragon Boat races of China's South were and are honored with other traditional "cakes," glutinous rice dumplings, either plain, savory, or sweet, wrapped in small bundles of bamboo leaves and boiled.

Traditions begun in those times have lasted. Enjoyed throughout China to this day are round glutinous rice dough dumplings, *tong yeun,* filled either with sweet bean paste, with sweetened black sesame seed paste or a paste of sesame seeds, crushed peanut, and sugar. These are boiled and served in sweet soups called *tong soi,* which translate simply as "soup of sugar water." They may be hot soups or cool, clear or purees, but they share a common base of water in which sugar has been dissolved. Several sweet soups, traditions of the South, have over the years moved north. These include *fan seuh tong soi,* diced sweet potatoes cooked and softened in a sweet soup, as well as a similar preparation, *wu tao tong soi,* made with diced taro root. I remember the workers in the fields around my home in Sun Tak being given these *tong soi* for breakfast because of the energy they provided.

There is even a sweet in which a dough made of both rice and wheat flours is steamed, rolled into sausage shapes, and sliced, then added to a *tong soi.* And in Shanghai glutinous rice balls are boiled, then combined with wine rice and sugar into a sweet, often with fresh eggs broken into it. Other sweet soups had cloud ears added to them, in addition to various fruits, nuts, herbs, even the blossoms of such as lotus, cassia, or chrysanthemum flowers. To the Chinese these are not desserts but rather tonics and are not only tasty but considered advantageous to one's health simply because of the energy imparted by the sugar. They help, it is said, to make the body *ching bo leung,* or "clean and clear." These examples illustrate the basic nature of Chinese sweets, which is sweetened food rather than pure confection. Other popular sweets include candied watermelon rind and ginger, walnuts and pecans, and lotus seeds and roots, as mentioned earlier.

The peanut came into China during the

latter part of the Ming dynasty, in the six- teenth century, and it was an import of pro- found significance. The Chinese call the peanut *lo hua sheng,* or "dropping flower gives birth," to describe how the peanut plant pro- duces a pod that plants itself by going into the soil. The crushed peanut, used in many sweets, is also the source of China's most highly regarded cooking oil, the oil of choice in all parts of the country except in the North, where rapeseed oil is used. Ground peanuts make their way into pastries, cakes, and can- dies as sweet fillings and are the bases for sweet soups. I recall as a child *far sun tong,* a peanut brittle we would either make or buy from our sweet shop in Sun Tak.

We would buy as well *chau mai bang,* rice kernels dry-fried until they popped, then spread into a thin layer with a thick sugar syrup. When this hardened, we would cut it into squares and serve it as a sweet rice cake. My family also loved *sot kei mah,* pieces of wheat dough, cut into strips, deep-fried, then placed in a glaze of honey and sugar, all of it poured into a shallow pan and smoothed out. Once it was cooled, we cut it into sweet squares. And there were our *dan san,* or "honey bow," deep-fried pieces of wheat flour dough in the shapes of bows, then glazed with honey and sugar—another of our sweet treats that we enjoyed with our tea.

From writings we learn that the favorite sweets of the Ching dynasty, China's last, included eggs steamed with sugar and grated almonds; and in Sichuan during that period, a tradition arose of a custardlike pudding made from walnut paste and sugar. It was during this dynasty that another sweet food tradition was born, the candies for which Suzhou is famed to this day. These semihard candies,

usually fashioned into geometric shapes, are variously flavored with black sesame seeds, dates, plums, walnuts, almonds, dates, lico- rice, even roses and jasmine flowers, and sweetened with sugar. Embossed on them are symbols and words wishing long life and good fortune. These sweets are believed by the peo- ple of Suzhou, and elsewhere in China, to help in lowering the body's temperature, a belief that was strengthened when, it is said, the dowager empress of the Ching dynasty, Ci Xi, ate their candy.

The story told in that beautiful city of gardens and canals is that at one point in her reign, Empress Ci Xi took ill and sought the services of a highly regarded doctor from Suzhou. He came to Beijing with all manner of gifts, among them some of these candies. The empress ate them, became stimulated, and she decreed them to be a tribute of health. The candies came to be thought of not only as treats but as sweet medicine and are so regarded to this day.

Also well known for their sweets and sweet soups are the people of Fujian, particu- larly in the main city of Fuzhou. This eastern seacoast province, with Guangdong below it and the Shanghai region above, has sent its people and many of these dishes to Singapore and elsewhere in Southeast Asia. They make long, deep-fried crullerlike pastries they call, in their dialect, *hua tzu,* and sweet custardlike puddings, *bah bau yu nee,* made from mashed yams, pumpkins, and lotus seeds. To celebrate the onset of the Lunar New Year they make *dong zhi,* glutinous rice dumplings filled with ground peanuts, soybeans, and brown sugar that are added to sweet soups; and *mung gau,* chunks of rice flour and sugar dough steamed in banana leaves. As they steam they expand,

and to the people of Fujian they symbolize that things will become ever bigger and better.

Elegant sweet soups were quite the norm in the imperial court of Beijing—soups made with fruits, either fresh or cooked and pureed; others with those pearls fashioned from tapioca flour cooked with coconut milk and rock sugar; still others with red beans, lotus seeds, ginkgo nuts, and mung beans, all of these sweet. A court luxury was bird's nest soup, in which the strands of the nest of the swift, really saliva, were cooked in water with sugar and ginseng. Another was a sweet soup, the main ingredient of which were ovaries of snow frog. Both of these soups were and are regarded as beneficial to the skin and are said to confer the glow of youthful health to one's complexion. Bowls of them are eaten in shops for those reasons, expensive snacks indeed.

Traditionally, all of these sweets were eaten, along with cups of tea, during afternoons in teahouses. I recall afternoon teas at Ah Paw's house when sweet cakes and sweet soups would be served, but these were special occasions. Even more special were the family occasions when we had tables laden with sweets, the New Year, weddings, birthdays, feast days, and religious observances. We even offered sweet foods such as *jin dui* and *lin goh*, oranges, tangerines, and pomegranates to our ancestors at our family altar. For most of our year, however, we usually went to our Sun Tak teahouse for afternoon *yum cha,* to drink tea and enjoy a sweet. Over the last decades teahouse menus became longer, and restaurants, particularly in Shanghai, Guangdong, and Hong Kong, later in Taiwan and Singapore, began offering sweets as desserts in the Western order, as

a course to end a meal. And they have become most exotic.

Bird's nest is double-boiled in sweetened coconut milk or with sweetened almond cream. Ovaries of snow frog are double-boiled with whole red dates and lotus seeds in a sweet soup, essentially a *tong soi.* Almond cream, walnut cream, and pureed mango set into gelatin are offered as puddings. Sweet thickened creams made from sago, a palm pith starch, are adorned with pieces of cantaloupe or honeydew melon or that very special melon from Xinjiang, *hami gua,* a hard, crisp pink-orange melon that is exquisitely sweet. Red beans are made into soups and cooked with fresh lily bulbs, cooked and mashed into pastes to be folded into pastries and pancakes. As always, the emphasis of Chinese sweets is food, enhanced, sweetened, decorated. Yet even with these often extravagant, occasionally exotic, sweets offered, there will always be fresh fruit, artfully arranged, often sculpted, to conclude a meal or banquet.

In the home there are few elaborate sweets, except on special occasions. Instead the Chinese family will eat variations of those *tong soi,* sweet soups, simple to make, enjoyable hot or cool, satisfying and healthful, and they will eat prepared sweets made from various nuts, candied fruits, cookies, and small sweets that are bought in sweet shops. The recipes I set down here are traditions, classics. You will not find any hybrids, no Western-style layer cakes or pound cakes, no almond cookies, surely no fortune cookies—only those sweets enjoyed in the teahouses and in the home with tea. No desserts—for to conclude a meal the Chinese eat fruit, a custom, a tradition, that I am sure will never be abandoned.

GLUTINOUS RICE AND WHEAT SOUP

Nor Mai Mok Juk

*T*his was a treat in my family as a child, a different kind of sweet that we called a congee *because of its glutinous rice content. In Guangdong, China's most fertile rice-growing region, we had little contact with wheat except as milled into flour or made into dough and fashioned into noodles. So we would look to this sweet soup eagerly when the cooks in our family and that of Ah Paw, my grandmother, made it. I had often thought about it, yet it was only recently that I discovered, on a shelf of a* Chinese grocery, a package of wheat kernels. I took it home and re-created a sweet childhood memory.

½ cup wheat kernels, soaked in hot water for 4 hours and drained
9 cups cold water
½ cup glutinous rice, washed 3 times and drained
¼ pound sugarcane sugar (2 bricks), each broken into thirds, or brown sugar

1. Place the wheat and cold water in a large pot and bring to a boil over high heat. Lower the heat to simmer, cover the pot, leaving the lid cracked, and cook for 1 hour, stirring often.

2. Raise the heat back to high. Add the glutinous rice, stir well, and return to a boil. Lower the heat to a simmer, cover the pot, leaving the lid cracked, and cook for 30 minutes or until the mixture becomes creamy, stirring 3 or 4 times. Turn the heat up to medium, add the sugar, stir well, and cook until the sugar dissolves. Taste for sweetness. Turn off the heat, ladle into individual bowls, and serve.

MAKES 4 TO 6 SERVINGS

SWEET BIRD'S NEST SOUP
Yin Wor

*T*his is perhaps the most esteemed sweet soup in the Chinese kitchen. Expensive to be sure, because its ingredient is the nest of the tiny swift, a bird that nests mostly along craggy cliffs throughout Southeast Asia and whose nests are rare and obtained only with great effort. Its nests sell for exorbitant amounts of money not only because of their status but also because the Chinese believe that eating them enhances one's complexion and regenerates body cells. What is actually eaten are the strands of the swift's saliva, which bind the nests together. This sweet soup is served usually at the end of a banquet or festive meal, just before the fresh fruit. Or it can be taken as a snack in teahouses, restaurants, or snack shops that specialize in this sweet soup.

Whole nests are preferred for this classic soup of great elegance and repute, and to serve it is to offer honor to one's guests. After soaking the whole nests, the strands are steamed in a simple soup of sugar and water. White sugar is the choice because the whiteness of the nests and the clear soup is desired. This is the traditional way of serving the nests, but in other preparations fresh coconut milk is often added; in fact on occasion the soup is cooked inside of a coconut. Other sweets made with bird's nests include simmered nests sweetened with rock sugar, as well as nests simmered with rock sugar and rice to create a sweet pudding.

In some parts of southern China, in the Fujian area, bird's nest soup is eaten, as in other parts of the country, for beauty and health, but it is consumed with a bit of ritual. The sweet soup is made and saved. The children are sent to bed. After they have slept for a suitable time, they are awakened and given bowls of soup. It is believed that the soup, when consumed while the body is at rest, will be at its most beneficial.

Bird's nests are also used in nonsweet dishes. Often the strands are cooked in chicken or superior stock and boiled pigeon eggs are added; or julienned chicken; or julienned chicken and Yunnan ham; or strands of shark's fins, to mix with the nest strands. But the most famous rendering is this clear, sweet soup, basically a stylish tong soi.

Bird's nests are also sold in packages that contain pieces of nests. These are considerably cheaper than whole nests, but their quality is generally poor. Often muddy tan in color, they also contain many bits and pieces of twigs, feathers, leaves, and other impurities that must be picked out after the pieces of nest have been softened, an arduous process. In addition, these pieces of nests, even after hours of soaking and cooking, never become soft and silken as do the strands of whole nests. They stay chewy. Avoid them.

It is best, to experience what the Chinese believe to be one of their great gastronomic experiences, to use whole nests softened to silkiness. A simple dish, of great refinement. Usually one whole nest will serve 2 people.

continued

2 bird's nests of fine quality
(about 1½ ounces)
3 cups hot water

½ cup sugar
1 quart boiling water

1. To soak the nests, place them in a bowl, add the 3 cups hot water, and soak 4 to 4½ hours, until they loosen, separate into strands, and become soft. Rinse well and strain off. Repeat the rinsing.

2. Place the strands of nest into a steamproof porcelain deep dish that has been tempered (see tempering, page 63). Add the sugar. Pour in the boiling water and stir to mix well until the sugar dissolves.

3. Place the dish in a steamer, cover, and steam for 20 minutes (see steaming, page 64). Turn off the heat. Ladle the bird's nest soup equally into individual bowls and serve.

MAKES 4 TO 6 SERVINGS

SWEET WINE RICE SOUP

Jau Long Tong

This very special sweet soup, made in a particular, precise way, is a classic from Shanghai. It is flavored with that sweet wine rice so loved in Shanghai and was taught to me by Mrs. Kwai Woo Chui Fung, the mother-in-law of San Yan Wong, whom I regard as my personal calligrapher. She is a fine cook and interpreter of the foods of Shanghai. As with other preparations of the Chinese kitchen, this soup has traveled and is now quite common in Hong Kong, even in restaurants and teahouses that consider themselves Cantonese, proof that a fine food knows no boundaries.

½ cup glutinous rice powder
¼ cup warm water
4 large eggs
2½ cups cold water
¾ cup Sweet Wine Rice (page 69)
¼ cup sugar

1. Mix the glutinous rice powder with the warm water by placing the powder on a work surface, making a well in its center, and slowly adding the water, mixing with your fingers until the water is absorbed. Knead into a dough. Make 20 glutinous rice balls, slightly larger than the size of a marble, about ½ inch in diameter. Reserve.

2. Break each egg and slide it, without breaking the yolk, into an individual small bowl.

3. Pour the cold water into a wok and bring to a boil. Add the sweet wine rice and sugar and heat through for 2 minutes or until the sugar dissolves. Add the eggs, one by one, and continue cooking until they are somewhat poached. The eggs should be cooked, but the yolks not hardened. Add the glutinous rice balls and cook for 2 to 3 minutes, until they become translucent and float to the top. Taste for sweetness.

4. Serve in individual bowls. Each bowl should contain an equal measure of soup and wine rice, 1 egg, and 5 glutinous rice balls.

MAKES 4 SERVINGS

RED BEAN SOUP WITH LILY BULBS

Hung Dau Bok Hop Juk

This sweet soup is known and enjoyed throughout China. It is a favorite symbolic soup of the Lunar New Year because the name for the lily bulbs, bok hop, *translates as "100 things will go right." Lily bulbs are regarded as a calming food that helps eliminate nervousness and restore serenity; red beans as neutral food that builds one's blood without increasing bodily heat. A perfect dish, good taste. Good fortune, good health.*

One 14-ounce package Chinese
   red beans
8¾ cups cold water
6 ounces rock sugar (rock candy)
1 cup lily bulbs, fresh petals preferred
   (or ⅔ cup dried lily bulbs, soaked in
   hot water for 2½ hours until
   softened, brown spots trimmed)

1. Wash the beans well. Place them in a mesh strainer and place the strainer in a bowl. Run warm water through the beans, stirring with your fingers to rinse them of any grit. Drain and place in a pot.

2. Add the cold water to the pot, cover, and bring to a boil over high heat. Lower the heat and simmer the beans for 1½ to 1¾ hours, stirring often to prevent sticking, until the beans become soft and can be broken with a spoon. Add the sugar, mix well, and cook until the sugar dissolves. Turn off the heat. Add the lily bulb petals and stir to combine. Before serving, taste for sweetness and test for thickness. Add the sugar if needed and add boiling water if the soup is too thick. (If dried and soaked bulbs are used, cook the beans as directed, but add the lily bulbs to the cooking beans 15 minutes before adding the sugar.) Serve in individual bowls.

MAKES 4 TO 6 SERVINGS

STEAMED PEACHES WITH HONEY DATES

Mut Jo Jing Toh

*T*his is a sweet of my own creation but based on the traditional method of steaming sweets in China. Fruit and the preserved Chinese dates, called mut jo, or "honey dates," have classically been used in sweets and in soups, often combined, double-boiled with chicken, squab, or shin of beef. Often these dates are boiled in water to make a sweet, tealike infusion. Elders believe these dates are lubricants, beneficial to one's digestion and health.

6 cups cold water

3 tablespoons distilled vinegar

6 large peaches, 5 to 5½ ounces each, ripe but hard

6 Chinese honey dates or preserved sweet dates

9 tablespoons dark brown sugar

Six 6-ounce Pyrex dishes, tempered (page 63)

1. Place the cold water and vinegar in a bowl and mix. Keep at hand.

2. To prepare the peaches, cut across the top of each peach, just above the point where the pit begins. Place the tops in the vinegar-water mixture to prevent them from turning brown. Core the peaches in this manner: Cut a cylindrical hole in the center around the pit. Do not cut below the bottom of pit; the hole should not go through the peach. Remove the pit and widen the cavity in the peach with a grapefruit knife, taking care not to cut into the surface of the peach. Repeat with all peaches. As you prepare each, place in the bowl of vinegar water.

3. Place each peach in a small Pyrex bowl. Into each peach, place 1 date and 1½ tablespoons of brown sugar. Place the reserved tops back on the peaches. Place the bowls in a steamer, cover, and steam for 45 minutes (see steaming, page 64) or until the peaches are soft but not falling apart. Turn off the heat and serve individually in the bowls in which they were steamed. There will be a bit of sweet soup in the bowls as well, the result of condensation.

MAKES 6 SERVINGS

POACHED PEARS WITH HONEY, LEMON BALM, AND RAISINS

Ling Mon Heung Yip Boh Lei

*T*his sweet is a perfect example of a cooling, or yin, preparation. It is cooling for the system on several levels, conceptually and in a true bodily sense. Pears possess cooling energy and are often prescribed for those with overheated systems. The combination of honey and water is a tradition in China, believed to ease coughs and to soothe the throat. Lemon balm, as an infusion, is often prescribed as cooling as well, and raisins are essentially cool in nature. Cooking all of these together in the process of poaching, itself essentially cooling, is ideal. Any effort to cool down the dominance of yang, or heat, is believed by the Chinese to be conducive to longevity.

13 cups cold water
½ lemon
Four 6-ounce firm Bosc pears
One 10- by 20-inch piece of cheesecloth
5 tablespoons honey
**2 pieces dried tangerine peel, 1 by
    2 inches, soaked in hot water for
    20 minutes, until softened**
½ cup raisins
**18 sprigs lemon balm (1 to 2 bunches),
    about 7 inches long**
4 sprigs fresh mint

1. To prepare the pears, place 6 cups of the cold water in a bowl. Squeeze the juice from the ½ lemon into the bowl and add the lemon too. Core the pears from the bottom and peel, leaving the stems intact. As you peel each pear, place it in the bowl to prevent it from discoloring. Also place the cores and small pieces in the bowl. After the pears are peeled, wrap the cores and small pieces in the cheesecloth, folded double, and tie tightly with string.

2. Place the remaining 7 cups of cold water and the honey in a pot and stir to dissolve the honey. Add the tangerine peel, raisins, lemon balm, and cheesecloth bundle, together with the pears. Cover the pot and bring to a boil over high heat. Lower the heat and poach the pears at a low boil for 1½ hours, leaving the lid cracked.

3. Touch the pears with the tip of a chopstick. A properly poached pear should give a little; the pears should be soft and have taken on a light beige color. Turn off the heat. Remove the lemon balm, tangerine peel, and cheesecloth bundle from the pot and discard. Transfer each pear to an individual soup plate, sitting it upright, stem up. Divide the sweet soup equally among the plates. There should be about 4½ cups of soup. Divide the raisins equally as well. Garnish each pear by inserting a sprig of mint into it at the stem and serve.

MAKES 4 SERVINGS

APPLES STEAMED
WITH LOTUS SEED PASTE

Don Ping Gua

This is another sweet created by those inventive chefs of Shanghai, and they make it in a variety of tastes, substituting at will red bean paste, sweetened black bean paste, chestnut puree, or mashed dates as fillings for the apples. Most traditional is red bean paste, but I find that the lotus seed paste perfectly complements the tartness of the apples.

6 cups cold water
3 tablespoons distilled vinegar
Six 7-ounce firm Granny Smith apples
12 tablespoons lotus seed paste
Six 8-ounce Pyrex bowls, tempered
(page 63)

1. Place the cold water and vinegar in a bowl and mix. Keep at hand.

2. Cut the tops off the apples, about a quarter of the way down. Reserve the tops in the vinegar-water mixture to prevent them from turning brown. Scoop out the core of the apple and a bit of the inside to create a cavity. As each is cored, place it in the vinegar-water mixture.

3. When the apples are prepared, remove them from the bowl, dry, and fill each cavity with 2 tablespoons lotus seed paste. Place each apple in one of the small bowls, place the tops back on the apples, arrange in a steamer, and steam for 30 minutes (see steaming, page 64). The apples are done when they are slightly soft to the touch. Serve the apples in the bowls in which they were steamed. There will be a bit of condensed sweet soup in each bowl.

MAKES 6 SERVINGS

FRIED FRAGRANT BANANAS

Jah Heung Jiu

*I*n China the banana is jiu, *but there are so many different kinds of bananas that often they are given different, descriptive names. Those small, very sweet bananas in southern China and in Southeast Asia are called* fat jee jiu, *or "Buddha's fingers bananas." Another, a red-skinned banana, is called* hung jiu *to describe its color,* hung, *or red. Still another, quite like a plantain, is called* dai jiu, *or "large banana." The* heung jiu *of this recipe, or "fragrant banana," is grown widely in Guangdong and has a pleasant, perfumelike aroma when growing and is quite sweet when peeled. It is this fragrant banana that is used in this traditional preparation from Canton; thus its name. In other parts of China, such as Beijing and Shanghai, a sugar syrup is often poured over the bananas when they are served. There is no need for this, for the bananas are sweet enough, and I find the syrup cloying. The traditional way of preparing them is without any syrup.*

For the batter
1½ cups Pillsbury Best All-Purpose Flour
1 tablespoon baking powder
⅓ cup sugar
10 ounces water at room temperature
2 tablespoons peanut oil

3 large firm bananas, about 7 inches long
6 cups peanut oil

1. Mix together all the batter ingredients in a bowl until well blended. The batter should have the consistency of pancake batter. If too dry, add a bit more water. Peel the bananas, trim the ends, and break each into 4 equal pieces, about 1¼ inches long. Place in the batter and coat well and evenly.

2. Heat a wok over high heat for 1 minute. Add the peanut oil and heat to 350°F. Place 6 pieces of battered bananas into the oil and deep-fry, turning, for 3 to 4 minutes or until they turn golden brown and the crust is crisp. Remove and drain on paper towels. Repeat with the other 6 pieces. When completed, turn off the heat and serve.

MAKES 4 TO 6 SERVINGS

SHANGHAI RED BEAN CRÊPE
Dau Sah Wor Bang

This sweet, quite like a crêpe, is a favorite of Shanghai, where it originated and where it is fine art. It is also a favorite sweet in Beijing and Taiwan. The batter for it, depending on individual taste and custom, can be as thick as pancake batter or as thin as a crêpe. I prefer the latter for its delicate texture. Like all Chinese sweets, this is best enjoyed with tea, but in Taiwan, for example, it is often offered on a dim sum *menu*. It is also served, on occasion, as part of a festive banquet, as the course just before fresh fruit.

½ cup Pillsbury Best Bread Flour
1 large egg
¾ cup cold water
½ cup peanut oil
9 tablespoons red bean paste

1. Place the flour in a mixing bowl. Place the egg in another bowl and beat until smooth. Add the water to the egg and beat until smooth and thin. I like to call this mixture by its Chinese name, *don soi*, or egg water.

2. Add the egg water to the flour and mix well with a whisk. The batter should be smooth and thin, without any lumps.

3. Heat a 10-inch nonstick skillet over low heat for 10 seconds. Brush the bottom lightly with peanut oil (do not use all the oil at this time). Heat for 20 to 30 seconds, until the pan is hot. Add one third of the batter to the pan and tilt it to ensure the batter covers the bottom in an even layer. Allow to set. Then add 3 tablespoons bean paste, spread gently into a rectangular shape in the middle of the crêpe, leaving an inch at each end of paste. Fold one side of the crêpe over the bean paste, then overlap with the other side and fold up the ends to create a rectangle. Add the remaining peanut oil to the pan, raise the heat to medium, and fry the crêpe for 3½ to 4 minutes, until it is browned and slightly crisp. Prick the crêpe at intervals with a toothpick as it fries. Turn over the crêpe and fry for another 3½ to 4 minutes, until browned, pricking it again. Turn off the heat, remove the crêpe to a Chinese strainer, and drain.

4. Empty the oil from the skillet into a bowl. Wipe the excess oil from the skillet but leave a film. Repeat the frying process twice more to create 2 more crêpes. As each is made, place in a warm oven. When 3 crêpes are made, slice each into 4 pieces and serve.

MAKES 4 TO 6 SERVINGS

EIGHT-TREASURE GLUTINOUS RICE CAKE

Bot Boh Nor Mai Fan

A most special sweet, a classic from Shanghai that has come to be a festive dish throughout all of China, particularly in Nanjing and Suzhou. It consists of glutinous rice steamed with a variety of sweet ingredients. Historically the "8 treasures" included lotus seeds, almonds, red dates, sweet bean paste, and pieces of preserved or candied fruit, over which a sugar syrup was poured at serving.

Though it is not a cake in the strict sense of the word, it resembles a cake or a pudding when steamed. In Shanghai the preparation, though large and cakelike, became a staple of that city's dim sum repertoire, although it is far indeed from being a dumpling. Traditionally it was also served as the penultimate course of a banquet, just before the fresh fruit. Over the years it has evolved into a preparation of fancy, with different chefs, from different parts of China, adding different ingredients, the only stipulation being that there be 8 "treasures." This applies also to the West, where this cake has become a special sweet course at transplanted Chinese banquets.

It requires some effort to make and involves steaming rice twice, so it is rarely,

if ever, a dish made in the home. Rather it is eaten in restaurants, usually ordered in advance. It is, however, a wonderful and satisfying dish to prepare, and my adaptation of this classic uses a selection of dried fruit as its 8 treasures rather than those colored cubes of citron most often found in it. The false, sugared tastes of citron detracts, I believe, from the elegant tastes and texture it ought to have. Here is my Eight-Treasure Glutinous Rice Cake, worth the effort to make, for it is beautiful to see, delicious to eat. Enjoy it.

¼ *cup dried apricots*
¼ *cup dried pears*
¼ *cup dried mango*
¼ *cup dried pineapple*
⅛ *cup dried peaches*
¼ *cup honey dates or preserved dates,*
  pitted
⅛ *cup raisins*
2½ *cups cold water*
2½ *cups glutinous rice*
1½ *tablespoons peanut oil*
1 *cup red bean paste*

1. Cut all dried fruit, except the raisins, into ⅓-inch dice. Place all fruit, including the raisins, in a large bowl. Reserve.

2. Wash the glutinous rice 4 times in room-temperature water and drain well. Place in a cake pan. Add 2½ cups cold water to the rice. Place the cake pan in a steamer, cover, and steam for 30 to 40 minutes, until the rice is cooked (see steaming, page 64). It will

acquire a glaze and be translucent. Turn off the heat. Scoop out the rice, add to the bowl of fruit, and mix well to combine all ingredients thoroughly.

3. Coat a steamproof bowl, 1½-quart size, with 1½ teaspoons of peanut oil, making certain the bowl is well coated. Coat the hands as well, so the glutinous rice may be handled. Pick up half of the rice-fruit mixture, coat it with the remainder of the peanut oil, and pack it into the bowl, pressing it to the sides. Place the red bean paste in the center of the rice mixture and spread it a bit. Place the remainder of rice on top and press down gently.

4. Place the bowl in a steamer, cover, and steam for 45 minutes (see steaming, page 64). Turn off the heat. Remove the bowl and allow to cool for about 5 minutes. Pass a blunt dinner knife around the edge of the rice to loosen it. Place a serving plate, inverted, on top of the bowl, and upend it. The cake should slip out easily. Its fruit-dotted texture will glisten.

Use a large spoon to divide among individual bowls. Because of its texture, the steamed glutinous rice is virtually impossible to slice as one might a cake. Often a sugar syrup is poured over Eight-Treasure Glutinous Rice Cake when served. It is not at all necessary, because the various fruits, their sugars concentrated from drying, and the red bean paste are sufficiently sweet.

MAKES 10 OR MORE SERVINGS

With these sweet treasures I conclude this collection of the many foods and tastes of China. I trust that you the reader, you the cook, will note that they are true to Chinese tradition, for it was my intent when I embarked upon this book to demonstrate the history and breadth of the true Chinese kitchen. It was my desire—more a mission perhaps—to spread the message of the purity of the foods of China to show that much of what is often represented as Chinese food is not, that it is often bowdlerized beyond belief. I regard the purity of my food, my kitchen, my memories as sacred. Please enjoy it or, as we used to say in our family, ho ho sik, *a heartfelt wish for very good eating.* ◆

An Afterword About Wines

再談西洋酒

THE QUESTION IS OFTEN POSED, MORE AND MORE THESE DAYS, AS TO WHAT WESTERN WINE OUGHT TO BE DRUNK WITH CHINESE FOOD. THIS, HOWEVER, IS A LIMITED QUESTION SINCE IT PRESUPPOSES THAT THERE IS ONE PARTICULAR WINE THAT CAN BE COMPATIBLE WITH THE BREADTH OF THE CHINESE KITCHEN, WITH ALL OF ITS TASTES. Which, of course, is impossible. Rather the question to be raised should be what wines should be drunk with which of China's foods. Note the plurals.

There really is no one Western wine, with the exception of Champagne, that most versatile and elegant of wines, that might marry with all of the tastes of China's foods. I mention this in the context of an annual Christmas tradition in my family, where we serve a wide range of Chinese foods and serve only the best of Champagne with them. There are, to be sure, other wines that I have found to be compatible with different Chinese flavors, with individual dishes, gentle and fruity wines from France and Italy, whites and light reds from Switzerland, Germany, and Austria, others from Spain and South America.

Historically and traditionally, wines, *chiews* based on rice or grains such as sorghum, have been the accompaniments of choice in China, whether they were the refined, carefully fermented vintages of Shao-Hsing or Mei Kuei Lu Chiew, wines often scented with flowers, served at imperial banquets or important feasts, or the rice-based *chiews* enjoyed daily by the larger population. Often teas, of differing leaves and fermentation, many of them also flavored, were matched and drunk with food as well. Just as often beers, of German style, of different kinds and strengths, were served with food.

For generations many Chinese have favored brandy as the drink of choice with festive meals, drinking it with all courses. And the favorite brandy has traditionally been Cognac. Of late these brandy lovers have been drinking a good deal of Armagnac as well with meals. Others have favored Scotch whisky. But wines, matched with foods, have become more prevalent with each passing year.

Anyone who has been invited to be either a guest or a participant at a banquet in China will testify to the fact that Chinese official-dom, constantly, as a polite effort to satisfy all of those invited and to embarrass no one, sees to it that at one's right hand is set a virtual parade of glasses of different sizes. There's one glass each for rice and plum wines, others for soft drinks, beer, local brandies, and stronger spirits such as Mao Tai, and tea. No one, it is felt, should feel out of place and should have a glass of his or her choice when a toast is offered.

Yet, as the awareness of more of the different foods of China increases in the West, as they become increasingly more varied, more subtle, the question of Western wine persists. Which wines do indeed marry well with the various Chinese foods, with the different styles of cooking in the Chinese kitchen? The first, quick, reactive answer will be white wines as a genre, for white wines, particularly those with some gentle acidity and fruit, are in general most compatible with most Chinese foods. Utmost care must be taken with reds, since the big wines of Burgundy and Bordeaux are, in general, often too powerful for Chinese tastes. Nevertheless, fine pairings are possible. I have, for example, matched a sturdy Pinot Noir with a dish I often make just because of its affinity for red wine, thin scallops of veal sautéed in a sauce flavored with black pepper and shallots. My preference is for the lighter, clean style of Pinot Noir that one finds in Alsace.

My picks of wines to go with my foods are usually white, in most cases Alsatian, from the slightly acidic Sylvaners, which I like quite well with steamed or poached shellfish, to the fine Rieslings from that region of France, which at best are direct and flowery and complement steamed fish very well indeed. To go through the remainder of the Alsatian palette, I might suggest the Muscat, not sweet as it is in other regions, but fruity and dry, with a collection of appetizers and small dishes, even with *dim sum*, although I still prefer a tea such as Bo Lei with the latter. A gentle and round Pinot Blanc from Alsace I might match with a chicken and vegetable stir-fry; a Pinot Gris Tokay with a preparation that might have the sweetness of hoisin sauce among its salient ingredients. Finally I enjoy an Alsatian Gewürztraminer with most dishes that have dominant spices such as ginger and garlic. Smooth and rich at its best, it never is lost when married to a preparation in which various spices and herbs are combined. For my taste, and my food marriages, the best of Alsace is bottled by Trimbach and Leon Beyer and Domaines Schlumberger.

I realize that there are many and varied opinions about matching wines with foods, particularly white wines. I have tried Sancerres and found them good with some foods, likewise good Chablis and Meursaults, the latter favored by my husband. I can advance only those that I find complementary to my foods. Let me give an example of a marvelous food and wine pairing that I arranged with Moët & Chandon and Dom Pérignon in Singapore. I was asked to orchestrate a banquet of ten courses to go with Moët's Champagnes, including Dom Pérignon. Here is my menu, which I devised with the assistance of my husband, who insists that I identify him as an Officier of L'Ordre des Coteaux de Champagne.

Shrimp Marinated in Chinese Rose Wine
and Sesame Oil
Served with Beluga Caviar
CUVÉE DOM PÉRIGNON 1990

Salad of Barbecued Duck and Fresh
Cantaloupe Melon with Crisp Vegetables

Scallops and Yunnan Ham Steamed and
Scented with Scallion Oil
MOËT & CHANDON BRUT IMPÉRIAL 1992

Sweet Eggplant Stuffed with
Pungent Ginger Pickle and Sweet Onion,
Coated and Fried into
"Faux" Vegetarian Oysters

Fresh Sliced Fish and Spinach
in Superior Stock
MOËT & CHANDON
BRUT IMPÉRIAL ROSÉ 1993

Aromatic Smoked Chicken with
Lichee Black Tea and Rice,
Served with Steamed Buns

Buddhist "Squab" of Minced Soybean Cakes,
Flavored with Anise and
Cinnamon, Brushed with Hoisin Sauce,
Wrapped in Lettuce Leaves
MOËT & CHANDON BRUT IMPÉRIAL

Medallions of Veal Marinated in Shallot Oil,
Sautéed in Crushed Black Peppercorns

Fried Rice with Piquant Sun-dried Tomatoes,
Broccoli Stems, and Coriander

Poached Fresh Pears and Raisins, Scented
with Honey and Lemon Balm
MOËT & CHANDON NECTAR IMPÉRIAL

Chinese Petits Fours

Selection of Chinese Teas

Here is another food and wine matching banquet I devised for an American wine society, one designed to demonstrate not only the compatibility of the selected wines with Chinese foods but to show that such matches could be accomplished with a broad range of American wines.

Sweet Honey Walnuts and
Batter-Fried Oysters
ROBERT HUNTER SONOMA VALLEY
BRUT DE NOIRS

A Selection of Dim Sum
LANDMARK CHARDONNAY, SONOMA

Sautéed Chicken Breasts with Watercress
STRATFORD CHARDONNAY, NAPA

Poached Sea Bass
MOUNT EDEN VINEYARDS SANTA CRUZ
MOUNTAINS CHARDONNAY

Spicy Lobster
SIMI GEWÜRZTRAMINER, MENDOCINO

Shark's Fin Soup with Shredded Chicken
and Snow Peas
WICKHAM VINEYARDS NEW YORK STATE
JOHANNISBERG RIESLING

Yangzhou Fried Rice
VICHON NAPA CABERNET SAUVIGNON,
FAY VINEYARD

Peking Duck
SANFORD VINEYARDS SANTA MARIA VALLEY
PINOT NOIR, SANTA BARBARA

Cold Fresh Fruits
FREEMARK ABBEY EDELWEIN GOLD
SWEET JOHANNISBERG RIESLING

Beef Satay Marinated in Honey
RUTHERFORD HILL GEWÜRZTRAMINER,
NAPA

Lettuce in Oyster Sauce and Steamed Sea Bass
KENWOOD DRY CHENIN BLANC, SONOMA

Steamed Rice in Lotus Leaves
SAINTSBURY PINOT NOIR, CARNEROS, AND
EDNA VALLEY VINEYARD PINOT NOIR,
SAN LUIS OBISPO

For the purposes of this banquet dinner I altered what would have been the traditional order of the foods to accommodate the wines. Peking Duck would normally be served as the second or third course of such a meal, but we would have had to go from a Pinot Noir to perhaps a Chardonnay, which would have been disastrous for the latter. As rearranged, the two reds of the dinner were served just before the cold fruit and sweet dessert wine, a choice I made for wine harmony.

Subsequently I arranged another dinner, this matching Chinese foods with California wines only, at the request of the Wine Institute and Winegrowers of California. Let me offer this menu as well. With hors d'oeuvres of steamed shrimp dumplings and vegetarian oysters, a Schramsberg Blanc de Blancs was served, then we sat down to this planned matching banquet:

Sliced Chicken Stir-Fried with Honeydew and Cantaloupe Melons
MORGAN CHARDONNAY, MONTEREY

Roast Duck with Pistachios
FIRESTONE VINEYARD JOHANNISBERG
RIESLING, SANTA YNEZ VALLEY

With most of these seven wines, the pairings were straightforward, but those dining were asked to set down preferences. Most kept their wines and sampled different wines with different courses. For example, for the dessert course of Fried Ice Cream, most diners went back to the Firestone Vineyard Johannisberg Riesling. It was an interesting, instructive tasting that proved once again the compatibility of different wines with Chinese food.

There is perhaps no more highly regarded Italian winemaker than Angelo Gaja of the Piedmont. With him I did an unusual pairing of four of his finest wines with Chinese food, a matching he thought initially would not be possible. Here is my menu with his wines, which we drank from glasses supplied by Georg Riedel, who also attended our small dinner.

Steamed Shrimp Dumplings
Steamed Chive Dumplings
Vegetarian Spring Rolls

*Pan-Fried Pork Dumplings and Baked
Stuffed Curried Conch*
GAIA & REY CHARDONNAY 1990

Steamed Sea Bass with Ginger and Scallions
ALTENI DE BRASSICA SAUVIGNON BLANC
1990

*Cup of Duck Consommé
Roast Duck with Stir-Fried Broccoli Rabe*
BARBARESCO 1988

Veal with Snow Pea Shoots and Black Pepper
DARMAGI CABERNET SAUVIGNON 1988

Fresh Cold Fruit

When the meal was concluded, Gaja told me that the only other time he had matched his wines with Chinese foods had been with a chef of a Chinese restaurant near the Dorchester in London but that this dinner had exceeded the first and was "utterly magnificent." I will accept his opinion.

Nor are these the only marriages I have performed. I created a small Chinese New Year food and wine pairing for the German winemaker Deinhard, to mark a Year of the Rooster. I fashioned a veal dumpling shaped like a cockscomb, which I called Rooster Crest to go with Deinhard's Lila Brut Sparkling Wine; chicken stir-fried with a mélange of mixed vegetables matched with its Deinhard Riesling Dry; and a spicy shrimp stir-fry with red, yellow, and green peppers, with jalapeños that went beautifully with the winemaker's Forster Ungeheuer Riesling Spätlese. Fine matches all.

There are those who prefer the tart wines of Switzerland with dishes that contain sweetness and spices. Others, with similar preferences, occasionally suggest highly acidic wines such as a Muscadet or a Vouvray from the Loire. But I prefer such wines with shellfish, stir-fried or steamed, simply because of the contrast they provide. There have also been recommendations that Bordeaux of great lineage match well with that most well-known of banquet preparations, Peking Duck. I disagree. A prime ingredient in the Peking Duck service is hoisin sauce, sweet and thick, to brush on the duck skin before it is wrapped in a thin pancake for serving. This sweetness clashes with the Bordeaux. I would urge instead that a Pinot Noir be tried, if a red wine is your choice. Otherwise I suggest a Gewürztraminer of depth and spice for a fine mating.

The fact that wines of the West have become more available, more accessible, in China, Hong Kong, and Taiwan is undeniable. In recent years giant wine expos have been held in Hong Kong and Shanghai, where the wines of France and Italy have dominated. And figures record that China is importing ever more Western wines. These to complement the growth of its own Western-style wine industry, with many whites being grown and bottled these days, in particular the Dynasty brand, a Muscat-based wine that is the product of a French-Chinese joint venture.

As with all wine and food matching, much depends on one's individual palate. One person's marriage is another's divorce. What I have offered is a personal overview based on my experiences in matching the foods and flavors of China with the wines of the West. Be adventuresome.

Index